CW01629470

WILD WOMEN

The First 10 Years 2015 - 2025

News stories, match reports, photos and statistics for the first 10 years of the Widnes Wild Women's team.

The majority of the reviews, interviews and match reports in this book have been previously published on the widneswild.co.uk ice hockeyreview.co.uk websites and in the Widnes and Weekly News and Runcorn newspapers.

The lists of fixtures / results, league tables and player statistics are based on information taken from the eiha.co.uk and Fixtures Live websites, Elite Prospects and Gameday online system as well as paper gamesheets compiled by the author although they have not been published anywhere in this layout before.

This edition published in Great Britain in November 2025 by Ice Hockey Review, which is an imprint of Posh Up North Publishing, Wallasey, United Kingdom

ISBN: 978-1-909643-70-3

Intellectual rights to all works used herein remain with their originators and any perceived infringement of copyright is completely unintentional. Any errors in this regard will be corrected at the earliest possible opportunity.

© 2025 Paul Breeze & Posh Up North Publishing

All rights reserved. No part of this publication may be reproduced or copied in any manner without the prior permission in writing of the copyright holders.

British Library cataloguing in publication data.

A catalogue record for this book is available from the British Library

Front Cover Photos
Widnes Wild Women - September 2015 (for names see page 21)- photographer unknown
Widnes Wild Women, League Champions 2025 – Photo by Stuart Cutting

Back Cover: Paul Breeze – Photo by @haganovaphoto

CONTENTS

PB announcing the MVPs on the ice after a Wild Women's home game (Photo by Andrew Shutt)

INTRODUCTION

I have always been a keen follower of women's ice hockey, going all the way back to the early 1980s when my local Peterborough Ravens team won the first modern day English League title.

One of the Ravens players – Helena Perkins - was in my year at school and Debbie Jeffers - who was a bit older than me - used to live a few doors down my road.

In later years, Tracey Nicholls played on the same rec team that I did and I actually bought some secondhand kit off Kim Strongman – before she went on to be a Queen Bee Elite player and long standing GB international!

Kim Strongman (far left) and Tracey Nicholls (2nd right) with the Peterborough Ravens ca 1987 (Photo by Francis Page)

Our rec team – the Peterborough Spartans - used to play a "friendly" game against the Ravens once a year and, would you believe, they were the most violent encounters you could possibly imagine!

I only ever played in one such game and I distinctly remember early on having the opportunity to dispossess one of the Ravens' players of the puck by – obviously - splattering her against the boards.

But, with me being a somewhat robust 6' 4" and her being "only a girl", I thought I'd better take the more chivalrous option and try and out-play her instead.

The next thing I knew, I was flat out on the ice and she was homing in on goal ready to score.

By the end of the game, one of our guys had his chin split open and another had to go to hospital with a dislocated shoulder.

On top of that, Peterborough Pirates player Jim Ryan – who was guesting for us - had to miss the British League Premier Division game on the Sunday due to an ankle injury. So don't you go telling me "it's ONLY girls..."

Anyway, coming up to date, when we found out that Widnes was going to have a women's team, Lucy and I jumped at the chance to go along and support them.

I initially wrote match reports for the women's games on my Ice Hockey Review website and they also got picked up by the Widnes Weekly News paper. On the strength of this, I was then asked to do the same for the Wild NIHL team which saw me posting match reports and news items on the official Wild website as well.

Through an amusing set of circumstances – which you can read about later - Lucy and I ended up sponsoring the MVP awards for the home games – and still do to this day.

I have been the official match announcer for Wild women games since 2017 and am also the official scorer. I also take occasional photos and still do match reports for my website and the newspaper - so can't complain that life is in any way dull!

Having been present at the Wild Women's first home league game in February 2016 and been at pretty much every other home game since in some capacity or other, I feel a real affinity for this team.

I am proud to have been able to follow and support them through their 2 league title winning seasons - and all the others in between - and I hope you enjoy reading this special souvenir of their first 10 years.

Paul Breeze, 2025

Blackpool Blades (Photo by Blackpool Gazette)
Back Row (l to r): Emma Williams, Michelle Couch, Joanne Munroe, Rachael Linton, Ruth Aspinall, Sarah Hutchinson, Charlotte Porter, Sarah Brown. Front Row (l to r): Gaynor Lilley, Kim Marley, Ursula Wilson, Nikki King, Dawn Hayton.

IN THE BEGINNING.

The first women's ice hockey team in the north west was set up in Blackpool in 1987 - initially as the Blackpool Barracudas and then as the Blackpool Blades.

They played in the Womens Summer League in 1988 as the Barracudas and then changed their name to the Blades and played in the north section of the Women's British League for the 1988/99 season.

The women's leagues were re-structured in 1989 with the formation of a new top tier Women's Premier League and the Blades were placed in Division 1 North for the 1989/90 season.

They finished bottom of the table in summer 1988 and season 1988/89 and then second bottom in 1989/90 – but their results got noticeably better as they went along.

They played in Division 1 North again for the 1990/91 season but we don't know where they finished in that one as the league records have mysteriously disappeared.

In 1991, the Blades fell foul of the Blackpool rink's decision to stop supporting ice hockey. The Blackpool Seagulls men's team and the junior sides all moved to play at the recently opened Blackburn rink instead but the Blades women's team couldn't muster enough players who wanted to make the move so they, sadly, folded.

Interestingly enough, Ruth Aspinall (now Leopold) and Rachael Linton (now Pearce) were leading players in the Blackpool team and they both ended up playing for the Widnes Wild Women in recent years, so we will hear more about them later.

Women's ice hockey eventually arrived in Blackburn in 1998 when the Blackburn Thunder team was founded.

They played in Women's Division 1 North for 19 seasons until 2018 when dwindling numbers also forced them to call it a day.

Notable players from the Thunder team who went on to play for Widnes include Catherine Fell, Amanda

Williams and Penny Fletcher - and Rachael Linton / Pearce also played for a while at Blackburn.

At the turn of the millenium, a new women's team was formed in Altrincham and the Altrincham Avalanche played for just one season in Division 1 North in 2001/02.

Familiar names on the Avalanche roster for that season include Charlene Chapman, Vanessa Crickmore-Clarke and Emma Pearson (then Brown).

With the original Altrincham rink due to close, the Avalanche team relocated to Deeside for the following season and played as the Flintshire Furies.

The Furies played for 8 seasons – from 2002/03 to 2009/10 with 3 seasons in the WPL and 5 in Division 1 North.

Their record appearance holder during that time was Emma Middleton who also went on to be an original Wild Woman - along with Megan Bowen, Katy Holliday, Beckie Elliot, Rachel Cartwright and, of course Charlene, Vanessa and Emma Pearson.

After the Furies finished in 2010, there was a gap until 2013 when the Manchester Phoenix Women's Team was formed to play at the new Altrincham rink.

They originally trained at the new Widnes rink that had recently opened in December 2012 - some 20 miles or so along the M56 - and actually played their home matches there for the 2013/14 league season.

They joined Women's Division 1 North and went on to finish 7th out of 9 teams in their first league season, with 4 wins and 2 draws from the 15 games that they played.

For their second season, the Manchester Phoenix team were able to play their home games at Altrincham and, having strengthened their squad with a couple of new players, they went on to win the league title with 16 wins and 1 draw from their 18 league games.

They also won the end of season play offs, beating Division 1 South winners Swindon 3-2 in a closely contested and nail-biting final.

The play-off win meant that Manchester earned promotion to the Women's Premier League for the following season but the Manchester Phoenix women never got to play in the WPL as the team moved permanently to Widnes to play as the Widnes Wild Women.

Flintshire Furies *- Back Row: Ellie Dawson, Katy Holliday, Nick Venables, Victoria Foster , Mike Lavery, Faye Andrews, Beckie Elliott, Charlene Chapman Front Row: Tegan Lavery, Zuzana Zavadilova, Lucy Kirkham, Vanessa Crickmore-Clarke, Emma Middleton, Linda Jones*

Blackburn Thunder – Season 2011/2012 (Photo by Nick Fletcher)
Back Row: Beckie Elliott, Penny Fletcher, Kimberley Derbyshire, Catherine Fell, Jakki Duncan, Sarah Eastham, Jade Bolton, Elizabeth Wright, Nicola Crompton. Front Row: Beatrice Fletcher, Megan Bowen, Elizabeth Aspinall, Dannielle Skelton, Amanda Williams, Sarah Wilson, Emma Lowe

Manchester Phoenix Women – League Champions 2014/15
Standing: Scott Dutton, Elizabeth Wright, Katie Hills, Jakki Duncan, Leen de Decker, Elizabeth Loss, Catherine Fell, Megan Bowen, Lucy Kirkham, Sammi Boyle, Beckie Elliott, Penny Fletcher, Mike Thomas. Kneeling: Rachel Cartwright, Emma Pearson, Charlene Chapman, Emma Middleton, Amanda Williams, Rebecca Wilde, Vanessa Crickmore-Clarke, Front: Stephanie Drinkwater. (Photo by Nick Fletcher)

2015: Time To Go Wild...

The Widnes Wild women's team came into being in the summer of 2015 when the hitherto Manchester Phoenix women's team moved en bloc from Altrincham Ice Rink.

Now, without getting too involved in recriminations and finger pointing, the background to this really needs a bit of explaining.

For a number of years, Manchester Phoenix had been the main men's team at Altrincham and, under their umbrella, they also operated the junior teams, the womens' team and the sledge hockey team.

Over time, rink operators Silver Blades (now part of Planet Ice) had become unhappy with the way that the overall Phoenix club was being run and cited such factors as questionable business relationships with outside parties and delays in ice rental payments.

This all came to a head in the summer of 2015 and the rink withdrew the ice contract from the Phoenix parent club. This meant that they could no longer train or play matches at the Altrincham rink and it had the knock-on effect of causing chaos among the various other teams involved, none of whom, to be fair, had actually done anything wrong.

The fall-out from this saw the Manchester Phoenix EPL team go off and play their home matches at Deeside for the 2015/16 season and the junior club had to hastily re-brand as Trafford Juniors.

The rink set up a new Manchester Storm club to play in the Elite League, resurrecting the name of a previous team, and the struggling NIHL Division 1 Manchester

Minotaurs team re-branded to play as Altrincham Aces in Division 2 instead.

The new ice time arrangements left the sledge team homeless and for the next couple of years they trained and played at whatever venue they could get ice time - and the women's team re-located to Widnes.

This wasn't a particular hardship as the Phoenix women's team had actually trained and played their games at the Widnes rink during the 2013/14 season anyway and many of their players had been part of the previous Flintshire Furies team that had played at Deeside from 2002 to 2010.

The Phoenix women's team had won the Women's Division 1 North league title in season 2014/15 and then went on to win the play offs, which brought them promotion to the Womens' Premier League.

Thus the new Widnes Wild women's team started life in the WPL – with most of the previous season's Phoenix players on their roster - for the 2015/16 league campaign.

And that is where we pick up the action.

16th August 2015: The Widnes Wild Ladies took on a "Ladies Select" team in a pre-season friendly match. The Widnes team were wearing the white Phoenix shirts from the previous season while the Select team were wearing the Phoenix black shirts. And a few Wild players turned out for the Select team as well - so it was all a bit confusing. The Select team won 0-3 by the way… (Photos by Nick Fletcher)

EIHA Women's Premier League – Season 2015/16

Team	GP	W	D	L	GF	GA	Pts
Swindon Topcats	14	12	2	0	76	20	26
Widnes Wild Women	14	8	3	3	62	36	19
Streatham Storm	14	6	4	4	40	31	16
Milton Keynes Falcons	14	7	2	5	52	30	16
Slough Phantoms	14	7	0	7	79	72	14
Whitley Squaws	14	5	1	8	58	68	11
Nottingham Vipers	14	1	3	10	42	101	5
Chelmsford Cobras	14	2	1	11	35	86	5

Top Points Scorers

Player	Team	GP	G	A	Pts	PIM
Rebecca Osman	Swindon Topcats	14	22	11	33	6
Stephanie Towns	Whitley Squaws	13	20	13	33	14
Rebecca Da Cova	Swindon Topcats	13	14	16	30	2
Robin Mullen	Nottingham Vipers	11	23	6	29	16
Katerina Lossnitzer	Slough Phantoms	10	19	8	27	29
Louise Wheeler	Slough Phantoms	4	14	12	26	6
Nicola Bicknell	Slough Phantoms	11	13	11	24	4
Amy Campbell	Whitley Squaws	12	20	4	24	14
Katie Hills	Widnes Wild	14	15	8	23	10
Rachel Piotrowski	MK Falcons	14	17	5	22	18
Samantha Bidmead	Slough Phantoms	13	7	13	20	20
Leen De Decker	Widnes Wild	14	15	4	19	2

Top Netminders

Netminder	Team	GPI	SA	GA	Sv%	SO
Gemma Davies	SWI	7	165	6	96.36%	2
Holly Steeples	NOT	4	174	10	94.25%	0
Rachel Moore	SWI	12	231	14	93.94%	1
Kayliegh Doyle	MKF	14	444	30	93.24%	1
Ruth Cattell	STR	12	366	27	92.62%	3
Stephanie Drinkwater	WID	13	326	33	90.80%	0
Sarah Boulton	WHI	9	142	17	88.03%	0
Jessica Kinghorn	WHI	11	348	43	87.64%	1
Sarah Gunstone	SLO	14	531	68	87.19%	0
Philippa Wheeler	NOT	10	48	8	83.33%	0
Cherry Hambelton	CHE	13	409	72	82.40%	0

Widnes Wild Women Player Statistics
Season 2015/16 – Women's Premier League

Player	GP	G	A	Pts	PIM
Katie Hills	14	15	8	23	10
Leen De Decker	14	15	4	19	2
Catherine Bowen Fell	13	10	4	14	4
Abigail Culshaw	8	7	4	11	6
Charlene Chapman	14	5	3	8	6
Amanda Williams	10	2	4	6	0
Lucy Kirkham	13	2	3	5	2
Emma Pearson	6	1	4	5	2
Madeleine Gustavsson	10	1	3	4	0
Megan Bowen Fell	12	1	2	3	26
Rachel Cartwright	3	2	1	3	0
Elizabeth Amy Wright	13	0	3	3	14
Jakki Duncan	6	0	2	2	2
Beckie Elliott	12	1	1	2	2
Sarah Hutchinson	3	0	2	2	4
Emma Middleton	4	0	2	2	0
Vanessa Crickmore Clarke	8	0	1	1	6
Emma Bevan	1	0	0	0	0
Samantha Joann Boyle	12	0	0	0	6
Jodie Alexandra Boyle	7	0	0	0	0
Stephanie Jade Drinkwater	13	0	0	0	0
Penelope Fletcher	1	0	0	0	0
Abigail Hayes	10	0	0	0	12
Katharine Holliday	4	0	0	0	0
Elizabeth Loss	1	0	0	0	0
Sophie Emma Sinclair-Reeks	3	0	0	0	0
Rebecca Jade Wilde	2	0	0	0	0

Widnes Wild Women Player Statistics
Season 2015/16 – Play Offs

Player	GP	G	A	Pts	PIM
Katie Hills	1	0	1	1	0
Leen De Decker	1	1	0	1	0
Catherine Bowen Fell	1	0	0	0	0
Abigail Culshaw	1	0	0	0	0
Charlene Chapman	1	0	0	0	0
Amanda Williams	1	0	1	1	2
Lucy Kirkham	1	0	0	0	0
Emma Pearson	1	0	0	0	2
Madeleine Gustavsson	0	0	0	0	0
Megan Bowen Fell	1	0	0	0	0
Rachel Cartwright	0	0	0	0	0
Elizabeth Amy Wright	1	0	0	0	0
Jakki Duncan	0	0	0	0	0
Beckie Elliott	0	0	0	0	0
Sarah Hutchinson	0	0	0	0	0
Emma Middleton	0	0	0	0	0
Vanessa Crickmore Clarke	1	0	0	0	0
Emma Bevan	0	0	0	0	0
Samantha Joann Boyle	1	0	0	0	0
Jodie Alexandra Boyle	1	0	0	0	0
Stephanie Jade Drinkwater	1	0	0	0	0
Penelope Fletcher	0	0	0	0	0
Abigail Hayes	1	0	0	0	0
Katharine Holliday	0	0	0	0	0
Elizabeth Loss	0	0	0	0	0
Sophie Emma Sinclair Rooke	1	0	0	0	0
Rebecca Jade Wilde	0	0	0	0	0
Bench	0	0	0	0	2

Widnes Wild Women Player Statistics
Season 2015/16 – Total – All Matches

Player	GP	G	A	Pts	PIM
Katie Hills	15	15	9	23	10
Leen De Decker	15	16	4	19	2
Catherine Bowen Fell	14	10	4	14	4
Abigail Culshaw	9	7	4	11	6
Charlene Chapman	15	5	3	8	6
Amanda Williams	11	2	5	6	2
Lucy Kirkham	14	2	3	5	2
Emma Pearson	7	1	4	5	4
Madeleine Gustavsson	10	1	3	4	0
Megan Bowen Fell	13	1	2	3	26
Rachel Cartwright	3	2	1	3	0
Elizabeth Amy Wright	14	0	3	3	14
Jakki Duncan	6	0	2	2	2
Beckie Elliott	12	1	1	2	2
Sarah Hutchinson	3	0	2	2	4
Emma Middleton	4	0	2	2	0
Vanessa Crickmore Clarke	9	0	1	1	6
Emma Bevan	1	0	0	0	0
Samantha Joann Boyle	13	0	0	0	6
Jodie Alexandra Boyle	8	0	0	0	0
Stephanie Jade Drinkwater	14	0	0	0	0
Penelope Fletcher	1	0	0	0	0
Abigail Hayes	11	0	0	0	12
Katharine Holliday	4	0	0	0	0
Elizabeth Loss	1	0	0	0	0
Sophie Emma Sinclair-Reeks	4	0	0	0	0
Rebecca Jade Wilde	2	0	0	0	0
Bench	0	0	0	0	2

Netminding Breakdown – Season 2015/16

Match	NM	GPI	Mins	SA	GA	GAA	SV%
12th Sept @ SLO	Drinkwater	1	60	30	3	3.00	90.00
11th Oct @ STR	Drinkwater	1	60	29	1	1.00	96.55
8th Nov @ SWI	Drinkwater	1	58.38	30	1	1.00	96.67
	Empty Net	1	1.22	0	0	0	0
21st Feb v MK	Drinkwater	1	58.42	22	2	2.00	90.91
	Empty Net	1	1.18	0	0	0	0
28th Feb v SLO	Drinkwater	1	60	23	2	2.00	91.30
25th Mar v SWI	Drinkwater	1	60	30	3	3.00	90.00
3rd Apr @ CHE	Drinkwater	1	45	15	2	2.67	86.67
10th Apr v CHE	Drinkwater	1	60	35	4	4.00	88.57
17th Apr @ NOT	Drinkwater	1	60	33	6	6.00	81.82
24th Apr @ WHI	Drinkwater	1	60	28	2	2.00	92.86
5th Mar v STR	Bevan	1	60	25	3	3.00	88.00
1st May @ MK	Drinkwater	1	60	24	1	1.00	95.83
8th May v WHI	Drinkwater	1	60	28	3	3.00	89.29
15th May v NOT	Drinkwater	1	60	29	3	3.00	89.66
POSF v STR	Drinkwater	1	45	18	2	2.67	88.89

Totals	Comp	GPI	Mins	SA	GA	GAA	SV%
Drinkwater	WPL	13	762.20	356	33	2.59	90.73
	POSF	1	45	18	2	2.67	88.89
	Total	14	807.20	374	35	2.59	90.64
Bevan	WPL	1	60	25	3	3.00	88.00
Empty Net	WPL	2	2.40	0	0	0	0

Notes:
The away game at Chelmsford on 3rd April was 3 x15 minute periods due to time constraints.
The Play Off semi final was played at iceSheffield and was also 45 minutes duration.

Widnes Wild Women's Team – Season 2015/16
EIHA Women's Premier League Results

Date	Comp	Home			Away	WDL
12.9.15	WPL	Slough Phantoms	3	4	Widnes Wild	W
11.10.15	WPL	Streatham Storm	1	3	Widnes Wild	W
8.11.15	WPL	Swindon Topcats	1	0	Widnes Wild	L
21.2.16	WPL	Widnes Wild	1	2	MK Falcons	L
28.2.16	WPL	Widnes Wild	7	2	Slough Phantoms	W
5.3.16	WPL	Widnes Wild	3	3	Streatham Storm	D
26.3.16	WPL	Widnes Wild	3	3	Swindon TopCats	D
3.4.16	WPL	Chelmsford Cobs	2	10	Widnes Wild	W
10.4.16	WPL	Widnes Wild	5	4	Chelmsford Cobs	W
17.4.16	WPL	Nottm Vipers	6	8	Widnes Wild	W
24.4.16	WPL	Whitley Squaws	2	10	Widnes Wild	W
1.5.16	WPL	MK Falcons	1	1	Widnes Wild	D
8..5.16	WPL	Widnes Wild	2	3	Whitley Squaws	L
15.5.16	WPL	Widnes Wild	5	3	Nottingham Vipers	W
28.05.16	POS	Streatham Storm	2	1	Widnes Wild	L

Charlene Chapman was the Wild Women's team captain for their first three seasons, 2015/16 to 2017/18 (Photo by Geoff White)

Widnes Wild Women - September 2015

Back Row: Sophie Sinclair Reeks, Penny Fletcher, Madeleine Gustavsson, Jakki Duncan, Abigail Hayes, Jodie Boyle, Vanessa Crickmore-Clarke, Sammi Boyle. Front Row: Elizabeth Wright, Leen de Decker, Katie Hills, Stephanie Drinkwater, Leanne Curry, Sarah Hutchinson, Charlene Chapman.

Leen de Decker scored the Wild Women's first ever league goal away at Slough (Photo by Flyfifer Photography)

12th September 2015 – Women's Premier League Slough Phantoms 3 - Widnes Wild Women 4

Period Scores: 1-0, 1-1, 1-2
Shots on goal: not recorded
Penalties In Minutes: Slough 10 - Widnes 0
Scoring: Widnes – Leen de Decker 2+1, Rachel Cartright 1+1, Charlene Chapman 1+0, Emma Middleton 0+2, Abigail Culshaw 0+1

The Widnes Wild women's team made a winning start to their first ever season in the Women's Premier League with a 3-4 win away at Slough Phantoms – who were a top-flight team last season.

Slough took the lead after seven minutes with the only goal of the first period and struck again on 36.54 to give the hosts a two goal cushion. A powerplay goal from Wild's Belgian international record holder Leen De Decker in the last minute of the period halved the deficit and gave Widnes hope going into the final third.

A goal from Wild captain Charlene Chapman straight from the restart put the teams on level pegging and a second strike from De Decker put Widnes ahead for the first time less than 2 minutes later.

Slough tied the game up with a their 3rd goal at 54.48 but almost straight from the face off, Wild's Rachel Cartright picked up on a Leen De Decker pass to slot home the winning goal just 9 seconds later.

The Widnes Wild team for this first ever women's game was:

#1 Stephanie Drinkwater (NM)
#3 Charlene Chapman (C)
#4 Rachel Cartwright (A)
#5 Leen De Decker
#6 Abigail Culshaw
#24 Emma Middleton
#27 Lucy Kirkham
#33 Emma Pearson (A)
#37 Megan Bowen Fell
#66 Katie Hills
#73 Catherine Bowen Fell
#85 Katharine Holliday
#91 Elizabeth Wright
#92 Jakki Duncan &
#96 Rebecca Wilde

Catherine Bowen Fell scored twice away at Streatham
(Photo by Flyfifer Photography)

11th October 2015 – Women's Premier League Streatham Storm 1 – Widnes Wild Women 3

Period Scores: 0-1, 1-2, 0-0
Shots On Goal: Streatham 29 – Widnes 51
Penalties In Minutes: Streatham 4 - Widnes 6
Widnes Scoring Widnes Scoring: Catherine Bowen Fell 2+0, Rachel Cartwright 1+0, Kate Hills 0+2

The Widnes Wild Women made it two wins from two starts with a hard fought 1-3 victory away to Streatham Storm.

Catherine Bowen Fell opened the scoring for the Wild on 8 minutes and the score remained 0-1 at the first period break.

A second goal from Bowen Fell on 28 minutes doubled the Wild lead and they went 0-3 up with a goal from Rachel Cartwright 4 minutes later.

Streatham finally found the back of the net themselves on 38 minutes but that was the last goal of the game and the Wild Women held on to record an impressive win away in South London.

Rachel Cartwright (Photo by Flyfifer Photography)

Swindon Wildcats 1 – Widnes 0 (Photo by Carol Light)

8th November 2015 – Women's Premier League Swindon Topcats 1 – Widnes Wild Women0

Period Scores: 0-0, 1-0, 0-0
Shots On Goal: Swindon 30 – Widnes 26
Penalties In Minutes: Swindon 8 - Widnes 2

The Widnes Wild women lost out by the narrowest of margins in 1-0 defeat away to league title favourites Swindon Topcats.

After a very tense and closely fought goal-less first period, Swindon eventually took the lead on 30 minutes.

Despite numerous chances for both sides, the score remained 1-0 heading into the last minutes of the game and Widnes removed netminder Drinkwater in favour of an extra attacker for last 90 seconds.

Unfortunately, they were unable to make the extra player count and the score remained 1-0 at the final buzzer.

Wild Women 1 – Milton Keynes 2 (Photo by Paul Breeze

Sunday 21st February 2016 – Women's Premier Lge Widnes Wild Women 1 – Milton Keynes Falcons 2

Period Scores: 0-2, 1-0, 0-0
Shots on Goal: Widnes 41 – MK 22
Penalties: Widnes 20 – MK 4
Widnes Scoring: Leen De Decker 1+0

The Widnes Wild ladies team put on a battling display in their first home game of the season but ended up losing 1-2 to the Milton Keynes Falcons.

The Wild actually scored first in the 2nd minute but the goal was disallowed by the referee and insult was heaped on injury as the Falcons immediately went down to the other end and scored for themselves.

The game was very close with chances for both sides but then - in the dying seconds of the first period, the Falcons scored again with a breakaway goal that gave them a somewhat flattering 0-2 lead going into the break.

Widnes fans finally had something to cheer in the 27th minute when Belgian international player Leen De Decker scored a fine solo effort to get the Wild back in the game.

Things began to get physical as the second period wore on and the Wild started pressing for an equaliser. They began clocking up penalty minutes but, despite being short-handed on numerous occasions, they managed to defend their net and looked most likely to score again.

The third period remained goalless and was a very tense affair throughout. The Wild pulled their netminder for the last minute of the game to throw on an extra attacker in an attempt to force a late goal but to no avail.

Overall, the Wild outshot their opponents by almost two to one (41 to 22) and the MK netminder Kayleigh Doyle played a blinder for the visitors.

The Wild Women have now played 4 games in their Women's Premier League campaign this season and have won two and lost two.

The Widnes team for this first ever home game was:

#1: Stephanie Drinkwater
#3: Charlene Chapman
#5: Leen De Decker
#9: Jodie Boyle
#11: Sarah Hutchinson
#13: Katie Hills
#14: Penelope Fletcher
#21: Samantha Boyle
#22: Madeleine Gustavsson
#27: Lucy Kirkham
#37: Megan Bowen Fell
#44: Beckie Elliott
#71: Amanda Williams
#73: Catherine Bowen Fell
#91: Elizabeth Wright
#92: Jakki Duncan
#97: Abigail Hayes

Widnes Wild Women v Slough Phantoms (Photo by Paul Breeze)

Sunday 28th February 2016 – Women's Premier Lge Widnes Wild Women 7 – Slough Phantoms 2

Period Scores: 0-1, 5-0, 2-1
Shots on Goal: Widnes 44 – Slough 23
Penalties In Minutes: Widnes 2 – Slough 4
Widnes Scoring: Leen De Decker, Katie Hills, Catherine Bowen-Fell all 2+0, Madeleine Gustavsson 1+0, Sarah Hutchinson, Jakki Duncan both 0+2

The Widnes Wild women's team picked up their third win of the season - and their first at home – with a thrilling 7-2 victory over Slough Phantoms at the Silver Blades Ice Rink in Widnes on Sunday evening.

For the fans who had witnessed the previous week's game against Milton Keynes, the first period must have been a bit of "déjà vu" with the Wild dominating for long periods and then Slough rushing up to the other end to score the opening goal of the game. That goal came when the visitors were shorthanded due to a tripping penalty and came very much against the run of play.

Whatever was said during the period break obviously had an effect as the Wild responded with 5 unanswered goals

– three in just over 3 minutes – as they battered the Phantoms' goal with 18 shots compared to the six that Widnes' Stephanie Drinkwater had to deal with.

In fact, much praise has to go to the Phantoms netminder Sarah Gunstone who performed heroics in her own net and probably kept the score a lot lower than it might otherwise have been.

By the time that the Phantoms managed to strike again at 53.41 (Hadden asst Bicknell), the Wild had already scored their 6th of the game (Hills unassisted 45.08) and the contest was well and truly out of reach of the battling Slough team.

A second unassisted goal for Hills at 56.54 was the icing on the cake and the ensuing 7-2 scoreline sees the Wild Women move up to 5th place in the Women's Premier League Table, where they have games in hand over all the other teams.

Madeleine Gustavsson (Photo by Steve Pollitt)

Leen de Decker scores against Streatham (Photo by Steve Pollitt)

Saturday 5th March 2016 – Women's Premier League
Widnes Wild Women 3 – Streatham Storm 3

Period Scores: 2-1, 0-0, 1-2
Shots On Goal: Widnes 28 – Streatham 25
Penalties In Minutes: Widnes 6 – Streatham 6
Widnes Scoring: Leen De Decker 2+0, Katie Hills 1+0 Lucy Kirkham, Amanda Williams, Elizabeth Wright all 0+1

It is really difficult to set down on paper what a closely fought, exciting and tense game of ice hockey this was to watch. The match was played at a tremendous pace throughout and Streatham were definitely the best visiting women's team seen so far at the Hive this season.

Widnes took the game to Streatham from the off but as has been the case in all 3 women's home games this season so far, the visitors scored first – through Polish player Monika Suchanek (asst Catherine Pinder) - with just 1.32 on the clock.

That lead however, lasted just 99 seconds as Leen De Decker (asst Elizabeth Wright) levelled the score on 3.11 and added a second on 10.21 (asst Amanda Williams) to give the Wild the narrow lead that their work rate certainly deserved.

The rest of the period was goal-less and was followed by whole period of goal-lessness as the scores remained the same at the second break. The second period was so close that both netminders had exactly the same number of shots each (9) to contend with.

When Katie Hills managed to break the deadlock for Widnes in the 45th minute (44.02 asst Lucy Kirkham) to put them 3-1 up, one might have hoped that they would start to press home their home advantage and gradually start to pull away.

However, instead of crumbling at that point, Streatham upped their game and scored a second goal through Danielle Hogan (45.23 asst Sarah Audsley) to pull their way back into the game.

The match was up and down throughout and Streatham drew level on 50.29 with an unassisted goal by Suchanek and the final 10 minutes were agonisingly tense to watch as both sides chased the win.

Widnes had the greater possession but Streatham looked increasing dangerous on their breakaways. Wild's GB international Sarah Hutchinson took a tactical tripping penalty in the last minute to break up one such attack and the short-handed Widnes team weathered the Storm to secure a hard-earned point.

18 year old netminder Emma Bevan – playing her first game for Widnes, having played for Sheffield Shadows in National Division 1 North division this season –

deservedly received the MVP award for her heroics in the Widnes net.

Following this result, the Widnes Wild Women's team are 5th in the Women's Premier League with 7 points from their 6 games to date, with games in hand over all the teams above them.

They are next in action against league leaders Swindon Topcats – who beat them 1-0 away earlier in the season – on Saturday 26th March at Silver Blades, Widnes in a 4.30pm face off.

Emma Bevan makes a save in the Widnes goal
(Photo by Steve Pollitt)

Wild Women v Swindon Topcats (Photo by Paul Breeze)

Saturday 26th March 2015 – Women's Premier Lge Widnes Wild Women 3 – Swindon Topcats 3

Period Scores: 1-1, 1-2, 1-0
Shots on goal: Widnes 35 – Swindon 30
Penalties In Minutes Widnes 4- Swindon 6
Widnes Scoring - Abigail Culshaw 2+0, Leen de Decker 1+0, Katie Hills, 0+1, Catherine Bowen Fell 0+1

The Widnes Wild women's team picked up a well-deserved point against league leaders Swindon Topcats in an entertaining and highly competitive 3-3 draw at Silver Blades Widnes on Saturday.

The table topping Topcats arrived on Merseyside with an unbeaten record so far this season – having only dropped one point in their 8 games – in a 2-2 draw away at Nottingham Vipers.

The Wild women took the game to the visitors from the off but, once again, it was the away side who found the back of the net first – with the opening goal from Topcats' top scorer Rebecca Da Cova (assist Rebecca Inker) coming after just 2.43 of the match.

Widnes outshot Swindon 11 to 8 in the first period but it was another 10 minutes before Belgian international Leen De Decker scored the equaliser for the Wild (12.46 - unassisted). The score remained the same at the end of the first period. The match was finely poised and, with the confident way that the Wild women were playing, an upset was possibly on the cards.

The Wild women took the lead right sat the start of the second period with an excellent strike from Abigail Culshaw (20.54 - asst Catherine Bowen Fell) scoring her first goal for Widnes.

The lead lasted less than 3 minutes as Captain Rebecca Inker pulled the Topcats back level on 23.43 with an unassisted goal and then Swindon retook the lead on the halfway mark with a goal from player coach Rebecca Osman (30.41 – assts Sarah -Jane Fletcher & Rebecca Da Cova).

To their credit, however, the Widnes women dug deep and that was the last time that the visitors found the back of the net.

The final period was extremely close and you couldn't get a proverbial cigarette paper between the two teams. Then Abigail Culshaw broke through and lifted the puck over the Topcats' netminder to put Widnes back on level terms.

Neither team sat back settling for the draw and both teams had countless chances to win the game. A slashing call on Widnes' Abigail Hayes in the dying minutes kept hearts in mouths and the Wild on the back foot as they managed to keep the Topcats out shorthanded for almost two minutes and claim a well-earned point.

Katie Hills scored 5 goals away at Chelmsford
(Photo by Perry Tomlinson)

Saturday 3rd April 2016 – Women's Premier Lge Chelmsford Cobras 2 - Widnes Wild Women 10

Period Scores: 1-3, 1-5, 0-2
Shots on goal: Chelmsford 15 - Widnes 38
Penalties In Minutes: Chelmsford 2 - Widnes 2
Widnes Scoring: Katie Hills 5+0, Abigail Culshaw 1+2, Leen de Decker & Amanda Williams 1+1, Lucy Kirkham & Beckie Elliott 1+0, Charlene Chapman & Elizabeth Wright 0+1

The Widnes Wild women's team moved up to third place in the Women's Premier League after a comprehensive 2-10 win away at Chelmsford Cobras.

They join Streatham Storm and Slough Phantoms on 10 points but have a superior playing record and games in hand over both teams.

The Wild took control of the game from the start outshooting their hosts 12 to 2 in the opening period but it wasn't until the 9th minute that they scored the first goal of the game through Lucy Kirkham (8.48, asst Charlene Chapman).

Two more quick goals came from Katie Hills (10.03 unassisted) and Beckie Elliot (11.58 no asst) before the Cobras finally pulled a goal back after 17 minutes through Tereza Plankova (asst Tara North & Nicola Hull) to end the first period 1-3 down.

Chelmsford scored first in the second period through Jennifer Bolton (asst Zara Scott) to narrow the margin to just one goal but a quick brace from Katie Hills (25.18 & 27.58) and powerplay goal from Leen de Decker (37.23 assists Amanda Williams and Abigail Culshaw) put the Wild well and truly back in the driving seat.

Two more unassisted goals from Culshaw (38.22) and Hills (39.50) before the end of the second period pretty much put the game out of reach of the Cobras and Katie Hills scored again after the restart (42.47 - asst Elizabeth Wright) to bring her personal tally to five for the game.

Amanda Williams rounded off the scoring for the Wild at 44.08 to bring the two points home to Merseyside.

Wild's Leen De Decker battles in front of the Chelmsford net. (Photo by Perry Tomlinson)

Wild Women v Chelmsford Cobras (Photo by Paul Breeze)

Sunday 10th April 2016 – Women's Premier Lge Widnes Wild Women 5 - Chelmsford Cobras 4

Period Scores: 2-0, 1-1, 2-3
Shots on goal: Widnes 42 - Chelmsford 35
Penalties In Minutes: Widnes 8 - Chelmsford 4
Widnes Scoring: Katie Hills 2+1, Abi Culshaw 2+0, Charlene Chapman 1+0, Leen de Decker, Madeleine Gustavsson, Lucy Kirkham, Amanda Williams all 0+1

The Widnes Wild women's team moved up to second place in the Women's Premier League table after a hard fought 5-4 win at home to Chelmsford Cobras on Sunday night.

They are one of 4 teams tied on 12 points but, because of a superior playing record against 3rd place Streatham, they currently occupy the runner's up slot – albeit a fairly distant 8 points adrift of leaders Slough Topcats – who won 1-7 away at Whitley Bay.

The game against Chelmsford was a gritty affair – and a complete contrast to the game away in Essex 7 days earlier that the Wild had won at a romp.

The Cobras had much of the play in the first period and spent most of their time camped in the Widnes end with the Wild attack consisting mainly of brief counters out of defence. The first goal of the game came when Katie Hills – who had scored 5 away in the last game - got on the end of a Leen de Decker clearance and slotted home on 15.12 to give the Wild a fortunate lead.

Then, in the dying seconds of the period, Abigail Culshaw, taking advantage of a hooking penalty fired in a power play goal (19.06 – asst Hills & Madeleine Gustavsson) to give Widnes a 2 goal cushion at the first break.

The second period saw more one-way traffic as the visitors outshot their hosts by 19 to 6. Stephanie Drinkwater performed heroically in the Widnes net and kept everything out until she was beaten for the first time at 25.30, however the Cobras' goal was disallowed as the referee had been in the process of blowing for a high sticks penalty against Chelmsford's Lucy Jarvis on the edge of the blue zone at the moment the goal went in.

The Cobras' breakthrough did, eventually come 4 minutes later with a well worked unassisted goal from experienced Russian player Tereza Plankova on 29.24.

Just 3 minutes later, it looked as if Chelmsford might score again but the attacking player was adjudged to have been brought down unfairly and a penalty shot was awarded. Netminder Drinkwater stood her ground, however, and saved the penalty and the score remained a narrow 2-1 in favour of the Wild.

The Widnes team managed to give themselves a little breathing space at the end of the period as Katie Hills scored her second goal of the game (39.55 asst Amanda

Williams) and the Wild women went into the second break with a 3-1 lead.

When Abi Culshaw added a fourth goal at 41.07 (unassisted) you might have thought that the game was pretty much over but that was far from the case.

The plucky Cobras continued to push forward and a second goal for Plankova (43.12 asst Law) put them right back into it again.

Enter Bethany Hill – just back from winning a bronze medal with the GB team at the World Championships in Slovenia - with two stunning goals on 48.17 (unassisted) and 51.31 (asst Plankova) and the scene was set for a nail biting finale.

The Cobras seemed to have the initiative and it could only be matter of time before they scored again to take the lead but the Widnes women dug deep and managed to keep them at bay. Just when it looked as if the match was heading for a draw – which would have been the Wild's third in a row at home – team captain Charlene Chapman put them back in front (54.36 assist Lucy Kirkham) with what would turn out to be the game winning goal.

The last few minutes involved more hard defending as the Cobras surged forward in search of a late equaliser. However, despite several icing calls that took play back into the Wild zone in the last minute, they did not pull their netminder in favour of an extra attacker and the clock slowly ticked down to a Widnes victory.

Sunday 17th April 2016 – Women's Premier Lge
Nottingham Vipers 6 – Widnes Wild Women 8

Period Scores: 1-4, 0-4, 5-0
Shots on goal: Nottingham 33 - Widnes 48
Penalties In Minutes: Nottingham 35 - Widnes 20
Widnes Scoring: Leen De Decker 2+0, Katie Hills 2+0, Megan Bowen Fell, 1+ 1, Amanda Williams 1+1, Abigail Culshaw 1+1, Vanessa Crickmore Clarke 0+1, Catherine Bowen Fell 1+0, Elizabeth Amy Wright 0+1, Charlene Chapman 0+1

Widnes remain in second place in the Women's Premier League table after a sensational 6-8 victory away at Nottingham Vipers on Sunday evening. Earlier in the day, fellow contenders for the runners-up spot Streatham Storm had beat Chelmsford Cobras 2-0 to move ahead on points so a win was vital for the Wild women to maintain their position.

Whitley Squaws beat Milton Keynes 3-1 in their first win since November meaning that the Falcons are now two points off the pace in 4th.

Despite an otherwise fairly evenly balanced first period, the Wild women scored three early goals and were leading 1-4 by the first break and then added a further 4 unanswered goals in the second period to go into the final third with a 1-8 advantage.

However, the Vipers upped their game for the final period. A goal straight from the restart initiated a goal fest that saw them score 5 unanswered goals to pull the score back to 6-8, with team captain Robyn Muller scoring 4 straight between 40.08 and 49.35.

The Widnes Wild women were kept goalless for almost the whole of the second half of the game but managed to hold on to register an important victory.

On Saturday, league leaders Swindon Topcats are away to Slough Phantoms while MK Falcons are at home to Nottingham Vipers.

On Sunday the Widnes Wild women are away to Whitley Squaws in a 4.30pm face off while 3rd place Streatham Storm entertain the MK Falcons. Nottingham and Chelmsford meet at the National Ice Centre for a bottom of the table clash.

The Widnes Wild women's team are next at home on Sunday 8th May when they entertain Whitley Squaws at Silver Blades Widnes in a 5.30pm face off.

Above Left: Jodie Boyle Above Right: Jakki Duncan
(Both photos by Geoff White)

Beckie Elliott (Photo by Flyfifer Photography)

Sunday 24th April 2016 – Women's Premier Lge Whitley Squaws 2 – Widnes Wild Women 10

Period Scores: 1-3, 1-6, 0-1
Shots on Goal: Whitley 28 – Widnes 57
Penalties In Minutes: Whitley 6 – Widnes 6
Widnes Scoring: Catherine Bowen Fell 3+0, Katie Hills 2+5, Charlene Chapman 2+0, Leen De Decker 1+1, Lucy Kirkham 1+1, Emma Pearson 1+1, Madeleine Gustavsson 0+2, Beckie Elliott 0+1

The Widnes Wild women's team took a step closer to securing the runners up spot in the English Women's Premier League after a comprehensive 2-10 win away at Whitley Squaws.

With fellow contenders for second place Streatham Storm and Milton Keynes Falcons drawing 0-0 against each other, it means that the Wild women are now 1 point clear of both teams with games in hand and a game away at MK next Sunday.

If they win away at MK next week, the Wild women will be assured of second place.

In the bottom of the table clash, Nottingham Vipers beat Chelmsford Cobras 4-2 to leapfrog them off the bottom spot.

Whitley actually scored first – after just 1.48 – in a first period that saw them heavily outshot by 6 to 20 and, once the Wild women got in their stride, there was no stopping them. Emma Pearson opened the Widnes account with her first goal for the club on 3.28 and goals from Charlene Chapman and Catherine Bowen Fell gave them a 1-3 lead at the first break.

A 1-6 second period put the game way beyond Whitley's reach and Lucy Kirkham rounded off the scoring at 58. 43 to give the Wild a 2-10 win.

Catherine Bowen Fell was Widnes' top markswoman with 3 goals while Katie Hills weighed in with 2+5.

The Wild women are away at Milton Keynes next Sunday and then finish off their first ever Women's Premier League campaign with two successive home games – against Whitley Squaws on Sunday 8th May and Nottingham Vipers on Sunday 15th May at Silver Blades Widnes.

Both games face off at 5.30pm and admission is free.

Abi Culshaw scored the Wild Women's equalising goal away at MK (Photo by Lucy McGill Photography)

Sunday 1st May 2016 – Women's Premier Lge Milton Keynes Falcons 1– Widnes Wild Women 1

Period Scores: 0-0, 1-0, 0-1
Shots on Goal: MK 24 – Widnes 40
Penalties In Minutes: MK 6 – Widnes 6
Widnes Scoring: Abi Culshaw 1+0, Catherine Bowen Fell 0+1

The Widnes Wild women's team took a step closer to securing the runners up spot in the Women's Premier League with a close- fought 1-1 draw away at Milton Keynes Falcons.

Looking for revenge over the only team to have beaten them at home this season, the Wild women had the upper hand in the first period – outshooting their hosts by more than 2 to 1 but were unable to make a breakthrough.

Milton Keynes eventually scored first during a more evenly balanced second period with their only goal of the game coming from Sarah Carter at 35.53 (asst Kirsten Noble).

Despite battering the MK goal again in the third period, it took until 53.36 for Widnes to find the back of the net when Abi Culshaw picked up from Catherine Bowen Fell to slot in a well-deserved equaliser.

Penalty calls on both sides made the last few minutes interesting and Widnes had a powerplay opportunity in the last 2 minutes of the match but were unable to force in that all-important game winning goal.

Sharing the points means that the Widnes women's team are not yet assured of finishing in second place as both they and MK still have a game to plays.

Streatham Storm, however will not be overtaking them as they drew their final game of the season 1-1 away at Nottingham Vipers and finish up with 16 points from their 14 games. They are currently in 3rd but could be overtaken by MK if they win their last game of the season at home to champions Swindon Top Cats next weekend.

That draw was Nottingham's third of the season and the first time they have gone unbeaten in back to back fixtures all year.

As expected, Swindon Top Cats secured the league title after their 9-0 shut out of Slough Phantoms ensured they couldn't be caught by any of the chasing pack with games in hand. They are unbeaten in all their 13 league season but face a tricky away trip to Milton Keynes for their last game of the campaign.

Wild Women v Whitley Squaws (Photo by Paul Breeze)

Sunday 8th May 2016 – Women's Premier Lge
Widnes Wild Women 2 – Whitley Squaws 3

Period Scores: 1-1, 0-1, 1-1
Shots On Goal: Widnes 32 – Whitley 28
Penalties in Minutes: Widnes 16 – Whitley 10
Widnes Scoring: Leen de Decker 1+0, Charlene Chapman 1+0, Emma Pearson 0+1, Catherine Bowen Fell 0+1

The Widnes Wild women's team secured second place in the EIHA Women's Premier League in their first season at this level, despite losing at home to Whitley Squaws 2-3 on Sunday in a hard fought and entertaining game at Silver Blades, Widnes.

With challengers Milton Keynes Falcons narrowly losing at home to champions Swindon Topcats in their last league game later in the day, it meant that the Wild women couldn't be caught and that the scoreline in their own game was – luckily - immaterial.

With Widnes having won 2-10 away in the North East a few weeks ago, you might have expected this return match to be a largely one-sided affair but that was far from the case. With a few players missing, and some having to play out of their normal positions, the Wild team seemed to missing a certain spark whereas the Squaws looked very well organised and played with determination and spirit throughout the game.

Despite this, the game started very evenly and Whitley opened the scoring at 6.55 when Melissa Gough slotted away a pass from team captain Amy Campbell. The home side rallied from this early set back and got themselves back on level terms with a goal from Leen de Decker on 14.23 (asst Emma Pearson).

The score remained level at the first break and Widnes came out all fired up for the second period but were unable to make the most of the pressure that they were putting on the Whitley net.

This turned out to be the most penalty littered of games that we have seen from the Wild women at home this season and it was unfortunately, the penalty count that led to their downfall on this occasion.

Whitley's second goal of the game (25.58 – Campbell, asst Stephanie Towns) came from a powerplay opportunity, while the Wild were shorthanded from a holding penalty and their third goal (47.50 – Towns, asst Campbell) came on a tripping powerplay.

Widnes captain Charlene Chapman battled through to put the Wild women back in the game on 53.50 (asst Catherine Bowen Fell) and, with the pressure that followed, one might have expected a dramatic late equaliser and another 3-3 home draw. But it was not to be. The Squaws upped their game again and defended most resolutely.

Widnes pulled their netminder for that last 30 seconds or so but were unable to take any advantage from the extra player and Whitley held on to pick up their first away victory since November and only their 4th win of the season overall.

The Squaws are at home next Sunday in their last game of the season – with Chelmsford Cobras the visitors. Whitley are assured a 6th place finish in the WPL irrespective of the result although they will undoubtedly be keen to finish the season on a winning note.

Chelmsford - who lost 3-5 at home to Slough Phantoms - need a positive result to give them any chance of hauling themselves off the bottom of the table. Nottingham Vipers are level on points with them but have the better playing record between the two teams.

The Vipers provide the opposition at Silver Blades Widnes next Sunday for the Widnes Wild women's team's last game of the season. Face off is 5.30pm and admission is free.

Wirral-based writer, broadcaster and historian Lucy London was on hand to present the MVP awards at the end of the Widnes v Whitley game.

Elizabeth Wright was the Wild Women's recipient (Photo by Paul Breeze)

Wild Women v Nottingham (Photo by Paul Breeze)

Sunday 15th May 2016 – Women's Premier Lge Widnes Wild Women 5 – Nottingham Vipers 3

Period Scores: 0-1, 2-2, 3-0
Shots on Goal: Widnes 56 – Nottm 29
Penalties in Minutes: Widnes 6 – Nottm 41
Widnes Scoring: Catherine Bowen Fell 2+1, Leen de Decker 2+0, Katie Hills 1+0, Emma Pearson 0+2, Charlene Chapman & Megan Bowen Fell 0+1

The Widnes Wild women's' team finished off their first ever EIHA Women's Premier League campaign on a winning note with a hard fought 5-3 home victory over Nottingham Vipers.

The Wild team had a point to prove after a disappointing defeat at home to Whitley Squaws the week before while Nottingham needed a positive result in order to stay ahead of Chelmsford Cobras and avoid finishing bottom of the table.

As it turned out, it was the Nottingham team who were quickest off the blocks and shocked the home crowd into silence with a goal after just 36 seconds of the game.

Obviously rocked by this early setback it took the Wild women a while to reorganise themselves and while they enjoyed lots of possession in the first period, they were unable to make any sort of breakthrough. Two power play opportunities came and went and the first period ended with Nottingham leading 0-1.

Things did not improve greatly for the home side as the second period got underway. While pushing up to take advantage of another powerplay situation, the Wild allowed Nottingham captain and top scorer Robin Mullen through to score a shorthanded goal.

Then when Catherine Bowen Fell finally slotted home to score Widnes' first goal of the game (26.02 – asst Emma Pearson), a defensive mix up right from the restart saw the puck trickle beyond the despairing reach of netminder Stephanie Drinkwater and edge across the line to restore the Vipers' 2 goal advantage.

But that was as good as it got the for the visiting Nottingham team. They started picking up penalties and Widnes were able to gradually pull themselves back into the game.

A second goal from Bowen Fell on a powerplay for hooking call made it 2-3 (31.25 – asst Pearson) and when a Nottingham player was given a 5+game for checking and another picked up a checking minor soon afterwards, you just felt that the Wild team would make something of the resulting 5 on 3 play. The Vipers defended most resolutely however and the score remained 2-3 at the end of the second period.

The third period was a very closely contested and tense affair. Widnes equalised on 44.27 with another powerplay goal (Leen de Decker, asst Charlene Chapman) and the scene was set for a nail-biting finale.

The turning point came when Widnes found themselves on the wrong end of a 3 on 5 with both Katie Hills and Catherine Bowen Fell banished to the penalty box for minor penalties at the same time.

The Wild women fought a brave rear-guard action to keep the rampaging Vipers at bay during this crucial period of the game and as the penalties expired (53.50), both played players sprinted up the ice to combined for the go-ahead goal that put Widnes in front for the first time in the game (53.53 - Hills, asst Bowen Fell).

A second goal from Leen de Decker (57.29 – asst Megan Bowen Fell) finally put some daylight between the two teams and the game finished 5-3 to the Widnes Wild women.

The result means that the Widnes Wild women's team finish in second place with 19 points from their 14 games, 7 points behind champions Swindon Topcats who didn't lose a single game all season.

Perhaps more importantly, they finish ahead of Streatham Storm, Milton Keynes Falcons and Slough Phantoms who had all played in the Premier League last season and who all boast very fine pedigrees in women's hockey.

At the bottom of the table, Chelmsford Cobras lost 13-1 away at Whitley Squaws, meaning that they pick up the wooden spoon, with Nottingham Vipers finishing above them based on games between the two sides.

The top four teams in the WPL now meet in the play-off weekend which will take place at iceSheffield on 28th and 29th May. The semi-finals will be held on the Saturday and the final played on the Sunday.

Megan Bowen Fell (Photo by Flyfifer Photography)

Widnes Wild Women - April 2016 (Photo by Geoff White)

Back Row: Emma Pearson, Jakki Duncan, Madeleine Gustavsson, Lucy Kirkham, Katherine Holliday, Catherine Bowen Fell, Beckie Elliott, Amanda Williams, Charlene Chapman. Front Row: Leen de Decker, Katie Hills, Stephanie Drinkwater, Elizabeth Wright, Abi Culshaw, Abi Hayes.

28th May 2016 - WPL Play Off Semi Final
Widnes Wild Women 1- Streatham Storm 2

Period Scores: 0-1, 0-1, 1-0
Shot On Goal: Widnes 21 – Streatham 18
Penalties In Minutes: Widnes 6 – Streatham 2
Widnes Scoring: Leen de Decker 1+0, Amanda Williams & Katie Hills 0+1

The Widnes Wild women narrowly lost out 2-1 to Streatham Storm in the semi final of the WPL Play Offs at Sheffield over the weekend.

Streatham took the lead on 10 minutes and then doubled the advantage with a second goal 4 minutes into the second period.

Widnes pulled a goal back through Leen de Decker 25 seconds into the 3rd period but they were unable make any further headway and the score finished 2-1 to Streatham.

Sarah Hutchinson (Photo: Geoff White) is the only Widnes player to have played as a full Great Britain international while a Wild Women's player.

She took part in the Div2A of the World Championships in Slovenia during April 2016.

Abi Culshaw played for the GB Women's Under 18 team at the 2016 World Championships while she was a Widnes player and went to be a regular senior international in later years.

Amanda Williams in action at the Swindon Tournament
(Photo by Flyfifer Photography)

Swindon Tournament 2016

by Leen de Decker

Last weekend on Saturday June 18th to Sunday June 19th the Widnes Wild Women's team played in the 20th British Women's Ice Hockey Friendship Tournament in Swindon.

The tournament uses a 12 minute game with running clock format, so it really forced the girls to get straight into the game and play hard from the first shift.

Widnes ended the first day in 3rd place with 3 wins and 3 draws out of 6 games which put them in a great position to reach the knock-out stages of the tournament.

The 2nd day, Widnes started strong with a very convincing win over Nottingham, but lost the following game to Solihull, the only team out of the Elite league to play in the tournament.

The next three games were crucial for Widnes to secure a place in the semi-finals and they did so with 2 draws and a win.

This meant Widnes finished third in the overall standing and played in the first semi-final to 2nd place and host team Swindon.

In a very tense game with plenty of chances on both sides, the game finished 0-0 after the 15 minute regular playing time format used for the knock-out stages.

This meant the game would have to be decided on a penalty shout-out and the home team Swindon emerged as match winners. Swindon eventually went on the win the tournament after beating Solihull in the final.

Abi Hayes was voted MVP for Widnes Wild based on the 12 games played inc. the Semi final.

A special thanks and congratulations go to Swindon from the Widnes team for organising a great tournament yet again. Huge thanks to thc organising team for all their efforts in making the weekend such a success and we hope to be there again next year.

EIHA Women's Premier League - Season 2016/17

Final Table	GP	W	D	L	GF	GA	PIM	Pts
Streatham Storm	12	9	2	1	92	23	96	20
Chelmsford Cobras	12	7	3	2	58	49	74	17
Milton Keynes Falcons	12	6	4	2	57	30	102	16
Widnes Wild Women	**12**	**5**	**2**	**5**	**45**	**45**	**136**	**12**
Slough Phantoms	12	5	2	5	43	60	65	12
Kingston Diamonds	12	2	0	10	27	44	225	4
Nottingham Vipers	12	1	1	10	24	95	48	3

EIHA WPL Top Points Scorers – Season 2016/17

Player	Team	GP	G	A	Pts	PIM
Rachel Piotrowski	MK Falcons	11	24	7	31	12
Bethany Ruth May Hill	Chelmsford Cobras	10	18	5	23	6
Nicola Bicknell	Slough Phantoms	11	10	12	22	6
Jennifer Bolton	Chelmsford Cobras	12	12	10	22	4
Carolyn Scott	Streatham Storm	10	13	8	21	12
Amy Hadden	Slough Phantoms	10	15	4	19	4
Danielle Hogan	Streatham Storm	12	7	12	19	0
Fiona King	Streatham Storm	11	14	4	18	0
Joanna Li How Cheong	Streatham Storm	11	8	10	18	2
Tereza Plankova	Chelmsford Cobras	11	9	8	17	28
Elizabeth Archer	MK Falcons	11	6	10	16	22
Leen De Decker	Widnes Wild Women	11	11	5	16	2
Katie Hills	Widnes Wild Women	10	9	6	15	28
Melissa Reidelberger	Streatham Storm	11	7	8	15	0

EIHA WPL Top Netminders– Season 2016/17

Netminder	Team	GPI	SA	GA	Sv%
Lucy Jarvis	Chelmsford Cobras	7	23	1	95.65%
Michaela Walker	Slough Phantoms	6	145	10	93.10%
Kayliegh Doyle	MK Falcons	12	367	30	91.83%
Ruth Cattell	Streatham Storm	12	265	23	91.32%
Charlotte Cook	Kingston Diamonds	12	484	44	90.91%
Stephanie Drinkwater	Widnes	7	254	26	89.76%
Sarah Gunstone	Slough Phantoms	7	330	38	88.48%
Rachel Fairbairn	Widnes	7	84	12	85.71%
Cherry Hambelton	Chelmsford Cobras	11	334	48	85.63%
Summer Cramer	Nottingham Vipers	10	505	74	85.35%
Ruth Palmer	Nottingham Vipers	3	139	21	84.89%

Widnes Wild Women Results – Season 2016/17

Date	Comp	Home		Away	H/A	Res
11.09.16	WPL	Widnes Wild	1	MK Falcons	5	L
25.09.16	WPL	Chelmsfd Cobras	7	Widnes Wild	6	L
23.10.16	WPL	Widnes Wild	3	Slough Phantoms	3	D
30.10.16	WPL	Widnes Wild	3	Nott'm Vipers	2	W
27/11/16	WPL	Widnes Wild	6	Kingston Dias	4	W
11.12.16	WPL	Nottm Vipers	4	Widnes Wild	2	L
08.01.17	WPL	Streatham Storm	5	Widnes Wild	1	L
15.01.17	WPL	Widnes Wild	2	Streatham Storm	3	L
12.02.17	WPL	Widnes Wild	4	Chelmsfd Cobras	4	D
30.04.17	WPL	Slough Phantoms	2	Widnes Wild	9	W
07.05.17	WPL	MK Falcons	4	Widnes Wild	5	W
27.05.17	WPL	Kingston Diamds	2	Widnes Wild	3	W
03.06.17	POS*	Widnes Wild	1	Streatham Storm	6	L

**Play Off Semi Final played at iceSheffield*

Sal (Sarah) Roberts, left and Sav (Savannah) Sumner, right, were the first Widnes born and trained players to play league ice hockey when they made their debuts at the start of the 2016/17 season (Photos by Flyfifer Photography)

Head Coach Owen Tennant talks tactics during a period break. (Photo by Geoff White)

Widnes Wild Women Season Summary - 2016/17

The Widnes Wild women's team were always going to be hard pushed to replicate the previous season's success where they finished runners up in the Women's Premier League and qualified for the end of season play offs at a canter.

That was the first season of women's ice hockey at Widnes, with the former Manchester Phoenix women's team making a last minute switch from Altrincham to Widnes in the wake of the Red Hockey / Phoenix upheavals in the summer of 2015.

This season was very much one of transition with several of the former Phoenix players either moving on to other teams or giving up playing all together.

Swedish player Madeleine Gustavsson went back home to play in Swedish women's Division 1 west for Kallhalls IF, Elizabeth Wright switched to play for the Widnes based recreational teams while Team GB international player Sarah Hutchinson went off to play with the Altrincham Aces men's team in the Laidler Conference and Kingston Diamonds in the Women's Elite League.

Of the returning players, several were unavailable for long periods of the season either due to injury, work or other reasons - but all was not doom and gloom!

The nucleus of the team returned, led again by experienced captain Charlene Chapman, and Katie Hills and Leen de Decker were back to resume their duel at the top of the team's scoring tables.

Sophie Sinclair Reeks – who enjoyed a successful breakthrough campaign last season - became a full time member of the team – and also went on to represent GB at under 18 level in the Women's World Championships in Poland.

In addition, the team was able to bring in a new crop of girls from the Widnes area who all did very well in their first ever season of competition. Sav Sumner was an ever-present in the side, Sal Roberts went on to be stand-in captain in the absence of Chapman and Rachel Fairbairn looks to be a very good prospect.

The team also had a new coaching team in the shape of Head Coach Owen Tennant and fellow former Deeside player Matt Humphreys.

The WPL season started with a disappointing 1-5 defeat at Silver Blades Widnes to MK Falcons where nothing went right for the Wild women. They outplayed the visitors for much of game, outshot them throughout and had what might have been a pivotal early goal disallowed - whereas everything that MK touched seemed to end up in the back of the of the net!

This was followed up with a 7-6 defeat away at Chelmsford Cobras, after having led 0-2 early in the game. This seemed to be a disappointing result at the time as the Cobras had finished bottom of the WPL the previous season but they went on to lead the table for much of this campaign and were a much stronger proposition all round.

The Wild Women finally picked up their first point of the season with a 3-3 draw at home to Slough Phantoms in October. Having led 2-1 earlier in the game, the Wild women fell behind with just 3 minutes to go and only snatched the draw in dramatic fashion with a goal by Leen de Decker in the very last second of the game.

Two more wins came in consecutive homes games – as the Wild women beat Nottingham Vipers 3-2 and bottom team Kingston Diamonds 6-4 - but the calendar year ended with a 4-2 defeat away at Nottingham, which would ultimately turn out to be the Vipers' only win all season.

The New Year opened with back to back games against emerging title contenders Streatham Storm over consecutive weekends. The away trip – with a very short Widnes bench – ended in a 5-1 win for the home team but hopes were high for the return game at Silver Blades Widnes the following week when more players were expected to be available for the Wild women.

Unfortunately, during the week prior to the game, the Silver Blades rink arranged to stage a Manchester Phoenix EPL game the same day and the face-off time for the women's game was brought forward from 5.30pm to 4pm.

This late change caused problems for the Wild team as some players were unable to manage the earlier start time and they had to play with a weaker team than expected.

The game started off pretty much to form with Streatham well in command. They outshot the hosts by almost 2 to 1 and led 0-2 at the end of the first period. Widnes gradually dragged themselves back into the game and goals from Charlene Chapman and Leen de Decker drew them level with just 6 minutes left to play.

The Wild women pushed forward trying to force a winning goal but were caught out at the back as Streatham broke through some two minutes later to retake the lead. The last 4 minutes were as exciting ice hockey as you could hope to see anywhere as Widnes tried to snatch a late goal but it was all in vain and the Storm took the win 2-3.

A creditable 4-4 draw with Chelmsford Cobras followed in the Wild women's last home game of the season in mid-February and they then had an incredibly long wait until the end of April to finish their league campaign.

By this time that they took to the ice again, results among the other teams meant that, despite having had a comparatively disappointing season thus far, the Wild women still had an outside chance of finishing in 4th place in the WPL table and reaching the end of season play off weekend.

To do this, however, they would have to win their last three games – all away from home.

The play off run-in in kicked off with an incredible 2-9 win away at Slough Phantoms on their temporary ice surface and then continued with a 4-5 win at Milton Keynes Falcons who had already secured third place in the table.

The decisive game away at Kingston Diamonds was very close and it took a dramatic late winner from Wild's Amanda Williams to score the win and ensure a fourth place finish for the Widnes team.

Widnes Wild Women - Player Statistics
Season 2016/17

	Regular Season					Play Offs*				
Player	**GP**	**G**	**A**	**Pts**	**PIM**	**GP**	**G**	**A**	**Pts**	**PIM**
Leen De Decker	11	12	5	17	2	1	1	0	1	
Katie Hills	10	10	6	16	42	1	0	1	1	
Charlene Chapman	10	6	6	12	0	0	0	0	0	
Lucy Kirkham	11	4	4	8	0	1	0	0	0	
Amanda Williams	9	4	4	8	0	0	0	0	0	
Emma Pearson	12	2	5	7	4	1	0	0	0	
Abigail Culshaw	2	3	2	5	0	0	0	0	0	
Sophie Sinclr-Reeks	10	3	2	5	6	1	0	0	0	
Abigail Hayes	9	1	2	3	2	1	0	0	0	
Savannah Sumner	12	1	2	3	10	1	0	1	1	
Vanessa C-Clarke	6	2	0	2	0	0	0	0	0	
Beckie Elliott	12	0	2	2	0	1	0	0	0	
Emma Bevan	2	0	0	0	0	0	0	0	0	
Megan Bowen Fell	7	0	0	0	64	0	0	0	0	
Steph Drinkwater	7	0	0	0	0	1	0	0	0	
Rachel Fairbairn	7	0	0	0	0	0	0	0	0	
Elizabeth Loss	1	0	0	0	0	0	0	0	0	
Emma Middleton	4	0	0	0	0	0	0	0	0	
Sarah Roberts	10	0	0	0	2	1	0	0	0	
Cath Bowen Fell	1	0	0	0	0	0	0	0	0	
Tegan Lavery	1	0	0	0	0	1	0	0	0	

**Note: Complete player statistics were not made available for the Play Off Semi Final*

Netminder Statistics - Season 2016/17

Netminder	Comp	GPI	Mins	SA	GA	GAA	Save %	SO
Steph Drinkwater	WPL	7	400	254	26	3.90	89.76	0
Emma Bevan	WPL	2	120	71	5	2.50	92.96	0
Rachel Fairbairn	WPL	3	140	90	12	5.14	86.67	0
Tegan Lavery	WPL	1	60	39	2	2.00	94.87	0
	POS	1	60	40	6	6.00	85.00	0
	Totals	2	120	79	8	4.00	89.87	0

Netminding Break Down – Season 2016/17

Match	Netminder	GPI	Mins	SA	GA	GAA	Sv %
11th Sep v MK	Drinkwater	1	60	40	5	5.00	87.50
25th Sep @ CHE	Fairbairn	1	60	38	7	7.00	81.58
23rd Oct v SLO	Bevan	1	60	37	3	3.00	91.89
30th Oct v NOT	Bevan	1	60	34	2	2.00	94.12
27th Nov v KIN	Drinkwater	1	40	23	3	4.50	86.96
27th Nov v KIN	Fairbairn	1	20	13	1	3.00	92.31
11th Dec @ NOT	Drinkwater	1	60	42	4	4.00	90.48
8th Jan @ STR	Drinkwater	1	60	34	5	5.00	85.29
15th Jan v STR	Drinkwater	1	60	53	3	3.00	94.34
12th Feb v CHE	Fairbairn	1	60	39	4	4.00	89.74
30th Apr @ SLO	Drinkwater	1	60	29	2	2.00	93.10
7th May @ MK	Drinkwater	1	60	33	4	4.00	87.88
27th May @ KIN	Lavery	1	60	39	2	2.00	94.87
3rd June POSF*	Lavery	1	60	40	6	6.00	85.00

**Play Off Semi Final against Streatham played at iceSheffield*

HOME
GUEST
20:00
BAUER
BAUER
Reebok
Reebok

Leen de Decker
(Photo by Paul Breeze)

Katie Hills(Photo by Geoff White)

Stephanie Drinkwater
(Photo by Geoff White)

Charlene Chapman
(Photo by Lucy McGill)

8th September 2016: Season Preview, 2016/17

The Widnes Wild Women's ice hockey team get their Women's Premier League season underway with a home game against Milton Keynes Falcons this Sunday at Silver Blades Widnes.

This is the Wild team's second season at WPL level and last season they finished runners up in the league standings to the all-conquering Swindon Top Cats who went the whole season unbeaten.

The Wild women were one of only two teams to take a point off the eventual champions and, with the Top Cats now having been promoted to the Women's Elite League, there are hopes that the Widnes team might be able to go one better this time around.

Assistant Captain Emma Brown said:"The women's team is largely unchanged from last season with the majority of players re-signing. We have a couple of new faces who haven't played on a women's team before, Sav Sumner and Sal Roberts, but who are looking forward to the new challenge and are fitting in well with the existing team. We also have a new coach, Owen Tennant, who has brought a new dynamic to our on Ice sessions and we are hopeful he can help us build on our previous success.

Last season Widnes competed well against MK with a draw and a very closely fought loss. We are hoping to improve on these results and get a win in our first game of the season, starting as we mean to go on."

The WPL has 7 teams this season as opposed to last season's 8, due the Whitley Bay Squaws dropping out at a late stage in the summer. Last season's champions Swindon have been promoted to the WEL and Kingston

Diamonds - who won the Division 1 North v Division 1 South Play Off at iceSheffield - have moved up into the WPL.

The Widnes Wild women's team Women's Premier League fixtures for the 2016/17 season are as follows (home games in bold):

11th September - home v Milton Keynes Falcons
25th September - away @ Chelmsford Cobras
23rd October - home v Slough Phantoms
30th October – home v Nottingham Vipers
27th November – home v Kingston Diamonds
11th December: away @ Nottingham Vipers
8th January: away @ Streatham Storm
15th January: home v Streatham Storm
4th February: away @ Slough Phantoms
12th February: home v Chelmsford Cobras
7th May: away @ Milton Keynes Falcons
27th May: away @ Kingston Diamonds

The Wild women's team's first home game of the season is against Milton Keynes Falcons this Sunday. Face off is at 5.30pm - and admission is free!

Katie Hills scores the Wild Women's only goal against MK
(Photo by Geoff White)

Sunday 11th September 2016 – Women's Premier Lge
Widnes Wild Women 1 - Milton Keynes Falcons 5

Period Scores: 0-1, 0-1, 1-3
Shots on Goal: Widnes 47 – Milton Keynes 40
Penalties in Minutes: Widnes 2 - Milton Keynes 16
Widnes Scoring: Katie Hills 1+0, Abigail Culshaw 0+1

The Widnes Wild Women's ice hockey team had a disappointing start to their Women's Premier League season as they crashed to a surprise 1-5 defeat at home to Milton Keynes Falcons on Sunday at the Silver Blades rink in Widnes.

The Wild women were runners up in the league last season and have more or less the same team in place for the new campaign - with the addition of few new faces - but they were given a lesson in finding the back of the net by a useful looking Milton Keynes side who arrived as early season league leaders following a 3-3 win away at Chelmsford in their first game last weekend.

Setting the scoreline aside for a moment, this was actually a very closely contested game overall and very entertaining to watch. Widnes had by far the most possession of the puck in the first period – outshooting the Falcons by 21 to 12 – but it was the visitors who took the lead after 9 minutes.

As the period ticked down, the Wild increased the pressure of the Milton Keynes goal and, in the dying seconds, it looked as if they had finally managed to force home an equaliser but the buzzer for the end of the period sounded just before the puck crossed the goal line and the goal did not count.

The second period was a much closer affair in terms of possession with Widnes making the early running but still not managing to make any significant breakthrough.

The first penalty of the game came at 29.36 as a Falcons' player was called for hooking but Widnes were unable to gain any advantage from the resulting powerplay. Buoyed by their strong defensive performance while a player short, the Milton Keynes team upped their efforts and had the upper hand for much of the rest of the period.

They also seemed to be getting all the lucky breaks as, with just 57 seconds to go in the period, the puck took an unfortunate bounce off a Wild defender and looped down onto the stick of an attacker. The Falcons' forward Elizabeth Archer looped it straight back towards the goal and the puck flew over the despairing grasp of Wild netminder Stephanie Drinkwater and dropped into the back of the net.

Even at 2-0 down, the Wild team looked as if they might be able to drag themselves back in to the game and they spent most of the third period pushing forward in search of that elusive breakthrough goal. Unfortunately, this meant they left space at the back and Milton Keynes hit a third goal with 44.35 on the clock.

The Widnes players will probably have realised that it was not going to be their night when, on 53 minutes and while they had a player advantage on a powerplay after the Falcons had been caught with too many players on the ice during a line change, they conceded a penalty shot which was slotted away by Milton Keynes Canadian player Rachel Piotrowski.

The Wild women called a time-out to re-gather their composure but even that backfired as, straight from the re-start, Milton Keynes went straight down the Widnes end and scored again!

At 0-5 down, with less than 5 minutes remaining on the clock and Milton Keynes looking very solid in all areas of the ice, it seemed very unlikely that Widnes would be able to salvage anything in the time remaining.

However, the home fans did eventually get something to cheer about when Abigail Culshaw went on a darting run forward and knocked in a perfect cross for last season's top points scorer Katie Hills to fire in a consolation goal at 57.35.

A bizarre occurrence just 40 seconds from the final buzzer saw Falcons' Archer pick up a 10 minute misconduct penalty for abuse of an official but she returned to the ice after the match to pick up the MVP award for the Falcons while the Wild award went to Sarah Roberts who was playing in her first ever competitive game.

Leen de Decker (#5) and Abi Culshaw (#98) attack the goal away at Chelmsford Cobras (Photo by Perry Tomlinson).

Sunday 25th September 2016 – Women's Premier Lge Chelmsford Cobras 7 – Widnes Wild Women 6

The Widnes Wild women's team suffered heartbreak on the road at Chelmsford as they lost out to a late rally in a 13 goal thriller.

The Wild women took a two goal lead early in the first period but were gradually pegged back and found themselves 5-4 down after two periods.

Abi Culshaw hit her hat-trick goal on 53 minutes to pull the Wild level again, however, two unassisted goals from Chelmsford's GB women's international Bethany Hill – her 3 rd and 4 th of the game- put the Cobras into an unassailable lead and a goal by Wild's top scorer from last season Katie Hills in the last 30 seconds of the match was not enough to take a share of the spoils.

The last-second equaliser at home against Slough Phantoms captured on video by the Wild's official videographer Colin Ellis.

Sunday 23rd October 2016 – Women's Premier Lge
Widnes Wild Women 3 – Slough Phantoms 3

Period Scores: 0-1, 2-1, 1-1
Shots on Goal: Widnes 63 – Slough 37
Penalties In Minutes: Widnes 2 – Slough 10
Widnes Scoring: Leen de Decker 2+1, Sophie Sinclair-Reeks 1+1, Katie Hills 0+1, Abigail Hayes 0+1

The Widnes Wild women's team picked up their first point of the new season in dramatic fashion as a last minute equaliser salvaged a 3-3 draw against Slough Phantoms at Silver Blades Widnes on Sunday.

The result saw the Wild women end the visiting Phantoms' unbeaten start to the season and also get their own Women's Premier League campaign well and truly under way.

The Wild team was slightly understrength with a few regular players missing – including regular captain Charlene Chapman who was replaced as skipper by

Emma Pearson - and the also team used their 3rd netminder in 3 games with Emma Bevan being called in as cover from the North 1 Sheffield team.

The first period was very even with chances going to both sides but first blood eventually went to the visitors who scored the opening goal after 10 minutes – a lead that they held until the first break.

The second period was one of end to action and excitement with the Wild women laying siege to the Slough goal for long periods at a time. They outshot the Phantoms by over two to one (29 shots to 14) in the middle third and the incessant pressure finally began to pay off.

With the clock at 24.28 two Slough players picked up penalties at the same time – one for cross checking and one for hooking – which gave the Wild a two player advantage. They made the most of this opportunity and within 90 seconds were back on level terms as former Belgium international player Leen de Decker fired in a pass from Sophie Sinclair-Reeks for a superbly worked powerplay goal.

Less than two minutes later at 27.39, Widnes took the lead as Sinclair–Reeks – fresh back from international duty with the Team GB Under 18 team in Hungary – scored her first senior goal to leave the game well and truly there for the taking with over 30 minutes still to play.

More Widnes pressure led to more Slough penalties and the Phantoms called a timeout at 31.03 when faced with another 5 on 3 powerplay. The tactic worked and the Widnes momentum was lost. Slough then scored an equalising goal with 4 minutes left on the clock - leaving the score at 2-2 after 40 minutes.

The third period saw more of the same with Widnes once again battering the Slough goal and outshooting their visitors by 22 to 8. However Slough shut up shop and neither side was able to make much of a breakthrough. The Wild conceded their only penalty of the game as Megan Bowen Fell was called for hooking at 53.26 but they weathered the storm and killed off the Slough powerplay.

A subsequent timeout called by the Wild at 55.50 had the undesired effect of breaking up their pattern of play and Slough subsequently raced down the ice and scored at the other end within seconds of the restart – somewhat against the run of the play.

The remaining 4 minutes once again saw Widnes besieging the Slough goal in search of an equaliser.

They didn't give up but, just as it seemed as time was going to run away from them - and with JUST 1 SECOND LEFT in the game, Leen de Decker slotted the puck away for her second goal of the game to give the Wild women a thoroughly well-earned point.

After the game, Coach Owen Tennant said: "The final goal was a long time coming and well deserved. The effort put in by the girls was deserving of a win but we will take away the positives and work on the negatives in training to make sure we get the win next time."

The result means that Widnes are now off the mark with 1 point from their 3 games to date and are in 5th place in the Women's Premier League table, ahead of both Kingston Diamonds and Nottingham Vipers.

Lucy Kirkham (Photo by Steve Pollitt)

30th October 2016 – Women's Premier League Widnes Wild Women's Team 3 – Nottingham Vipers 2

Period Scores: 2-1, 1-0, 0-1
Shots on Goal: Widnes 26 – Nottingham 34
Penalties in Minutes: Widnes 4 – Nottingham 6
Widnes Scoring: Lucy Kirkham 2+0, Charlene Chapman 1+1, Beckie Elliott 0+1

The Widnes Wild women's team picked up their first win of the season – a 3-2 triumph over Nottingham Vipers - at home at Silver Blades Widnes on Sunday.

The team was bolstered with the return of regular captain Charlene Chapman who had missed the previous week's home draw with Slough Phantoms and Vanessa Crickmore-Clarke, who was making her first appearance of the season, while Emma Bevan retained her place in goal.

The Vipers team were very well organised both defensively and in attack and certainly did not look like a team that had let in 30 goals in their last 3 games. In fact, they even achieved a feat that no other visiting team had managed since the start of last season as they actually outshot the Wild women on their own ice 34 to 26 overall.

After a tense opening, the first goal of the game came on the cusp of 9 minutes with a brilliant solo effort by Widnes' Lucy Kirkham to score her first goal of the new season.

With just under 5 minutes to go in the first period, the scores were level after a well taken strike by Nottingham captain Megan Rathbone but Kirkham was on target again before the break (18.35 assisted by Beckie Elliot and Charlene Chapman) to ensure that the Wild women went back to the dressing room with their lead intact.

In the second period, the Nottingham team turned up the pressure in search of another equaliser but it was the Widnes team who were next to score when Charlene Chapman put them two goals ahead with an unassisted strike just after the half way mark. That was the goal that would ultimately win the game for the Wild women but they had to weather a late onslaught – particularly after Vipers' Rathbone halved the deficit with just 3½ minutes still to play.

The Widnes women's team held on to notch up their first victory of the season and now have a break until their next WPL match which is at home to Kingston Diamonds on 27th November.

Vanessa Crickmore-Clarke was on target against Kingston (Photo by Steve Pollitt)

Sunday 27th November – Women's Premier League
Widnes Wild Women 6 – Kingston Diamonds 4

Period Scores: 5-1, 0-1, 1-2
Shots on Goal: Widnes 43 – Kingston 36 (19-8, 15-13, 9-15)
Penalties In Minutes: Widnes 2 – Kingston 20
Widnes Scoring: Charlene Chapman, Leen de Decker 1+1, Vanessa Crickmore Clarke, Emma Pearson, Katie Hills, Amanda Williams all 1+0, Lucy Kirkham 0+2, Sophie Sinclair-Reeks 0+1

The Widnes Wild women's team picked up their second win in succession with a tense and hard fought 6-4 victory over Kingston Diamonds in the Women's Premier League at Silver Blades Widnes.

Coming off the back of a draw and a win in their two previous home games, the Wild women were keen to extend their unbeaten run and were quickest out of the blocks.

After team captain Charlene Chapman combined well with Leen de Decker to fire Widnes ahead in the 5th minute, they raced to an impressive 4-0 lead with further goals from Vanessa Crickmore Clarke, Emma Pearson (assist Sophie Sinclair-Reeks) and Amanda Williams (asst Lucy Kirkham) before Kingston finally managed to get on the scoresheet themselves at 18.17.

The Wild women had been having problems in previous games with turning their superior possession into goals but not so on this occasion and they quickly bounced back to restore their 4 goal margin with de Decker netting from a Chapman pass just 22 seconds from the restart.

The Diamonds team began picking up penalties in the second period as the game seemed to be slipping away from them but they pulled a second goal back just prior to the half way mark. However a 2+10 penalty for a check to the head for Kingston's Reagan Downing broke their momentum and there was no further scoring during the period.

The visitors upped their game in the third period and Widnes hearts were in mouths as they gradually began closing the deficit.

The returned-to-the-ice Downing hit a sensational unassisted short-handed goal on 46.30 to make it 5-3 and then Kingston's Hannah Gibson (who also plays for the Diamonds' Elite league team and Bradford Bulldogs in the men's Laidler Conference AND is also a match official...) fired home to make it 5-4 with over 10 minutes remaining in the game.

It was a nervy final phase of play with Kingston pushing forward to try and force an equaliser and the Wild keen to defend their lead and then, in the 57th minute with Kingston shorthanded due to a tripping penalty, last season's top points scorer for the Wild, Katie Hills, fired in a valuable powerplay goal (assist Kirkham) to settle the nerves and, indeed, settle the game.

The resulting two points mean that Widnes remain in 5th place in the Women's Premier League table but have drawn level on points with 4th place Slough Phantoms, who didn't play at the weekend.

Looking back at the game, Coach Owen Tennant said: "I think the score after the first period says it all really. The momentum seemed to shift during the second period and Kingston came out strong in the third. After the timeout mid-way through the third period, the girls went out and did exactly as was asked. They have the capability to beat any team in the league and that showed."

The Wild women are on the road for their next two fixtures – away at Nottingham Vipers on 11th December and then at Streatham Storm on 8th January. Their next home game at Silver Blades Widnes will be on Sunday 15th January when they will face Streatham in a 5.30pm face

Abigail Hayes (Photo by Geoff White)

11th December 2016 – Women's Premier League
Nottingham Vipers 4 – Widnes Wild Women's Team 2

Period Scores: 0-2, 0-0, 4-0
Shots on Goal: Nottm 42 - Widnes 37(13-13, 17-12, 12 12)
Penalties in Minutes: Widnes 0 – Nottm 0
Widnes Scoring: Charlene Chapman 1+0, Vanessa Crickmore – Clarke 1+0, Savannah Sumner 0+1,Abigail Hayes 0+1

A plucky Widnes Wild women's team made the long trip to Nottingham for a late face off game against the Vipers, hoping to avoid the potential banana skin that was the league's bottom team who had lost all 5 of their previous matches.

Unfortunately, the Wild women were seriously short benched and could only muster 10 skaters and they were particularly disadvantaged by the absence of leading goalscorers Katie Hills and Leen de Decker – the latter being away on international duty in Taiwan with the Belgian national team.

Despite all this, the game started well for the Wild team and they raced to a two goal lead by the end of the first period. Vanessa Crickmore-Clarke opened the scoring after 10 minutes with an assist from Savannah Sumner – her first ever point in a competitive game, having just joined the team this season - and then team captain Charlene Chapman doubled the lead, assisted by Abigail Hayes in the 18th minute.

The second period was incredibly tense with both teams having lots of possession but neither being able to make a breakthrough and, despite an amazing 29 shots on goal in total, the score remained 0-2 going into the final third.

The Wild women began to tire as the game went on and will have rued their missed chances in the second period as Nottingham began to make their strength in numbers count. The game was completely turned on its head by 4 straight goals from Jessica Urquhart – a former GB under 18 international who currently also plays for the Nottingham (men's) Under 20 team and is the daughter of former Nottingham Panthers import player Mike Urquhart and Laura Urquhart – herself a prominent women's player and also former GB international and coach.

The first goal came just 30 seconds into the third period and was followed by further strikes after 48, 52 and 56 minutes for which the depleted Wild team had no answer.

Leen de Decker (right) at the World Championships in Taiwan

Leen de Decker At The World Championships

Widnes Wild women's team player Leen de Decker (above, right) was in action for her native Belgium in a World Championships Qualifying tournament in Chinese Taipei (Taiwan) just before Christmas.

The Belgian team beat South Africa 8-1, Hong Kong 7-0 and Bulgaria 6-0 before losing out 1-2 in their last group game against the hosts, the result which decided the outcome of the group as both teams had previously been unbeaten. The result meant that Chinese Taipei finished top of the 5 team group and Belgium finished second.

De Decker scored 4 goals and 1 assist in her 4 games and was the top scorer on the Belgium team – and 5th in terms of goals for the whole tournament overall.

We caught up with Leen and asked her about her experience at the WCQs and her overall involvement in ice hockey to date....

How was your overall experience at the WCQs in Taiwan?

I had a great experience in Taipei. I love playing hockey and this was a great chance to help out my national team. I was asked to bring some experience to what is a very young team and I was happy to do so. It was great to see some of the younger players on the team growing throughout the tournament.

What was the level of competition like from the other teams and how disappointing was it to lose out in the very last game to the hosts?

It was the qualification level, which we were obliged to enter as Belgium - by deciding to not go to the Worlds last year - were automatically relegated. Hong Kong, Bulgaria and South-Africa, whilst having great spirit, unfortunately, do not have a great hockey tradition in their country and that does get reflected in the skills of the teams.

Taipei, on the other hand, has taken a very professional approach to ice hockey in their country and - due to funding - were able to have a great preparation for this championship. We were very matched in skill and teamplay, but with Taipei having some referee decisions go their way, and the crowd behind them, just had the upper hand. To lose with a very contested goal (puck never did cross the line, we believe) was hard to take.

You hadn't played for Belgium for a while – was that a personal choice or a selection issue…?

I hadn't played since 2013. This was due to not being able to combine work and career that easily anymore. I was asked, but could not commit to the time required. This year I was able to take the time off work to attend.

How did you first get into playing hockey in Belgium?

The classic story: my brother played (and still does) so I wanted to play as well.

What brought you to England and how hard was it to find a team to play with?

I first played in England when I was studying at Hull University. I then returned to Belgium to start my career in an international firm and a few years later ended up in Manchester due a re-location of my department. And I'm still here 8 years on.

How would you compare the women's game in Belgium with the game here, ie playing standards, organisation etc

No comparison, there currently is no women's competition in Belgium.... something I highly regret and keep lobbying the federation to change. When I started playing there was a Dutch-Belgian joint women's competition on top of a Belgian cup competition with the 6 women's team we had in Belgium. However due to some ice-rinks closing and no support from the Belgian federation for a long period of time, the competition was not organised anymore and the teams folded with a lot of girls quitting the sport as they did not want to play in the men's teams.

What are your hopes for the Widnes Wild women's team?

My hopes for the team are to remain a greatly competitive team that can challenge the top teams in our league and offer exciting hockey to our fans. It's great to see the younger players getting better year on year and, hopefully, we'll be able to attract and develop some great players so we can become an established name in women's hockey under the Widnes Wild name!

What are your own long term goals in ice hockey?

I love the sport so I just want to keep playing as long as I can. Further to that I would love to be involved in the development of women's hockey in Widnes. Why not dream to have 2 women's teams (Elite and Premier League) or even a junior women's team? This will be a very long term goal, but I believe with the right support and help around us, we can make this happen.

Emma Middleton and Stephanie Drinkwater
(Photo by Flyfifer Photography)

Sunday 8th January 2017 – Women's Premier League
Streatham Storm 5 - Widnes Wild Women 1

Period Scores: 2-1, 0-0, 3-0
Shots On Goal: Streatham 34 – Widnes 31
Penalties in Minutes: Streatham 4 – Widnes 2
Widnes Scoring: Leen de Decker 1+0, Katie Hills 0+1

The Widnes Wild women's team suffered a 5-1 defeat in their first game of the New Year at the hands of Streatham Storm down in South London on Sunday.

The team travelled short benched due to an unfortunate combination of injuries and international call ups and were only able to ice two full playing lines with netminder Rachel Fairbairn playing out of goal to give the Wild women an extra skater.

In view of the lack of numbers – and the long journey down - the Widnes team gave a very good account of themselves and, despite the final score, it was a very closely fought game throughout with the home side only really pulling away in the latter stages.

In fact, it was Widnes who scored the first goal of the game in a first period that saw them outshoot their hosts by 17 to 10. Belgian international player Leen de Decker – recently returned from international duty with her national side in the World Championship Qualifiers in Taiwan – fired the Wild women into the lead with 10 minutes gone on the clock – with an assist from last season's top scorer Katie Hills.

Widnes were pegged back by a Streatham equaliser after 16 minutes and then fell foul of a checking call – their only penalty of the game – which saw them concede a powerplay goal with just 30 seconds left to play in the first period.

The second period was incredibly tense with both teams enjoying periods of possession and pressure but neither side managed to score and it was only in the third period that Streatham were able to make their superior numbers count as the Widnes players - quite understandably - began to tire.

Two goals 60 seconds apart made sure of the win for the Storm and a 5th strike with some 3 minutes left on the clock completed the scoring.

Looking back at the game, Coach Owen Tennant said:

"The result away at Streatham wasn't the best start to the year and definitely doesn't reflect the performance as the girls are very proud of their gameplay. We had a very promising training session on Thursday showing that the girls are more than capable to get the win at home next Sunday.

Again, short lines due to injuries, illness and international duties don't help, but these things are unavoidable. With more players, I have no doubt we will pull off the win this weekend."

The Wild women have an early chance of revenge against the Storm as they play the return Women's Premier League fixture at home at Silver Blades Widnes this Sunday 15th January. The game faces off at 5.30pm and admission is free.

Sammi Boyle (Photo by Steve Pollitt)

Charlene Chapman (#3) scores the Wild's first goal at home to Streatham. (Photo by Geoff White)

15th January 2017 – Women's Premier League Widnes Wild Women 2 – Streatham Storm 3

Period Scores: 0-2, 1-0, 1-1
Shots On Goal: Widnes 28 – Streatham 53 (11-20, 9-17, 8-16)
Penalties In Minutes: Widnes 18 – Streatham 16
Widnes Scoring: Charlene Chapman 1+1, Leen de Decker 1+0, Katie Hills 0+2, Emma Pearson 0+1

The Widnes Wild women's team put up a plucky performance in their Women's Premier League game at Silver Blades Widnes on Sunday before eventually succumbing to a 2-3 defeat to high-flying Streatham Storm.

The face-off time for this game had been brought forward from its scheduled 5.30 start time to 4pm in order to accommodate the Manchester Phoenix EPL game which had been switched to Widnes at short notice during the week. Unfortunately, this late change meant that certain Wild women's players were unable to take part and the Widnes team were subsequently at a disadvantage but the team that played gave a very good account of themselves.

After a fairly even opening, the visiting Storm took the lead after 13 minutes when a long shot from just inside the blueline beat Wild netminder Stephanie Drinkwater. Worse was to come when just over two minutes later, Widnes lost the puck from a face off in the Streatham zone and the Storm broke away to score a second goal to give them a 0-2 lead going into the first break.

The second period began much as the first had finished with the Storm laying siege to the Widnes goal and it seemed only a matter of time before the floodgates began to open. However, the Wild defence valiantly kept the attackers at bay and netminder Stephanie Drinkwater performed heroics to stop multiple close range shots.

The storm was weathered somewhat and, just after the half-way point in the game, the Wild women's fortunes changed. Katie Hills stole the puck off a Streatham player near the half way line, skated the length of the ice and crossed for team captain Charlene Chapman to fire in the opening Widnes goal.

After this breakthrough, the Wild women seemed to play with a bit more self-belief and the game opened up. At the end of the second period, the score was still 1-2 with everything to play for.

The third period was incredibly tense and, after increasing periods of pressure, Widnes finally got their just desserts after a long shot from Sav Sumner bounced around the Streatham goalmouth before Wild's Belgian international player Leen de Decker fired through a melee of players to put the home side on level terms on 53 minutes.

The Wild women pushed forward trying to force a winning goal but were caught out at the back as Streatham broke through some two minutes to retake the lead. The last 4 minutes were as exciting ice hockey as you could hope to see anywhere as the Wild women tried to snatch a late goal.

Women's games don't tend to be all that physical as body checking is not allowed and the play is usually more based upon skating and passing skills rather than the more physical aspect of the men's game.

However, tempers flared in the dying moments of this game when Widnes' Katie Hills received a roughing penalty with just 22 seconds left on the clock. Her penalty expired once the buzzer sounded for the end of the match and Hills raced out of the penalty box to take issue with one of the Streatham players who subsequently ended up on the floor.

There was a lot of pushing and shoving among the players and Hills was given a further 2+10 minutes for cross checking. A Streatham player got 10 minutes for incitement and Wild's Sav Sumner received 2 minutes for roughing in the same incident.

The result saw Streatham move level on points at the top of the league with leaders Chelmsford Cobras who drew 3-3 away at Nottingham. The Wild women remain in 5th place with 7 points from their 8 games to date.

After the game, Coach Owen Tennant said:

“We got off to a bit of a slow start which made it tough to come back from. The girls put in a fantastic effort throughout the second and third periods and deserved more than the 2 goals they pulled back. It was just one of those games - we didn't do much wrong but the slow start cost us.”

“As I've said previously, it's extremely hard for a team to play with a short bench but I think the girls deserve a big well done for carrying on with the situation they were put in, and still showing a great performance.”

Having already watched and reported on the Widnes women’s team since they started in 2015, I made my Wild Women’s announcing debut at the game against Streatham on 15th January 2017. You can read more about my involvement with the Wild Women later on...

(Photo by James Birtwistle)

Sophie Sinclair-Reeks
(Photo by Mandy Sinclair)

Team GB Under 18 Call Up For Sophie Sinclair-Reeks

The Widnes Wild women's team can boast another international player in their ranks after Sophie Sinclair-Reeks was selected to play for the Team GB Under 18s team at the World Championships in Poland in January.

The team took part in Division 1B of the WCs in Katowice between 8th to 14th January in a 6-team group and lost 0-3 to Italy, 5-1 to Denmark and 2-1 to Poland before beating China 2-1 and Kazakhstan 4-2 to finish fourth in the group, just outside the medal positions.

Sophie had already played for the GB Under 18s in the 4-team Friendship Tournament in Hungary back in October and then also had to take part in a trial match at Bradford before the final WC selection was made.

The GB team lost 11-0 to Poland and 10-0 to hosts Hungary before beating last year's tournament winners Spain 4-2 in their final game and Sophie was appointed one of two Alternate Captains for the tournament.

We started off by asking Sophie how it felt when she heard that she had been picked to play for the GB under 18 team in Hungary.....?

"I honestly just couldn't believe it, my mum got the email while I was at work, when she picked me up she told me and I was genuinely blown away! Confidence has always been a huge struggle of mine; it was beyond imagination that they had chosen me!"

For people who don't know how it works, what sort of process did you have to go through to be selected?

"Initial trials were held last January (2016), where the original squad was cut from. Monthly we have training camps at ice Sheffield where players can be cut, or new players added if they have been scouted from games or recommended."

What does it mean to you to represent your country?

"Pride. When I came home from the Hungary trip, I honestly just kept crying! There is genuinely nothing like standing on the blue line with the national anthem playing after a win. Since I was 5 it has been my dream to play for my country, and I genuinely couldn't believe I was doing it!"

You were appointed Alternate Captain for the 4 team tournament – how did that come about? And how did you find the experience?

"We were kitting up for our first training session in Budapest when I was pulled out the changing room! My first reaction was I thought I was going to be sent home! Turns out I wasn't in the end! We had a brief conversation about the prior training camps and how I had impressed both on and off the ice. Then I was asked how I felt about being given the A. Probably the hardest thing was trying not to cry! The experience was difficult to begin with, primarily because it was so completely unexpected. It gave me an incredible opportunity to show

my leadership qualities and bond with the team. It was an incredible honour."

How did you get on with the other Team GB girls?

"I was nervous before I went, I hadn't done England girls so I didn't know many of them, but it took less than an hour to get to know each and every person. I honestly feel as though I've made friends for life there, there's no mates like hockey mates! Everyone becomes so close in a matter of days; you eat together, play together and sleep together."

It has already been a long journey from the 4 year old whose first ever experience on ice was on the Trump ice rink in New York City's Central Park while on a family visit.

Sophie's mum Mandy takes up the story at this point:

"She got into hockey a couple of months later at Deeside when a steward spotted her and suggested she tried ice hockey at their novice night. As soon as she got hold of a stick and puck she was hooked and joined the Deeside U10 squad."

She played her first game age 5 and played for Deeside U10s for 3 seasons when she moved to Manchester Phoenix where she captained the U10s and played up for the U12s. More recently she decided to switch to the girls game and the following season played for Sheffield Shadows U16s whilst also training with the Widnes Women.

As soon as she reached 16 she started playing for the Widnes Women and was also successful in being selected for the GB U18s."

So what comes next for Sophie? Well, she is still studying A Level Economics, Politics and Business Studies at school in Chester.

She is keen to enjoy success with the Widnes Wild women's team and has also joined the Deeside Under 18s to get more ice time and practice.

Wild Women Sophie Sinclair Reeks with Team GB at the U18 World Championships in Poland

Netminder Rachel Fairbairn in action in the 4-4 home draw with Chelmsford Cobras. (Photo by Geoff White)

12th February 2017 – Women's Premier League Widnes Wild Women 4 – Chelmsford Cobras 4

Period Scores: 1-2, 1-1, 2-1
Shots On Goal: Widnes 39 – Chelmsford 33 (13-14, 14-10, 12-9)
Penalties in Minutes: Widnes 2 – Chelmsford 6
Widnes Scoring: Lucy Kirkham 2+0, Leen de Decker 1+0, Sophie Sinclair-Reeks 1+0, Emma Pearson, Beckie Elliott Amanda Williams all 0+1

The Widnes Wild women's team staged a sensational fight-back to take a point off current Women's Premier League leaders Chelmsford Cobras in a 4-4 draw in their final home game of the season at Silver Blades Widnes on Sunday.

The Cobras arrived with an unbeaten record and had only dropped points to Milton Keynes Falcons and

Nottingham Vipers all season who whom they had drawn 3-3. They were missing the league's top scorer so far this season - Team GB international Bethany Hill – but still had impressive firepower in the form of Russian player Tereza Plankova.

The Wild women had only very narrowly lost the away fixture in Chelmsford 7-6 back in September, despite having led 1-3 early in the first period and were keen to continue the progress they had shown in recent games.

The opening to this game was incredibly close with both teams testing each other's strengths and weaknesses but with neither side able to make much of an impression. The first goal came after 8 minutes when Widnes got caught out in defence and the puck dropped to an unmarked Cobras player on the right post who was able to guide it into the net.

The lead didn't last long – however – as, a little over 3 minutes later, the Wild women were back on level terms. They had a powerplay opportunity after Chelmsford's Plankova was sent to the box for a cross checking penalty and Lucy Kirkham fired in a long shot through a scrum of defenders to beat the netminder.

Widnes pushed forward trying to build on this breakthrough but were unable to make their offensive pressure count. They were eventually undone by a breakout from the Cobras' defence that saw an unmarked Plankova power through the Wild defence and fire past the netminder to put the visitors back in front.

There were more chances for both teams in the closing minutes of the period but both netminders played especially well to keep the scores at 1-2 at the first break.

The second period started off being contested as fiercely as the first had finished and Widnes began to find their game. Chelmsford edged further ahead with a goal after 28 minutes although this was rather controversial as Wild netminder Rachel Fairbairn, having already made a great save from point blank range, appeared to have her glove over the puck when it was poked into the net by the Cobras' attacker. Despite the subsequent protestations, the referee allowed the goal to stand and the Cobras went into the second half of the game 1-3 in front.

Widnes dug deep at this point and showed a lot of character to overcome this setback and pull themselves back into the game. The breakthrough came on 35 minutes when a Chelmsford attack broke down and Wild's Kirkham stole the puck off a Cobras' player, skated the whole length of the ice and fired in a superb unassisted goal to halve the deficit.

Hopes were high in the third period but the Wild suffered an early setback as Cobras' Plankova skated through the whole Widnes defence to score her hattrick goal – and the visitors' 4th – less than two minutes into the period. Once again, the Wild women regrouped and set out to pull themselves back into the game.

On 48 minutes, they did just that when a rasping blueline slapshot by Sophie Sinclair Reeks - recently returned from international duty with the Team GB women's under 18 team – flew into the back of the net and gave Widnes hope of a late fight back.

The next 10 minutes were incredibly tense as both teams tried to force their way through and create an opening. Then with just under 90 seconds remaining, the chance came for Widnes. Beckie Elliott carried the puck out of the defensive zone and, with a precision slide-rule pass, found Wild's Belgian international and season top scorer Leen de Decker homing in on goal. She calmly fired the puck past the despairing netminder to tie the scores at 4-4.

A frantic last minute or so saw the Wild goal come under intense pressure as the league leaders tried to snatch a late winner but the Widnes defence held firm and the Wild women picked up a very creditable draw against a very good Chelmsford side.

After the game, Coach Owen Tennant said:

"I couldn't be happier with the performance from the girls. We got off to a bit of a slow start but that was always going to be a problem when playing Chelmsford for any team, but our determination allowed us to pull it back."

"The girls listened to the advice from both me and assistant coach Matt Humphreys on the bench and put in to play what we have been working on in training. This showed through the growing intensity as the game progressed. For the girls, only positives should be taken from this and they should be very proud of their performance."

This was the Widnes Wild women's team's last home game of the Women's Premier League season, although they have three away games still to play. Their next game is away to Slough on 30th April, they then travel to Milton Keynes on 7th May and round off the campaign with a trip to Hull to play Kingston Diamonds on 27th May.

If the Wild women are able to manage a 4th place finish in the WPL table, they will qualify for the EIHA Womens' Champions tournament weekend in Sheffield at the beginning of June, which features the play off competitions for the top teams in all 4 women's divisions.

Wild Women after the 9-2 win away at Slough
(Photo by Owen Tennant)

Back Row: Beckie Elliott, Abi Hayes, Leen de Decker, Amanda Williams, Sophie Sinclair Reeks / Middle Row: Charlene Chapman, Katie Hills, Lucy Kirkham, Emma Pearson / Front Row: Sav Sumner, Stephanie Drinkwater

Sunday 30th April 2017 – Women's Premier League Slough Phantoms 2 – Widnes Wild Women's Team 9

Period Scores: 0-3, 0-2, 2-4
Shots on Goal: Slough 29 – Widnes 44 (5-10, 6-18, 18-16)
Penalties in Minutes: Slough 2 – Widnes 4
Widnes Scoring: Katie Hills 3+1, Charlene Chapman 2+1, Leen de Decker 1+2, Amanda Williams 1+1, Abigail Hayes & Sophie Sinclair Reeks both 1+0, Emma Pearson 0+2, Savannah Summer & Lucy Kirkham 0+1

The Widnes Wild women's team made a return to winning ways with a sensational 2-9 win away at Slough Phantoms in the Women's Premier League on Sunday.

It was the Wild women's first competitive game since mid-February and even playing on the unfamiliar surface of Slough's new temporary ice rink – installed by operators Silver Blades as cover while the main rink is being refurbished – didn't faze the girls, who came home with their biggest win of the season so far.

Things just seemed to click for the Wild team who had not notched up a single point on their travels all season. The opening goal came in the 8th minute from Widnes' Belgian international player Leen de Decker and this was followed up less than 2 minutes later by a strike from Katie Hills. A third goal - from Amanda Williams - gave the Wild a 0-3 lead going into the first break and they looked to be on a roll.

They had outshot their hosts by 10 to 5 in the first period and the barrage continued in the second with a massive 18 shots being fired at the net of Phantoms loanee netminder Heidi-Jane Radburn who usually plays for Oxford in the lower Division 1 South. Stephanie Drinkwater in the Widnes goal had just 6 shots to contend with over the same period, all of which were duly dealt with.

Second period goals from Hills, again, and team captain Charlene Chapman with nothing in reply from the Phantoms meant that Widnes were leading 0-5 at the second break and the third period looked to be little more than a formality.

The Slough team did manage to up their game in the final 20 minutes and outshot the Wild women 18 to 16 but, by the time their captain Amy Hadden managed to score their opening goal of the game on 48 minutes, Widnes had already extended their lead even further with a goal from Wild's GB under-18 international Sophie Sinclair Reeks.

The Wild response was swift and the 6-goal cushion was restored less a minute after the Slough goal with a second goal of the game from Chapman and then two further strikes within 40 seconds of each other from Katie Hills and Abigail Hayes – both shorthanded while Widnes' Emma Pearson sat out at 2 minute interference penalty – rounded off the scoring for the visitors.

A late strike by Slough's Hadden with just 10 seconds left on the clock was the last piece of action in the game and the Wild women were able to celebrate their first away win of the season.

The result sees the Widnes team move to within 2 points of Slough who are currently occupying the fourth and final play-off place in the Women's Premier League table. Both teams have two games left to play – Widnes' are both away while the Phantoms' remaining games are both at home.

If they can manage to finish in the top 4, the Wild women will qualify for the end of season play off weekend which will be held at iceSheffield on 4th and 5th June and will feature the top teams from the Women's Premier League, Women's Elite League, National Divisions North & South and Under 16s leagues.

Looking back at the game, team coach Owen Tennant said:

"The trip to Slough was an interesting one. We knew that the rink we would be playing on was a temporary one whilst the other one is getting refurbished, what we didn't anticipate however was how small the rink would be. This meant that we would have to change our style of play completely as the pace of the game would be fast and intense."

"Before the game the girls and I had a discussion about how they would need to approach the game, so all that was left for them to do was to go out and execute the plan. With a 9-2 win, I don't think I need to say much more!"

"The girls played outstandingly and made me a very proud coach. All the training has paid off and we are confident going into the final two games of the season that we can come away with another two wins."

The Wild women's next game is next Sunday 7th May away at Milton Keynes Falcons, face off 6.30pm.

The Falcons are in third place in the league table with 12 points from their 9 league games to date. They picked up a creditable 3-3 draw against title contenders Streatham Storm at the weekend which almost certainly secured their own place in the end of season play offs and means that the title race will go to the wire.

Current league leaders Storm travel to second place Chelmsford Cobras in the last league match of the season for both teams on Sunday 14th May and the winners of that game will win the league title. If the match is drawn, Streatham will take the title by one point.

Sunday 7th May 2017 – Women's Premier League Milton Keynes Falcons 4 – Widnes Wild Women 5

Period Scores: 0-2, 2-2, 2-1
Shots on Goal: Milton Keynes 33- Widnes 31 (6-7, 13-16, 14-8)
Penalties In Minutes: Milton Keynes 14 – Widnes 4
Widnes Scoring: Leen de Decker 2+0, Katie Hills 2+0, Savannah Sumner 1+0, Amanda Williams 0+2, Lucy Kirkham & Emma Pearson both 0+1

The Widnes Wild women's team gave their play-off hopes a boost with a sensational 4-5 win away at third place Milton Keynes Falcons in the Women's Premier League on Sunday.

The Wild women had lost 1-5 at home to the Falcons earlier in the season but were on a roll after their 2-9 win away at Slough the previous week and are still in with a chance of snatching 4 th place, if results go their way over the next couple of weeks.

This was a very evenly fought game throughout with both teams having plenty of chances. Widnes took the lead after just 25 seconds with a strike from their Belgian international player Leen de Decker and the advantage was doubled on 16 minutes while the Wild women were on a powerplay for a Falcons' penalty. Katie Hills picked up on an Amanda Williams pass and slotted the puck into the net to make the score 0-2 to Widnes at the first break.

The home team's penalty woes continued into the second period and Hills and Williams combined again with another powerplay goal to punish a slashing call on 25 minutes to give the Wild women a three goal lead.

Once the Falcons were returned to full strength, they finally managed to score their first goal of the game through leading scorer Rachel Piotrowski but the brief rally did not last long as Widnes restored their three goal advantage on 29 minutes with a first ever goal from Savannah Sumner who is playing her first season of competitive ice hockey.

The Falcons rallied again after this and Piotrowski scored her second goal of the game on 34 minutes - but the Wild women were still looking good for their lead and went into the second break with a 2-4 advantage.

Things looked even better for the Wild women at the start of the third period as, within 90 seconds of the restart, Leen de Decker scored her second goal of the game - and Widnes' fifth - to give them a commanding lead.

The home side upped their game in the third period and finally began to take advantage of their numerical superiority on the bench as the Wild players gradually began to tire. The Wild were outshot for the first time in the game – by 14 to 8 – but netminder Stephanie Drinkwater was outstanding in the Widnes goal.

The pressure paid off for Milton Keynes in the 47th minute when Piotrowski scored her hat trick goal to narrow the score down to 3-5 and then another Falcons' goal came with just 8 minutes left to ensure that the game had a nail-biting finish.

The Wild women held on to record their 4th victory of the season and notch up their 3rd game in a row unbeaten.

After the game, team coach Owen Tennant said:

"What a game of hockey! As in the previous game, the girls put in an outstanding performance short benched and were deserving of the win. Training sessions really shone through as you could pick out the plays that we continue to work on. The work ethic of every one of the girls is fantastic, both in matches and training."

"It was a real team performance, something I feel is becoming a stronger attribute every game.

With one more game for us to win, and a bit of luck that other results go our way, playoffs are definitely within our grasp."

Widnes are still in 5th place in the Women's Premier League table but are now just 2 points behind Slough Phantoms who occupy the final play off place. Both teams have one game left to play and the Wild travel to Hull to face the Kingston Diamonds on Saturday 27th May in their final league game of the season.

However, their play-off fate might already have been decided for them by then as Slough are at home to Milton Keynes next Saturday 13th May and, if they win that game, they will not be able to overtaken by Widnes.

Widnes could then, theoretically, still finish on the same number of points as Milton Keynes if the Falcons were to lose their last game at home to second bottom team Nottingham Vipers on 28th May but, even under that scenario, Milton Keyes would still finish above Widnes as they have a superior record in head to head games between the two teams.

Wild players celebrate a goal in their last league game away at Kingston Diamonds. (Photo by Tony King Photography)

Saturday 27th May 2017 – Women's Premier League Kingston Diamonds 2 – Widnes Wild Women 3

Period Scores: 1-2, 1-0, 0-1
Shots on Goal: Kingston 39 – Widnes 39
Penalties in Minutes: Kingston 26 – Widnes 47
Widnes Scoring: Leen de Decker, Katie Hills & Amanda Williams all 1+0

The Widnes Wild women's team rounded off their regular season with a sensational 2-3 win away at Kingston Diamonds to snatch the last place in the Women's Premier League play offs.

The Wild women had been set the task of winning their last three games of the season – all away from home – in order to finish in 4th place above Slough Phantoms. This was quite a tall order as they had hitherto only actually won two games all season – both at home - but road wins away at Slough and Milton Keynes in their last two games set up this fascinating season finale.

The team was boosted by the return of Megan Bowen Fell - who hadn't played since February – and Catherine Bowen Fell, who was making her first appearance of the season. Sarah Roberts took over as captain for the day in the absence of regular skipper Charlene Chapman and goaltending duties were taken up by 18 year old Tegan Lavery who usually plays for Deeside Dragons juniors and was making her first appearance at WPL level.

The game was very close and closely fought throughout and the opening goal was scored after just 2 minutes by Kingston top scorer Reagan Downing – who is a Team GB international and also plays for the Diamonds Elite League team – who fired in a long shot through players which crept past the possibly unsighted netminder Lavery.

Kingston adopted a rather physical approach to this game and there were quite a few penalties handed out to both teams. The first Widnes goal came as result of powerplay for a 2+2 penalty for roughing on the Diamonds' Alternate Captain Clara Ashton and Wild's Katie Hills fired in the equaliser in the 18th minute.

The Wild then took the lead – albeit in rather fortunate circumstances - in the dying seconds of the period after Belgian international player Leen de Decker found the loose puck at her feet after a mêlée in the Kingston goal crease and duly poked it into the net. With several players of both sides clearly encroaching and the Diamonds netminder left flailing on the ice, it was open to question as to whether the goal should have been allowed to stand but the referee was in a perfect position to see and Widnes left the ice leading 1-2 at the first break.

The home side's robust play continued in the second period and included a 2+10 penalty for a check from behind but it was the Diamonds who scored the next goal – Downing again, on 29 minutes – to tie the score at 2-2 with 30 minutes of the game remaining.

There was no more scoring in the second period and the game was on a knife edge when the teams came back out for the third period with the players all keyed up for the challenge. Within seconds of the restart, Katie Hills was banished to the box on 2+2 penalty for roughing plus 10 minutes for misconduct, brought on by a clash with the Kingston captain Bethany Barwell.

In the aftermath of these penalties, Wild's Megan Bowen Fell was handed a match penalty for a kick, leaving the Widnes bench somewhat short for the rest of the period but despite this, with a little over 10 minutes to go, Widnes re-took the lead with a fine strike from Amanda Williams who picked up the puck outside the Kingston blue line and skated past several defenders to fire the puck into the roof of the Hull net.

The tension was unbelievable around the Hull Arena as the clock slowly ticked down and the Wild women hung on for a well-earned 2-3 victory – and a place in the WPL play offs.

After the game, coach Owen Tennant said:

"It was a tough game that could have gone either way. Some debatable calls were/were not made, all of which I will be reviewing personally. That aside, I guess in the end it just came down to who wanted it more. Knowing that the win would take us to the playoffs definitely played a big part in us coming away with the win."

"Being able to say that we have made the playoffs is a great feeling and the girls should be very proud of themselves. The work they put in week in week out is the reason that they have the chance to compete in the playoffs. I believe that the girls can put in a great performance over the weekend and I see no reason why we shouldn't be aiming to win the competition."

The Wild women will be now be taking part in the WPL Play Offs as part of the EIHA Women's Trophy Weekend at iceSheffield next weekend – Saturday 3rd and Sunday 4th June – where they will have the somewhat daunting prospect of playing league champions Streatham Storm for a place in the WPL final.

The Wild women lost to Streatham at the same stage of competition last season and lost to the home and away in the league this season as well, albeit with a team depleted by injuries and player availability.

However, their recent form – of 3 away wins in their last 3 games – plus the return to the team of some of the missing players suggests that they may have every chance in a one off game on neutral ice next weekend.

The Widnes team celebrate Leen de Decker's goal against Streatham in the Play Off Semi Final. (Photo by MyTeamPhoto)

Saturday 3rd June 2017 – Play Off Semi Final Streatham Storm 6 – Widnes Wild Women 1

(Played at iceSheffield)

The Widnes Wild women's team can hold their heads up with pride after an heroic performance against league champions Streatham Storm at the Women's Premier League play offs in Sheffield at the weekend.

Unfortunately, the Wild team – who had struggled with numbers through injuries and player unavailability all season – were further affected by international call ups and had to travel to Sheffield with just 10 players, of which one was the goaltender.

18-year old Deeside junior netminder Tegan Lavery stepped in between the pipes in what was only her second ever game at this level, having previously played for the Wild in the win at Kingston Diamonds - while Sal Roberts stood in as team captain.

Needless to say, only having 9 skaters to play a 60 minute game that is designed to be played using two or more alternating lines of 5 players each is far from ideal and the Wild women were up against it right from the start. The buoyant – and more numerous - Streatham team were much too strong for the Widnes girls but they battled away and managed to keep the score to - in the circumstances - a very respectable 6-1 defeat.

The Widnes goal was scored by Belgian international player Leen de Decker, bringing her total to 12 goals and 5 assists from 12 games this season. The goal was assisted by Katie Hills who finishes the season as the Wild women's second highest scorer behind de Decker with 9+7 and Sav Sumner who finishes with 1+4 in her first season of competitive hockey, during which she was ever-present in the team.

The other semi-final saw Milton Keynes Falcons beat league runners up Chelmsford Cobras and the final on the Sunday saw a bit of an upset as the third place finishing Falcons beat the Storm to take the Play-Off Title.

Looking back on the season as a whole, Coach Owen Tennant said:

"The season has brought many positives as well as some negatives. The negatives are the things we can address at training and the positives are confidence boosts. Obviously the start of the season was tough; a number of factors contributing including the change of coach. The girls have adapted to my style of coaching really well and, likewise, I have tried to adjust certain aspects of my coaching to suit the team. I feel that we have worked well together over the past season and they have most definitely done themselves and me proud."

"Although we finished the season with a loss, I would still say we finished on a high. Three fantastic away wins proved the quality of the team and I have no doubt that form can be carried on into next season."

The short benched Widnes team that valiantly battled against league champions Streatham Storm in the Play Off Semi Final at iceSheffield. Left to right. Sav Sumner, Sophie Sinclair Reeks, Tegan Lavery, Abigail Hayes, Beckie Elliott, Leen de Decker, Lucy Kirkham, Katie Hills, Sarah Roberts & Emma Pearson.

(Photo by MyTeamPhoto.com)

2017 Tournament Runners Up: *Back Row: Amanda Williams, Catherine Bowen Fell, Beckie Elliott, Abi Hayes, Megan Bowen Fell, Lucy Kirkham, Sophie Sinclair Reeks, Katie Hills. Front Row: Sal Roberts, Leen de Decker, Abi Culshaw, Emma Pearson, Sav Sumner, Stephanie Drinkwater*

17th / 18th June 2017 - Swindon Tournament

The Widnes Wild women's team ended the season on a high note as they finished runners up in the annual British Women's Ice Hockey Friendship Tournament which was held at Swindon over the weekend.

The tournament – now in its 21st year – involves women's teams from different leagues from across the country and even had a team from Finland taking part. This year there were 12 teams in the senior tournament and 4 teams in the under 16s competition and, with each team playing all the other teams in a preliminary qualifying group before proceeding to semi-finals and final, that meant an eye watering 90 games had to be fitted in over the two day event.

Obviously, having staged this tournament for many years now, they have got this down to a fine art now at Swindon. The group games are just 12 minutes each in duration and the next game follows immediately afterwards with a brief pause for ice cutting at certain points during the day.

Over the course of the Saturday - and the early part of Sunday, all the teams playing each other and the top four in the group go on to play in semi-finals and then a final – played with slightly longer match times - on the Sunday evening.

The Wild women made a slow start to the competition but, by the end of the Saturday, were in 5th place in the group with 3 wins and 1 draw from their 6 games. The Sunday went even better as they went unbeaten through the rest of the group stage, winning 2 and drawing 3. Draws against group leaders Streatham and 4th place Milton Keynes saw the Wild women manage to usurp the Falcons team for 4th place and book their place in the semi-final.

The semi-final saw the Wild women take on Streatham – who had beaten them in the WPL Play Off semi-final two weeks beforehand and who had gone right though the group stage of the Swindon tournament unbeaten. It was an end to end game throughout and Streatham were, obviously favourites, but the Wild women managed to notch up a hard fought 1-0 victory – with the only goal of the game coming from Emma Pearson, assisted by Katie Hills.

The final was played against the Swindon Elite team, who not only had home advantage but were also the highest ranked team in the tournament league-wise so it was not a huge surprise that they went on to win the game 3-0, although all three goals came in the final minutes of the game - when the Widnes team were beginning to tire.

The Wild women still had cause to celebrate, however, as they won the Hockey Skills competition! This was held on the Saturday morning as a precursor to the group games and was in the form of a relay race between teams with each leg using a particular skill.

Katie Hills in the Skills Competition (Photo by Flyfifer Photography)

It involved fastest skate from the goal line to the far blue line (with Amanda Williams skating for the Wild women), shooting the puck at 4 targets (Sophie Sinclair-Reeks hit 2 out of 4), stick-handling (Katie Hills) and netminders skating & shooting on goal, in which Wild's Stephanie Drinkwater was the only netminder to score!

EIHA Women's Premier League - Season 2017/18

Final Table	GP	W	D	L	F	A	+/-	PIM	Pts
Swindon Topcats	12	11	1	0	85	7	78	42	23
Chelmsford Cobras	12	8	1	3	62	37	25	58	17
Milton Keynes Falcons	12	8	0	4	57	26	31	107	16
Kingston Diamonds	12	5	1	6	36	47	-11	92	11
Bracknell Firebees	12	5	1	6	58	52	6	75	11
Widnes Wild Women	12	1	2	9	28	57	-29	110	4
Nottingham Vipers	12	1	0	11	14	114	-100	75	2

EIHA WPL Top Points Scorers – Season 2017/18

Player	Team	GP	G	A	Pts	PIM
Rebecca Da Cova	Swindon Topcats	10	19	17	36	2
Rebecca Osman	Swindon Topcats	11	16	18	34	6
Tereza Plankova	Chelmsford Cobras	12	20	8	28	20
Rachel Piotrowski	MK Falcons	12	16	11	27	8
Jennifer Bolton	Chelmsford Cobras	12	19	5	24	6
Margeurite Laffitte	Bracknell Firebees	10	7	12	19	2
Sarah-Jane Fletcher	Swindon Topcats	11	2	16	18	8
Monica Petrosino	MK Falcons	9	12	6	18	6
Lucy Anna Beal	Bracknell Firebees	6	6	9	15	0
Reagan Downing	Kingston Diamonds	11	9	6	15	20
Claire Fay	Bracknell Firebees	11	10	5	15	8
Rebecca Inker	Swindon Topcats	11	9	6	15	2

EIHA WPL Top Netminders – Season 2017/18

Netminder	Team	GP	TOI	SA	GA	SA%	SO
Kayliegh Doyle	MK Falcons	12	38	288	26	90.97%	3
Steph Drinkwater	Widnes Wild	10	30	459	48	89.54%	1
Charlotte Cook	Kingston Diamonds	10	54	345	38	88.99%	0
Summer Cramer	Nottingham Vipers	11	45	761	92	87.91%	0
Cherry Hambelton	Chelmsford Cobras	11	45	270	37	86.30%	2
Meryia Throop	Bracknell Firebees	12	30	364	52	85.71%	1

Wild Women Netminder Statistics - Season 2017/18

Netminder	Comp	GPI	Mins	SA	GA	GAA	Sv%	SO
Steph Drinkwater	WPL*	10	600	459	48	4.80	89.54	1
Rebekah Scott	WPL*	2	120	84	9	4.50	89.29	0

*Note: *Mins (ie Time On Ice) are estimated)*

Widnes Wild Women Results – Season 2017/18

Date	Comp	Home			Away	Res
15.10.17	WPL	Widnes Wild	3	5	Nottinghm Vipers	L
5.11.17	WPL	Widnes Wild	0	3	Swindon Top Cats	L
3.12.17	WPL	Widnes Wild	4	6	MK Falcons	L
17.12.17	WPL	Nottingham Vipers	0	2	Widnes Wild	W
14.01.18	WPL	Widnes Wild	5	6	Chelmsfd Cobras	L
10.02.18	WPL	Bracknell Firebees	6	1	Widnes Wild	L
11.02.18	WPL	Swindon Top Cats	5	1	Widnes Wild	L
18.02.18	WPL	Kingston Diamds	3	1	Widnes Wild	L
25.02.18	WPL	Widnes Wild	1	5	Kingston Diamds	L
18.03.18	WPL	Widnes Wild	4	4	Bracknell Firebees	D
15.04.18	WPL	MKeynes Falcons	8	0	Widnes Wild	L
06.05.18	WPL	Chelmsfd Cobras	6	6	Widnes Wild	D

Player Statistics – Season 2017/18

Player	GP	G	A	Pts	PIM
Amanda Williams	9	7	3	10	0
Leen De Decker	9	4	5	9	0
Katie Hills	5	6	3	9	2
Lucy Kirkham	12	3	4	7	0
Charlene Chapman	12	3	2	5	4
Abigail Hayes	8	2	1	3	6
Emma Pearson	10	1	2	3	33
Savannah Sumner	12	2	0	2	6
Catherine Bowen Fell	7	0	1	1	4
Samantha Joann Boyle	9	0	1	1	2
Katherine Fairclough	11	0	1	1	29
Pauline Hayward	10	0	1	1	0
Sarah Roberts	7	0	1	1	6
Sophie Emma Sinclair-Reeks	11	0	1	1	2
Megan Bowen Fell	6	0	0	0	6
Vanessa Crickmore Clarke	9	0	0	0	2
Stephanie Jade Drinkwater	10	0	0	0	2
Beckie Elliott	2	0	0	0	0
Alice Horsfield	7	0	0	0	0
Charlotte McPhee	5	0	0	0	0
Rebekah Scott	2	0	0	0	0

Widnes Wild Women - Season 2017/18 (Photo by Geoff White)

Back Row: Gary Sumner (Sponsor), Owen Tennant, Megan Bowen Fell, Beckie Elliott, Vanessa Crickmore Clarke, Catherine Bowen Fell, Abi Hayes, Leen de Decker, Sal Roberts, Sammi Boyle, Katie Fairclough, Mikey Gilbert, Jordan Sumner (Sponsor). Front Row: Stephanie Drinkwater, Sav Sumner, Emma Pearson, Charlene Chapman, Sophie Sinclair Reeks, Lucy Kirkham, Amanda Williams

The Widnes Wild women's team have announced their fixtures for the 2017/18 season in the EIHA Women's Premier League.

The WPL features two new teams this season as the Swindon Topcats drop down from the Women's Elite League – where they finished bottom after a difficult single season stay – and Bracknell Firebees step up from National League Division 1 after winning promotion via the play offs at the Trophy Weekend in June.

Last season's WPL champions Streatham Storm are promoted to the WEL this season and the WPL finds itself another team down after the Slough Phantoms announced that they would be unable to enter a side this time around due to a lack of player numbers.

The Wild women's team's fixtures for the 2017/18 WPL season are as follows:

15th October 2017: Home v Nottingham Vipers
5th November 2017: Home v Swindon Topcats
3rd December 2017: Home v Milton Keynes Falcons
10th December 2017: Away @ Milton Keynes Falcons
17th December 2017: Away @ Nottingham Vipers
14th January 2018: Home v Chelmsford Cobras
10th February: Away @ Bracknell Firebees
11th February 2018: Away @ Swindon Topcats
18th February 2018: Away @ Kingston Diamonds
25th February 2018: Home v Kingston Diamonds
18th March 2018: Home v Bracknell Firebees
6th May 2018: Away @ Chelmsford Cobras

Home games (in bold) are played on Sundays at Silver Blades Widnes. Face off time for home games is 5.30pm and admission is free.

Katie Fairclough makes her league debut for the Wild Women (Photo by Geoff White)

15th October 2017 – Women's Premier League Widnes Wild Women's Team 3 – Nottingham Vipers 5

Period Scores: 1-3, 2-1, 0-1
Shots on Goal: Widnes 47- Nottingham 53 (10-19, 21-19, 16-15)
Penalties In Minutes: Widnes 4 – Nottingham 4
Widnes Scoring: Leen de Decker 1+1, Emma Pearson & Amanda Williams both 1+0, Sarah Roberts 0+1

The Widnes Wild women's team suffered defeat in their first Women's Premier League game of the season as they lost out 3-5 to a well organised Nottingham Vipers side on Sunday at Silver Blades Widnes.

The game saw the welcome return to the team of Samantha Boyle - who did not play last season - as well as the senior Women's debut of Wild junior player and GB under-16 inline hockey international Katie Fairclough, who made a very good impression in what was her first ever competitive game on ice.

After a fairly even start, the Vipers took the lead with two strikes within 80 seconds of each other to lead 0-2 after just 10 minutes of the game.

The Wild women managed to hit back with a well-taken goal of their own some 40 seconds later as Vanessa Crickmore-Clarke fired in a furious shot from the blue-line which was parried by the Nottingham netminder. Emma Pearson picked up the rebound and duly slotted the puck into the net to pull the Wild back into contention.

The Wild women upped the pressure on the Vipers' goal in search of an equaliser but were caught out at the back as the visitors scored again on 16 minutes to take a 1-3 lead into the first break.

The Wild came out the stronger for the second period, visibly upping their work-rate and out-shooting the visitors 21 to 19. They were rewarded with a goal from Amanda Williams after 28 minutes, which, once again, brought them to within touching distance of the Vipers. However, Sav Sumner then picked up a roughing penalty to leave the home side a player short and, shortly afterwards, Sal Roberts was called for tripping, meaning that the Wild would have to defend 3 on 5 for over a minute of play.

Netminder Stephanie Drinkwater made some incredible saves during this period and her heroics certainly helped keep the Wild in contention.

They killed off the Sumner penalty and, during a clumsy player change by the Vipers, Leen de Decker stole the puck and raced down the ice to fire in an amazing short handed goal to put Widnes back on level terms.

The Wild were back to full strength 40 seconds later and immediately looked to fire themselves into the lead for the first time in the game but, once again, they were caught out by a quick Nottingham break-away and the Vipers scored again to make it 3-4 at the end of the second period.

A 5th goal for the visitors within 90 seconds of the start of the third period effectively killed the game off and, while they had numerous chances, the Wild attack were unable to penetrate the stubborn Nottingham defence.

After the game, coach Owen Tennant said:

"The game against Nottingham showed a lot of strengths but also weaknesses in our game. The positive of this is that all the weaknesses shown can be worked on and we can make sure to improve before our next game.

The girls scored three good goals, working plays we had discussed and used in training so I was especially pleased with that.

The overall performance however did not display the quality we have within the team. We are focusing on the positives and will be addressing the downfalls during training over the next few weeks."

The Wild women play their second game of the new Women's Premier League season on Sunday 5th November at Silver Blades Widnes – 5.30pm face off.

Sophie Sinclair-Reeks (Photo by Geoff White)

5th November 2017 – Women's Premier League Widnes Wild Women's Team 0 – Swindon Top Cats 3

Period Scores: 0-1, 0-2, 0-0
Shots on Goal: Widnes 33 – Swindon 32
Penalties In Minutes: Widnes 4– Swindon 6

The Widnes Wild women's team suffered a "shut out" as they lost 0-3 at home to the Swindon Top Cats in the Women's Premier League at Silver Blades Widnes on Sunday.

The forward-looking team handed WPL debuts to 16 year old netminder Rebekah Scott, who has previously only played Scottish league under-16 games, and to Widnes based recreational player Pauline Hayward - who was playing her first competitive league game.

The Top Cats had been relegated from last season's Women's Elite League and are favourites to win the WPL title this time around but the Wild women gave them a good run for their money and were actually on top for long periods of the game.

The visitors took the lead in the 6th minute and the score remained 0-1 at the end of the first period. The Wild Women put the Top Cats under a lot of pressure in the second period – out-shooting them by 15 to 8 - but were unable to convert any of that attacking play into goals.

The Cats, by contrast, scored with 2 of their 8 shots either side of the half way mark and were 0-3 up by the 32nd minute.

The Wild women battered the Swindon goal again in the third period but were unable to get past netminder Rachel Moore - who picked up her third shut out from the 4 games that the Top Cats have played so far this season.

Swindon move to the top of the WPL table with this win, having won all 4 of their games to date and only have conceded 1 goal in total, while the Wild women occupy 6th position with two defeats from their two games.

The Wild women are next in action on Sunday 3rd December when they take on last season's play off champions Milton Keynes Falcons at Silver Blades Widnes – 5.30pm face off.

Amanda Williams top scored for the Wild Women against Milton Keynes (Photo by Flyfifer Photography)

Sunday 3rd December 2017 – Women's Premier Lge Widnes Wild Women 4 – Milton Keynes Falcons 6

Period Scores: 0-1, 3-3, 1-2
Shots on Goal: Widnes 27 – Milton Keynes 52
Penalties In Minutes: Widnes 10 – Milton Keynes 35
Widnes Scoring: Amanda Williams 2+0, Katie Hills 1+2, Lucy Kirkham 1+0, Charlene Chapman, Pauline Hayward, Sophie Sinclair Reeks & Katie Fairclough all 0+1

The Widnes Wild women's team put in a good performance in their Women's Premier League game against reigning play off champions Milton Keynes Falcons before eventually running out of steam in a 4-6 defeat at Silver Blades Widnes on Sunday.

The first period was a rather one-sided affair with the home side being out-shot by 22 to 4 but they managed to hold out until the 12th minute of play before Monica Petrosino opened the scoring for the Falcons.

Thanks to some solid defending by the Wild women - and excellent saves by netminder Rebekah Scott, the score was still 0-1 at the first period break, leaving Widnes still in with a chance of making something of the game.

When Milton Keynes top scorer Rachel Piotrowski put the Falcons 0-2 ahead in the very first minute of the second period, it all looked doom and gloom for the Wild women. However, they visibly upped their game at this point and fired in two quick-fire goals themselves – through Lucy Kirkham and Amanda Williams - to draw Widnes level.

A 26th minute powerplay goal - conceded while Megan Bowen Fell was sitting out a holding penalty - edged the Falcons back in front but the Wild equalised again on 36 minutes when Katie Hills fired in a powerplay goal to take the score to 3-3

The Milton Keynes response was swift, however, and they retook the lead just 90 seconds later and maintained that advantage going into the second period break.

The third period was very tense and the Falcons were forced into taking defensive penalties as they battled to keep the renewed Wild attack at bay. However, the Wild were caught out in defence while pushing up to attack.

A 5th goal on 48 minutes put the visitors further ahead and then a 6th – shorthanded this time - some 3 minutes later pretty much killed the game off from a Widnes point of view.

The Wild women did find the net once more – Amanda Williams scoring her second goal of the game with just 5 seconds left on the clock – and the 4-goal haul represented the best Widnes return of the season so far.

The win sees the Falcons consolidate their third place in the Women's Premier League table with 6 points from 5 games. The Wild women have three defeats in three starts and are second bottom ahead of bottom team Bracknell Firebees on goal difference.

The Wild women's next game sees them travel to Milton Keynes for an early return fixture next Sunday 10th December – 6.30pm face off.

Rebekah Scott (Photo by David Law Photography)

Wild Women's GB prospect Katie Fairclough
(Photo by Stephen Fairclough)

Katie Fairclough Joins GB Squad

The Widnes Wild women's team could soon boast another international player on their roster as Katie Fairclough has been offered a place in the Great Britain Women's Under 16s squad after successfully negotiating the trials at Sheffield last Autumn.

She will now attend a series of training camps with the other girls who have also been selected, with a view to playing in international tournaments, although details of these have yet to be announced.

Katie is the latest Widnes Wild women's player to be selected for a national team, following in the footsteps of Leen de Decker who has played over 60 world championship games for her native Belgium, Team GB's Sarah Hutchinson - and Sophie Sinclair Reeks, who played for the GB Under 18s team at the World Championships in Poland last year.

Katie only started playing ice hockey in 2015 when she joined the women's hockey basics course at Silver Blades Widnes before joining the Wild Academy juniors set up.

In early 2017 she was invited to train with the Wild women's senior team and, in the summer, was given special dispensation to play league matches with them for the 2017/18 season, despite being a year younger than the normally permitted age of 16. She has played 3 matches so far and scored 1 assist.

However, this meteoric rise through the ice hockey ranks is only part of the story. Katie actually learnt to skate on wheels first before taking to blades when she started going to sessions at Wigan Roller Rink with her sister Caroline back in 2012.

She got involved with the junior inline hockey training there – which subsequently moved to the purpose-built hockey rink at Atherton. Since then, she has played for numerous inline teams at both her own age group and above and was selected to play for the Under 18 Junior Women Inline Hockey GB team at the 2016 FIRS World Inline Hockey Championships held in Asiago and Roana, in Italy.

Now in her third season of inline hockey, Katie signed for the under-14 and under-16 teams with the Blackhawks Junior inline team at Simply Skate in Rotherham and the season is part way through.

She also tried out for both the Women's Inline Hockey GB team again, who are going to compete in the World Skate Inline Hockey Championships Italy in 2018 and the World Roller Games in Barcelona in 2019 – and has been accepted for both junior and senior teams.

Leen de Decker and Sav Sumner celebrate a goal against Chelmsford (Photo by David Law Photography)

Sunday 14th January 2018 – Women's Premier Lge
Widnes Wild Women 5 – Chelmsford Cobras 6

Period Scores: 1-1, 3-2, 1-3
Shots on Goal: Widnes 32 – Chelmsford 52 (6-13, 12-20, 14-19)
Penalties In Minutes: Widnes 2 – Chelmsford 0

Widnes Scoring: Leen de Decker 2+1, Amanda Williams 1+2, Charlene Chapman & Sav Sumner 1+0, Lucy Kirkham 0+1

The Widnes Wild women's team came close to causing a major upset in their Women's Premier League against league leaders Chelmsford Cobras at Silver Blades Widnes on Sunday but ended up losing 5-6 in a thrilling match.

The Cobras arrived having won all of their 5 league games to date and having conceded just 3 goals in the process so the Wild women knew that they were in for a tough time. The home side were comfortably out-shot throughout the game, but this didn't stop them have a real go at the league leaders who had travelled with barely enough players to ice two full lines.

After a tense, end to end, start, it was the Wild who opened the scoring in the 12th minute through their Belgian international player Leen de Decker and, although Chelmsford equalised some three minutes later, the score of 1-1 at the end of the first period was a real credit to the Wild women.

They started the second period with two more goals – from De Decker, again, just 25 seconds from the restart, and then Sav Sumner just 90 seconds after that – to give the Wild a 3-1 lead. That advantage lasted less than a minute, however, as the Cobras fired in two quick goals themselves within 20 seconds of each other to tie the score at 3-3 with 37 minutes still left to play in the game.

Wild heads might have dropped at this point but they didn't and the Widnes players rallied and came out battling once again. Team captain Charlene Chapman put them back in the lead in the 38th minute and the Wild women took a highly deserved 4-3 scoreline into the final period.

The third period was very tense and there were chances for both sides. Chelmsford equalised with 10 minutes left to play and then edged themselves into the lead for the first time in the match with a powerplay goal in the 55th minute while the Wild's Megan Bowen Fell was sitting out the only penalty in the whole game for tripping.

An even-handed goal a minute later from Cobras' Tereza Plankova – who scored 4 in total – put the game tantalisingly beyond the Wild women's reach, and a strike by Widnes' Amanda Williams with just 13 seconds left brought the final score to 5-6.

This was the best performance by the Wild women this season so far and they can take heart from the fact that, not only did they lead the league leaders for 50 minutes of the game, but they also scored more goals against them in this one game than had been scored in all previous 5 league games put together.

The Wild women have three weekends without a game and then face three away trips in a row, playing Bracknell Firebees on 10th February, Swindon Topcats on 11th February and Kingston Diamonds on 18th February.

They are next at home on Sunday 25th February when they play Kingston Diamonds in the Women's Premier League at Silver Blades Widnes – 5.30pm face off.

Charlene Chapman (Photo by David Law Photography)

Wild's Stephanie Drinkwater (#1 netminder) and Sophie Sinclair Reeks (#16) defend a Swindon attack in Widnes' 5-1 defeat by the Topcats. (Flyfifer Photography)

10th February 2018 – Women's Premier League Bracknell Firebees 6 - Widnes Wild Women 1

Period Scores: 2-0, 1-0, 3-1
Shots on Goal: Bracknell 56 – Widnes 16 (19-4, 14-7, 23-5)
Penalties In Minutes: Bracknell 4 - Widnes 6
Widnes Scoring: Charlene Chapman 1+0, Amanda Williams & Leen de Decker 0+1

11th February 2018 – Women's Premier League Swindon Topcats 5 - Widnes Wild Women 1

Period Scores: 4-0, 1-1, 0-0
Shots on Goal: Swindon 62 – Widnes 13 (27-3, 18-4, 17-6)
Penalties In Minutes: Swindon 2 - Widnes 2
Widnes Scoring: Savannah Sumner 1+0, Emma Pearson & Samantha Boyle 0+1

The Widnes Wild women's team had a frustrating weekend on the road in the Women's Premier League, losing 6-1 away to Bracknell Firebees on Saturday and 5-1 away to Swindon Topcats on Sunday.

The Wild women were up against it from the start in Bracknell and were heavily out-shot throughout the match. The first goal came for the Firebees in the 6th minute and was followed by a second some 5 minutes later.

Bracknell scored once more in the second period and added three more goals in the third before the Wild women finally found the back of the net themselves with a goal by team captain Charlene Chapman.

In the game at Swindon on Sunday, the Wild women performed arguably better against a Topcats team who had been unbeaten in the league all season and are one of the favourites for the league title.

Despite being heavily out-shot once again, they actually matched the high flyers for the second two periods, notching up 1-1 and 0-0 period scores, and it was only due to a bad start in the first period that they found themselves 4-0 down after 20 minutes with too much ground to make up.

The Wild women's goal was scored by Sav Sumner at 32.54 – her second goal of the season.

The Widnes Wild women's team are away again this Sunday 18th February when they travel to Hull to face the Kingston Diamonds in a 12.30 face-off game. They are then at home to Kingston the following Sunday, 25th February, at Silver Blades Widnes - 5.30pm face off.

Katie Hills scored the only Wild goal against Kingston (Photo by Geoff White)

25th February 2018 – Women's Premier League
Widnes Wild Women 1 – Kingston Diamonds 5

Period Scores: 0-2, 0-2, 1-1
Shots on Goal: Widnes 37 – Kingston 45 (9-19, 16-11, 7-15)
Penalties in Minutes: Widnes 4 – Kingston 12
Widnes Scoring: Katie Hills 1+0

The Widnes Wild women's team lost 1-5 at home to Kingston Diamonds in their Women's Premier League match at Planet Ice Widnes on Sunday.

Missing several key players, they were unable to make any sort of real impression on the visitors from Hull and were heavily out-shot in the first period. Kingston went ahead after 10 minutes and added a second goal 3 minutes later to lead 0-2 at the first break.

The second period saw much better play from the Wild women. They enjoyed more spells of possession and out-shot the Diamonds but were unable to find a way past Kingston netminder Charlotte Cook.

Kingston scored two more goals –one on either side of the halfway point – and, although Widnes put their net under increasing pressure in the latter stages of the period, the lead remained 0-4 after 40 minutes of play.

The game was effectively killed off as a contest 3 minutes into the third period with a fifth goal for the Diamonds- a hat-trick goal for Sophie Campbell.

Seconds from the restart, the Wild's Katie Hills zigzagged her way through the Kingston defence to slot away a well taken individual goal but that was the last goal action in the game and Widnes slumped to a 1-5 home defeat.

The defeat leaves the Wild women second bottom of the WPL table with just 1 win from 9 starts. They have three games left this season – one at home followed by two away.

The Widnes Wild women's team have their last home game of the season on Sunday 18th March when they play the Bracknell Firebees in the Women's Premier League at Planet Ice Widnes - 5.30pm face off.

Wild Women v Bracknell Firebees (Photo by Geoff White)

Sunday 18th March 2018 – Women's Premier League Widnes Wild Women 4 – Bracknell Firebees 4

Period Scores: 1-1, 1-1, 2-2
Shots on Goal: Widnes 33 - Bracknell 32
Penalties In Minutes: Widnes 6 - Bracknell 6
Widnes Scoring: Katie Hills 3+0, Charlene Chapman 1+0, Lucy Kirkham, Emma Pearson, Abi Hayes & Catherine Bowen Fell all 0+1

The Widnes Wild women's team picked up their first home point of the season in a thrilling 4-4 draw against the Bracknell Firebees in the Women's Premier League at Planet Ice Widnes on Sunday.

The Firebees were making their first ever visit to Widnes after winning promotion from Division 1 South last season, and look set to qualify for the end of season play offs in their first season in this division.

They arrived on the back of a 4-game winning streak, having already beaten the Wild women 6-1 down in Berkshire back in February and, in their last game, trounced the league's bottom team Nottingham Vipers 22-0.

The Wild team are in transition this season, having introduced a number of new players to the squad so a 4-4 draw was, in fact, a very creditable outcome.

The game was very close throughout with both teams having numerous chances. The first goal of the game went to the visitors in the 9th minute, scored by Louise Beresford who is a GB under 18 international and also plays for the Bracknell Queen Bees Elite League team, but the score was levelled in the 16th minute with a fine strike by the Wild captain Charlene Chapman and the score remained at 1-1 at the first period break.

The Firebees edged back into the lead just 80 seconds after the restart with a second goal from Beresford but that was countered with a powerplay strike from the Wild's Katie Hills with just 3 minutes left of the period.

The Firebees took a 2-goal lead in the third period - with both being scored by Claire Fay – a highly experienced former Queen Bees player with 90 matches under her belt at top tier level – which left the Wild women with lots to do in the last 10 minutes.

The Wild's Katie Hills scored two sensational goals – giving her a hat-trick on the night – to tie the score with 5 minutes left, but try as they might, the home side were unable to find a late winner.

The shared points from the game see the Firebees move up into 4th place in the Women's Premier League table while the Wild women now have daylight between themselves and bottom club Nottingham.

That was the Wild women's last home game of the season. They have two away games left to play – against Milton Keynes Falcons on 15th April and Chelmsford Cobras on 6th May.

Vanessa Crickmore-Clarke (Photo by David Law Photography)

Sunday 15th April 2018 – Women's Premier League
Milton Keynes Falcons 8 - Widnes Wild Women 0

The Widnes Wild women's team had a disappointing trip to Buckinghamshire where they were shut out 8-0 by the Milton Keynes Falcons in their penultimate game of the Women's Premier League season. Their one remaining game is away to the title-chasing Chelmsford Cobras on 6th May.

The Wild Women away at Chelmsford (Photo by Steve Fairclough) Back Row: Sophie Sinclair-Reeks, Lucy Kirkham, Charlene Chapman, Leen de Decker, Charlotte McPhee Front Row: Katie Fairclough, Sav Sumner, Stephanie Drinkwater, Amanda Williams, Emma Pearson, Pauline Hayward. Laying Down: Abi Hayes

Sunday 6th May 2018 – Women's Premier League Chelmsford Cobras 6 – Widnes Wild Women 6

Period Scores: 1-0, 3-1, 2-5
Shots on Goal: Chelmsford 36 – Widnes 37
Penalties In Minutes: Chelmsford 4 – Widnes 4
Widnes scoring: Amanda Williams & Abigail Hayes both 2+0, Lucy Kirkham & Leen de Decker both 1+2

The Widnes Wild women's team ended their Women's Premier League season on a high note with a 6-6 draw away at league runners-up Chelmsford Cobras on Sunday.

The game was very closely contested throughout, completely belying the comparative league positions of the two teams – the Cobras already confirmed in second place in the league table with 8 wins from 11 games and the Wild women struggling down in second bottom with just 1 win and 1 draw from 11 starts.

There were numerous chances at both ends but the hosts just edged the first period 1-0 with a goal after 11 minutes.

The Wild women equalised just 5 minutes into the second period with a goal from Abi Hayes and the Widnes team had much more possession – out-shooting the Cobras by 13 to 8 - but not managing to capitalise on their efforts. The home team, on the other hand, managed to score 3 goals from their 8 shots in the period and headed into the second break with a 4-1 lead.

It was 5-1 to Chelmsford within 2 minutes of the restart but a goal from Amanda Williams pulled the Wild women back to 5-2 some 3 minutes later. The Cobras extended the lead once again making it 6-2 with 10 minutes to play and, looked at that time, to be cruising to victory.

With just 5 minutes left, Chelmsford's leading goalscorer Tereza Plankova picked up a hooking penalty and the Wild women pushed up to make the most of their ensuing two minute player advantage. Abi Hayes fired in the powerplay goal and this breakthrough sparked a revival among the Widnes team.

Just 50 seconds later, the Wild's Belgian international player Leen de Decker scored to make it 6-4. 80 seconds after that, Lucy Kirkham found the back of the net to close the gap to a single goal and set up a fascinating last two minutes of the league season.

The clock ticked down, both teams had chances and then – with just 21 seconds left to play - Amanda Williams fired into the Cobras' net to level the score and secure the Wild women a well deserved 6-6 draw.

The resulting point sees the Wild women finish the season in 6th place in the league table - 2 points clear of the relegation slot occupied by Nottingham Vipers.

Amanda Williams finishes the season as the Wild women's top points scorer with 7+3 in 9 appearances. Katie Hills and Leen de Decker tie in second with 6+3 and 4+5 respectively.

Lucy Kirkham, Sav Sumner and captain Charlene Chapman were ever presents for the season, each having played all 12 league games.

The season was notable for encouraging new talent with 5 new players – Katie Fairclough, Pauline Hayward, Alice Horsfield, Charlotte McPhee and Rebekah Scott - all making their WPL debuts for the Wild women.

Wild Women Fair Play Winners 2018
Back Row: Abi Culshaw, Stephanie Drinkwater, Pauline Hayward, Katie Fairclough, Abi Hayes. Front Row: Sav Sumner, Emma Pearson, Amanda Williams (Photo by Flyfifer Photography)

BWIH Friendship Tournament 2018

The Widnes Wild Women brought home silverware from the end of season Swindon Tournament for the second year running.

Last year, they won the Skills Competition and came second overall in the tournament, losing out to the host Swindon Elite League team 3-0 in the final.

This year they only finished mid-table in the group games but were awarded the Fair Play Trophy, which is also nice to have.

25th February 2018: Presentation Carnage at the Wild Women v Kingston home game - PB with Diamonds' Lois Tomlinson (Photo by Geoff White)

Paul & Lucy And The Wild Women

As I already mentioned earlier, I have always been a keen follower of women's ice hockey, going all the way back to my home town of Peterborough where the Ravens team were multiple title winners in the early 1980s.

So, when we found out that Widnes was going to have a women's team, Lucy and I jumped at the chance to go along and support them.

As women's hockey never gets as much attention as the men's games, I started off writing match reports for all their games. The home games were easier as we went to all of those and I then started closely studying the gamesheets for the away games and putting together reports for those as well.

The Wild Women played their first home game in the early months of 2016 and the game lacked a bit of atmosphere because there wasn't initially any music or announcing.

I had been doing the music and announcing at Blackpool Seagulls games at Cleveleys / Bispham since 2012 but had originally decided to have a "year off" from that – and also from radio and what's on news etc - when Lucy and I moved to the Wirral in the spring of 2015.

I did think about offering my services when I found out about the Widnes women's team but, by the time I got past my shyness, Patrick Sinclair had started doing the match calling using the rink's radio microphone so I decided to forget about it.

We had been in contact with original team captain Charlene Chapman about sponsoring something or other, albeit without really getting very far and, at the penultimate home game against Whitley Bay Squaws on 8th May, I suddenly took it upon myself to march in to the officials' booth and announced that she (Charlene) had said that Lucy could present the MVP awards.

She HAD touched upon it vaguely in a previous email but certainly nothing had been formally agreed so I wasn't really sure how this overture would go down.

The lady doing everything in the box peered at me over her glasses in a very severe and "who the bloody hell are you...?" sort of manner and then, indeed, did actually ask me who I was.

Slipping into safety default mode, I replied: "Paul & Lucy", somewhat oblivious to the fact that any casual onlooker might think this rather odd as I was standing there on my own at the time.

However, it is worth bearing in mind that being "Paul & Lucy" used to open a lot of doors for us in Blackpool and the surrounding area when we were doing our radio shows and our Best Kept Secrets website - and it also had the desired effect here as she realised that it was us who had been writing the match reports for the women's games.

She introduced herself as Mandy Sinclair – mother of the player Sophie Sinclair–Reeks - and said how much they all appreciated the work we had been doing on their behalf.

So, that was all arranged and, by the end of the game, I finally got round to telling Lucy that she was going to present the MVP awards.

I left it until the last moment on purpose so that she didn't have time to get nervous about it and think of all sorts of reasons why she couldn't possibly do it – and around we went. There was no photographer that day so I bravely ventured out onto the ice and took the presentation photos.

Now, the 15th January 2017 is another important date in this story as the Wild women were due to play Streatham Storm in the WPL at Widnes.

Through having written a story for the Wild website and the newspaper about Sophie Sinclair-Reeks having been selected to play for the Team GB Under 18 women's international team in Poland, I had picked up on the fact that Mandy and Patrick were going out to watch her and they were not going to be at the Streatham game.

This meant that there wasn't going to be anyone there to do the Electronic Gamesheet or to do the match announcements, although Rob Melvin would probably be there doing the clock as usual.

I pointed this out to the women's team and, having just successfully broken my announcing duck at Widnes by doing the Widnes Wildcats v Riverside Raiders Antony Morris memorial game the week before, I offered to step in and help out.

The run up to this game was a bit bizarre as the Manchester Phoenix team had been given permission to play the rest of their EPL games for the season at Widnes, rather than dragging their long suffering fans all the way to Blackpool to use the rather dubious Fylde Coast Ice Arena.

The first of these games took place on the same day as the Wild women v Streatham match and the women's game was moved to an earlier face off time to accommodate it.

The Women's team were up in arms about this late change as several of their players had got their work shifts arranged around a 5.30 pm face off and couldn't change them that easily – and the head coach at the time also went ballistic and provided me with few choice comments that I could never get away with printing anywhere!

The face off was supposed to be at 4pm so Lucy and I arrived at 3pm to get set up only to find that the skating session was still very much underway and not actually due to finish until 4pm.

There was a heightened air of tension around the place as nobody really knew what was going to happen with the Phoenix game – how many people would turn up and how it would all go. The rink manager Kirsty was prowling up and down and there was also another manager chappy who I didn't know and have never seen before or since who was also there helping to keep on top of things.

We got set up and managed to get sound-checked once the disco music had finished - and Joanne Gibson from Bradford came along and did the EGS for the game.

It was a very close and entertaining game and Streatham just won 2-3 with a late goal. You can watch Colin's highlights compilation on YouTube and one of the fascinating points about this game isn't so much the game at all but all of the people who kept wandering in and out of the rink as it went on.

The Phoenix game was due to start at 6.30 and all of their fans arrived in plenty of time. As it was free admission to the women's game, they all came into the rink and sat down or milled about in the walkways. So at the start of the video, there is hardly anyone there – as it was an odd face off time – and then by the end the place is absolutely heaving with all these Phoenix fans.

They were also planning to do a livestream of the game for fans who couldn't get to Widnes to watch and this was a big money earner for the hard up Phoenix team. It was important for them to get it working right and they had a huge amount of equipment to bring in and set up beforehand.

So, throughout the women's game, during which yours truly was trying to concentrate on playing the music and getting the announcements right (this was, after all, the first senior league game that I had ever worked on), a procession of Phoenix people kept coming along asking where they could set things up and plug things in.

Then the girl who was going to do the music for the Phoenix game came in and asked about linking up to the sound system. She also asked me rather enigmatically if anybody had spoken to me about announcing for their game – which they hadn't – and nobody ever did, so I don't really know what that was all about.

Then Neil Morris came along (you either know who he is or you don't - check out Stuart Latham's book about Manchester Phoenix to find out more about him...) and he also poked around and looked at the sockets for the sound cables and then asked me if I knew anywhere locally where you could buy audio leads. At 5pm on a Sunday...!

Needless to say, I politely replied in the negative while trying to carry on keeping up with the game that I was actually there for.

Now, what actually surprised me about all of this is that you have a team playing in the EPL - ie two divisions above Widnes Wild – being run by people who, apparently, organise huge international live events but, for some reason, nobody had thought to drop into the rink during the week before the game to check out the lie of the land, where the sockets were and what sort of leads they might need to bring with them....

But there you go. After the trials and tribulations of the women's game and the additional hassle of having to deal with all sorts of odd people and their random enquiries, Lucy and Iscuttled off to go and have a well earned McDonalds and left them all to it....

So, fast forward to 25th February 2018 when the Wild Women were at home to Kingston Diamonds

On this particular day, I had arranged to meet up with the Hull player Lois Tomlinson after the game and give her a copy of my latest book because she had kindly provided me with some photos to use in it earlier in the season.

As Geoff White the official Wild photographer was going to be there, we decided to make it part of the after match presentations and give it a bit of extra attention.

When I arrived, I went into the officials' booth and told Mandy what I wanted to do at the end of the game and she said "OK – you might as well present the MVP awards as well, in that case."

During one of the breaks, Geoff came up to me and said that Mandy had told him that I was presenting the MVP awards. He explained that he always had trouble getting the women's players to stand still long enough after they had been given the award to be able to take a decent photo and asked if I could try and do something about this for the presentation – so I gave it a bit of thought.

Now, I have to say that the presentation on the ice after this game was a thoroughly life changing experience – in a nice way, that is – more than I ever could possibly have imagined - and I learnt a huge amount of lessons as a consequence of it.

The first thing that you need to know is - if you have ever been on the ice – or stood at the door of the penalty box at the end of a game - it is a really thrilling experience, with the crowd cheering and the players skating round and shaking hands and the music blaring and the bustling activity behind the scenes.

In fact, the first time that I ever did this (in the "modern era"...) - when I presented the MVP awards at the Wild v Hull Jets men's game in March 2016, it took me a week to come down afterwards and the whole thing remains a sort of haze to this day.

The other thing that you won't know if you haven't been out on the ice is how the plexi glass affects the acoustics around the rink. If you are off the ice and somebody on the other side of the glass tries to talk to you, you can't hear what they say and you have to go to an opening in order to be able to communicate.

This means that you don't too hear much of what goes on between the players on the ice nor what the referee says to them.

When I first started watching ice hockey at Peterborough in the 1980s, there was no plexi glass at the rink - just netting that hung around the boards.

However, this meant that you could hear the interaction among the players and you could also clearly hear the referee's instructions. When the play was stuck against the board, you'd hear the ref shouting out "Play It ! Play It!" or you'd hear the linesman shouting "No Icing!" when he waved off a call after an end to end shot had clipped somebody on the way past.

And, when the referee blew to give a penalty – you could clearly hear him call out, for example "Number 2 White. Two minutes for cross checking " or whatever the call was for....

Now, knowing for a fact that this used to happen in the old days, when I became an off ice game official at games at Widnes and was involved with the announcing, occasionally scoring and keeping an eye on the scoreboard and penalty boxes, I was constantly surprised when a player would come into the penalty box, flop onto the bench, throw his gear on the floor and exclaim "What was that for...?".

I would then have to spend half the game patiently explaining to the various players what penalties they had been given and how long they would be sitting in the box.

I eventually asked one of the referees at a game one day if they still called out what the penalty was for when they blew the whistle out on the ice as I was rather surprised that the players never seemed to know what they had been penalised for.

He explained that usually, when the whistle got blown, the players would be all up in arms either pushing and shoving the opposition or arguing about the call with the officials - and would then whinge and complain all the way to the penalty box, which is why they never knew what the penalty had been called for.

Anyway, back to the end of February 2018 and I went round to the officials' bench at the end of the game to make the presentations. On my way onto the ice, a small box of chocolates was pressed into my hand to give as the MVP award and I stood there awaiting the verdict.

There was no music on this occasion – and only a fairly small crowd – so it was rather eerie and quiet out on the ice compared to usual and you could clearly hear all the whispers between the players on both sides.

At this time we were using the penalty box nearer to the away team for accessing the ice to do the presentations so I was right in the firing line in terms of comments from the visiting players - and they were moaning and complaining in my direction about something or other.

I think they were criticising the fact that the MVP award was a piffling box of chocolates rather than a trophy that they might usually have expected to receive. This was actually nothing to do with me as I had just had it sprung on me at the last minute so there wasn't much I could do about it.

There wasn't any microphone on the go for this game either - for some reason – and being the only one who could be audible across the ice because of my positioning and my loud, well-projected, voice - I ended up having to call out the winners of the awards as well.

Presumably, from the players' point of view, this made it look as if I had actually selected them, which I can guarantee you I did not - and, indeed, never have - because I would have trouble selecting an MVP even if there was only one player on the ice!

I touched on this earlier but it is worth explaining in full at this point so that you understand what I just said. It is true that, as a match announcer or scorer or whatever, you have a front row seat and often sit about 6 inches away from the action of the game.

But the very nature of the job – where you have to write everything down and get it properly entered on the game sheet – means that you don't always have the luxury of being able to watch / enjoy the game.

In fact, I probably spend as much time looking at the clock for how long is left until the next announcement is needed – or how long a penalty has left to run – or at the penalty box to make sure the right players are there and who is going out next etc – or where the person is with the results of the raffle that is due to be called out at the next period break – as I do actually watching the game.

So it was called out to me who the winner of the MVP award was for the Hull team (the away team always goes first) – and I in turn called this out across the ice.

It was Sophie Campbell who had scored 3+1 in the game and the game had finished 1-5 to the Kingston Diamonds so it wasn't an unreasonable call - and one I might even have arrived at myself based on a quick look at the scoring figures on the gamesheet - but the Hull girls were in full swing by this point and this announcement was received with a torrent of maybe not *abuse*, but certainly some rather sarcastic catcalls.

As Campbell came over to collect her box of chocolates, I enacted my masterplan to help the photographer get a decent MVP photo for once. As she approached, I asked her to take her helmet off for the photo. Luckily she was quite young and little and just did what I asked – probably in shock – and we got a nice posed photo taken.

She put her gloves and stick down on the ice so that she could undo her helmet and then took that off and laid it on the ice as well. My strategy was working quite well and after all that fuss and upheaval, she stood completely still, smiling sweetly for the shot. Had it been one of the other more vociferous players, I am not sure if it would have gone quite so well.

Then it was time for the Widnes MVP award winner to be announced. I looked up and saw all these eyes piercing and burning into me from behind the masks and face cages lined up along the other blue line.

At the time, I imagined that they were all looking at me hopefully, imploringly, desperately wishing to be called out as the MVP but I came to realise later that they were probably hoping that it wasn't them - and that there was no way they were going to take THEIR helmet off for a photo and box of chocolates.

But I was also in full swing by now and, in aloof "Important Person" mode, I ignored the crescendos of chuntering that were building up from both sets of players and I called out Sammi Boyle from the Wild women and got her to take her helmet off for the photo as well.

Then I called over Lois Tomlinson from the Hull team and that really set the cat among the proverbial pigeons as only she, me and Geoff knew about this one and there were surprised shouts of “Eh? What’s this for...?“ and so on....

So – mission accomplished. All awards presented – all photos safely taken, along with a great publicity shot for my book – and I went for a bit of a lie down!

I suggested to Patrick Sinclair that I actually had my sound equipment in the car as Lucy and I were doing the Halton Huskies game later that same evening and had we known in advance, I could have brought it in earlier for the women’s game and done the music.

The final Wild women’s home game of the season was scheduled for a few weeks later – against Bracknell Firebees, and once again we were due to do a Huskies game the same day - so we arranged to come in early and set up for the women’s game and I did the music and Patrick did the announcing.

We did the same thing again: taking the helmets off for the photos but this time we used the side closer to the Widnes blueline - and to be honest - the away players were less belligerent on this occasion.

The MVP winners were Claire Fay for Bracknell (Daniel Fay’s mum...) and Sav Sumner for Widnes – who did moan a bit about probably having “helmet hair”...

We don’t bother with the taking off of the helmets any more – for the following season Lucy devised an ever better strategy for getting the MVP photos done - and there are several very good reason for this:

1) It makes everybody HATE you
2) They have got used to the idea of MVP photos and don't skate off as quickly afterwards
3) There is a chance that the award winner might be under 18 and under 18s are not allowed to remove their helmets on the ice at any time – so best to be on the safe side

During the summer months (2018), I was looking back at the photos we had taken during the course of the season and in a Damask flash of inspiration (yes – I was at the dining table), I suddenly understood what the Hull players had been whining on about.

At the end of a men's game, each team usually gets presented with a crate of beer – with enough bottles or cans for one for each player. Fair enough. At most women's games they get a little statuette of some sort – but here was some bloke giving out little boxes of chocolates that didn't even have enough in them for one each among the players.

It seemed a little condescending and, in hindsight, I could fully appreciate why the Hull girls were a bit miffed about it.

That's not to say that I was criticising whoever had kindly provided the chocolates as it meant that there were, at least, prizes to give out and even 12 little boxes of choccies over the course of the season still costs money after all...

I pointed this out to Lucy and suggested the WE could sponsor the MVP awards for the next season. We could do it in the name of one of the First World War women that she was researching and it would be good publicity all round.

The Women's team were pleased with the idea as it removed a cost and an extra task for them to worry about for the next season and that is how it all came about.

Above: MVPs v Kingston 25th February - PB with Sammi Boyle, left, and Sophie Campbell, right
Below: MVPs V Bracknell, 18th March – Sav Sumner and Claire Fay
(All Photos by Geoff White)

EIHA Women's Premier League - Season 2018/19

Final Table	P	W	D	L	GF	GA	+/-	Pts
Nottingham Vipers	14	11	2	1	90	39	51	24
Whitley Squaws	14	10	1	3	80	44	36	21
Chelmsford Cobras	14	9	0	5	54	36	18	16
Kingston Diamonds B	14	7	1	6	48	53	-5	15
Sheffield Shadows	14	6	1	7	74	60	14	13
Bracknell Fire Bees	14	6	0	8	81	69	12	12
Milton Keynes Falcons	14	4	1	9	39	67	-28	9
Widnes Wild Women	14	0	0	14	16	114	-98	-2*

**2 points deducted for failing to fulfil a fixture*

EIHA WPL Top Points Scorers – Season 2018/19

Player	Team	GP	G	A	Pts	PIM
Robin Mullen	Nottingham Vipers	14	33	14	47	16
Stephanie Towns	Whitley Squaws	14	29	17	46	18
Abigail Culshaw	Whitley Squaws	14	23	17	40	4
Emily Harris	Bracknell Fire Bees	7	25	8	33	6
Madison Wright	Nottingham Vipers	13	17	15	32	26
Katherine Wiggins	Sheffield Shadows	10	15	14	29	8
Hazel Wilson	Sheffield Shadows	10	15	10	25	10
Lucy Beal	Bracknell Fire Bees	11	11	14	25	2
Marguerite Laffitte	Bracknell Fire Bees	10	15	6	21	14
Jennifer Bolton	Chelmsford Cobras	12	10	10	20	2

EIHA WPL Top Netminders – Season 2018/19

Player	Team	GPI	Mins	SA	GA	GAA	Sv%	SO
Emma Nichols	CHE	6	360	334	15	2.5	95.51%	0
Holly Steeples	NOT	13	780	501	37	2.84	92.61%	2
Robyn Maby	CHE	4	240	117	10	2.5	91.45%	1
Lucy Jarvis	CHE	9	540	23	2	0.22	91.30%	0
Liberty Bird	SHE	6	360	68	6	1	91.18%	2
Charlotte Cook	KIN	10	600	328	30	3	90.85%	2
Jess Kinghorn	WHI	13	780	361	34	2.61	90.58%	5
Dawn Dickinson	KIN	12	720	54	6	0.5	88.89%	0
Steph Drinkwater	WID	13	780	965	109	8.38	88.70%	0
Lucy Gruber	CHE	3	180	34	4	1.33	88.24%	0
Olivia Brooks	KIN	4	240	118	14	3.5	88.14%	0

Note: MINs played are estimated as full and concise date was unavailable. GAA figures are therefore also approximated so this table may differ from other official records, should they exist.

Widnes Wild Women Results – Season 2018/19

Date	Comp	Home			Away	Res
16.9.18	WPL	MK Falcons	10	3	Widnes Wild	L
13.10.18	WPL	Sheffield Shads	3	1	Widnes Wild	L
28.10.18	WPL	Nottinghm Vipers	11	2	Widnes Wild	L
11.11.18	WPL	Kingston Diamds	6	0	Widnes Wild	L
9.12.18	WPL	Widnes Wild	1	9	Whitley Squaws	L
6.1.19	WPL	Bracknell Firebs	7	0	Widnes Wild	L
20.1.19	WPL	Widnes Wild	3	9	Nottinghm Vipers	L
10.2.19	WPL	Widnes Wild	2	9	Chelmsfd Cobras	L
3.3.19	CH	Solway Sharks	7	7	Widnes Wild	D
10.,3.19	WPL	Widnes Wild	1	4	MK Falcons	L
7.4.19	WPL	Widnes Wild	2	14	Bracknell Firebs	L
21.4.19	WPL	Chelmsfd Cobras	5	0	Widnes Wild	LA*
28.4.19	WPL	Widnes Wild	1	13	Kingston Diamds	L
19.05.19	WPL	Widnes Wild	0	8	Sheffield Shads	L
26.05.19	WPL	Whitley Squaws	7	0	Widnes Wild	L

Note: The away game at Chelmsford was awarded as a 5-0 forfeit after Widnes refused to travel due to a late change in venue and much later face off time.*

Emma Pearson was appointed the new captain of the Wild Women for the 2018/19 season after the retirement of original skipper Charlene Chapman

(Photo by Flyfifer Photography)

Widnes Wild Women Player Statistics
Season 2018/19

Player	Women's Premier League					Challenge Match				
	GP	G	A	Pts	PIM	GP	G	A	Pts	PIM
Savannah Sumner	12	6	2	8	8	1	2	0	2	0
Emma Pearson	13	2	6	8	16	1	0	0	0	0
Amanda Williams	11	3	2	5	4	1	0	0	0	0
Leen De Decker	3	3	0	3	0	0	0	0	0	0
Jemma Brown	12	0	2	2	2	1	0	0	0	0
Elizabeth Loss	11	1	1	2	0	0	0	0	0	0
Danielle Skilander	10	1	1	2	0	0	0	0	0	0
Katherine Fairclough	12	0	1	1	4	1	0	0	0	0
Laura Marcroft	12	0	1	1	0	1	0	2	2	0
Sophie Sinclair-Reeks	8	0	1	1	4	1	0	1	1	0
Victoria Venables	7	0	1	1	8	0	0	0	0	0
Katie Adshead	13	0	0	0	2	1	1	0	1	0
Karyn Cooper	11	0	0	0	2	1	0	0	0	0
Vanessa Crickmore Clarke	8	0	0	0	2	0	0	0	0	0
Stephanie Drinkwater	13	0	0	0	4	1	0	0	0	0
Pamela England	9	0	0	0	0	0	0	0	0	0
Kathryn Garner	12	0	0	0	2	1	0	1	1	2
Pauline Hayward	12	0	0	0	4	1	0	0	0	0
Daisy Lloyd-Hazlegreaves	12	0	0	0	2	0	0	0	0	0
Charlotte McPhee	13	0	0	0	0	1	2	0	2	0
Josie Moran	10	0	0	0	0	1	0	0	0	0
Philippa Wheeler	11	0	0	0	4	1	1	0	1	0

Netminder	Comp	GPI	Mins	SA	GA	GAA	Sv%
Steph Drinkwater	WPL	13	780	965	109	8.38	88.70%
	Chal	1	60	44	7	7	84.10
	Total	**14**	**840**	**1009**	**116**	**8.29**	**88.50%**

Widnes Wild Women - Season 2018/19 (Photo by Geoff White)
Back Row: Michael Parkin, Leen de Decker, Elizabeth Loss, Jemma Brown, Amanda Williams, Kat Garner, Karyn Cooper, Charlotte McPhee, Josie Moran, Laura Marcroft, Katie Adshead, Phil Pearson.
Front Row: Katie Fairclough, Danielle Skilander, Emma Pearson, Stephanie Drinkwater, Vanessa Crickmore-Clarke, Pauline Hayward, Daisy Lloyd-Hazlegreaves, Pamela England

SATURDAY, 30 JUNE 2018

Join The Wild Women For the 2018/19 Season

www.icehockeyreview.co.uk

The Widnes Wild women's team are recruiting for the 2018/19 season and are keen to attract new players as well as a new head coach.

The Wild Women play in the EIHA's Women's Premier League and are the only women's team in the north west to play at that national level.

They have been in the WPL for three seasons, qualified for the end of season play offs in two of those years and finished runners up in 2015/16.

While, obviously, wishing to remain competitive, the Wild women are keen to encourage new talent and nurture prospective players. As such, last season saw them hand WPL debuts to a number of players who had never played senior league hockey before, coming from backgrounds such as junior teams elsewhere, university hockey or even roller hockey.

There is a wide range of ages and experience on the current Wild women roster with players aged from 15 to 60 - and seasoned internationals sharing line duties with season debutants.

Wild women training starts again in August and prospective new players are asked to get in touch with the team via Facebook or Twitter.
Facebook: www.facebook.com/widneswildwomen
Twitter: www.twitter.com/widneswildwomen

June 2018: Join The Wild Women for the 2018/19 Season

The Widnes Wild women's team are recruiting for the 2018/19 season and are keen to attract new players as well as a new head coach.

The Wild Women play in the EIHA's Women's Premier League and are the only women's team in the north west to play at that national level.

They have been in the WPL for three seasons, qualified for the end of season play offs in two of those years and finished runners up in 2015/16.

While, obviously, wishing to remain competitive, the Wild women are keen to encourage new talent and nurture prospective players. As such, last season saw them hand WPL debuts to a number of players who had never played senior league hockey before, coming from backgrounds such as junior teams elsewhere, university hockey or even roller hockey.

There is a wide range of ages and experience on the current Wild women roster with players aged from 15 to 60 - and seasoned internationals sharing line duties with season debutants.

The Wild women are also looking for a new Head Coach for the 2018/19 season. The requirements are as follows:

Must hold a valid EIHA Level 2 licence.
Ability to plan and lead weekly training sessions, with the support of Assistant Coaches.
Available to travel with the team to bench coach a 14-game season (7x home, 7x away).

Wild women training starts again in August and prospective new players or coaches are asked to get in touch with the team via Facebook or Twitter.

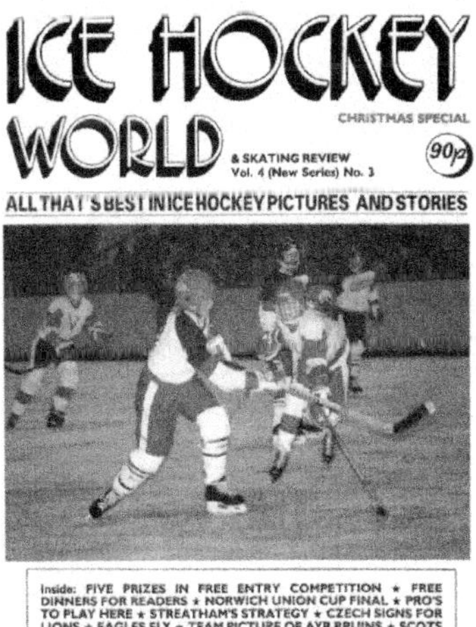

On A Personal Note:

A lot of people don't realise there is such a thing as women's ice hockey and those who do are often disparaging about it for one reason or another.

I have always been interested in women's hockey – dating right back to the days in the 1980s when the Peterborough Ravens were the first English league champions.

In fact, the rec team that I used to play for had regular "friendly" games against the Ravens - although these were anything but friendly and usually ended up with us getting battered both physically and score-wise!

Women's hockey isn't quite that aggressive these days and is played on a "non-checking" basis.

While it may come across as tame in comparison with men's league games, this means that there is a lot more emphasis on skating, passing and positioning techniques, which in a lot of ways makes the games more interesting.

There are not so many stoppages, less niggly posturing and arguing and the game flows much more freely.

I have been reporting on the Wild women's games since they started playing at Widnes three years ago and can safely say that I enjoy those matches just as much as the Wild NIHL games.

If you have the chance to go and watch a women's game at your local rink, do go along and give them your support.

There are many women's teams across the country playing in Elite League, Premier League and D1 North & South and also U16s teams in some areas as well.

Paul Breeze

The new look Wild Women's team after their first game away to Milton Keynes (Photo by Wild Women IHC)

16th September 2018 – Women's Premier League
Milton Keynes Falcons 10 – Widnes Wild Women 3

Period Scores: 4-1, 2-0, 4-2
Shots on Goal: Milton Keynes 70 – Widnes 34 (16-14, 24-8, 30-12)
Penalties In Minutes: Milton Keynes 6 – Widnes 6
Widnes Scoring: Leen de Decker 2+0, Sav Sumner 1+1, Amanda Williams 0+1

The Widnes Wild women's team opened their 2018/19 EIHA Women's Premier League campaign with a 10-3 defeat away to the Milton Keynes Falcons and, while a defeat is always disappointing, this match must be looked at in a wider context.

The Wild team had 6 brand new players on their bench – 5 of whom had never played competitive hockey at this level before. They handed WPL debuts to Josie Moran, Katie Adshead, Kathryn Garner, Danielle Skilander and

Laura Marcroft and back up netminder Philippa Wheeler also made her first appearance in Wild colours, having made the move from Nottingham Vipers.

Despite the somewhat one-sided final scoreline, the new look Wild women gave a very good account of themselves and the first period was very closely matched with lots of chances for both sides.

The home team took the lead after 5 minutes and went two up after 9 but then the Wild's Belgian international player Leen de Decker fired in a powerplay goal to halve the deficit.

Two more goals followed for the Falcons and the 4-1 scoreline at the end of the first period probably flattered them somewhat.

The second period, however, was nearly all Falcons and they out-shot the Wild women by 24 to 8. Two home goals during the period effectively finished the game off as a contest and they had added three more by the time de Decker scored the Wild's second goal of the game at 51.28.

Sav Sumner added a third for Widnes with 2 and half minutes left on the clock and Milton Keynes rounded off the scoring with their 10th goal of the game at 58.47.

The Wild women have three more away games before their first home game of the new season. They travel to Sheffield on 13th October, Nottingham on 28th October and Kingston (Hull) on 11th November before playing at home to the Whitley Squaws on Sunday 9th December at Planet Ice Widnes.

13th October 2018 – Women's Premier League Sheffield Shadows 3 – Widnes Wild Women 1

Period Scores: 2-0, 0-1, 1-0
Shots on Goal: Sheffield 44 – Widnes 28 (13-14, 19-6, 12-8)
Penalties In Minutes: Sheffield 12 – Widnes 4
Widnes Scoring: Leen de Decker 1+0, Amanda Williams 0+1

The Widnes Wild women's team came away with their heads held high after a narrow 3-1 defeat in the Women's Premier League against newly relegated Sheffield Shadows on Saturday.

This season, the Wild women are continuing with their ambitious player development policy and, following on from their previous game where they had six new players on the bench, the team for the Sheffield game included 4 more brand new players.

Karyn Cooper and Daisy Lloyd-Hazlegreaves all made their competitive debuts having never played any women's league matches before and Jemma Brown also made her first Widnes appearance, having previously played WPL hockey with the Kingston Diamonds team and before that, gaining junior experience with teams in Hull, Trafford and Blackburn.

Victoria Venables – who had previously played 1 season with the Altrincham Avalanche and 8 more with Flintshire Furies – also made her Wild Women debut.

The Wild women actually outplayed their hosts in the first period – out-shooting them by 14 to 13 - but it was the Sheffield team who made the most of their opportunities in front of goal and they scored in the 2nd and 10th minutes to take a 2-0 lead into the first period break.

Widnes scored the only goal of the second period when Leen de Decker halved the deficit with a strike in the 27th minute and the game remained finely balanced for the rest of the period.

Sensing that they could still take something from the game, the Wild women pressed forward in the third period and forced the Shadows into taking defensive penalties. They couldn't make the most of their powerplay opportunities, however, and the Shadows' third goal in the 52nd minute effectively killed off the game.

After the game, Amanda Williams said:

"Sheffield were a very young team with some strong skaters whose constant movement challenged our defensive game."

"I'm really pleased that everything we've worked on in training for the past weeks showed in the game. The team is in a great place right now having 22 players signed up. Our development players are getting regular ice time and improving every game."

"To ice a team where 50% of players are playing in their first season of competitive ice hockey and come away with a 3-1 defeat is a credit to how hard the players are working."

The Wild women have two more away games before their first home game of the new season. They travel to Nottingham on 28th October and Kingston (Hull) on 11th November before playing at home to the Whitley Squaws on Sunday 9th December at Planet Ice Widnes.

28th October 2018 – Women's Premier League
Nottingham Vipers 11 – Widnes Wild Women 2

Period Scores: 4-1, 4-0, 3-1
Shots on Goal: Nottingham 73 – Widnes 20 (30-4, 11-9, 32-7)
Penalties In Minutes: Nottingham 6 – Widnes 4
Widnes Scoring: Amanda Williams 2+0, Jemma Brown, Elizabeth Loss & Laura Marcroft all 0+1

The Widnes Wild women's team came back from the Lace City on the wrong end of an 11-2 defeat, having lost to the Nottingham Vipers in the Women's Premier League on Sunday.

As with their previous games, this result needs to be put into context as half of the Wild team had never even played competitive hockey before this September and, as such, this season should be looked upon as one of player development and team re-building.

That being the case, one of the most pleasing aspects was to see new players Jemma Brown, Elizabeth Loss and Laura Marcroft all getting on the scoresheet with an assist each.

The Vipers have a very strong line-up this season with a few Team GB internationals and some overseas players on their roster and it was Canadian Robin Mullen who did the most damage scoring 4+2 for Nottingham with Czech-born Renata Mudrakova adding 2+2 and hockey gene rich Jessica Urquhart 2+1.

Amanda Williams scored her first goal of the season for the Wild after 12 minutes to pull the score back 3-1 and then added her second in the 55th minute to round off the scoring for the game.

After the game, Amanda said:

“Nottingham are a much stronger side this season. We knew this going into the game but continued our season's aim of developing new players and therefore we still played 4-line hockey.”

“The team played a well-disciplined game and there was some brilliant offensive play. Several players had stand out performances, but Philippa Wheeler earnt the MVP for a great game against her former team. We've lots to work on, but it's very pleasing to see the benefits of our on-ice training and crossfit sessions coming across in games.”

The Wild women are away to Kingston Diamonds in Hull on Sunday 11th November and then have their first home game of the season when they host the Whitley Bay Squaws on Sunday 9th December at Planet Ice Widnes – face off 5.30pm

Philippa Wheeler (Photo by Conor McGill)

A minute's silence for Remembrance Sunday before the game in Hull (Photo by Rachel Stork)

11th November 2018 – Women's Premier League Kingston Diamonds 6 – Widnes Wild Women 0

Period Scores: 3-0, 2-0, 1-0
Shots on Goal: Kingston 62 – Widnes 15 (26-3, 24-4, 12-8)
Penalties In Minutes: Kingston 4 – Widnes 8

The Widnes Wild women's team put in a battling performance but came away without reward with a 6-0 defeat in the Women's Premier League against Hull-based Kingston Diamonds on Sunday.

In a season that has already seen them ice new players in double figures, they gave another WPL debut out in this game – to Pamela England, another successful graduate of the Widnes hockey basics training course.

A healthy bench of 18 players travelled the length of the M62 for the mid-day face off, although match experience is still a little on the short side as only 6 of those were playing regular league hockey before this season. Jemma Brown was Wild captain for the day against her old team-mates and, while the statistics may look rather one sided, the enthusiastic Wild women gave a good account of themselves.

Despite being heavily out-shot in the first period 26 to 3, the Wild women kept the Kingston attack at bay until the 8th minute of play. Two more goals handed the hosts a 3-0 lead at the first break and, by the second break, they had built up a 5-0 advantage.

The Wild carried on pushing forward in search of a consolation right up until the final buzzer and were unlucky to concede a sixth goal in the closing stages. However, it is all good match experience and it will be interesting to see how this ambitiously constructed new-look team develops as the season progresses.

After the game, Amanda Williams said:

“We made the short trip to Hull missing a number of key experienced players. We know how Hull play and we were expecting the physical encounter. All 4 lines worked hard for each other, stood up to the challenge and battled until the final buzzer.”

“The girls can take pride in their performance, with only 1 of 6 goals coming from a clear shot rather than a goal mouth scramble. A special mention must go to Pamela England, who made her debut after stepping up from Learn To Play and rec hockey. We now have a month to heal some injuries and get back to training before our first home game on December 9th.”

The Wild women’s next game is on Sunday 9th December when they play their first home game of the season against the Whitley Bay Squaws at Planet Ice Widnes – 5.30pm face off.

Widnes Wild Poet In Residence Lucy London with Wild Women's player Kat Garner (photo by Paul Breeze)

Poet Lucy Sponsors MVP Awards

There will be a new name on the MVP awards for the Widnes Wild women's team's home games this season and, rather than being one of the players, it will be the name of a World War One Heroine!

The Wild's Poet In Residence Lucy London is sponsoring the match awards and is using the opportunity to spread the word about Sarah MacNaughtan – who was quite well known prior to the First World War but is all but forgotten today.

Lucy explains the story behind this:

Since 2012, I've been researching the role of women in the First World War for a series of commemorative exhibitions. Having commemorated the First World War all my life it was not until I began researching for this project that I began to discover what women accomplished before they were allowed to vote.

Women served in many of the theatres of the conflict and many of them died or were killed. Yet there are many of those women whose names do not appear on the Commonwealth War Graves Commission List of Female Casualties and, I have just found out that some of them may not even have graves, let alone a mention on a war memorial.

Sarah MacNaughtan is particularly interesting yet not many people have heard of her these days. She was 50 when war broke out; she was a successful writer with several books to her name and was a wealthy woman. Sarah was no stranger to war zones, having been in Rio de Janeiro in Brazil during the 1893 – 1894 bombardment.

She also helped tending the wounded in South Africa during the Boer Wars and in The Balkans during The Balkan Wars.

In September 1914, Sarah travelled to Antwerp in Belgium with Mabel St. Clair Stobart's ambulance unit to tend wounded French and Belgian soldiers. When Antwerp was evacuated, Sarah ordered a special mobile kitchen from Harrods in London and had it sent over so she could set up a soup kitchen in northern France.

Sarah noticed the plight of wounded French and Belgian soldiers who were often left for days without attention in stations waiting for treatment because the most seriously wounded were tended to first.

After a speaking tour of England, Scotland and Wales, Sarah went to help out in Russia and Persia (now called Iran) in September 1915. During that time she continued to write books and have them published. Sarah returned to England exhausted and ill and died on 24th July 1916.

In sponsoring these Most Valued Player Awards, I wanted to make sure that Sarah's name was remembered."

You can read more about Sarah MacNaughtan and other fascinating women on Lucy's Inspirational Women website at:

http://inspirationalwomenofww1.blogspot.com/2016/12/sarah-broome-macnaughtan-1864-1916.html

– and follow Lucy's "Poet In Residence" Facebook page at www.facebook.com/lucy-poet-in-residence.

The Sarah MacNaughtan Memorial MVP award for the 2018/19 season (Photo by Paul Breeze)

Victoria Venables was the Wild Women's MVP against Whitley (Photo by Paul Breeze)

Sunday 9th December 2018 – Women's Premier Lge Widnes Wild Women 1 – Whitley Bay Squaws 9

Period Scores: 0-3, 0-6, 1-0
Shots on Goal: Widnes 5 – Whitley 74 (3-22, 1-27, 1-25)
Penalties In Minutes: Widnes 4 – Whitley 4
Widnes Scoring: Amanda Williams 1+0, Danielle Skilander and Vicky Venables both 0+1

The Widnes Wild women's team played their first home game of the Women's Premier League season, losing 1-9 to Whitley Bay Squaws at Planet Ice Widnes on Sunday.

The Wild women had played their first 4 games away from home and, with an ambitious new development policy in place this season where they have given league debuts to over a dozen players who have never played competitive ice hockey before, this was going to be a very significant first ever home game for a lot of players.

The game was very much the proverbial game of three periods. The first period ended 0-3 to the visitors but Widnes had their best spell in terms of shots on goal. In the second period, Whitley romped away with the game scoring 6 unanswered goals whereas, in the third period, the only goal went to the Wild women who defended resolutely and kept the Squaws attack at bay for the final 20 minutes.

The biggest cheer of the night came in the 50th minute when the Wild's Amanda Williams broke away to fire in the first and only Widnes goal of the game – to a crescendo of noise around the rink.

Strangely enough – according to the match statistics (which never lie but often don't tell the full story either), that was the Wild women's ONLY shot on goal for the whole of the third period which, as it beat back up netminder Megan Quigley who had only come on for the last 20 minutes, left the poor Whitley goalie with an incredibly rare "0%" save percentage record for a game which her team actually won by a large margin.

The statistics show that this was a one sided game but, for the sizeable crowd watching, it really didn't feel like that. The Wild players carried on with boundless enthusiasm for the whole game, regardless of the score and enjoyed lots of puck possession which they sadly were unable to convert into sustained attacks and shots on goal.

But for a team, most of whom had not played league ice hockey before this September, to keep out an experienced side such as the Squaws who had several regular GB players in their ranks for even 20 minutes of the game shows the potential that there is in this new-look Wild women squad and can only bode well for the future as they get more games and experience under their belts.

After the game, Amanda Williams said:

"It was a tough game for us, but played with good sportsmanship throughout. Whitley move the puck really well and we struggled to get any possession for most of the game, but the girls kept working hard and were rewarded with a clean sheet in the 3rd period. Steph (netminder) was outstanding; the work she and Netminder Coach Philip Pearson are putting in to practice and game preparation is really showing."

The Wild women are away to the Bracknell Firebees on Sunday 6th January and are next at home on Sunday 20th January when they host the Nottingham Vipers at Planet Ice Widnes.

Danielle Skilander (Photo by Copper Tree Photography)

Katie Fairclough in action for the GB Women's U18 team (Photo by Angela Reid - https://reidysphotos.smugmug.com)

Katie Fairclough Makes GB Debut

Widnes ice hockey can boast another international player after women's team player Katie Fairclough played for the Team GB Women's Under 18 team in the annual 4-team tournament in Sosnowiec in Poland at the weekend.

She joins an ever-growing list of players who have represented their country at some level or other while playing for Widnes including current women's senior internationals netminder Nicole Jackson who played one season for the Wild NIHL team and Sarah Hutchinson who previously played for the Wild women's team, Wild woman Leen de Decker who plays internationally for Belgium and Sophie Sinclair Reeks who has also played for the Team GB U18 women's team.

Wild NIHL players Matt Croyle and Mike Mawer have also played international hockey when they were selected for the GB Universities team.

This was the fourth time that the women's under 18 tournament has been held and teams look upon it as a good opportunity to try out new players and formations ahead of the World Championships in January.

The GB Under 18 team lost to Hungary 2-1 and Poland 3-2 before beating Spain 3-0 in their final game but it was all good experience for the players, some of whom were with the team for the first time.

Talking about her first international ice hockey experience, Katie said:

"It was an amazing experience, overwhelming at first, but all the players, coaches and staff were really nice and helpful. It's such a buzz playing at that level for your country."

"The games were really good, very fast and exciting. We were unlucky against Hungary, getting an early lead, but then they pulled it back. It was a similar game against Poland, very close and I think we were a bit unlucky.

The last game against Spain it came together, we played really well and controlled the game. Our net-minder Ella was brilliant and we came away with a 3-0 win – a great way to end the tournament."

Talking about Katie's achievement, Amanda Williams from the Widnes Wild women's team said:

"We were all very proud to see Katie representing the Wild as a member of the GB u18 squad in Poland. Katie is very dedicated and, with the support of her parents, barely has a night off from training. Katie is always pushing herself to improve, having recently also started training with Manchester Storm Academy U18s and attending our weekly Crossfit sessions. It's great to see Katie's efforts rewarded with an opportunity to play internationally."

"These experiences are invaluable - both on and off the ice. They also help at club level, as players bring back a broader view of the game, plus the confidence and motivation required to achieve at the higher level."

The GB team will be taking part in the IIHF Women's Under 18 World Championships in Dumfries in January and Katie will be hoping that she made a sufficient impression on the coaches to qualify for the final squad selection.

Amanda Williams (Photo by David Law Photography)

December 2018: The Wild Women's Season So Far

Interview with Amanda Williams – Player /Coach of the Widnes Wild Women.

The Widnes Wild women's team had their first home game of the 2018/19 Women's Premier League season just before Christmas and, while they may have lost 1-9 to a very strong and highly experienced Whitley Bay Squaws side – their fifth defeat in five starts this season - nobody on the Wild camp is panicking and they are, in fact, pretty happy with the current situation as whole.

Having run a wide-reaching recruitment campaign for new players over the course of the summer, the Wild women have been able to take on a lot of new faces this season and they have taken the bold step of plunging them all right in at the deep end – and putting them straight into the team for the WPL season.

This means that, while being built around a core of long term experienced players, a large percentage of the new-look team had never played any competitive league ice hockey before this season and, in some cases, never even played any ice hockey at all! So when you look at things in that context, "only" losing 1-3 away to a Sheffield Shadows team who were playing in the higher Elite League last season, isn't really a bad achievement.

Women's team player coach Amanda Williams explained how the whole thing came about:

"Like most Women's teams in the UK, each year we'd tend to have a squad of around 12-14 players. With every season that's gone by, it has become increasingly difficult to both fulfil the EIHA league rules for minimum bench sizes (or forfeit matches); and also to afford the cost of ice rental, referees etc - all of which is funded from the players' monthly subscription fees."

"This is an all too familiar situation in the Women's game and, unfortunately, it has resulted in the loss of several teams and talented players over the past couple of seasons. As things are now, there just isn't the luxury of a large number of female players in the UK. So the Summer just gone, a lot of our free time was spent on recruitment to bring more females into the game and ensure we could continue operating the team and still give women in the North West a place to play ice hockey."

"We managed to secure a more sociable training slot and were lucky that the Learn To Play sessions held at

Widnes had already interested a number of potential players. The decision to ice every new player regularly in the WPL is where we may differ to some other teams in our league, but to us it is a no brainer."

"All players need ice time in games to learn, improve and enjoy their hockey – factors that are all crucial to the survival and success of our team."

And five games down the line, albeit climbing a rather steep learning curve in a lot of cases, the new players are definitely showing signs of progress:

"I've been really impressed with how quickly they are developing and that's largely due to their effort and enthusiasm. Leen (de Decker – Belgian international player) and I have taken training back to basics to bring everybody onto the same page as well as doing some work on individual skills, but we've also massively upped the intensity compared to the past couple of seasons and that has benefited everybody."

"We have yet to win a game, but you've just got to keep in mind the bigger picture and focus on other victories – and there have been many of those. The dressing room is really positive and fun to be a part of. Everyone is supportive of one another - it's definitely the best atmosphere we've had in the 5 years I've been with the club."

In contrast to most of the new players, summer signings Jemma Brown and Philippa Wheeler both had previous league experience, having played with Kingston Diamonds and Nottingham Vipers respectively. Speaking of those two new arrivals, Williams said:

Jemma made the move to get regular ice time, so we will see her improve with confidence as the season goes on.

Philippa has proved to be a versatile player, having been played in defence and forward positions for games. Vickie Venables (nee Foster) had also played previously before taking a lengthy break from hockey when her team folded, so she has been a great addition to our team and was deservedly appointed one of our Alternate Captains."

Having lost their first five games of the season, the emphasis for the Wild women's team this season is - obviously - firmly upon player development rather than challenging for trophies. They do still, however, have goals to try and achieve for the season and beyond:

" We hope to finish the season with all the players we have recruited still with us and thinking that taking up ice hockey was the best decision they've ever made! Joking aside, we'll carry on taking it one game at a time and continue to head in the right direction. It would be nice to retain our place in the WPL, but our longer-term goal of building a sustainable future for the team is far more important."

Despite the WPL season starting back in September, the Wild women only played their first game at home at Planet Ice Widnes in December. Having played away games in Milton Keynes, Sheffield, Nottingham and Hull, finally being able to play a league game at home was a great experience – particularly for all the new players, Amanda explained:

"It was great for them to finally play in front of family and friends. We had really good support at that game. The initial run of away games was probably nerve-wracking for the new players, but the long road trips meant that we got to spend more time getting to know each other and it

really helped with regards to team building to have that so early on in the season."

"Now we have more home games left than away so that will be a huge boost. The team will continue to improve game upon game, but the support we get at home games gives everybody an extra lift."

For anybody who hasn't seen a women's game before – or may even be interested in taking up this exciting team sport, Amanda explains as follows:

"We don't have body checking in the women's game, but it is not without contact and, at our level (WPL), there is quite a mix of player ability throughout each team. The games are still competitive like in the men's league, but play tends to be slower which allows spectators to follow it better.

There is a growing number of female players in the UK who are now playing in 'men's leagues', whilst others go abroad to pursue women's hockey at a higher level."

The Wild women's next game is away to Bracknell Firebees on Sunday 6th January and, following that, they are at home to current league leaders Nottingham Vipers on Sunday 20th January at Planet Ice Widnes – 5.30pm face off.

Sunday 6th January 2019 – Women's Premier League Bracknell Firebees 7 – Widnes Wild Women 0

Period Scores: 2-0, 3-0, 2-0
Shots on Goal: Bracknell 68 – Widnes 13 (24-4, 19-4, 25-5)
Penalties In Minutes: Bracknell 0- Widnes 4

The Widnes Wild women's team's lost their "bottom of the table" clash 7-0 away to the Bracknell Firebees on Sunday down in Berkshire.

The Wild team travelled with a shorter bench than in previous games due to a bout of illness in the camp and several of the more experienced players were missing from the line–up, so it was always going to be an uphill struggle against a Firebees side who, like the Widnes team, were also looking for their first points of the season.

Most of the damage was caused by the Firebees' French international player Marguerite Laffitte who scored 5 of the Bracknell goals and assisted on one other. She also plays for the Queen Bees in the Women's Elite League and the Bracknell male Under 20 team and she has also won medals at international level for France.

The Wild women actually started the game well, keeping out the Bracknell attack for over 7 minutes before conceding two quick goals within 60 seconds of each other.

A third goal just 30 seconds from the start of the second period put the home side further ahead and, with two more goals added before the second break, a home win was already a near certainty.

Two further goals in the third period made sure of the result for the Firebees and the Wild women now have time to regroup before their next game.

After the game, assistant coach Leen de Decker said:

"It was a hard fought game with many players for Wild missing due to injury and illness, but a quick paced game saw the players improve tremendously yet again. Bracknell had one particularly talented young player (5 goals and 1 assist) and she made the difference. We hope to give them a good game with a full team present when they visit us in Widnes."

The Wild women are next in action on Sunday 20th January when they host the Nottingham Vipers at Planet Ice Widnes – face off 5.30pm.

Pauline Hayward

(Photo by David Law Photography)

Post-match Wild Women's team group (Photo by Geoff White)

Laura Marcroft was the Wild Women's MVP against Nottingham (Photo by Geoff White)

Sunday 20th January 2019 – Women's Premier Lge Widnes Wild Women 3 – Nottingham Vipers 9

Period Scores: 2-1, 0-3, 1-5
Shots on Goal: Widnes 17 – Nottingham 75 (4-25, 10-21, 3-29)
Penalties In Minutes: Widnes 4 – Nottingham 16
Widnes Scoring: Emma Pearson 1+1, Sav Sumner 1+1, Danielle Skilander 1+0

The Widnes Wild women's team put in a brave and thrilling performance in front of an enthusiastic and sizeable crowd before eventually succumbing 3-9 to league leaders Nottingham Vipers at Planet Ice Widnes on Sunday.

The Wild women had lost 11-2 away to Nottingham back in October and, with them icing a largely inexperienced development line-up this season, this match would have marked down as an away win on most people's pools coupons prior to the game.

The Vipers took the lead after just 15 seconds of play but, demonstrating how far they have come in such a short space of time - with many of the Widnes players on the ice never having played a competitive game before this season - the Wild womens' heads did not drop and they immediately fought back.

Sav Sumner fired in an equalising goal in the 6th minute and then, after a tense and entertaining spell of end to end action, Widnes took the lead through team captain Emma Pearson on 16 minutes. This was, in fact, the first time that the Widnes team had taken the lead in any league game this season so far and the score remained 2-1 at the first period break.

The score was still 2-1 10 minutes into the second period and the Wild women looked confident on the puck and were having lots of possession. But then on 33 minutes, Nottingham's Canadian born player Robin Mullen scored her second goal of the game to tie the score.

Two more goals late in the period – from Madison Wright and a hat trick strike from Mullen – turned the game on its head and the score stood at 2-4 after two periods of play.

Widnes hopes were raised once again with a great goal from Danielle Skilander to halve the deficit on 45 minutes but Nottingham's Jessica Urquhart scored just 3 minutes later and two more goals from Robin Mullen put the Vipers firmly in control.

The game was held up for a few minutes while Wild netminder Stephanie Drinkwater needed treatment on the ice after a collision but she bravely got up and played on for the remaining 10 minutes or so during which time Nottingham struck again to round off the scoring at 3-9.

Despite the eventual scoreline, this was a really good display from the Wild women who showed character and courage throughout against considerably stronger opposition and will undoubtedly continue to make progress as the season goes on.

The Sarah Macnaughtan Memorial awards for most Most Valuable Player went to Laura Marcroft for Widnes and Alice Haddleton for Nottingham and were presented by the Wild's Poet in Residence Lucy London.

After the game Wild women's player coach Amanda Williams said:

"Overall, I was really pleased with how the game went. This was the first time we've met a team for the second time this season, so it was always going to be interesting to see how we've progressed since early in the season."

"We were immediately a goal behind in the first period before the girls switched on but, to their credit, they focussed and deservedly took the lead through 2 great finishes from Sav and Emma. The 2nd period remained close, but we got caught out by a couple of stretch passes and were punished on the breakaway. It's all part of the learning curve. In regular play, our lines weren't too badly matched."

"Unfortunately the score was racked up a bit in the 3rd. We got tired and left Steph (who was injured with 10mins left in the game) vulnerable to further one on one chances. All in all, it was an enjoyable game and good to see training is paying off."

Katie Adshead was the Wild Women's MVP against Chelmsford (Photo by Paul Breeze)

Sunday 10th February 2019 – Women's Premier Lge Widnes Wild Women 2 – Chelmsford Cobras 8

Period Scores 0-3, 2-4, 0-1
Shots On Goal: Widnes 23 – Chelms 59
Penalties In Minutes: Widnes 4 – Chelms 12
Widnes Scoring: Sav Sumner 2+0, Emma Pearson 0+2, Jemma Brown 0+1

The Widnes Wild women's team slumped to a 2-8 defeat against likely title challengers Chelmsford Cobras in a good tempered and highly entertaining game at Planet Ice Widnes on Sunday.

The Wild women are undergoing a season of transition and over half of the team on the ice for this game had not played competitive league ice hockey before the start of this season but they gave a very good account of themselves and held their own for long periods of the game.

Chelmsford took the lead in the 4th minute and were 0-3 up at the first break. An excellent second period for the Wild women saw Sav Sumner score two goals for Widnes but four more for the visitors saw the Cobras leading 2-7 after 40 minutes of play.

The third period was a much closer affair with both teams having lots of chances. The Wild matched their opponents for shots on goal during this period and, on another day, might well have bagged a few more goals. As it was, Chelmsford scored the only goal of the period and came out 2-8 winners.

Sophie Sinclair Reeks in action against Chelmsford (Photo by Geoff White)

The two teams together after the Wild Women's first ever trip to Scotland (Photo by Solway IHC)

Sunday 3rd March 2019 – Challenge Match
Solway Sharks Ladies 7 – Widnes Wild Women 7

Period Scores: 2-4, 0-2, 3-3
Shots on Goal: Solway 44 - Widnes 33 (15-11, 12-9, 17-13)
Penalties In Minutes: Solway 2 - Widnes 2
Widnes Scoring: Charlotte McPhee 2+2, Sav Sumner 2+0, Katie Adshead 1+2, Josie Moran 1+1, Philippa Wheeler 1+0, Laura Marcroft 0+2, Sophie Sinclair Reeks & Kathryn Garner both 0+1

The Widnes Wild women's team took a break from their league campaign to play a challenge game away against the Solway Sharks ladies team on Sunday, which ended in a thrilling 7-7 draw.

The Wild women were quickest off the blocks with Charlotte McPhee opening the scoring after just 15 seconds. Two goals from Sav Sumner saw the Wild leading 0-3 after just 8 minutes but two quick goals for Solway pulled them back into contention. A goal for Philippa Wheeler edged Widnes further ahead again and the score stood at 2-4 at the first period break.

A goal-less second period for the Wild women and two goals for the hosts saw the game tied at 4-4 after 2 periods and an even third period of three goals each – with goals from McPhee, Josie Moran and Katie Adshead for the Wild - ensured an entertaining game right up to the final buzzer.

After the game, Wild women player coach Amanda Williams said:

“This extra game for us at the weekend was a really valuable exercise with emphasis given to further developing our newer players by encouraging them to have more time on the puck and build their confidence. They accepted the challenge and we were rewarded with first ever goals for Charlotte McPhee (2), Josie Moran and Katie Adshead. Philippa Wheeler's goal was also her first for the Wild.

Hopefully we can get a return game with the Sharks ladies set up in the near future.”

“The mood is positive going into our league game versus MK this weekend. Leen and I are looking forward to seeing what the team can bring, as we look to fight to retain our spot in the Premier league.”

The Wild women now turn their attentions to their home game this Sunday 10th March when they take on the Milton Keynes Falcons in the Women’s Premier League at Planet Ice Widnes – 5.30pm face off.

First time scorers Katie Adshead, Josie Moran and Charlotte McPhee celebrate their maiden strikes for the Wild women away at Solway (Photo by Wild Women IHC)

Stephanie Drinkwater was the Wild Women's MVP against Milton Keynes (Photo by Paul Breeze)

Sunday 10th March 2019 – Women's Premier League
Widnes Wild Women 1 – Milton Keynes Falcons 4
The Widnes Wild women's team's roller-coaster season of transition and new player development continued with a highly entertaining and hard fought 1-4 defeat at home to the Milton Keynes Falcons at Planet Ice Widnes on Sunday.

The Wild women – many of whom had never played a competitive game before the start of this season – are improving with every game they play and are certainly heading in the right direction and, if points were given out for commitment and enthusiasm, they would be top of the league by now.

They matched their more experienced opponents for long spells of the game and were unfortunate not to be able to convert more of their possession into shots and goals.

Milton Keynes took the lead on 6 minutes and doubled the advantage 7 minutes later to lead 0-2 at the first period break. The second period was goal-less and the longer the score remained at 0-2, the more it felt as if the Wild women might be able to stage a fightback.

The Falcons scored again on 49 minutes to make the score 0-3 but then Widnes finally got the breakthrough they had long been threatening and, on 53 minutes, top scorer Sav Sumner made a break from the half way line and fired a rocket shot under the MK netminder.

This lifted the team and they swarmed forward trying to push for another goal. Unfortunately, this left them open at the back and the Falcons scored their 4th goal on 55 minutes, rounding off the scoring for the evening.

The Sarah Macnaughtan Memorial awards for most Most Valuable Player went to netminder Stephanie Drinkwater for Widnes and Kirsten Noble for Milton Keynes.

After the game, Wild women player coach Amanda Williams said:

"Our preparation for the game was spot on - playing games on back to back weekends really helps. Again, we ran 4 lines and the girls should be pleased with their performance earning the 4-1 result, especially given that 6 months ago in MK we lost 10-3. We need to work on upping our shots for and reducing shots against. Had we managed to get our goal earlier in the game it could've been a different story."

Stephanie Drinkwater makes one of her 74 saves against Bracknell (Photo by Geoff White)

Sunday 7th April 2019 – Women's Premier League Widnes Wild Women 2 – Bracknell Firebees 14

Period Scores: 1-3, 1-8, 0-3
Shots On Goal: Widnes 16 – Bracknell 88
Penalties In Minutes: Widnes 10 – Bracknell 2
Widnes Scoring: Elizabeth Loss 1+0, Sav Sumner 1+0, Emma Pearson 0+2, Katie Fairclough 0+1

The Widnes Wild women's team were served up a tough lesson in finishing when they lost out 2-14 to the Bracknell Firebees in the Women's Premier League at Planet Ice Widnes on Sunday.

The Wild women actually scored first in this game – a first ever WPL strike from Elizabeth Loss – in the 7th minute but, while they were pushing forward to build on this lead, they were caught out by the impressive skating and finishing abilities of Firebees' Emily Harris who, despite being only 17, has over 30 games at Women's Elite League level under her belt and has also played 15 times for the GB Under 18s women's team.

Harris equalised for Bracknell in the 10th minute and then added two more solo efforts by the first break for a score of 1-3. She scored 4 more goals in the second period and, by the time that Sav Sumner had fired in a second goal for the Wild at 34.15, Bracknell already had got eight in the bag and went on to lead 2-11 after two periods.

The third period was goal-less for Widnes and saw Bracknell hit 3 more for a final score of 2-14. The game as a whole was not as one sided as the scoreline suggests and the Wild women put together a lot of plays that, unfortunately, broke down before they could finish them off.

The Sarah Macnaughtan Memorial awards for most Most Valuable Player went to Elizabeth Loss for Widnes and Emily Harris for Bracknell.

After the game, Wild women player coach Amanda Williams said:

"Not our best performance, but I felt we improved over the 60 minutes. Bracknell had one stand out player doing the damage, but playing as a unit on the ice we should be able to shut individual players down. We just lost focus of our own game and it was disappointing to end up on the wrong end of a high scoreline in an otherwise competitive match. The fans are always loud and proud at Widnes, but this game especially and it gave the team the boost they needed to keep working until the final buzzer. Their support is much appreciated."

Elizabeth Loss was the Wild Women's MVP against Bracknell (Photo by Paul Breeze)

Wild Women's Off Ice Officials during the 2018;19 season: Mandy Sinclair, Howard Hughes, Patrick Sinclair, Shannon Holt, Lucy London – and PB, out on ice taking photos.

Sunday 21st April 2019 – Women's Premier League Chelmsford Cobras 5 - Widnes Wild Women 0 (forfeit)

The Widnes Wild women's team's away game with Chelmsford Cobras on Easter Sunday was cancelled with the points being awarded to Chelmsford.

The game had originally been scheduled to be played in Chelmsford with a lunchtime face-off but, with the Riverside rink currently closed for refurbishment, all of the various Chelmsford teams' remaining games have been moved to other venues at different times.

In view of the early face off time, the Wild players had arranged hotel accommodation in Chelmsford for the night before so they would be fresh and ready for the game the next day.

Unfortunately, the game was moved – with relatively short notice - to Lee Valley ice rink in East London with a 6.30pm face off time and the later finishing time and journey home meant that several players and coaches would not be able to make the journey.

Commenting on the decision to forfeit the game, Wild women's player coach Amanda Williams said:

"We were always going to be short-benched for a game scheduled for Easter weekend, but several of our players selflessly rearranged their plans around the midday face off in Chelmsford to ensure that we could raise the minimum number of players to play the fixture."

"Due to the refurbishment of Chelmsford ice rink, the game was recently moved to an evening face off out of Lee Valley on the same Sunday. Unfortunately, the later face off time meant that a number of players with prior commitments had to drop out and also left us with no Level 2 coach available. We are disappointed to lose out on the game time, as we always have good, competitive matches against the Cobras."

The game was awarded as a 5-0 win to Chelmsford and Widnes also received a 2 points deduction on their league record for failing to fulfil the fixture.

The Wild women's next game is on Sunday 28th April when they entertain Kingston Diamonds at Planet Ice Widnes. The face-off time for that game is slightly later than usual - at 6pm instead of the normal 5.30.

Daisy Lloyd-Hazlegreaves was the Wild Women MVP against Kingston (Photo by Geoff White)

Sunday 28th April 2019 – Women's Premier League Widnes Wild Women 1 – Kingston Diamonds 13

Period Scores: 1-3, 0-5, 0-4
Shots on Goal: Widnes 13 – Kingston 76 (6-25, 0-32, 7-19)
Penalties In Minutes: Widnes 4 – Kingston 6
Widnes Scoring: Emma Pearson 1+0

The Widnes Wild women's team's roller-coaster experimental season continued with a slightly disappointing 1-13 defeat at home to the Hull-based Kingston Diamonds at Planet Ice Widnes on Sunday.

As with previous games, the Wild women had lots of puck possession but were unable to convert that into goals, while the Diamonds had great strength in depth – with 8 different players finding the back of the net and three more adding assists.

While many of the Wild players are only in their first season of competitive ice hockey and are learning as they go, the vast experience of the visitors clearly showed - with several players having GB caps and many of them having played for the Diamonds Elite League team – and they made the most of their chances on goal.

Kingston opened the scoring after just 90 seconds of the game but Widnes equalised on 9 minutes with a great goal from team captain Emma Pearson. At that point, the game looked very evenly balanced and, had the Wild women been able to build on that breakthrough, things might have gone differently. Unfortunately, Kingston scored three quick-fire goals within 60 seconds of each other just before the break and the Wild women found themselves 1-4 down at the end of the first period.

The Diamonds moved up a gear in the second period, scoring 5 unanswered goals, and then hit 4 more in the third period but the final score of 1-13 was probably a little harsh on the Wild women who battled hard throughout and chased the game until the final buzzer.

The Sarah Macnaughtan Memorial awards for most Most Valuable Player went to Daisy Lloyd-Hazlegreaves for Widnes and Ketziah Robinson for Kingston.

The Wild women's team are next in action on Sunday 19th May when they take on the Sheffield Shadows in what will be their last home game of the season. They then finish their league campaign with a visit to Whitley Bay Squaws on Sunday 26th May.

Emma Pearson scores the only Widnes goal against Kingston
(Photo by Geoff White)

This was the last game as Match Scorer for Mandy Sinclair
(Photo by Geoff White)

The Wild Women's team after their last home game of the season (Photo by Paul Breeze)

Sunday 19th May 2019 – Women's Premier League Widnes Wild Women 0 – Sheffield Shadows 8

Period Scores 0-2, 0-4, 0-2
Shots On Goal: Widnes 14 – Sheffield 84
Penalties In Minutes: Widnes 8 – Sheffield 12

The Widnes Wild women's team rounded off their home programme for this year's Women Premier League with a battling but ultimately disappointing 0-8 defeat against the Sheffield Shadows at Planet Ice Widnes on Sunday.

Following a coaching change in recent weeks and a reshuffle of lines and player positions for this game, the Wild women looked quite dangerous in the first period and looked to be matching their opponents in terms of puck possession and opportunities.

Sheffield opened the scoring somewhat against the run of play in the 10th minute but Widnes heads did not drop and the Wild women continued to press forward. A second goal in the dying seconds of the first period came as a bitter blow for the Wild women, although they continued to battle and were still in with a chance at the midway point of the game.

However, three goals within two minutes of each other put an end to any Widnes hopes of a result in their last home game of the season and three more strikes followed to give the visitors an 0-8 win.

While there was little to cheer about result-wise, the was still something to sing about as the team left the ice to a song written especially for the Wild women by poet in residence Lucy London, who also presented the MVP awards.

The Widnes Wild women's team play the last game of their WPL season away to Whitley Bay Squaws this Sunday 26th May – 12.15pm face off.

Wild MVP against Sheffield, Charlotte McPhee (Photo by Paul Breeze)

Sunday 26th May 2019 – Women's Premier League Whitley Bay Squaws 7 – Widnes Wild Women 0

Period Scores: 3-0, 1-0, 3-0
Shots On Goal: Whitley 120 – Widnes 10
Penalties in Minutes: Whitley 0 – Widnes 6

The Widnes Wild women's team rounded off their roller coaster Women's Premier League season with a 7-0 defeat away to Whitley Bay Squaws on Sunday.

Any defeat is always disappointing but "only" losing 7-0 to the league runners up who have several Great Britain international players in their ranks is certainly no disgrace and the Wild women can hold their heads high, having put in another battling performance in one of the more tricky away rinks to play in.

Netminder Stephanie Drinkwater had a particularly impressive game and, while 7 shots might have beaten her, she actually faced an incredible 120 shots over the course of the game - meaning that she SAVED 113 shots in 60 minutes.

The Squaws took the lead in the 6th minute of the game and were 3-0 up by the end of the first period. The second period saw them limited to just one strike but 3 more in the third period handed them a 7-0 win in the last game of the WPL season.

The Wild women's team finish the season in bottom place in the Women's Premier League table with "minus two points" due to a points deduction from when they refused to travel away to play Chelmsford on Easter Sunday after the fixture had been switched at very short notice to an alternative venue and much later face off time.

Canadian musicians Jason Moon and Jaime April helped with the music and made a professional recording of "The Girls...!" song.

"The Girls ...!" Song by Lucy London

Towards the end of the 2018/19 Women's Premier League season, Lucy was inspired to write a song for the Wild Women's team.

The final recording was finished just in time to be played at the last home game of the season against Sheffield Shadows on 19th May 2019.

Here's the full story of the song, taken from the TTN Records Press Release in June 2019:

Wirral-based poet, writer and broadcaster Lucy London– who is probably better known for her World War One exhibitions, research websites and related books – has written a new song to celebrate women in sport to coincide with the women's football world cup in France and other female sporting events which tend to get overlooked by the mainstream media.

Lucy was the in-house researcher for the Wilfred Owen Story Museum and Gallery on Argyle Street in Birkenhead from 2012 to 2018 and produced many WW1 commemorative exhibitions on different topics which helped the venue win the Wirral Horn award in 2018.

She is also the "Poet-In-Residence" at the Planet Ice rink in Widnes and this is where the idea for the song first came about, as Lucy explains:

"I am always trying to find ways to highlight the involvement of women in WW1 and to this end sponsored the 2018 - 2019 Season's Most Valued Player Awards for Widnes Wild Women's Ice Hockey Team in memory of Sarah Macnaughtan, a writer who went to help look after the wounded troops in Belgium and France."

"I am always coming up with ideas, jotting down lines for poems and songs and I like to write things to support the various ice hockey teams at Widnes."

"At a recent women's team match, somebody from the visiting team expressed surprise that we were putting so much effort into the game day experience as it was "only women…". "

"I immediately put him straight and told him that we don't differentiate at Widnes and that we try and put on the same show, whether it be men's games, women's games, junior games or rec games. However, it still irked me for a few days afterwards and in the end, I came up with the words to a song to celebrate women's involvement in sport."

Determined that the song should be a rousing anthem to celebrate women's sport, Lucy contacted Canadian musician friends Jason Moon and Jaime April - originally from Prince Albert, Saskatchewan, but now residing in Liverpool - to help out with the tune.

Jason and Jaime came up with a superb rousing tune to go with the lyrics and also produced a professional recording of the song

Lucy has appeared regularly at public events talking about her research work and has made numerous appearances on local radio.

Sheet music for "The Girls...!" song.

You can see a full readable and playable version in "The Lucy London Songbook" ISBN 978-1909643444.

You can listen to the full recorded version of "The Girls...!" on Soundcloud if you know where to look...

The Girls…!

The boys! The boys! They may be back in town
But the girls haven't exactly been waiting around!
When there's stuff to be done, the girls don't shirk
They get their sleeves rolled up and get to work

Chorus
The girls! The girls! The girls are here to stay
The girls! The girls who haven't been away
You can count on us to get things done
Come on girls let's have some fun.

Just because we're girls shouldn't mean we get left out
Life is for living – that's what it's all about.
We can climb mountains and play football too
And cricket and ice hockey – just like the boys do.

Chorus

The Girls! The Girls! Don't dismiss as as "only"
Without us the world would be very lonely.
We're the girls, the girls don't push us away
We're the girls, the girls and we're here to stay.

Chorus x 3 to fade….

Lyrics by Lucy London © Copyright 2019
Music by Jason Moon and Jaime April
Musical Notation by Richard Lawrence
Music Publishing by Posh Up North Publishing

WNIHL Division 1 North – Season 2019/20

Final Table	P	W	D	L	F	A	+/-	PIM	Pts
Widnes Wild Women	**10**	**8**	**1**	**1**	**74**	**28**	**46**	**96**	**16**
Solway Sharks Ladies	10	7	0	3	74	36	38	109	14
Telford Wrekin Raiders	10	6	2	2	54	25	29	65	12
Sheffield Shadows	10	3	0	7	53	55	-2	58	6
Grimsby Wolves	10	2	3	5	28	48	-20	72	4
Nottingham Vipers	10	0	2	8	7	98	-91	50	0

Note: season suspended on 16th March 2020.
Grimsby v Nottm 4th April, Nottm v Widnes 18th April, Grimsby v Telford 25th April and Telford v Grimsby 9th May all awarded 0-0 draw with 0 points by EIHA

Leading Points Scorers – Season 2019/20

Player	Team	GP	G	A	Pts	PIM
Kimberley Breingan	Solway Sharks Ladies	10	29	15	44	2
Emma Pearson	Widnes Wild Women	9	21	15	36	22
Leen De Decker	Widnes Wild Women	7	20	8	28	0
Katie Reid	Sheffield Shadows	10	15	6	21	0
Michelle Croucher	Solway Sharks Ladies	10	11	8	19	14
Michelle Madziak	Telford Wrekin Raiders	8	10	9	19	0
Heather Metcalf	Telford Wrekin Raiders	8	14	5	19	12
Amanda Murdoch	Solway Sharks Ladies	10	7	11	18	20
Hazel Wilson	Sheffield Shadows	6	13	5	18	8
Emma Taylor-Lonsdale	Grimsby Wolves	7	7	8	15	10
Savannah Sumner	Widnes Wild Women	9	7	7	14	6

Leading Netminders – Season 2019/20

Player	Team	GP	SA	GA	Sv%	SO
Stephanie Drinkwater	Widnes Wild Women	7	215	14	93.49%	0
Teagan Hyatt	Telford Wrekin Raiders	7	59	6	89.83%	1
Courtney Smith	Grimsby Wolves	7	541	58	89.28%	0
Charlotte Jackson	Widnes Wild Women	8	104	14	86.54%	0
Rebekah Scott	Solway Sharks Ladies	7	171	24	85.96%	2
Jodie Alderson	Telford Wrekin Raiders	8	132	19	85.61%	0
Shannon Schneider	Sheffield Shadows N1	9	377	55	85.41%	0
Bethany Brown	Solway Sharks Ladies	6	60	12	80.00%	1
Caitlin Woolley	Nottingham Vipers N2	7	397	81	79.60%	0

Widnes Wild Women's Team Player Statistics
Season 2019/20

	WNIHL Div 1 North					Challenge Matches				
	GP	G	A	Pts	PIM	GP	G	A	Pts	PIM
Emma Pearson	9	21	15	36	22	2	3	1	4	0
Leen de Decker	7	20	8	28	0	0	0	0	0	0
Savannah Sumner	9	7	7	14	6	2	4	3	7	2
Sarah-Louise Aspinall	9	5	4	9	0	2	1	1	2	2
Catherine Bowen Fell	7	6	3	9	4	1	1	1	2	0
Kathryn Garner	9	1	5	6	2	2	1	0	1	2
Katherine Fairclough	9	2	3	5	20	2	2	1	3	4
Emma Martin	9	2	2	4	0	1	0	1	1	0
Victoria Venables	8	1	3	4	8	1	0	1	1	0
Shannon Holt	4	1	2	3	2	0	0	0	0	0
Daisy Lloyd-Hazlegreaves	6	1	2	3	2	0	0	0	0	0
Elizabeth Loss	9	2	1	3	0	2	1	1	2	0
Laura Marcroft	8	1	2	3	4	2	0	0	0	0
Danielle Skilander	9	1	2	3	0	2	1	0	0	0
Katie Adshead	8	0	2	2	12	2	0	0	0	0
Jemma Brown	8	1	1	2	10	2	3	2	5	0
Karyn Cooper	9	0	2	2	0	2	0	0	0	0
Vanessa Crickmore Clarke	4	0	0	0	4	0	0	0	0	0
Stephanie Drinkwater	7	0	0	0	0	1	0	0	0	0
Pauline Hayward	7	0	0	0	0	2	0	0	0	0
Charlotte Jackson	8	0	0	0	0	2	0	0	0	0
Charlotte McPhee	8	0	0	0	0	2	0	0	0	0
Suzanne Miller	4	0	0	0	0	0	0	0	0	
Josie Moran						1	0	0	0	0
Phillippa Wheeler						1	1	3	4	0

Netminder Statistics - Season 2019/20

Netminder	Comp	GPI	Mins	SA	GA	GAA	Save%	SO
Steph Drinkwater	D1N*	7	360	215	14	2.33	93.49%	0
	Chall	1	90	17	2	1.33	88.24%	0
	Totals	8	420	232	16	2.29	93.10%	0
Charlotte Jackson	D1N*	8	240	104	14	3.50	86.54%	0
	Chall	2	90	50	12	8.00	76.00%	0
	Totals	10	360	154	26	4.33	83.12%	0

Note: MINS played and GAA are estimates as the EIHA's otherwise superb "Fixtures Live" system didn't record them properly.*

Widnes Wild Women's Team Fixtures & Results Season 2019/20

Date	Comp	Home			Away	WDL
11.08.19	Chall	Solway Sharks	6	10	Widnes Wild Women	W
22.09.19	Chall	Widnes Wild Women	8	8	Solway Sharks	D
06.10.19	D1N	Widnes Wild Women	7	2	Sheffield Shadows	W
16.11.19	D1N	Telford Wr Raiders	7	2	Widnes Wild Women	L
15.12.19	D1N	Widnes Wild Women	9	5	Solway Sharks	W
21.12.19	D1N	Sheffield Shadows	5	9	Widnes Wild Women	W
05.01.20	D1N	Widnes Wild Women	15	1	Nottingham Vipers	W
11.01.20	D1N	Grimsby Wolves	3	8	Widnes Wild Women	W
16.2.20	D1N	Widnes Wild Women	12	2	Grimsby Wolves	W
01.03.20	D1N	Widnes Wild Women	8	1	Telford Wr Raiders	W
14.03.20	D1N	Solway Sharks	2	4	Widnes Wild Women	W
18.04.20	D1N	Nottingham Vipers	0	0	Widnes Wild Women	Da*

Note: season suspended on 16th March 2020. Away game at Nottm awarded 0-0 draw with 0 points by EIHA*

Fundraising at a Wild NIHL game in November 2019. Charlotte Jackson, Elizabeth Loss, Emma Pearson, Pukka the Penguin, Sarah Aspinall, Karyn Cooper, Laura Marcroft & Kat Garner.

Widnes Wild Women's Team – Season 2019/20 (Photo by Geoff White – www.gw-images.com)
Back Row: Michael Parkin (coach), Laura Marcroft, Shannon Holt, Danielle Skilander, Victoria Venables, Leen de Decker, Karyn Cooper, Kat Garner, Catherine Bowen-Fell, Emma Martin, Jemma Brown, Daisy Lloyd-Hazlgreaves, Charlotte McPhee, Daniel Fay (Coach), Philip Pearson (Coach). Front Row: Pauline Hayward, Elizabeth Loss, Charlotte Jackson, Vanessa Crickmore-Clark, Emma Pearson, Savannah Sumner, Stephanie Drinkwater, Sarah Aspinall, Katie Fairclough

MEET THE WILD WOMEN!
Preview to the 2019/20 WNIHL North Season

#1. Stephanie Drinkwater – sponsored by Martin Naden

Net Minder Stephanie Drinkwater was the most over-worked goalie in the Women's Premier League last season, facing 965 shots but stopping 856 of them for an overall save percentage of 88.70%. She was an "ever-present" in the Team last year and overall has played 45 matches for the Wild Women's Team.

Stephanie started playing competitive ice hockey in the 2013/2014 season when she joined the Manchester Phoenix Women's Team, where she played for two seasons before moving to the Wild.

#4. Sarah Louise Aspinall – sponsored by Varlden Clothing

Sarah Louise Aspinall is a new signing for the 2019/2020 season. Sarah originally learnt her hockey in Altrincham and played for the Manchester Phoenix Women's Team in the 2013/2014 season, making 4 appearances and contributing 1 assist. She has more recently played Rec. Hockey with the Widnes-based Earle Road Elks team.

Stephanie Drinkwater #1 (Photo by Geoff White)

Sarah Louise Aspinall #4 (Photo by Geoff White)

#5. Leen de Decker

Leen de Decker is one of the most experienced players on the Wild Women's roster, having been with the team since they moved from Altrincham for the 2015/6 season.

She learnt her hockey in her native Belgium and then played for Kingston Diamonds in Hull in the Premier League for 8 seasons before switching to the Manchester Phoenix women's team in 2014.De Decker holds the record number of international appearances for Belgium in the World Championships and also has the highest number of international goals. She has three bronze medals from the WCs – from 2001, 03, 05 & 07 and silver medal from 2017.

#6. Vanessa Crickmore-Clarke

Vanessa Crickmore-Clarke started playing ice hockey in her native north east, icing for some 9 seasons with the Sunderland Scorpions, during which time the team won the British League Northern Division on two occasions and Premier Division 3 times.

She then played for the Altrincham Avalanche team in 2001/2002 and had 6 seasons with the Flintshire Furies, before switching to the Phoenix Women's Team in 2013, once again winning league titles with each. Vanessa has had an impressive playing career of over 200 competitive games but, unfortunately, the closure of the Sunderland club means that her stats are not properly recorded.

Vanessa has played 32 games for the Wild Women Team, scoring 2 goals and 1 assist from her defensive role.

Leen de Decker #5 (Photo by David Law Photography)

Vanessa Crickmore Clark #6 (Photo by Steve Fairclough)

#7 Shannon Holt

Shannon is new to the women's team for this season, having learnt her hockey through the adult hockey basics sessions at Planet Ice Widnes.

She has previously helped out as penalty box judge and timekeeper at women's games and recreational matches is also a match night volunteer with the Wild NIHL team.

#8. Suzie Miller – sponsored by Outpost Paintball

Suzie is also new to women's team this season. She only started learning to ice skate in January 2019 and took part in the hockey basics course at Deeside before joining the Wild women.

#10 Daisy Lloyd-Hazlegreaves

Daisy joined the Wild women last season and played in 12 Women's Premier League games, mainly in defence. She also has a wide experience of university ice hockey and has played 62 games for Birmingham and Leeds teams over the past 5 seasons.

Shannon Holt #7 (Photo by Paul Breeze)

Suzie Miller #8 (Photo by Geoff White)

Daisy Lloyd-Hazlegreaves #10 (Photo by Geoff White)

Katie Fairclough #11 (Photo by David Law Photography)

#11. Katie Fairclough – sponsored by A.J. Bell Trust

Despite being only 17 years old, Katie will be playing her third season of competitive women's hockey for the Wild Women's team, having been given special dispensation to play a year early for the 2017/2018 season.

Katie originally started off playing Roller Hockey and was a GB International in that sport before switching to playing on ice. Since taking up ice hockey, Katie has also been selected to play for her country and has gained international honours at GB Women's Under 18 level.

In her two seasons to date with the Wild Women, Katie has played 24 matches, scoring 2 assists and picking up 33 Penalty Minutes.

#14. Emma Martin

Emma Martin spent six months playing for the Royal Navy Destroyers Development side in her early twenties. She then took a break from the game and started playing novice adult hockey at Deeside about three years ago.

She has been playing for the Sealand Aces Recreational Team and has joined the Wild Women this season because she would like to try a more competitive level of ice hockey.

Emma Martin #14 (Photo by Geoff White)

Emma Pearson #33 (Photo by Geoff White)

#33. Emma Pearson – sponsored by CrossFit Widnes

Team Captain Emma Pearson was an "ever-present" in the Wild Women's Team last season in the Women's Premier League, taking part in all League and Challenge games.

Pearson first started playing for the short-lived Altrincham Avalanche Team, which only ran for one season due to the closure of the old Altrincham rink in 2002. She then played three seasons with the Flintshire Furies – based at Deeside – two seasons with Kingston Diamonds and seven seasons with Sheffield Shadows, before returning to Manchester with the Phoenix Women's Team in 2013.

Overall, Pearson has played over 200 competitive games – including 18 for the Manchester Metros University Team – and has scored 84 + 82. Pearson has also played on numerous occasions for the Scotland representative team.

#34. Elizabeth Loss – sponsored by Cakes by Lucy

Elizabeth Loss originally played for the Manchester Phoenix Women's team and played a couple of WPL games for the Wild Women before really making her mark last season when she played 11 League games, scoring 1 goal and 1 assist.

#54. Charlotte Jackson – sponsored by The Wild Fans

While being a new player for the Wild Women's Team, Charlotte Jackson is already a very familiar face around

Elizabeth Loss #34 (Photo by Copper Tree Photography)

Charlotte Jackson #54 (Photo by David Law Photography)

the Widnes Planet Ice Rink, as she is the younger sister of long-serving Wild NIHL player Tom Jackson.

She has played Roller Hockey since the age of 8 – the last six years as a net minder – and has recently also taken up Ball Hockey and was selected for the GB Team at the World Championships in the Czech Republic. This coming season will be Charlotte's first ever playing on ice.

#55. Victoria Venables – sponsored by CUL-FIT Personal Training

Victoria Venables was Alternate Captain for the Wild Women last season, playing 7 games and notching up 1 assist. She missed half of the season through injury and will be hoping to make a greater impression this season.

Venables played the 2001/2002 Season for the Altrincham Avalanche Team, then spent the next 8 seasons with the Flintshire Furies. In all, she has played 115 games and has picked up 5 goals and 10 assists from her primarily defensive position.

#63. Charlotte McPhee – sponsored by G. Sumner Property

Charlotte McPhee returns for her third season in Widnes colours, having joined the Wild Women during the 2017/2018 season.

She has played 19 League games to date for the Wild Women and scored 2 + 2 in a Challenge game away to Solway mid-way through last season.

Victoria Venables #55 (Photo by Geoff White)

Charlotte McPhee #63 (Photo by David Law Photography)

#64. Pauline Hayward – sponsored by Femme Luxe

Pauline Hayward is one of the many "graduates" from the highly successful Hockey Basics course at the Widnes Planet Ice Rink.

In her two seasons with the Wild Women, she has played 23 leading Challenge games, scoring 1 assist and picking up 4 penalty minutes.

#65. Karyn Cooper – Sponsored by Design Wellness

Karyn Cooper has played University hockey for the Manchester Metros Team, making 43 appearances and scoring 1 + 2.

She made her League debut for the Wild Women last season and featured in 12 WPL and Challenge matches.

#66. Jemma Brown – sponsored by Bench Buddy Apparel

Jemma Brown is a veteran of some 70 competitive matches, having learnt her hockey with junior teams at Blackburn and Altrincham.

She also played for Kingston Diamonds Under 16s in the Girls North League, before going on to make 20 appearances for the Diamonds Senior Team in the Women's Premier League.

Jemma joined the Wild Women's team last season and played 13 League and Challenge games, picking up 2 assists.

Pauline Hayward #64 (Photo by Copper Tree Photography)

Karyn Cooper #65 (Photo by Copper Tree Photography)

Jemma Brown #66 (Photo by Geoff White)

Katie Adshead #71 (Photo by David Law Photography)

#71. Katie Adshead – sponsored by Ian Foulkes

Katie Adshead started off playing competitive hockey with the Manchester Metros University Team, playing 24 games in all and scoring 2 + 2. She was an "ever-present" in the Wild Women's Team last season, playing in all 14 games and scoring 1+2.

#72. Sav Sumner (AC)– sponsored by G. Sumner Property

Sav Sumner was the Wild Women's top goal scorer last season, 6 goals and 2 assists in 12 WPL games, plus 2 goals in the 7 – 7 friendly draw away to Solway Sharks.

Sumner was the first Widnes-born and trained player ever to play a competitive match for the Wild when she and fellow local girl Sal Roberts took to the ice against Milton Keynes Falcons in the first game of the 2016/2017 season. In her three seasons to date for the Wild Women, Sumner has played 37 games, scoring 11 goals and 4 assists.

#73. Catherine Bowen-Fell (AC)

Catherine Bowen-Fell is back for her fourth season with the Wild Women. She didn't play last season but in her previous three seasons with the Team, Catherine played 21 games and scored 10 + 5.

Bowen-Fell began playing hockey with the Blackburn Thunder team in 1999 season and played 8 seasons with them and 6 seasons with the Deeside-based Flintshire Furies, before joining the Manchester

Sav Sumner #72 (Photo by David Law Photography)

Catherine Bowen-Fell #73 (Photo by John Lewis)

Phoenix Women's Team for their 2014/2015 Division 1 North winning season.

Overall, Bowen-Fell has played 210 competitive matches, scoring 193 + 97.

#88. Kat Garner – sponsored by Kip's Skate Workshop

Kat Garner made her competitive debut for the Wild Women last season, playing primarily in defence. She played 13 matches and scored 1 assist.

#89. Danielle Skilander – sponsored by Alchemist Beauty

Danielle Skilander comes from a Roller Hockey background and made her ice hockey debut for the Wild Women's team last season.

Danielle played in 10 Women's Premier League games, scoring 1 goal and 1 assist – her sole strike being a spectacular solo effort against eventual League Champions Nottingham Vipers.

#93. Laura Marcroft – sponsored by Newton Bookkeeping Service

Laura Marcroft was another of the brand new players to ice for the Wild Women last season – she made 13 appearances in her debut campaign, contributing 3 assists.

Kat Garner #88 (Photo by Copper Tree Photography)

Danielle Skilander #89 (Photo by David Law Photography)

Laure Marcroft #93 (Photo by David Law Photography)

Wild Netminder Charlotte Jackson saves a penalty shot in her first ever game on ice. (Photo by Copper Tree Photography).

11th August 2019 - Challenge Match
Solway Sharks Ladies 6 – Widnes Wild Women 10

The Widnes Wild Women's team got their preparations for the new WNIHL season off to a great start with a 6 – 10 challenge match win over the Solway Sharks Ladies team away in Dumfries on Sunday.

The new Division 1 North League Season does not get under way until October and this friendly match was the ideal opportunity for the team to get some useful game time under their belts.

The Sharks were runners up in the Division last season and narrowly missed out on promotion to the Women's Premier League in the Play Offs and are expected to be title contenders this time around, so this was a very useful workout for the Wild Women.

Two new players were given their Wild Women debuts – Sarah Louise Aspinall and Charlotte Jackson, who is the younger sister of the long-term Widnes Wild defenceman Tom Jackson.

The game was very even in the first period and the score was tied at 3 – 3 at the first break. The Wild Women took control in the second period, scoring 5 unanswered goals and then the Sharks hit back to take the third period 3 – 2 in what was a highly entertaining game.

Jemma Brown (2), Laura Marcroft and Katie Fairclough all scored their first goals for the Wild Women and the other Wild Women goal scorers were Sav Sumner (2), Philippa Wheeler, Emma Pearson, Elizabeth Loss and Danielle Skilander.

The MVP Award for the Wild Women went to Netminder Charlotte Jackson, who was playing her first ever game on ice, having come from a Roller and Ball Hockey background and who also managed to save a penalty shot.

Inspector Victoria Holden and Superintendent Louise Harrison from Merseyside Police present the match puck to Solway and Widnes team captains Karen Craig (left) and Emma Pearson (right). (Photo by Paul Breeze).

Sunday 22nd September 2019 – Challenge Match: Widnes Wild Women 8 – Solway Sharks Ladies 8

The Widnes Wild women's team played their first home game of the new season in a challenge match with Solway Sharks Ladies, which ended in a thrilling 8 – 8 draw at Planet Ice Widnes on Sunday 22nd September.

Having drawn 7 – 7 against the Sharks' Team last season and won 6 – 10 in another Challenge game back in August, this game always looked likely to be full of goals and that is exactly what happened.

Kat Garner opened the scoring for the Wild after just two minutes – her first ever goal for the team – but two strikes from Solway's Kimberly Breingan on 4 and 10 minutes edged the Sharks ahead.

A short-handed goal from Wild Captain Emma Pearson just 70 seconds later levelled the score at 2 – 2 and then Jemma Brown fired the home side into the lead with just 10 seconds left in the period.

The second period was even more eventful, as Breingan equalised for the Sharks in the 25th minute and Katie Fairclough scored for the Wild Women just two minutes later to restore the lead.

A brace from Breingan within 20 seconds of each other around the midway point of the game, edged Solway 4 – 5 ahead and then a goal from the Wild's Catherine Bowen-Fell just 24 seconds later, levelled the score again.

A second goal for Emma Pearson and a first strike of the game for Sav Sumner gave the Wild a 2 goal cushion but Solway Captain Karen Craig halved the deficit with just 45 seconds to go in the period and the score stood at 7 – 6 after 40 minutes of play

The third period, while not quite the "goal fest" that the second had been, was similarly exciting. Sav Sumner scored her second goal of the game on 51 minutes, handing the Wild Women a 2 goal lead. The Solway team upped the pressure in the closing stages and Karen Craig pulled them back into contention with a goal with 90 seconds left on the clock.

The Wild Women found themselves on the back foot, as they desperately tried to defend their one goal lead but were caught out with a goal from the Sharks' Michelle Croucher with just 40 seconds left.

Widnes had a couple of chances right at the end but were unable to make the late pressure count and the match finished in a highly creditable 8 – 8 draw.

Despite the intensity of the game, there were only 4 minutes of penalties handed out for minor infringements and the Sharks Ladies went through the whole game penalty free.

The game saw the launch of the Edith Smith Memorial Trophy for the MVP Awards for the season. Edith Smith was Britain's first ever Warranted Woman Police Officer. Born in Oxton, Wirral, Edith was buried in St. Mary's Churchyard in Halton.

Inspector Victoria Holden and Superintendent Louise Harrison from Merseyside Police presented the match puck at the start of the game and Wirral Historian Bob Knowles presented the MVP Awards at the end. Catherine Bowen-Fell was named player of the match for the Wild, while Kimberly Breingan picked up the accolade for the Sharks, after her 5 goal haul.

The Widnes Wild Women's team are next in action on Sunday, 6th October 2019, when they take on the Sheffield Shadows in their first league game of the season at Planet Ice Widnes.

Widnes Scoring: Emma Pearson 2 + 1, Sav Sumner 2 + 1, Jemma Brown, Catherine Bowen-Fell, both 1 + 1, Katie Fairclough 1 + 0, Kat Garner 1 + 0, Emma Martin 0 + 1, Vickie Venables 0 + 1.

Netminders: Charlotte Jackson 25 shots/6 goals (40 mins), Stephanie Drinkwater 17 shots / 2 goals (20 mins)

MVP VIPS - L to R: Insp Victoria Holden, Catherine Bowen Fell, Emma Pearson, Sav Sumner, Lucy London, Kat Garner, Supt Louise Harrison, Bob Knowles, Carolyn Knowles (Photo by Paul Breeze

Edith Smith Memorial Awards For Most Valuable Player

The Edith Smith Memorial MVP Awards for the Widnes Wild Women's Team 2019/2020 Season were launched at the first home game on Sunday, 22nd September 2019 at Planet Ice, Widnes.

Edith became Britain's first ever Warranted Woman Police Officer during the First World War and she later worked as a nurse at a nursing home in Runcorn and died there in 1923 aged just 46. She was buried at St Mary's Church in Halton.

Lucy London – Poet in Residence at the Planet Ice Rink in Widnes – decided that she would like to commemorate

Edith and name the MVP Awards for the 2019/2020 Season in her honour.

Inspector Victoria Holden and Superintendent Louise Harrison of Merseyside Police had been instrumental in ensuring that Edith had a proper headstone and they, along with Wirral Historian Bob Knowles, were invited to the match to help launch the Award.

They all met some of the players before the game and Inspector Holden and Superintendent Harrison presented the match puck to get proceedings off to a flying start.

Bob Knowles has written a book about Edith and brought some copies along, together with some interesting items about Edith to display during the match. Bob presented the MVP Awards at the end of what turned out to be a very entertaining and exciting game.

VIP visitor Bob Knowles presents the MVP award to Catherine Bowen Fell (Photo by Paul Breeze):

Wild Women v Sheffield Shadows (Photo by John Lewis)

Sunday 6th October 2019 – WNIHL Div 1 North
Widnes Wild Women 7 – Sheffield Shadows 2

The Widnes Wild women's team got the new WNIHL Division 1 North season off to the best possible start with a 7 – 2 win over the Sheffield Shadows ladies team at Planet Ice Widnes on Sunday.

Following a couple of seasons of team re-building and new player development, it was actually the first time that the Wild Women had won in the league since their 0 – 2 win away at Nottingham Vipers in December 2017 and the first win at home since November 2016, when they beat Kingston Diamonds 6 – 4 in the Women's Premier League – so the result was very warmly welcomed.

The game was played at a furious pace throughout and was highly entertaining to watch. Sheffield took the lead with a goal on 5 minutes but the Wild were level less than 60 seconds later, with a great strike from Catherine Bowen-Fell.

Two quick-fire goals within 30 seconds of each other from team captain Emma Pearson towards the end of the period handed the Wild Women a 3 – 1 lead at the first break.

Last season's top goal scorer Sav Sumner further extended the lead with a goal just 1 minute and 13 seconds into the second period. Both teams had numerous chances but the period remained goalless until Sheffield scored a goal with 30 seconds to go.

However, the Wild Women countered almost immediately with a hat-trick goal for Emma Pearson and the score stood at 5 – 2 at the second period break.

Sheffield upped their game in the third period and bombarded the Wild net with shots but Stephanie Drinkwater pulled off some excellent saves as the Widnes defence managed to keep the Shadows' attack at bay.

A fourth goal for Emma Pearson in the 50th minute edged the Wild further ahead and the scoring for the evening was rounded off by Catherine Bowen-Fell with just 3 minutes left to play.

The Edith Smith Memorial MVP awards were presented by junior mascot Jacob Downe and match volunteer Lauren Holt, with netminders Shannon Schneider and Stephanie Drinkwater the respective recipients for the Shadows and the Wild.

The Wild women's team are next in action on Saturday 16th November when they travel away to face last season's champions Telford Wrekin Raiders and they are next at home on Sunday 15th December when they entertain the Solway Sharks Ladies Team at Planet Ice Widnes.

Widnes Scoring: Emma Pearson 4+1, Catherine Bowen-Fell 2+0, Sav Sumner 1+3, Katie Fairclough 0+2, Karyn Cooper and Kat Garner 0+1. Netminder: Stephanie Drinkwater 53 shots / 2 goals (60mins)

Wild women netminder Stephanie Drinkwater receives the MVP award from mascot Jacob Downe and match volunteer Lauren Holt (Photo by Paul Breeze).

16th November 2019 - WNIHL Division 1 North
Telford Wrekin Raiders 7 – Widnes Wild Women 2

The Widnes Wild women's team lost ground at the top of the WNIHL Division 1 North league table after a 7 – 2 defeat away to reigning champions Telford Wrekin Raiders on Saturday.

Telford took the lead in the fourth minute and were 2 – 0 up by the end of the first period. They went 3 – 0 ahead on 28 minutes but the Wild Women struck back with a short-handed goal from team captain Emma Pearson on 32 minutes to give themselves hope of a fightback.

Unfortunately, Telford re-established their 3 goal lead just 60 seconds later and edged further ahead with a fifth goal to lead the game 5 – 1 at the second period break.

Two more quick-fired goals within 30 seconds of each other in the 49th minute, put the game well beyond Widnes's reach and a second goal for Emma Pearson in the 58th minute rounded off the scoring for the game.

The result sees Telford move to the top of the league table with three wins from three games to date, while the Wild Women have one win and one defeat from two matches.

The Widnes Wild women are next in action on Sunday 15th December, when they take on the Solway Sharks ladies team at Planet Ice Widnes.

Widnes Scoring: Emma Pearson 2+0, Sav Sumner 0+1
Netminder: Charlotte Jackson – 55 shots / 7 goals (60 mins)

Emma Pearson receives her Oddballs Player of the Month prize from coaches Daniel Fay and Phil Pearson (see next page)

Netminder Stephanie Drinkwater (left) has been named Wild women's team's Player Of The Month for October

While not featuring in the short list for the national league award for October, Drinkwater is the Wild women's team's own Player of the Month and was presented with a "Puck Yeah" winners' sweatshirt.

Emma Pearson #33 (Photo by Paul Breeze)

EMMA NAMED WNIHL PLAYER OF THE MONTH

Widnes Wild women's team captain Emma Pearson has been named Oddballs' WNIHL Division 1 North Player of the Month for November.

Awards are made for the top player in all four divisions in the Women's league this season, along with similar awards for the five divisions in the men's competition.

Nominations for the women's awards are made by the coaches of each team and a monthly choice is made from those nominees

Emma is the first Widnes player to receive a league Player of the Month award since Wild player-coach Ollie Baron won the inaugural men's award for the Laidler Division in October 2017.

Leen de Decker (#5) scored 2+2 in her first game back for Widnes and also received the MVP award (Photo by Geoff White)

Sunday 15th December – WNIHL Div1 North
Widnes Wild Women 9 – Solway Sharks Ladies 5

The Widnes Wild women's team gave their title hopes a huge boost with a 9 – 5 win over league leaders Solway Sharks Ladies at Planet Ice Widnes on Sunday.

The two pre-season friendly games between these two teams had produced 16 goals each time and this first ever competitive game between the two sides turned out to be just as eventful.

The game was very closely fought throughout and it took until the 11th minute for the first breakthrough, which fell to the Sharks. Widnes drew level 3 minutes later with a power play goal from team captain Emma Pearson but Solway pulled ahead again with 90 seconds to go in the period and took a 1 – 2 lead into the first break.

The second period was just as close as the first, with Solway significantly out-shooting the Wild Women but Widnes net-minder Stephanie Drinkwater put in an amazing performance to keep the visitors' attack at bay.

The Sharks scored again and were 1 – 3 ahead in the 32nd minute but once again Widnes countered almost immediately with a goal from Leen de Decker who was back playing her first game after 14 months away. Another Solway goal and another Widnes reply – the second of the night for Emma Pearson – racked up the tension and the score stood at a tantalisingly close 3 – 4 at the second period break.

The game was completely turned on its head in the first minute of the third period with quick-fire goals from Leen de Decker and Sav Sumner within 8 seconds of each other to dramatically propel Widnes into the lead.

This seemed to unsettle the Solway team and they proceeded to pick up a stream of penalties in the third period – some clear cut and some maybe less so – and the Wild women were able to capitalise, firing in 3 powerplay goals – from Sumner again, Katie Fairclough – with her first goal of the season – and Emma Martin, with her first ever competitive goal, to build up a commanding lead.

A further goal from Emma Pearson – her hat-trick goal – gave Widnes a 9 – 4 lead heading into the last 2 minutes of the game. A late strike by Solway's Kimberley Breingan – Sharks' top scorer for the night with 2 + 3 – was too little too late to spark any type of comeback.

The resulting 9 – 5 victory sees the Wild women climb to fourth place in the Division 1 North Table, level on 4 points with Sheffield Shadows, who they play in Sheffield next Saturday.

Telford and Solway still jointly top the league table both level on 8 points but the Wild women have games in hand over all the teams above them.

The Edith Smith memorial MVP awards were presented by game mascot Corey Miller and went to Michelle Croucher for Solway and Leen de Decker for Widnes.

Widnes Scoring: Emma Pearson 3+2, Leen de Decker 2+2, Sav Sumner 2+0, Katie Fairclough 1+0, Emma Martin 1+0, Daisy Lloyd Hazlegreaves, Catherine Bowen Fell & Kat Garner all 0+1

Netminder: Stephanie Drinkwater 40 shots / 5 goals (60 mins)

Mascot Corey Miller presents MVP awards to Leen de Decker (Photo by Geoff White)

Kat Garner, Catherine Bowen Fell and Jemma Brown away at Sheffield. (Photo by Angela Reid https://reidysphotos.smugmug.com)

Saturday 21st December 2019 - WNIHL Div 1 North Sheffield Shadows 5 – Widnes Wild Women 9

The Widnes Wild Women's team moved up to third place in the Division 1 North table with a 5 – 9 win away to Sheffield Shadows at Ice Sheffield on Saturday.

The Wild Women had already beaten Sheffield 7 – 2 in the first meeting between the two teams at Planet Ice Widnes – and were on a high after beating erstwhile league leaders Solway Sharks Ladies 9 – 5 at home last weekend – but trips to Sheffield are always difficult affairs and nothing can be taken for granted in ice hockey.

The Wild Women took the lead in the fifth minute with a goal from Belgian international player Leen de Decker. Sheffield equalised three minutes later but a strike from

Catherine Bowen-Fell and a second for de Decker put Widnes 1 – 3 up after 13 minutes. A second goal for Sheffield, with just 2 minutes left in the first period, kept the game on a knife-edge.

Widnes scored again just 70 seconds into the second period with a goal from Sav Sumner but, despite being heavily out-shot throughout the game, the home team refused to give in and they pulled a goal back on 28 minutes.

A strike from team captain Emma Pearson at the half-way stage of the game edged the Wild Women further ahead but the Shadows struck back once more and, at the second break, the score of 4 – 5 meant there was still a lot for the Wild Women to do in the third period.

Widnes widened the gap once again with a fine strike from Jemma Brown 90 seconds into the third period but once again Sheffield countered within minutes. Two goals within a minute of each other – from Bowen-Fell and Pearson – finally put the game beyond Sheffield's reach and a goal with just 59 seconds left to play handed Emma Pearson her hat-trick and the Wild Women a 5 – 9 victory.

Widnes Scoring: Emma Pearson 3+2, Leen de Decker 2+1, Catherine Bowen-Fell 2+1, Jemma Brown 1+1, Sav Sumner 1+1, Sarah Aspinall, Victoria Venables, Katie Adshead & Kat Garner all 0+1

Netminder: Charlotte Jackson 26 shots / 5 goals (60 mins)

Married couple Phil and Emma Pearson iced on the same Wild team in the Midland Cup game away at Sutton (Photo by Mike Clancy)

Hockey History Made As Wild Ice Married Couple

The YKK-sponsored Widnes Wild team made an unusual bit of history in their Midland Cup game away to Sutton Sting at Ice Sheffield on Saturday 21st December when a husband and wife played on the same team in a competitive game for the first time.

There have been numerous instances of married match officials refereeing a game together, or husbands and wives playing in charity games – or matches for different teams within one club – but this is the first time that a husband and wife have played together in a competitive senior fixture – certainly in the history of the NIHL – and probably ever.

Philip Pearson is the Wild's first choice netminder and he was joined on the team roster for the away game at Sutton by his wife, Emma Pearson.

Emma is the captain of the Widnes Wild women's team and is their top scorer with 12 goals and 5 assists so far this season in WNIHL Division 1 North.

Emma has played over 200 competitive games for women's teams and has also played on numerous occasions for the Scotland representative team. She has played "mixed" hockey for the Manchester Metros university team but this was the first time she had ever played in a competitive men's league game.

After the game, Emma said:

"Being allowed the opportunity to ice in the Wild game on Saturday was incredible. I was really nervous before the game as I have never played at that level before. The lads were so supportive and I am really grateful to Mike Clancy for allowing me to have the experience of playing against a team like Sutton."

"Training with the Wild and icing in the game has helped me develop as a player and, hopefully, I will get more chances again in the future."

Emma also played for the Wild NIHL team in their home league game against the Blackburn Hawks 2 team on 29th December and then, in a bizarre twist, signed for the Hawks 2 for the rest of the season to help keep her match sharpness up for the remainder of the Wild women's title challenge.

She made her Hawks debut in the 0-23 home drubbing by the Wild on 19th January on and was named the "Man of the Match" for Blackburn!

Pearson went on to play 7 Laidler Division games in total for the Hawks2 scoring 1 goal and 1 assist.

Above: Daisy Lloyd-Hazlegreaves, Shannon Holt and Emma Martin in the 15-1 home win over Nottingham. (Photo by David Law Photography)

Sunday 5th January 2020 - WNIHL Div 1 North Widnes Wild Women 15 – Nottingham Vipers 1

The Widnes Wild women's team moved level on points with the league leaders at the top of the Division 1 North table after a comprehensive 15 – 1 win over Nottingham Vipers at Planet Ice Widnes on Sunday.

The Vipers are a new team to this division this season, having been formed during the summer of 2019 as a consequence of the main Vipers team being promoted to the Women's Elite League.

This Vipers second team is more of a development team, aimed at giving younger players and less experienced players more ice time than they would get if they were stuck on the fringes of the Elite League Team.

As such, a win always looked very much on the cards for the Wild women on Sunday, but it was a good opportunity to give plenty of ice time to all the players in the squad in preparation for the title push ahead.

The Wild took the lead in the fourth minute with a goal from team captain Emma Pearson. Strikes from Leen de Decker, Sarah Aspinall – her first ever league goal – Pearson again, Sav Sumner, Elizabeth Loss and Victoria Venables had the Wild Women 7 – 0 up at the first period break and the game was already over as a contest.

A goal from Laura Marcroft just 39 seconds into the second period put Widnes further ahead but Nottingham fired in their first goal just 90 seconds later and the game tightened up somewhat.

The Nottingham team were buoyed by this goal and upped their game in search of a second. However, the Widnes defence played very well throughout and kept the Vipers shots on Charlotte Jackson's goal down to single figures.

After a goal-less spell of some 12 minutes, Aspinall scored again for the Wild Women, leaving the score 9 – 1 at the end of the second period.

Three minutes into the third period Aspinall scored her hat-trick goal and the lead was further extended with a second strike of the night from Loss and a fine effort from Emma Martin.

A fourth goal from Aspinall, a first ever goal for Widnes from Daisy Lloyd-Hazlegreaves and a last-minute strike from Danielle Skilander rounded off the scoring for the Wild women and handed them their highest ever winning margin.

The Edith Smith Memorial MVP Awards were presented by match volunteer Julia Shutt and game mascots Henry Pearson and Lilly Miller and they went to Linaia Trusswell for Nottingham and Sarah Aspinall for Widnes.

A League debut was handed to Shannon Holt, who is a graduate of the Widnes Adult Hockey Basics Programme and has been training with the Wild Women and helping out behind the scenes at matches this season. Shannon picked up an assist and 2 penalty minutes in her first ever game and looks to be a promising asset to the Wild women's team.

The win sees the Wild women join joint league leaders Telford Wrekin Raiders and Solway Sharks Ladies on 8 points at the top of the Division1 North table.

They are next in action this Saturday 11th January when they make their first ever visit to Lincolnshire to take on the Grimsby Wolves – 4.00 p.m. face off.

The Wild women are next at home on Sunday 16th February with the return match against Grimsby at Planet Ice Widnes – face off 5.30 p.m

Widnes Scoring: Sarah Aspinall 4+1, Emma Pearson 2+2, Elizabeth Loss 2+1, Laura Marcroft 1+2, Leen de Decker 1+0, Emma Martin 1+1, Danielle Skilander 1+1, Sav Sumner 1+1, Daisy Lloyd-Hazlegreaves 1+0, Victoria Venables 1+0, Kat Garner, Shannon Holt, Karyn Cooper all 0+1

Netminder: Charlotte Jackson - 8 shots / 1 goal (60 mins)

Saturday 11th January 2020 – WNIHL Div 1 (N)
Grimsby Wolves 3 – Widnes Wild Women 8

The Widnes Wild women's team moved to the top of the Division 1 North table after a comprehensive 3 – 8 victory away to Grimsby Wolves on Saturday.

It was the Wild Women's first ever game at the Lincolnshire rink and the Wild Women didn't seem to be overly troubled by the venue's famously compact ice pad.

Despite significantly out-shooting the hosts throughout the game, it took the Wild Women almost six minutes to take the lead with a well-taken strike from Leen de Decker. The advantage was doubled four minutes later with a goal from team captain Emma Pearson but the Wolves pulled a goal back with just 80 seconds left in the first period to keep the game close at the first break.

A second goal for Pearson just eleven seconds into the second period, then a second goal for de Decker and a debut goal at the half-way point in the game for Shannon Holt – playing only her second ever competitive match – effectively put the game out of the reach of the Grimsby team and the Wild Women were able to enjoy a 1 – 5 lead at the second period break.

A goal for Sav Sumner in the 46th minute edged Widnes further ahead and then the Wolves scored their second goal of the game just short of 48 minutes. Two more goals for the Wild Women – a short-handed strike on 54 minutes by Emma Pearson to give her her hat-trick and then a hat-trick goal for Leen de Decker with just 90 seconds left to go in the game saw the Wild Women coasting towards victory.

A third goal for Grimsby with just one second left on the clock gave the home side something to cheer about but it was the Wild Women who went home happiest and they now move two points clear of the chasing pack at the top of the league table, albeit having now played more games.

Shannon Holt received the “Spirit of the Game” award for the Most Valued Player and Emma Pearson now tops the scoring standings for the Division with 17 goals and 8 assists from 6 games.

The Wild Women now have five weeks before their next league game on Sunday 16th February, when they take on the Grimsby Wolves at home at Planet Ice Widnes.

Widnes Scoring: Leen de Decker 3+2, Emma Pearson 3+1, Sav Sumner 1+0, Shannon Holt 1+0, Sarah Aspinall & Katie Adshead both 0+1 Netminder: Stephanie Drinkwater - 30 shots / 3 goals (60 mins)

Sunday 5th January 2020: Widnes 15 - Nottingham Vipers 1

Match volunteer Julia Shutt and mascots Henry Pearson and Lilly Miller present MVP award Sarah Aspinall

(Photo by Paul Breeze)

The Widnes Wild women's team have announced their Player of the Month for January as Kat Garner (left).

The previous Wild Women's Players of the Month this season have been Pauline Hayward (above) for December, Emma Pearson for November and Stephanie Drinkwater for October.

Pearson went on to win the overall national league Player Award for the month of November.

Wild's Catherine Bowen-Fell (#73) shoots against Grimsby (Photo by John Lewis)

Sunday 16th February 2020 – WNIHL Division 1 North Widnes Wild Women 12 – Grimsby Wolves 2

The Widnes Wild women's team moved level on points at the top of the Division 1 North table after a comprehensive 12 – 2 win over Grimsby Wolves at Planet Ice Widnes on Sunday.

The Wolves took the lead with a goal straight from the face off from Ketziah Robinson with just seven seconds gone on the clock and there followed plenty of end-to-end hockey, as both sides tested out the other's strengths and weaknesses.

Widnes drew level on six minutes with a goal from Kat Garner – her first competitive goal for the Wild women. Former Belgium international player Leen de Decker put Widnes ahead in the 9th minute and edged them further into the lead with her second goal of the game in the thirteenth minute.

Just 60 seconds later, Sav Sumner scored for the Wild, putting Widnes very much in control of the game.

A third goal from de Decker on 19 minutes and a second strike from Sumner with just two seconds left in the period left the Wild women with a very healthy 6 – 1 lead at the first break.

Over the course of the first period, the Wild women had outshot the visitors by 22 to 6 and the onslaught continued in the second period. Two goals from team captain Emma Pearson on 21 and 24 minutes put the game well beyond the reach of the Grimsby team and two more strikes from de Decker on 30 and 32 minutes put the Wild Women into double figures with a 10 – 1 lead at the second break.

For the most part, the game was played in good spirits but there was an incident in the 35th minute that, while not especially game-changing, did leave its mark on proceedings.

Some pushing and shoving in the Grimsby goal mouth led to a lengthy stoppage while the match officials decided what penalties to hand out. Among others, the Wolves captain ended up receiving a match penalty for a check to the head, plus an additional match penalty for making abusive gestures as she left the ice.

The third period was somewhat quieter in terms of incidents and the next goal did not come until the 55th minute, when Catherine Bowen-Fell fired the Wild women further ahead. The Grimsby team's heads did not drop, however, and they carried on battling for the whole 60 minutes. Their efforts were rewarded with a power play goal on 56 minutes – scored once again by Ketziah Robinson.

The scoring for the evening was rounded off with just 10 seconds left on the clock with a goal from Sav Sumner to complete her hat-trick. This was a very good all-round performance by the Wild women's team and every player on the bench was able to play a part in this important victory.

Charlotte Jackson came on to replace Stephanie Drinkwater in goal at the mid-way point of the game and both netminders put in solid performances.

The Edith Smith Memorial MVP Awards were presented by match scorer Nicky Jackson and went to Abbie-Jane Mercer for the Grimsby Wolves and Leen de Decker for her five-goal haul for the Wild women.

The win sees the Wild women go level at the top of the WNIHL Division 1 North league table, along with Solway Sharks Ladies – with both teams now having 12 points.

Widnes Scoring: Leen de Decker 5+1, Sav Sumner 3+1, Emma Pearson 2+2, Catherine Bowen Fell 1+1, Kat Garner 1+1, Shannon Holt, Daisy Lloyd-Hazlegreaves, Katie Fairclough, Victoria Venables & Danielle Skilander all 0+1.

Netminders: Stephanie Drinkwater 14 shots/1 goal (24 mins), Charlotte Jackson 15 shots/1 goal (35 mins).

Photo above: The Wild Women's team after their win over Grimsby (Photo by Howard Smith)

Left: Elizabeth Loss attacks the Grimsby goal (Photo by John Lewis)

Match volunteer Nicky Jackson present the MVP award to Leen de Decker (Photo by Paul Breeze)

Sunday 1st March – WNIHL Div 1 North
Widnes Wild Women 8 – Telford Wrekin Raiders 1

The Widnes Wild women's team moved clear on points at the top of the women's Division 1 North table after a convincing 8 – 1 win over title rivals Telford Wrekin Raiders at Planet Ice Widnes on Sunday.

With three teams tied on 12 points before the game, this was a very important result as it overturned the 7 – 2 defeat away to Telford back in November and it means that, should the two teams finish on the same number of points at the end of the season, Widnes would take the higher position.

Telford actually scored first in this game, winning the face off and firing the puck into the net on their very first attack. The Wild Women equalised in the sixth minute with a well taken goal from Leen de Decker and then edged into the lead a minute later with an unassisted goal from Catherine Bowen-Fell.

While the Telford team had plenty of puck possession and shots on goal, they weren't able to make the most of their chances and Widnes moved further ahead with a goal on 16 minutes from team captain Emma Pearson.

The second period played out in similar vein, with the visitors looking constantly dangerous in attack but Wild netminder Stephanie Drinkwater put in a very solid performance and performed heroics to keep the puck out of the net.

The Wild women extended their lead on 26 minutes with a short-handed goal from de Decker and then an incredible spell saw them score three more goals in the space of 66 seconds – two more from de Decker to bring her total for the game to four and a second for Emma Pearson – to put the game well and truly beyond the reach of Telford.

The third period saw just one goal scored when GB Women's Under 18 international Katie Fairclough fired in a rocket shot from some distance to make the score 8 – 1. The Wild Women thought they had scored again with just 90 seconds left on the clock but the goal was disallowed by the match officials.

The Edith Smith MVP Awards were presented by match night volunteer Julia Shutt and went to Rachel Logan for Telford and netminder Stephanie Drinkwater for Widnes.

This victory means that the Wild women finish their home season with a 100% record of five wins in five league games.

They have two more games to play – away to Solway Sharks Ladies on Saturday 14th March and away to Nottingham Vipers on Saturday 18th April with both the league title and promotion play offs firmly in their sights.

Widnes Scoring: Leen de Decker 4+1, Emma Pearson 2+1, Katie Fairclough 1+0, Catherine Bowen Fell 1+0, Emma Martin & Victoria Venables both 0+1.

Netminder: Stephanie Drinkwater – 32 shots / 1 goal (60 mins).

Widnes MVP Stephanie Drinkwater with Julia Shutt and mascots Henry Pearson, Jacob Downe and Lilly Miller (Photo by Paul Breeze)

Leen de Decker (#5) celebrates the goal that clinches the league title for the Wild Women away at Solway (Photo by Steve Fairclough)

Saturday 14th March 2020 - WNIHL Div 1N
Solway Sharks Ladies 2 – Widnes Wild Women 4

The Widnes Wild Women team secured the WNIHL Division 1 North League title with a 2 – 4 win over Solway Sharks Ladies in Dumfries on Saturday.

The previous meetings between these two teams had been full of goals, with the Wild's 9 – 5 league win over Solway back in December the lowest scoring game among them but this was a much closer affair and it took until the eighteenth minute for the deadlock to be broken.

The Wild's former Belgian international player Leen de Decker put Widnes into the lead but they were pegged back just 15 seconds later with an equaliser from

Solway's top goal scorer Kimberley Breingan. The score remained 1 – 1 at the first period break and the Wild women still had a lot of work to do.

They edged back into the lead again with a second goal from de Decker on 25 minutes and a goal from Sarah Aspinall doubled the Wild advantage on 30 minutes.

With a 1 – 3 lead at the second period break, there was finally daylight between the two teams but the Sharks were in no mood to give up and Breingan scored their second goal of the game on 45 minutes to set up an incredibly tense finale.

Solway outshot the Wild women by a considerable margin throughout the game but Stephanie Drinkwater put in an heroic display in the Widnes goal to keep them at bay. Leen de Decker scored her third goal of the game on 57 minutes and that was enough to secure both the win and the league title.

The result mans that the Wild women now have a total of 16 points and a game yet to play. Solway Sharks have played all their league games for a total of 14 points.

The other title challenger in this fascinating three-way chase for the league title – Telford Wrekin Raiders – have two more games yet to play but, even if they win both of those, the best they can achieve is 16 points, level with Widnes, and the Wild women would still take the league title on the basis of results between the two teams.

They have the chance to finish clear on points at the top of the table when they finish their regular league schedule with a game away to bottom club Nottingham Vipers on Saturday 18th April.

The Wild Women have also made sure of a place in the end-of-season Play Offs – the be held at iceSheffield on 30th & 31st May – where they will take on the top teams from Division 1 South to play for a place in the Women's Premier League next season.

Widnes scoring: Leen de Decker 3+1, Sarah Aspinall 1+1, Emma Pearson 0+4.

Netminder: Stephanie Drinkwater 46 shots / 2 goals (60 mins).

Catherine Bowen Fell, Stephanie Drinkwater, Victoria Venables and Pauline Hayward in action away at Solway (Photo by Steve Fairclough)

The Wild Women celebrate winning the WNIHL North 1 league title after their away win over the Solway Sharks Ladies in Dumfries (Photo by Mo Muir)

WOMEN'S LEAGUES ROUND UP

The Widnes Wild women's team have had their WNIHL Division 1 North league title win formally ratified by the League Management Committee.

While there was never really much doubt that this would happen, the cancellation of league ice hockey across the country on 16th March due to concerns over the coronavirus pandemic has caused a huge upheaval and, with it, an administrative nightmare as to how to deal with unplayed games and the final league tables.

The Wild Women's 2 – 4 win away to Solway Sharks Ladies gave them enough points to secure the league title outright despite other teams still having matches to play but the fact that the D1 North competition was closer to completion anyway made that the simplest to wrap up first.

The League Management Committee's subsequent decision to record all outstanding fixtures as 0 – 0 draws with no points being given to either side, was, certainly from an administrative point of view the easiest way to resolve this situation, but it has created other problems across the leagues that now need resolving.

In the finalised Division 1 North table, Widnes finish top with 16 points, having completed nine of their ten league fixtures. Solway Sharks Ladies finish in second place with 14 points from ten games, having played all their games for the season.

Last season's League Champions, Telford Wrekin Raiders, now finish in third place with 12 points from eight games played. They had two more matches still to come – home and away against Grimsby Wolves – and would have probably expected to have won those two games had the season run its full course.

Realistically, Telford would have finished in second place in the league table had things turned out differently.

All of this leaves a question mark over the promotional play offs – which were due to be held at iceSheffield at the end of May but which have now, obviously, been cancelled.

The top two teams in Division 1 North were to have met the top two teams in Division 1 South to play off for a place in the Women's Premier League next season.

With automatic promotion between the Women's Premier League and the Women's Elite League also to be finalised, further decisions will have to be made as to how these promotion and relegation issues are to be resolved.

The two national leagues above Division 1 North were not as advanced in their playing seasons and most of the teams have had to see 5 or more games written off.

The Women's Elite League saw Solihull Vixens awarded the league title with 26 points from 13 games played whereas perennial winners of the title, Bracknell Queen Bees, were on 25 points with 6 games left to play when the league was suspended.

The Women's Premier League competition saw an equally frustrating finish, with Swindon Top Cats finishing in first place with 15 points with six games left to play, with Bracknell Firebees in second place, also on 15 points and three games left to play.

Behind them, came both Whitley Squaws and Chelmsford Cobras who had 11 points each at the time of the league curtailment and six games each left to play.

Leen de Decker
(Photo by Paul Breeze)

WILD PLAYERS CLINCH LEAGUE AWARDS

February 2020 was a good month for the Widnes Wild club with Wild players scooping both men's and women's Player of the Month awards.

Wild NIHL Netminder Philip Pearson was voted Player of the Month for the Laidler Division and Wild Women's team player Leen de Decker was awarded award for the Women's Division 1 North as well.

Belgian international appearances record holder de Decker missed most of last season but has been truly inspirational since she returned to the ice early in this campaign.

She scored 20 goals and eight assists in just seven games, including 4 + 1 in the important 8 – 1 win over Telford and a hat trick in the 2-4 title clinching game away to Solway.

Here again, the Wild Women have featured heavily in the Player of the Month Awards this season as Team Captain Emma Pearson won the Division 1 North Award for the Month of November 2019.

By virtue of her nomination for the League award, de Decker is automatically the Wild Women's own Player of the Month for February.

Wild Women's team captain Emma Pearson (#33)
(Photo by Paul Breeze)

WILD WOMEN CAPTAIN EMMA REFLECTS ON TITLE WINNING SEASON

Emma Pearson was one of the original Manchester Phoenix women's team that moved to play at Widnes in the summer of 2015 and has seen all the ups and downs of the past five seasons with the Wild women.

They made the end of season play offs in their first two seasons as a Women's Premier League club and then the team entered a slump that ended with them being relegated to Division 1 North at the end of last season.

Looking back over this successful title-winning season, Emma said:

"I was really pleased with how the season went. It was great to win all but one of our games and was a huge change from the previous season for us. It was good to see the energy and excitement in the changing room each week and I was so impressed with how much the girls improved over the course of the season. So many people scoring their first goals this year was amazing and I loved seeing the joy on their faces when it happened."

Unfortunately, the latter stages of the season were cancelled due to concerns about the cornonavirus pandemic so the Wild women were not able to take part in the promotion play off weekend in Sheffield. Pearson commented:

"It's very disappointing. From somebody who has been to play offs in the past, I was so excited for the newer players to experience this too. I have never had the honour of lifting the league trophy for the team as captain so that was a real disappointment. It can't be helped and hopefully we will get another go at it next season."

Emma finished the season as the Wild women's top points scorer – and second in the league overall – with 21 goals and 15 assists from 9 league games. In an eventful season, she also played 2 games for the Widnes Wild NIHL team and 7 games for the Blackburn Hawks 2 team, for whom she scored 1+1. This was her highest ever total for league points – the next highest having been the 2011/12 season when she scored 13+13 for the Sheffield Shadows.

She explained how it came about:

"I worked hard over the summer and through the season to improve on my shooting. Scoring goals has never been my strong point and I'm sure the coaches will agree that I

often panic when I have no need to. Playing senior men's hockey this season has also boosted my confidence, I had less time on the puck and feel this experience was really beneficial to my women's game."

In the summer of 2018, the Wild women's team launched a recruitment drive and made the very bold – and, indeed, unheard of in competitive ice hockey circles – move to take on almost a whole new team of largely inexperienced players. Looking back on how that experiment has worked, Pearson said:

"2 years ago we had a large number of existing players leave for a variety of reasons. We had been running the club on lower numbers at that point anyway, so when the other players left we were either going to have to fold the club as we didn't have the minimum numbers the league requires for a team to register – or we had to do a big recruitment drive."

"We decided to go with recruitment, knowing it wouldn't be an easy season but it paid off, we recruited lots of new players and they are all still with us this season which is amazing!"

"They have improved a lot and, although they were thrown in at the deep in by playing games in the Women's Premier League, I think this was a good thing looking back as this season they have come out flying!"

The Wild women's title ambitions were given a huge boost when senior player Leen de Decker was able to play for the team again after a year away.

Commenting on de Decker's contribution as a player, Emma said:

"Leen is a very experienced player, she brings a calmness to the ice when she plays, there is no panic in her game. She has a lot of knowledge that she shares with the other players too. Leen and I have played on teams together for many years so I was really pleased when she was able to play competitive games again."

Looking ahead to next season, Pearson commented:

"I hope we have a season first of all – who knows what the situation will be! We are working towards the new season like we always do. We normally have a summer break – which we are obviously taking early this year – but I know myself and the girls are working hard to stay fit and work on skills at home that will help to benefit our game when we can get back on the ice."

"I would love to win the league title again and get to play offs – that's our biggest aim and I know the coaches and team feel the same way."

"We have built up a great team, and the spirit and atmosphere around the team is amazing, so – as long as we can keep that going – I'm sure we will be fine."

Wild NIHL netminder Phil Pearson formed a successful coaching partnership with Daniel Fay to coach the women's team this season. (Photo by Geoff White)

NETMINDER PHIL HELPS COACH WILD WOMEN TO TITLE SUCCESS

The Widnes Wild women's team won the first trophy in their 5-year history with the Division 1 North league title back in March and part of the credit for that success must go to Wild NIHL players Phil Pearson and Dan Fay who stepped in at short notice to coach the team at the start of the season.

A rather strange set of circumstances led to Pearson coaching the Women's team this season, as he explains:

"I had been to the Wild women's team's sessions a few times over the past few seasons (because my wife Emma plays for the team) – when my training with Bradford

Bulldogs and babysitting had allowed – working with Stephanie Drinkwater. They had a set of coaches in place for this season and, with me having signed for Wild NIHL team and the women's training being on straight after the men's session, I said I would stop on afterwards work with the women's netminders."

"Then, the original coaches suddenly left and I was asked to step up and run a few sessions with the full team rather than just focusing on the 'keepers."

"I hadn't much experience coaching a full team before but I had worked with the goalies in the past, just giving pointers and running a few drills. I had just done my coaching course over the summer so I was pretty happy that I could put together some drills that the girls would enjoy."

"I got a few of the Wild players to help with some of the sessions – the main one being Dan Fay – and Dan and I have continued to coach the women throughout the season. The girls seemed to enjoy it so we have carried on with it. The experience has been great – especially seeing the team develop and win the league."

"We started working on the basics. As some of the women were quite new to the game we decided to start working on skating. Dan ran a lot of the skating drills and the women's skating really came on as we did it. The drills we ran followed the same principles but became more complex as the season went on as the players improved."

The Wild women's team lost just one of their league games – away to Telford Wrekin Raiders – and were able to secure the league title with a win away to Solway

Sharks Ladies on the last day of competition. Looking back over the successes of the season Phil commented:

"It feels great to have won the Division 1 North title at the first attempt. When Dan and I took over, the main aim was to make playoffs as Telford hadn't lost a game for a considerable length of time, so we knew they and Solway were going to be pushing for the league as well."

"It's just a shame that the season ended early as it means the women can't receive their trophy on the ice at the playoffs, which would have been a great experience for the girls."

So, now that he has got the coaching bug, are we going to see more of Phil Pearson the coach in the future?

"Most definitely. I have really enjoyed this season and hope to do it for a good few years yet.

We also have a title to defend so I would like to do that! I would like to attend some of the goalie coaching courses in the future as well."

Wild women's team captain Emma Pearson said of the coaching set-up for this season:

"Having Dan and Phil as coaches has been amazing for the team. The girls have a lot of respect for them and we all know that they have so much knowledge and playing experience that they can share with us."

"They have made training fun but hard work at the same time, put new lines together and worked out what areas we needed to focus on."

"As a team who has a large number of players relatively new to the sport, having them both as coaches has really helped those players as well as the more experienced

players to develop new and existing skills which has shown massively in the games this season."

"We had Mike Parkin, Howard Hughes and Gareth Davies, who helped us out on game days too, and they all have a wealth of knowledge and playing experience – so I feel we are really lucky to have this group of coaches to help us."

Netminders' Verdicts On Successful Season

Stephanie Drinkwater is one of the longest serving Wild women's players, having been part of the initial Manchester Phoenix team that moved to Widnes in the summer of 2015.

This is the first piece of silverware ever for the Wild women and, looking back at the season, Drinkwater said:

"To win the league after being relegated back to Division 1 last year felt amazing, I was lost for words after our final game at Solway. This year felt even better to win with a new bunch of hard working girls who always had your back no matter what."

Asked about having Phil Pearson as a specialist netminding coach, she commented:

"Having Phil as a coach has been the best, to actually have someone to tell you what you're doing right from wrong had really helped my game this year. He saw me on good days and bad days and no matter what he always helped me to keep my head in the game. Training sessions were tough – but it all paid off!"

For the first time this season the Wild women had a regular backup netminder on the bench in Charlotte Jackson – younger sister of the Wild's Tom Jackson.

During the previous Women's Premier League season, lone 'keeper Drinkwater faced more shots than any other netminder and is now happy to be able to share the workload:

"Last year was definitely a tough one, I've never faced so many shots! I have never been so happy to have another netminder on the team. Charlotte is an absolute superstar in net and I'm so glad she had the opportunity to play. She's such a talented keeper, never gives up and I hope she stays with us next year."

Charlotte Jackson's first season of competitive ice hockey was actually her first season of ice hockey full stop. Despite having played roller hockey at international level, she had never played on ice before the first game of this season! She explains the transition:

"I've played roller hockey since I was 8 so changing from wheels to blades was tricky at first. General netminding principles and kit are the same but I didn't realise the ice was so slippy! Moving across the net was a lot different because you have to get used to using your edges so that you don't accidentally jam your blade into the ice and fall over! I did this a lot in the beginning!"

"Phil has been very helpful – especially with my movement across the net and glove positioning. He may be fed up with repeating himself to me, though! I don't always get it first time (or second or third or fourth)..!

Asked about her overall experience of her first year of competitive ice hockey Charlotte said:

"It has been great to win the league – other than we haven't been able to really celebrate it yet due to lockdown so it doesn't feel real yet. We have also missed

out on the promotion playoffs and our end of season party, which is a shame."

"Sharing the net with Steph has been good for me and the team. We both want the team to do well but her work commitments prevent her playing all of the games. It's scary to step into her position for those games but, luckily, the whole team support me through this. Steph has been really supportive sharing her tips and helping me get it right."

"My experience so far at Widnes Wild Women has been brilliant. I've loved being part of the team (win or lose). All the girls are supportive to me and each other. The support for the women's team is increasing and it would be nice to see that grow more next year."

Daniel Fay in action for the Wild men's team (Photo by Geoff White)

Phil Pearson and Daniel Fay on the Wild Women's bench for the away win at Solway (Photo by Steve Fairclough)

DANIEL FAY ON COACHING THE WILD WOMEN'S TEAM

Daniel Fay is well known to all Widnes fans as a very solid defenceman and, since he joined the Wild two seasons ago, he has picked up numerous man of the match awards and end of season awards for his endeavours.

However, this season, he has another accolade to add to his – already bulging – trophy cabinet, and one that even he at the start of the season could hardly have imagined – that of having coached the Widnes Wild women's team to the Division 1 North League title.

By his own admission, Dan had never coached a senior team before and had only helped out with juniors teams and "learn to play hockey" sessions back in his native Bracknell, so it was an unusual step for him to take, as he explains:

"Obviously, at beginning of the season the women's team were without a coach and Phil Pearson stepped up to the role. He asked me and a few other guys from the Wild to give him a hand with it. Initially, I thought I'd be there to push pucks around and just help out at training. Following a few weeks of doing this – which I thoroughly enjoyed, with a great group of girls – Emma came to me saying that we could get it sorted for me to come on the bench and from there it just sort of happened."

When asked how he went about structuring the training sessions to make sure that everybody was included and everybody benefited, he said:

"There was a wide range of abilities within the team and we needed to make training easy enough for beginners but not boring for the more elite players."

"We had to try and work on different things for each person but a key aspect was the skating component. That Is probably the most important skill in the game and we wanted to improve that first."

"We ran skating drills for the first month of the season, along with stations and shooting practise. In order to be able to focus on systems and flow drills we then decided to do separate skating lessons on Wednesday nights in which many of the girls came down which showed their commitment to the team."

"Overall I felt we all did a good job here by running progression drills which developed over the season till the end where everyone was flying."

Talking about winning the league title at his first attempt at coaching, Faye said:

"It was a great achievement to win the D1N title but it was all down to the girls. They put so much effort and work into it and came together as a team throughout the season. It was a pleasure for me to coach them and I am so proud of each of them."

"I would love to continue coaching – especially these girls they make it enjoyable and are all great hockey players – and hopefully we can go and win more trophies!"

Commenting on the new coaching arrangements this season, Wild women's player Pauline Hayward said:

"Phil and Dan make a great coaching team. They adopted a very different style, going back to basics with the whole team and putting a strong emphasis on fitness. I thoroughly enjoyed every second of training this season."

"Their style has clearly brought us the results we wanted. They have worked hard on our skating skills too – with Dan even doing extra work with us during public sessions, encouraging us all to get as much ice time as possible."

"Phil has done a lot of netminder coaching too, between them they have really built up the confidence of the team that hard work and playing as a team will pay off – which of course it has."

"Hats off, too, to the more experienced "senior" players who have committed 100% to developing all of the players. We have the best and most generous team spirit possible where everyone can be happy and thrive."

Shannon Holt – who made her league debut in January, said:

"Phil and Dan have been brilliant coaches this season. They have not only worked with us as a team, but have worked with us individually to see what we can improve on and what we are doing well. The two have made a great difference to the game and have been a real asset to the team this season."

"The team works really well together. The more experienced players help us rookies out and give us hints and tips into the structure and playing of the game. Overall, I think that all the girls are a strong team, on and off the ice."

Season 2020/21: Coronavirus Lockdown

The 2020/21 season didn't happen for the Widnes Wild Women – nor for any of the other women's teams in the UK – due to the Coronavirus pandemic, lockdowns and other restrictions on gatherings and sports activities.

You can read a lot more about this period in the book "10 Years In The Wild" which goes into a lot more detail about the ice rink closures and other restrictions that were put in place and the EIHA's Return To Play programme that eventually got ice hockey back up and running again.

The women's leagues didn't start playing again until the late summer of 2021, but here is a brief summary of what the Wild Women did in the intervening period.

May / June 2020: Wild Women Doing 100 Squat Challenge For Charity

Members of the Widnes Wild women's team are keeping extra fit during the lockdown period and helping to raise funds and awareness for charity at the same time.

They are undertaking the "100 squats a day" a day challenge in aid of the Royal British Legion Industries – which means literally doing 100 squats every day over 30 days from 3rd May to 2nd June.

The girls who are taking part make a video of their 100 squats and the results are edited together in a light hearted short video montage and posted on the Wild women's Facebook page, which also has a link to their Just Giving page for the charity.

The Royal British Legion Industries charity originally stated in 1919 helping thousands of soldiers who were sent home for the First World War suffering with tuberculosis.

In 1920, Industrial Settlements Incorporated – as it was originally known – purchased Preston Hall which was home to 240 ex-servicemen and women and, after the Second World War, the name was changed to British Legion Industries (Preston Hall) Incorporated – becoming a sister charity of the British Legion.

As well as the squat challenge, the Wild women's players have been finding other ways to keep fit and connected as a team during this difficult period.

Pauline Hayward explains:

"Some of us train together using Zoom twice a week on Tuesdays and Saturdays, hosted by Laura Marcroft who is social secretary."

"I also train with Zoom doing a HIT class every Wednesday and walk, cycle, trampoline and do tons of gardening. I do some stick handling/ shooting practice too but not as much as I would like as I don't have anywhere to do it without the risk of smashing the fences to bits!"

Wild women's captain Emma Pearson adds:

"The Zoom workouts have been useful to get some of the girls together and it's been really good to keep the motivation going."

"During lockdown I have been following the home workout programmes set by Chris at CrossFit Widnes which have been great to keep me fit. I have also been going on a few runs just for the cardio aspect."

Screen shot of Wild Women players taking part in a Zoom fitness session during the lockdown (Source: Pauline Hayward)

The newest member of the Wild women's team, Shannon Holt – who only just made her league debut in January said:

"During the lockdown, I have been playing ball hockey in the garden. I have been working on stick handling and puck control mainly. It's important to still work on these skills even though I cannot be on the ice as it will help for when we are back out there again."

19th October 2020: Wild Women Update

Reigning league champions the Widnes Wild women's team are preparing for the new season as best they can under the current coronavirus restrictions.

There has been no indication as to when the next league season might actually commence and indoor sports and venues are constantly being faced with more and more curbs and regulations.

Under recent directives from the government, only teams with “Elite” status can train as normal and, as they don’t play in a high enough league to qualify, the Wild women have to fit in with the rules of 6 on the ice.

However, having restricted ice usage is a great improvement on having none at all – which was the case for 5 months when the ice rink was closed over the summer, so the Wild women – under head coach Wild NIHL netminder Phil Pearson - have devised the best way to keep busy.

Team captain Emma Pearson explained: “Phil has put all the players into bubbles of 6 and named them after the original 6 NHL teams. Each week, teams will compete in drills and challenges to win points and be team of the week. All the bubbles have to remain socially distanced, obviously, so this adds some fun and competitiveness to the sessions.

“We ensure all players wear masks at the rink until they get on the ice, we keep players distanced whilst changing etc. Phil has adapted all the drills to make sure players stick to bubbles and each have roughly a quarter of the ice to work in.”

Emma and Leen de Decker - who are both qualified coaches as well - are helping with the coaching while the sessions are being run in this manner as it wouldn’t be possible for one person to oversee all the various groups on their own.

Sav Sumner in action for the GB Women's University team in Sheffield (Photo by Rob Hutchinson Photography)

April 2021: Sav Sumner In GB Action

In April 2021, as part of the EIHA's "Return To Play" programme, the men's and women's Great Britain Universities teams each played a challenge match at iceSheffield on Friday 23rd April.

The men's GB team easily won 11-2 against NIHL South side Milton Keynes Thunder while the women's team - including the Wild Women's Sav Sumner – lost 0-6 to Women's Elite League champions Solihull Vixens.

Talking about her GB experience, Sumner said: "I was extremely honoured to have been selected for the Great Britain Universities squad. From the beginning it had been a firm goal of mine to represent my country, therefore I couldn't be any more delighted. It was a great experience to be out on the ice with the team for us to showcase all the hard work we have been putting in over the last year."

EIHA WOMEN'S PREMIER LEAGUE
Season 2021/22

Final Table	GP	W	D	L	F	A	+/-	PIM	Pts
Bristol Huskies	16	15	1	0	150	7	143	123	31
Sheffield Shadows	16	11	1	4	106	39	67	54	23
Kingston Diamonds	16	10	2	4	75	27	48	136	22
Queen Bees	16	8	2	6	67	44	23	115	18
MK Falcons	16	9	0	7	83	56	27	130	18
Chelmsford Cobras	16	7	1	8	90	110	-20	161	15
Slough Sirens	16	4	0	12	54	124	-70	118	8
Nottingham Vipers	16	3	2	11	41	119	-78	145	8
Widnes Ladies	16	0	1	15	31	171	-140	78	1

Leading Points Scorers

Player	Team	GP	G	A	Pts	PIM
Ila Hobbins	Bristol Huskies	13	21	19	40	6
Eleanor Cooper	Sheffield Shadows	13	22	17	39	2
Jennifer Bolton	Chelmsford Cobras	16	25	12	37	4
Katie Edginton	Bristol Huskies	14	21	10	31	37
Rebecca Osman	Bristol Huskies	16	13	18	31	10
Jodie Attrill	Slough Sirens	15	19	10	29	6
Charmaine Easton	Chelmsford Cobras	15	18	11	29	41
Amiee O'Brien	MK Falcons	16	24	5	29	28
Hazel Taylor	Sheffield Shadows	13	11	18	29	0
Ellie Wallace	Bristol Huskies	11	14	15	29	4

Leading Netminders

Netminder	Team	GP	SA	GA	Sv%	SO
Mali Easton	Bristol Huskies	8	54	0	100.00%	6
Liberty Bird	Kingston / Sheff	10	269	5	98.14%	9
Gemma Davies	Bristol Huskies	11	140	5	96.43%	6
Sophia Voslinsky	Firebees	12	301	27	91.03%	1
Dawn Dickinson	Kingston Diamonds	13	116	11	90.52%	1

Preston Gennoe (#53) topped the standings for goals, assists, points and PIM for the Wild Ladies team this season (Photo by Brian Noble)

Season Review 2021/22

The Wild Ladies team (rebranded from "Women" to "Ladies" for this season...) had an eventful 2021/22 season in the Women's Premier League, gaining many friends, if not many points.

At the end of the 16-match campaign, they finished bottom of the league table with just 1 draw from 16 starts but that solitary statistic doesn't really tell the full story.

One thing to bear in mind is that they actually finished this season with THREE more points than they had managed the last time they played at this level.

Yes – they finished the 2018/19 season on minus 2 points after declining to play an away game against

Chelmsford that had originally been scheduled to take place at mid-day in Chelmsford and then got moved to a Sunday night in East London at very short notice.

As seems to happen on a very regular basis, the team saw a sizable turnover of players during the summer with the arrival of a number of promising young talents to join the returning core squad.

However, a certain amount of experience was lost from the team as the top goal scorers from each of the past 2 seasons, Emma Pearson and Sav Sumner, along with Charlotte McPhee and Kat Garner, all left for pastures new. Preston Gennoe came in from Coventry to counter this and Olivia Wilson – formerly of Whitley Bay – also contributed some experience at league level.

Giving the season fair reflection as a whole, the Wild Ladies should probably have won both their games against Nottingham, having led both home and away - and they possibly should have got results in the home games against Slough and the Firebees, when they put in a few good spurts late on but had left themselves too much to do in the latter stages.

For the rest, they came up against teams packed with current Elite League players – or, at least, players with Elite League experience - so it was never really much of a level playing field.

A few unwanted records left their mark on a generally "character-building" season – like losing 41-0 on aggregate over two games to runaway champions Bristol Huskies and going 206 minutes and 48 seconds without scoring a goal in a spell that saw 3 consecutive shut-outs

But on the whole, it was an enjoyable and uplifting experience for all those who were involved with the Wild

Ladies team and, with all the promising young players who are now coming through from the impressive Wild Junior Academy – and who all gained much-needed game time this season - it will be fascinating to see how they might go onto to develop as a unit in the next few years.

Stephanie Drinkwater (#1) faced more shots in the WPL than any other netminder this season.

Player, coach and captain Leen de Decker was second highest points scorer for the season and her usual inspirational self both on and off the ice.

(Photos by Geoff White)

Widnes Wild Ladies - Season 2021/22 (Photo by Geoff White).

Back Row: Beckie Elliott, Shannon Holt, Olivia Wilson, Jennifer Hickey, Leen de Decker, Natalie Buckles, Preston Gennoe, Karyn Cooper, Catherine Bowen Fell, Katie Adshead, Daisy Winstanley, Vanessa Crickmore Clarke.

Front Row: Laura Marcroft, Danielle Skiander, Elizabeth Loss, Katie Fairclough, Emma Downe, Stephanie Drinkwater, Jemma Brown, Suzie Miller, Ellie-Bindi Walsh-O'Neill, Phoebe Patient, Ellen Tyrer.

Widnes Ladies Team - Fixtures & Results Season 2021/22

Date	Game	Home	H	A	Away	WDL
11/07/2021	Chall	Sheff Shadows	10	2	Widnes Ladies	L
24/07/2021	Chall	Widnes Ladies	7	9	Caledonia S Queens	L
28/08/2021	Chall	Widnes Ladies	1	11	Bracknell Firebees	L
10/10/2021	WPL	Chelmsfd Cobras	7	2	Widnes Ladies	L
30/10/2021	WPL	Slough Sirens	10	4	Widnes Ladies	L
06/11/21	WPL	Sheff Shadows	14	0	Widnes Ladies	L
14/11/2021	WPL	Nottm Vipers	5	5	Widnes Ladies	D
21/11/2021	WPL	Widnes Ladies	2	3	Nottingham Vipers	L
02/01/2022	WPL	Widnes Ladies	0	9	Kingston Diamonds	L
09/01/2022	WPL	Widnes Ladies	0	9	Sheffield Shadows	L
23/01/2022	WPL	Bristol Huskies	21	0	Widnes Ladies	L
06/02/2022	WPL	Widnes Ladies	4	13	Chelmsford Cobras	L
13/03/2022	WPL	Kingston Dias	15	0	Widnes Ladies	L
20/03/2022	WPL	Widnes Ladies	3	7	Firebees	L
03/04/2022	WPL	Widnes Ladies	4	7	Slough Sirens	L
01/05/2022	WPL	Widnes Ladies	0	20	Bristol Huskies	L
08/05/2022	WPL	Widnes Ladies	2	14	MK Falcons	L
15/05/2022	WPL	MK Falcons	9	3	Widnes Ladies	L
22/05/2022	WPL	Firebees	8	2	Widnes Ladies	L

Unofficial "Netminder Saves" Table – WPL 2021/22

Player	Team	SA	GA	Saves
Stephanie Drinkwater	Widnes Ladies	903	124	779
Gerry Park	Slough Sirens	642	78	564
Caitlin Woolley	Nottingham Vipers	586	86	500
Cherry Hambelton	Chelmsford Cobras	479	95	384
Kayliegh Doyle	MK Falcons	428	53	375
Kirsty Robson	Sheffield Shadows	368	39	329

Widnes Wild Ladies Team Player Statistics – Season 2021/22

	Women's Premier League					Challenge		Totals				
Player	**GP**	**G**	**A**	**Pts**	**PIM**	**GP**	**Pts**	**GP**	**G**	**A**	**Pts**	**PIM**
Preston Gennoe	12	7	4	11	26	1	1	13	8	4	12	26
Leen De Decker	14	6	3	9	4	1	0	15	6	3	9	4
Katie Fairclough	13	5	2	7	4	0	0	13	5	2	7	4
Catherine Fell	12	4	1	5	20	1	0	13	4	1	5	20
Jemma Brown	13	2	2	4	4	2	1	15	2	3	5	4
Charlotte Cramp	15	2	1	3	0	1	2	16	3	1	5	0
Kaitlyn Kerr	0	0	0	0	0	2	4	2	2	2	4	2
Karyn Cooper	14	0	2	2	0	1	0	15	0	2	2	2
Ellen Tyrer	14	1	1	2	2	1	0	15	1	1	2	2
Ellie Walsh-O'Neill	14	2	0	2	2	0	0	14	2	0	2	2
Jennifer Hickey	14	1	0	1	2	1	1	15	1	1	2	2
Danielle Skilander	8	0	1	1	2	1	1	9	1	1	2	2
Kathyrn Garner	0	0	0	0	0	1	2	1	2	0	2	0
Katie Adshead	13	0	1	1	2	2	0	15	0	1	1	2
Natalie Buckles	9	0	1	1	4	2	0	11	0	1	1	4
Beckie Elliott	7	1	0	1	0	0	0	7	1	0	1	0
Suzanne Miller	14	0	1	1	0	2	0	16	0	1	1	0
Phoebe Patient	14	0	1	1	2	1	0	15	0	1	1	2
Olivia Wilson	11	0	1	1	0	1	0	12	0	1	1	0
Daisy Winstanley	7	0	1	1	0	0	0	7	0	1	1	0
Laura Marcroft	14	0	0	0	0	2	1	16	0	1	1	0
Sav Sumner	0	0	0	0	0	1	1	1	1	0	1	0
Sarah Aspinall	1	0	0	0	0	1	0	2	0	0	0	0
Vanessa C-Clarke	9	0	0	0	0	0	0	9	0	0	0	0
Emma Downe	7	0	0	0	0	2	0	9	0	0	0	0
Steph Drinkwater	14	0	0	0	0	0	0	14	0	0	0	0
Pamela England	1	0	0	0	0	1	0	2	0	0	0	0
Pauline Hayward	2	0	0	0	0	0	0	2	0	0	0	0
Shannon Holt	12	0	0	0	0	1	0	13	0	0	0	0
Charlotte Jackson	8	0	0	0	0	2	0	10	0	0	0	0
Elizabeth Loss	10	0	0	0	0	1	0	11	0	0	0	0
Charlotte McPhee	0	0	0	0	0	1	0	1	0	0	0	0

Netminder Statistics

Netminder	Comp	GP	Mins	SA	GA	GAA	SA%	SO
Stephanie Drinkwater	WPL*	14	780	903	124	9.54	86.27	0
Charlotte Jackson	WPL*	8	180	220	47	15.67	78.64	0
Charlotte Jackson	Chall	2	120	98	20	10.00	79.59	0
Charlotte Jackson	Totals	10	300	318	67	13.40	78.93	0

Note – the player statistics for the challenge game away to Sheffield Shadows on 11th July have never been made available. The two challenge matches referred to here are 24th July v Caledonia Steel Queens and the informal training session on 28th August v Firebees. Neither of these games feature in the official EIHA statistics, so this is the only place that they are recorded.

Netminder Mins and GAA are estimated

Wild women's Kat Garner (#88) receives the MVP award from match timekeeper Rebecca Clayton (Photo by Paul Breeze)

Saturday 24th July 2021 – Challenge Match Widnes Wild Women's Team 7- Caledonia Steel Queens 9

The Widnes Wild women's team were involved in a highly enjoyable sixteen goal thriller in their pre-season challenge game against the Edinburgh-based Caledonia Steel Queens at Planet Ice Widnes on Saturday, narrowly losing out 7-9.

This was the first home game for the Wild women since 1st March 2020 due to the various rink closures and Covid lockdowns and was the first time that fans had been able to see the team in action since they won the Division 1 North league title away in Dumfries, before the 2019/20 season was curtailed.

The Wild women's team iced a largely inexperienced development team against the Steel Queens - with several players who are new to competitive ice hockey and, indeed, 4 were making their home Wild debuts.

The match started well for Widnes with new player Kaitlyn Kerr opening the scoring with her first ever Wild goal after just three minutes. The Steel Queens equalised on 13 minutes but Widnes edged back again just 90 seconds later with a second goal for Kerr.

The lead only lasted 13 seconds, however as the Scots equalised again and the score remained 2-2 at the first period break.

Widnes scored with a superb strike from Sav Sumner on 23 minutes to restore the lead but, once again, they were pegged back by a goal from the visitors some 4 minutes later. The same thing happened again at the mid-point of the game when Charlotte Cramp scored her first goal for Widnes on 32 minutes and the Steel Queens came back to level on 38 minutes.

Just when it looked as if the game would remain a stalemate heading into the second period break, the Wild women scored again with a goal from Kat Garner with just 70 seconds left on the clock. She repeated the feat just 12 seconds into the 3rd period to put Widnes 6-4 up and show daylight between the two teams for the first time in the game.

There were hopes that the numerically superior Widnes team might start to pull away at this point but the Caledonia team had other ideas and they pulled one goal back within 90 seconds.

The game was completely turned on it head in the 46th minute when a mix up in defence allowed the Steel

Queens to equalise and then they skated straight down the ice from the resulting face off to score again and take the lead. As if that wasn't bad enough, they did the same thing with their very next attack as well to score a third goal within 24 seconds of each other. This put them 6-8 in the lead and left the Wild women a lot to do in the latter stages of the game.

Widnes did pull a goal back through a Danielle Skilander strike on 53 minutes but any hopes of a late Wild fightback were dashed by another Steel Queens goal 3 minutes later.

Overall this was a very entertaining game – played in the very best of spirits and with only 2 PIM being handed out in total. The teams were for the most part pretty evenly matched and, save for the dramatic events of the 46th minute, the result could easily have gone either way.

The Edith Smith Memorial MVP awards were presented by match volunteer Rebecca Clayton and went to Mikanshi Ashok for the Steel Queens and Kat Garner for Widnes.

11th July 2021 – Challenge Match
Sheffield Shadows 10 – Widnes Wild Women 2

This challenge game saw a development-based Widnes team take on the Sheffield Shadows WPL team at iceSheffield.

No game sheet was made available but we are reliably informed that Katie Fairclough and Natalie Buckles scored the Wild goals.

The Wild women's team that played against the Caledonia Steel Queens. (Photo by Paul Breeze)

Back Row: Phil Pearson, Charlotte Cramp, Jemma Brown, Suzanne Miller, Kat Garner, Kaitlyn Kerr, Natalie Buckles, Emma Downe. Front Row: Jennifer Hickey, Pamela England, Laura Marcroft , Danielle Skilander, Elizabeth Loss, Charlotte McPhee, Sav Sumner, Katie Adshead. Reclining: Charlotte Jackson

MVPs Alissa Mailes and Preston Gennoe (Photos by Paul Breeze)

28th August: Wild Women – Bracknell Firebees

This was supposed to be a challenge game but, due to administrative difficulties at EIHA level, it was reclassified as a training session with players from Widnes and Bracknell all taking part as one big happy group.

Had goals been being counted, Bracknell would have won 1-11, with Preston Gennoe scoring for Widnes on her first appearance.

After the session, timekeeper Rebecca Clayton presented “Spirit Of The Training Session“ awards to Alissa Mailes from Bracknell and Preston Gennoe from Widnes.

Sunday 10th October 2021 – Women's Premier Lge
Chelmsford Cobras 7 – Widnes Wild Women 2

The Widnes Wild women's team put in a battling performance in their first game back in the Women's Premier League before ultimately losing out 7-2 to very a strong and experienced Chelmsford Cobras team away in Essex on Sunday.

The women's team has seen a lot of changes since they won the Division 1 (North) in their last league match all the way back in March 2020 and this game saw senior league debuts for Ellen Tyrer and Phoebe Patient - who had both previously played for the Wild Academy Under 15 mixed team - Jennifer Hickey and Charlotte Cramp.

Also new to the Wild women for this season were Preston Gennoe – formerly with Coventry Phoenix - Olivia Wilson who previously played with Whitley Bay and Beckie Elliott, who is back at Widnes after two seasons away.

Chelmsford were the first to score in this early face off game (12.15 start), taking the lead after just two minutes but Widnes were back on level terms just 4 minutes later with a goal from Beckie Elliott.

The Cobras edged ahead again on 9 minutes and the Wild women countered with an equaliser from Preston Gennoe on 15 minutes to leave the score standing at 2-2 at the first period break.

The Wild women were heavily outshot throughout this game but it took until 13 minutes into the second period for their stubborn defences to be breached again - when three quick-fire goals within 50 seconds of each other put the hosts well and truly in the driving seat.

At 5-2 after two periods, it looked as if the game was slipping away for the Wild women and they went further behind to a 6th goal on 44 minutes. The scoring was rounded off with a 7th goal for the Cobras with just 1 second left on the clock.

Netminder Stephanie Drinkwater performed wonders in the Wild goal to keep the score down in the latter stages, stopping an incredible 56 of the 63 shots that she faced.

By way of the vaguaries of statistics, she ended up with a better "Save Percentage" for the game - with 88.89% - than the Chelmsford netminder, who had ended up on the winning side but who only had a 75% Save Percentage.

Saturday 30th October 2021 – Women's Premier Lge Slough Sirens 10 – Widnes Wild Women 4

The Widnes Wild women's team slumped to a 10-4 defeat away to Slough Sirens in the Women's Premier League on Saturday.

With a new look team from the side that won the Division 1 North title last season, the Wild women travelled to Berkshire with several experienced players missing but gave league debuts to Daisy Winstanley and Natalie Buckles.

Slough took the lead in the 8th minute but Widnes equalised on 13 with a goal from Katie Fairclough.

Two more goals for the Sirens – including one with just 40 seconds to go in the period - saw them leading 3-1 at the first break.

Slough scored twice more to give themselves a 5-1 lead before Fairclough once again found the net for Widnes but two more home goals late in the period already looked to have pretty much settled the game in Slough's favour.

However, a goal just two minutes from the restart from Charlotte Cramp – her first ever league goal – gave the Wild women some hope and she repeated the feat in the 55th minute to narrow the score to 7-4.

Three late goals from Slough gave the score an undeservedly one-sided feel but the Wild women gave a good account of themselves overall and will be pleased with an improved "shots on goal" tally of 37 for the match.

Saturday 6th November 2021: Women's Premier Lge
Sheffield Shadows 14 - Widnes Wild Women 0

The Widnes Wild women's team's steep learning curve in life back in the WPL continued on Saturday with a 14-0 defeat away to Sheffield Shadows.

This is a greatly changed team from the Wild women side that won the Division 1 North title back in the 2019/20 season and the combination of losing the highest goal scorers from the two previous seasons during the summer and the fact that they are now playing in a higher division always suggested that this season might be a bit of a challenge.

Continuing their policy of encouraging new talent, the Wild gave a league debut to Ellie Walsh–O'Neill, who had previously played with the Academy Under 18 mixed team.

Sheffield opened the scoring in the 6th minute and led 2-0 at the first period break. 4 unanswered goals followed in the second period and 8 in the third, which made the final result look a little more one-sided than the game actually was. Despite the high scoring tally, Charlotte Jackson put in a good performance in the Widnes net and stopped 48 of the 62 shots that she faced.

Sunday 14th November 2021 – Women's Premier Lge Nottingham Vipers 5 – Widnes Wild Women 5

The Widnes Ladies team picked up their first WPL point of the season with an exciting and highly entertaining 5-5 draw away to Nottingham Vipers on Sunday.

This was the best performance of the season so far with the Wild women outshooting their opponents by 46 to 33 and clearly demonstrates that the new look team - with a lot of new players since last season - is beginning to gel on the ice.

Nottingham took the lead after just 60 seconds of the game but Widnes equalised with a goal from Jennifer Hickey – her first for the club – on 7 minutes.

The Wild took the lead just 90 seconds later through Preston Gennoe and the score remained at 1-2 at the first period break.

This was a very closely contested game throughout with both teams having their chances but it was the Vipers who eventually made the next breakthrough with an equalising goal on 28 minutes. They then went on to retake the lead with a short handed goal 4 minutes later.

Parity was restored on 34 minutes when Catherine Bowen Fell fired in a third goal for Widnes and the game remained on a knife-edge at 3-3 after two periods.

The Wild women visibly upped their game in the last period and peppered the Nottingham goal with shots. They were rewarded in the 44th minute when Bowen Fell scored her second goal of the game to edge Widnes back into the lead.

The advantage was extended to 3-5 with a second goal from Gennoe with just 3 minutes left in the game, and it began to look as if the Wild women were going to secure their first win at WPL level since they beat the Vipers back in December 2017.

But there was drama late on as Nottingham pulled a goal back with just 90 seconds left to play – and then levelled the scores once more 24 seconds later.

The clock ticked down and the game finished as a 5-5 draw with both teams taking a point, which sees the Wild women move off the bottom of the WPL table.

The Widnes Ladies will be hoping to build on this result when they take on the Vipers again next Sunday 21st November in their first home game of the season at Planet Ice Widnes – 4.15 pm face off.

Leen de Decker (#88) scores for the Widnes Ladies against Nottingham (Photo by Geoff White)

Sunday 21st November 2021: Women's Premier Lge Widnes Wild Ladies 2 – Nottingham Vipers 3

The Widnes Wild ladies team put in a battling performance in their first home game of the Women's Premier League season, narrowly losing out 2-3 to Nottingham Vipers at Planet Ice Widnes on Sunday.

After 4 away games in a row, this game had been keenly anticipated and there was a huge crowd in the rink to watch the resumption of rivalries between the same two teams that had drawn 5-5 in the Lace City last weekend.

This was a very good advert for women's ice hockey, with the two teams very closely matched throughout. The game could have gone either way and the result remained in doubt until the very last second.

After a tense opening phase, Widnes took the lead after 6 minutes with a goal from Belgian international Leen de Decker and, despite mounting pressure from the Vipers' attack, the score remained 1-0 at the first period break.

The game was littered with niggly penalties for both sides and this seemed to affect the Wild most as they found themselves having to defend shorthanded for sustained periods of play.

Nottingham scored their first goal of the game on a powerplay after just 46 seconds of the second period and then edged into the lead with a second strike 4 minutes later.

Widnes fought back and narrowly outshot the Vipers during the second period. Their mounting pressure was eventually rewarded when Jemma Brown fired in a goal on a delayed penalty call for slashing with just 26 seconds left in the second period – leaving the game on a knife edge with everything still to play for.

The third period continued in the similar end-to-end vein and Widnes were caught out at the back while pushing forward on a powerplay to concede a short handed goal in the 47th minute.

Both teams had numerous chances in the latter stages but impressive performances by the netminders at either end saw the rest of the game play out goal-less.

This result sees the Vipers move up into second place in the WPL table while Widnes remain 8th at this early stage of the season.

Paul Breeze presents the first Winifred Mabel Letts memorial MVP award of the season to Sarah Kimber of Nottingham Vipers (Photo by Geoff White)

WW1 HEROINE REMEMBERED IN WILD LADIES' MOST VALUABLE PLAYER (MVP) AWARDS

The Widnes Ladies team will be honouring First World War inspirational woman Winifred Mabel Letts this season, following Wild club Poet In Residence Lucy London's decision to sponsor the Most Valuable Player awards this season in her memory.

It is the third year in a row that Lucy has sponsored the MVP awards for the Wild women's home matches and, in keeping with her other main activity – that of researching and raising awareness of the roles of women in the Great War – Lucy has once again decided to dedicate this year's awards to the memory of another such woman.

For the 2018/19 season, the Wild women MVP awards were dedicated to the memory of Sarah MacNaughtan who single-handedly set up and operated soup kitchens in the war zones on the western front, and in 2019/20, the awards were in honour of Merseyside born Edith Smith who became the country's first female warranted police officer during WW1 and later worked as a nursing assistant at a hospital in Runcorn.

Winifred Mabel Letts was born in Salford and she went to be a successful writer. During the First World War, she joined the Volunteer Aid Detachment and worked as a nurse at Manchester Base Hospital. She then trained as a medical masseuse – that is a physiotherapist in modern parlance – with the Almeric Paget Military Massage Corps. Winifred worked at Army camps in Manchester and Alnwick, Northumberland.

Talking about her choice of Letts to commemorate for this season's awards, Lucy said;

"As the Wild club have a connection with the Physio Department at Salford University for this season, I felt it appropriate to commemorate Winifred as she was born in Salford and became a medical masseuse – which was the forerunner of physiotherapy."

The first Winifred Mabel Letts memorial MVP awards of the season were presented at the home game against Nottingham Vipers on Sunday. The presentation was made by Widnes off ice game official Paul Breeze and the awards went to Sarah Kimber for the Vipers and Preston Gennoe for Widnes.

Wild's Preston Gennoe (#53) receives the MVP award from match timekeeper Rebecca Clayton (Photo by Paul Breeze)

Sunday 2nd January 2022 – Women's Premier League Widnes Wild Ladies 0 – Kingston Diamonds 9

The Widnes Wild ladies team got the new year off to a low key start with a 0-9 defeat at the hands of the Kingston Diamonds at Planet Ice Widnes on Sunday.

The visitors opened the scoring straight from the face off with just 12 seconds gone on the clock and, having got that early boost, there was no stopping them.

They doubled the advantage on 6 minutes and were 0-3 up on 8 minutes – and a further goal late in the period saw Kingston leading 0-4 at the first break.

The Wild women visibly upped their game in the second period and enjoyed much more puck possession and shots on goal. However, they weren't able to make the most of their chances and were continually thwarted by a solid Diamonds defence and their netminder, who was in fine form.

Three straight goals in the second period for Kingston's Elizabeth Saunders put the game well beyond the reach of the Widnes side and, from then on, it was more of a case of damage limitation.

In the Widnes net, Stephanie Drinkwater pulled off some superb saves to keep the score down and was only beaten once more - in the 56th minute. The game finished 0-9 to Kingston but that scoreline makes it sound a little more one-sided than it actually was.

Looking at the positives, this is a new-look team playing in a higher division and the mix of youth and experience will continue to gel as the players get more games together under their belts. The match saw home WPL debuts for Charlotte Cramp and Daisy Winstanley and further promising performances from the young trio of Ellen Tyrer, Phoebe Patient and Ellie Walsh O'Neill - who are also all in their first season of senior competitive hockey.

The Winifred Mary Letts MVP awards – which have been sponsored this season by Wild Poet In Residence Lucy London in memory of the First World War poet and medic – went to Megan Day for Kingston and Preston Gennoe for Widnes and were presented by match volunteer Rebecca Clayton.

Wild's Phoebe Patient (#44) receives the MVP award from match volunteer Lynda Bird (Photo by Paul Breeze)

Sunday 9th January 2022 – Women's Premier League Widnes Wild Ladies 0 – Sheffield Shadows 9

The Widnes Wild ladies team put in a spirited performance but slumped to a 0-9 defeat at the hands of league leaders Sheffield Shadows at Planet Ice Widnes on Sunday.

The visitors opened the scoring with just 47 seconds gone on the clock and, having got that early boost, there was no stopping them. They doubled the advantage on 2 minutes and were 0-3 up on 5 minutes – and further goals late in the period saw Sheffield leading 0-5 at the first break.

The Wild women steadied the ship somewhat in the second period and put some good attacks together themselves but were unable to make the most of their chances. They managed to keep the Sheffield offence at bay for a good 13 minutes before the next goal went in on 33 minutes and this was followed up by another strike 90 seconds later and another 2 minutes after that.

Sheffield led 0-8 after two periods but, with their bench short on numbers, they began to lose steam in the final period – although their healthy lead by that time allowed them to ease off a bit.

The third period yielded just one goal – scored by Sheffield on 57 minutes and the game finished 0-9 to the visitors.

The Winifred Mabel Letts MVP awards – which have been sponsored this season by Wild Poet In Residence Lucy London in memory of the First World War poet and medic – went to Eleanor Cooper for Sheffield and Phoebe Patient for Widnes and were presented by match volunteer Lynda Bird.

The Widnes Ladies are next in action on Sunday 23rd January when they travel to take on the Bristol Huskies at the new Planet Ice rink in Bristol – face off 5.30pm – and are next at home on Sunday 6th February, when they entertain the Chelmsford Cobras at Planet Ice Widnes – face off 4.15pm.

Shannon Holt (#7) and Natalie Buckles (#9) in action against the Huskies away in Bristol (Photo by Flyfifer Photography)

Sunday 23rd January – Women's Premier League
Bristol Huskies 21 – Widnes Ladies 0

The WIdnes WIld LadIes team continued their steep learning curve in the Women's Premier League with a 21-0 drubbing away to Bristol Huskies on Sunday.

The Huskies are favourites to take the league title this season and have a 100% record with, now, 5 wins from their 5 games overall, having conceded just 2 goals in total.

The Wild women lost their two top goalscorers from the previous two seasons during the summer and have put together a completely new look squad for their return to this higher division - so this first ever trip to the new Bristol rink, taking on the relocated Swindon Topcats team containing several players with Elite League experience, was always likely to be a bit of a test.

Bristol took the lead after just 90 seconds of the game and were 10-0 up by the end of the first period. After two periods it was 17-0 and four more goals went in during the third.

In the Widnes goal, plucky Stephanie Drinkwater – who was just getting over an illness - faced an incredible 101 shots and impressively managed to save 80 of them.

The Wild Ladies are next in action on Sunday 6th February when they take on Chelmsford Cobras at Planet Ice Widnes, 4.15pm face off.

Overworked Wild netminder Stephanie Drinkwater (#1) in action away at the new Planet Ice rink in Bristol against the Huskies. (Photo by Flyfifer Photography)

The Widnes Ladies team away at Bristol.

Back row: Laura Marcroft, Katie Adshead, Catherine Fell, Olivia Wilson, Pauline Hayward, Charlotte Cramp, Natalie Buckles, Karyn Cooper, Katie Fairclough, Emma Downe, Ellie Walsh-O'Neill, Shannon Holt

Front row: Jennifer Hickey, Suzie Miller, Leen de Decker, Elizabeth Loss, Daisy Winstanley, Phoebe Patient, Ellen Tyrer. Front: Jemma Brown, Stephanie Drinkwater (Photo by Flyfifer Photography)

Wild's Elizabeth Loss (#34) receives the MVP award from match mascot Lilly Miller (Photo by Paul Breeze)

Sunday 6th February 2022 – Women's Premier League Widnes Ladies 4 – Chelmsford Cobras 13

The Widnes Wild Ladies team put in a much improved performance against the Chelmsford Cobras but unfortunately lost out 4-13 in a highly entertaining game at Planet Ice Widnes on Sunday.

The visitors took the lead after just 32 seconds but the roof of the rink was metaphorically raised at 6.22 when Katie Fairclough fired in an equaliser for the Wild, thus ending an extended goal drought for the Widnes team.

Having failed to score at all in their last 3 games – albeit against the leading teams in the division and very strong opposition – you have to go back to 21st November and 39 minutes 34 seconds into the home game against

Nottingham when the Wild women last found the back of the net – this was quite a momentous event for the players and their fans.

Indeed it represented an incredible 206 minutes 48 seconds of playing time without a goal – quite possibly some sort of unwanted Women's Premier League record - so you can easily appreciate why this Fairclough strike was so enthusiastically received.

Chelmsford hit back almost immediately, however, restoring the lead just 30 seconds later and went on to build up an impressive 1-5 advantage by the end of the first period.

A 6th goal for the Cobras 2 minutes from the restart edged them further ahead but Widnes heads did not drop and they went on to have their best spell of the game.

A goal for Ellen Tyrer – her first ever in senior competitive hockey – on 24 minutes received as big an ovation as Fairclough's earlier marker and then Catherine Fell fired in just 50 seconds later to draw the Wild ladies back to 3-6.

There then followed a highly frenetic 9 minute phase with both teams having plenty of chances on goal and Widnes looking ever likely to further narrow the deficit.

The next goal, however - when it came - fell to Chelmsford and they quickly scored two more follow up strikes. Preston Gennoe fired in for Widnes on 35 minutes leaving the score at 4-9 to the visitors at the second period break.

4 unanswered goals for Chelmsford in the third period made the overall scoreline appear more one-side than

the game actually was and the Wild women can draw a lot of positives from this performance.

The Winifred Mabel Letts memorial MVP awards sponsored by Poet In Residence Lucy London went to Tegan Hyatt for Chelmsford and Elizabeth Loss for Widnes and were presented by match mascot Lilly Miller.

The Widnes Wild Ladies team are next in action on Sunday 13th March when they travel to face Kingston Diamonds in Hull – 12.30 (noon) face off.

They are next at home on Sunday 20th March when they entertain the Firebees at Planet Ice Widnes, 4.15pm face off.

Sunday 13th March 2022 – Women's Premier League Kingston Diamonds 15 - Widnes Ladies 0

The Widnes Wild Ladies team had a difficult trip to Humberside in the Women's Premier League on Sunday, suffering a 15-0 drubbing at the hands of the Kingston Diamonds.

Kingston opened the scoring after just 45 seconds and were leading 6-0 by the first period break. 6 more unanswered goals followed in the second period and 3 more in the third.

In fairness to the Wild women, all but one of the Kingston goals were scored by players who also play regularly for the Diamonds Elite League team, so this was hardly an even-sided encounter.

Many of the Widnes players are in their first ever season of competitive hockey and very few others have much experience at WPL level. One positive note from the game was that netminder Charlotte Jackson managed to turn away an incredible 68 of the 83 shots that she faced during the 60 minutes.

The Wild Ladies team are at home on Sunday 20th March when they take on the Firebees at Planet Ice Widnes, 4.15 pm face off.

Charlotte Cramp (#29) and Preston Gennoe (#53) celebrate the latter's first goal against the Firebees (Photo by Geoff White)

Sunday 20th March 2022 – Women's Premier League Widnes Wild Ladies 3 – Firebees 7

The Widnes Wild Ladies team put in an impressive performance against the Slough-based Firebees at Planet Ice Widnes on Sunday and were ultimately unlucky to finish up on the wrong end of a 3 –7 scoreline.

After a close opening phase, the visitors opened the scoring in the 5th minute and raced to a 0-3 lead before Catherine Fell pulled a goal back for the Wild women with just 44 seconds left in the first period.

The second period was a much closer run affair with the Firebees being restricted to one single goal on 26 minutes, which was cancelled out by a superb strike by Preston Gennoe to leave the score standing at 2-4 at the second period break.

A second goal for Gennoe early in the third period narrowed the deficit to just one goal and Widnes really were flying.

As they pushed forward looking for an equaliser, however, they were caught out at the back and the Firebees struck again to make the score 3-5.

This was really a most entertaining game to watch and, although the visitors had the upper hand for long spells, the Wild Ladies never gave up and, on another day, might well have snatched a result.

As it was, two late goals gave the scoreline a more uneven feel than the game deserved but the Wild women have plenty of positives to look back on.

In the Widnes goal, Stephanie Drinkwater faced an incredible 93 shots but managed to turn away 86 of them for an impressive 92.7 save percentage.

The Winifred Mabel Letts memorial MVP awards sponsored by Poet In Residence Lucy London went to Phebe Dodd for the Firebees and Laura Marcroft for Widnes and were presented by off-ice match official Paul Breeze.

Laura Marcroft (#93) picked up the MVP award for the home game against the Firebees (Photo by Geoff White)

Jemma Brown (#66) receives the MVP award from match volunteer Tricia Holt (Photo by Paul Breeze)

Sunday 3rd April 2022 – Women's Premier League Widnes Wild Ladies 4 – Slough Sirens 7

The Widnes Wild Ladies team staged an heroic late comeback in their Women's Premier League home game against the Slough Sirens at Planet Ice Widnes on Sunday but, unfortunately, it wasn't quite enough to prevent them ultimately slipping to a 4-7 defeat.

This was a very entertaining game from start to finish and, apart from an unfortunately subdued middle period, was closely contested throughout.

Slough took the lead after 5 minutes but were otherwise kept at bay by some stubborn defending and a superb display of netminding by the Wild's Stephanie Drinkwater, who turned away 25 shots in the first period to keep the score at 0-1 at the first break.

The visitors scored again just 49 seconds into the second period and with the Wild women constantly pressing forward to try and break their duck but having no luck in front of goal, went on to add 4 more unanswered goals.

With the scoring standing at 0-6 after two periods, a rout looked on the cards but, 4 minutes into the third period, Ellie Walsh O'Neill fired in her first ever competitive goal for Widnes and the atmosphere around the rink noticeably lifted.

Slough scored again on 48 minutes to extend the lead to 1-7 but the Wild players had a definite spring in their step and looked a lot more dangerous going forward.

A goal from Jemma Brown on 52 minutes boosted the mood and further strikes - from Kate Fairclough and Leen De Decker on 55 and 58 minutes respectively – sparked further hopes of a dramatic late comeback but, unfortunately, the clock ticked down far too quickly.

Had the game gone on for an extra 5 minutes or so, the result might have been different - but the Wild Ladies can be especially proud of their performance in the latter stages as they out-shot their opponents by 22 to 15 and won the final period 4-1.

The Winifred Mabel Letts memorial MVP awards sponsored by Poet In Residence Lucy London went to Aniko Gaal - who previously played for the Budapest Stars in the European Women's Hockey League back in her native Hungary – and Jemma Brown for Widnes, and were presented by match volunteer Tricia Holt.

Charlotte Cramp (#29) receives the MVP award from match timekeeper Thomas Horner (Photo by Paul Breeze)

Sunday 1st May 2022 – Women's Premier League Widnes Wild Ladies 0 – Bristol Huskies 20

The Widnes Wild Ladies team put in a plucky performance against the table topping Bristol Huskies in their Women's Premier League game on Sunday at Planet Ice Widnes but ultimately slumped to a 0-20 defeat.

The new Huskies team have taken the league by storm this season, are undefeated in all 14 games they have played to date and only conceded 7 goals in the process so Sunday's game was always going to be a bit of an uphill struggle for the Wild women.

As it turned out, Widnes started the game very well and gave as good as they got in the opening minutes. It took the recently crowned league champions until the 9th minute to breach the Wild defences and two further goals saw them leading 0-3 at the first period break.

Despite the one sided scoreline, this was a very entertaining game to watch and the Wild players never let their heads drop once and kept battling right through to the final buzzer.

8 unanswered goals followed for the visitors in the second period and 9 more in the third but the Widnes netminding duo of Stephanie Drinkwater and Charlotte Jackson put in an heroic performance, stopping an incredible 79 shots out of the eye-watering 99 that they faced over the course of the game.

The Winifred Mabel Letts memorial MVP awards sponsored by Poet In Residence Lucy London went to Nora Egri for Bristol and Charlotte Cramp for Widnes, and were presented by match volunteer Thomas Horner.

The Widnes Wild Ladies team play their last home game of the season this Sunday 8th May when they take on Milton Keynes Falcons in the Women's Premier League at Planet Ice Widnes – 4.15pm face off.

Preston Gennoe (#53) joins in the celebrations for Leen de Decker's (#5) goal against Milton Keynes (Photo by Brian Noble)

Sunday 8th May – Women's Premier League Widnes Wild Ladies 2 – Milton Keynes Falcons 14

The Widnes Wild Ladies team put in a stirring performance in their last Women's Premier League home game of the season but it ultimately wasn't enough to prevent them slumping to a 2-14 defeat at the hands of the Milton Keynes Falcons at Planet Ice Widnes on Sunday.

It has been a difficult season for the Wild women, having been promoted to the higher division after previously winning the Division 1 North title and their new look – and largely youthful - team has regularly found themselves up against long established WPL teams, with some squads packed with players with Elite League experience.

The game on Sunday started well for Widnes and they matched the visitors blow for blow in the early stages.

Milton Keynes scored the first goal in the 5th minute but Widnes looked to have equalised shortly afterwards but were not quite able to force the puck over the goal line.

Had that goal gone in, things might have been a lot different but, instead, the Falcons struck back and scored two quick fire goals just 30 seconds apart around the 7 minute mark to give them a commanding early lead.

The Wild women kept plugging away but their efforts to push forward left them exposed at the back and they were susceptible to breakaways and long shots. Three more unanswered goals for the Falcons saw them leading 0-6 at the end of the first period, leaving Widnes with a lot of catching up to do.

The home side had a much better second period, keeping the number of shots down on embattled netminder Stephanie Drinkwater while putting more pressure on the Falcons' defence and goal. Two more Milton Keynes goals followed but then Widnes had their brief period of domination.

A superb strike from season top scorer Preston Gennoe gave the Wild women their opening goal of the game on 34 minutes and captain Leen de Decker made it 2 for Widnes just 30 seconds later.

This got the crowd on their feet and, despite the score standing at 2-8, there were still hopes of a Widnes comeback at this point as the Milton Keynes team had a very short bench and were quite likely to tire in the latter stages.

The home team pushed forward again in the hope of further reducing the deficit but, despite creating numerous chances in front of goal, were unable to make any of them count and it remained a 2-2 period.

A superhuman effort by the numerically challenged Falcons saw them edge further ahead in the third period with a 9th goal on 44 minutes and then a 10th 5 minutes after that. Widnes heads did not drop at any point and the team continued to battle until the final buzzer.

4 more unanswered goals in the final 10 minutes gave the final score a slightly more one-sided look than the game deserved but the Wild Ladies can still be pleased with what they have achieved this season.

Rhianna Holt presents the MVP award to Vanessa Crickmore-Clarke (Photo by Paul Breeze)

The Winifred Mabel Letts memorial MVP awards sponsored by Poet In Residence Lucy London went to Samantha Ruff for Milton Keynes and Vanessa Crickmore-Clarke for Widnes, and were presented by match volunteer Rhianna Holt.

Ellie Walsh-O'Neill (#3) opened the scoring for the Wild Ladies away at Milton Keynes (Photo by Brian Noble)

Sunday 15th May – Women's Premier League
Milton Keynes Falcons 9 – Widnes Wild Ladies 3

The Widnes Wild Ladies team continued their challenging Women's Premier League season with a 9-3 defeat away to Milton Keynes Falcons on Sunday.

Having lost 2-14 to the same opposition at home the previous weekend, this could definitely be viewed as an improvement - and that is testified by the increase in shots on goal that the Widnes team managed to create as well as the reduction in shots conceded over the course of the game.

The Wild actually scored first with a goal from Ellie Walsh-O'Neill in the 7th minute but that strike was cancelled out by an MK equaliser just 52 seconds later.

The Falcons edged ahead 3 minutes after that but a goal from Widnes captain Leen de Decker levelled the scores again on 12 minutes.

All was looking good until the hosts re-took the lead on 17 minutes and then a hammer blow just 11 seconds from the buzzer saw them take a 4-2 advantage into the first period break.

The second period saw Milton Keynes pile on the pressure and they were rewarded with 3 unanswered goals to lead 7-2 at the second break.

Widnes pulled a goal back through de Decker on 50 minutes but that was as good as it got for the battling Wild women as two late goals for the hosts rounded off the scoring and topped off a 9-3 victory.

Wild netminder Stephanie Drinkwater once again performed miracles in the Widnes goal to keep the score down and managed to save 50 of the 59 shots that she faced.

The Widnes Ladies play their last game of the season away to the Firebees in Slough next Sunday 22nd May – face off 6pm.

That game will have added significance for the Firebees as victory will confirm their place in the end of season playoffs.

The Wild Ladies team for their last game of the season away to the Firebees in Slough: Back row: Jennifer Hickey, Olivia Wilson, Charlotte Cramp, Leen de Decker, Karyn Cooper, Ellie Walsh-O'Neill Front row: Katie Adshead, Laura Marcroft, Ellen Tyrer, Katie Fairclough, Suzie Miller, Preston Gennoe, Shannon Holt. Front: Stephanie Drinkwater

Sunday 22nd May: Firebees 8 – Widnes Wild Ladies 2

The Widnes Wild Ladies team finished off their roller-coaster Women's Premier League season with an 8-2 defeat away to the Firebees in Slough on Sunday.

The home side took the lead 3 minutes into the game but Widnes drew level just 2 ½ minutes later with a superb goal from Katie Fairclough. Two more quick-fire goals followed for the Firebees just 40 seconds apart and then a further strike late in the period saw them leading 4-1 at the first break.

Widnes had a much better second period in terms of puck possession and shots on goal but found themselves caught out at the back as they pushed forward trying to narrow the deficit. This led to three answered goals, which gave the Firebees a commanding 7-1 lead at the mid-way point of the game.

Wild heads did not drop, however, and the continued Widnes pressure was eventually rewarded with a goal from team captain Leen de Decker on 38 minutes.

There was just one goal in the 3rd period – for the home side in the 44th minute to bring the score to 8-2 – and embattled netminder Stephanie Drinkwater put in another heroic performance in the Widnes goal to keep the score down.

In fact, she turned away an incredible 60 of the 68 shots that she faced over the course of the game and actually finished the match with a better overall "save percentage" than her opposite number on the winning team.

Another interesting statistic saw the Wild women not incur any penalties for the third game in a row – quite possibly some sort of record - and this was, indeed, the 7th out of 16 league games overall this season where they managed to go penalty free.

Sunday's win over Widnes meant that the Firebees made sure of a 4th place finish in the league table and thus clinched the final spot in the end of season play offs.

WILD WOMENS TEAM END OF SEASON AWARDS

Following the conclusion of the women's ice hockey season, the Wild Ladies team held their end of season awards night.

The award for most points for the season went to Preston Gennoe, who joined the club last summer. She finished the campaign with 8 goals and 4 assists from 13 league and challenge games and also topped the club standings in penalties with 26.

The Wild Ladies player, coach and captain Leen de Decker – who holds the all time goals and appearances record in the World Championships for her native Belgium – was named Best Forward of the Year while the Best Defence award went to Vanessa Crickmore-Clarke.

Overworked netminder Stephanie Drinkwater – who faced more shots in the WPL than any other netminder this season, but also made more saves than anybody else – was Players' Player of the Season and Charlotte Cramp was Coach's Player of the Season.

Ellie Walsh-O'Neill - playing her first season of senior competition - was named most improved player.

The Wild Ladies team are now taking a well –earned break and will resume training for the new season on 19th July. New players – especially anybody with league experience – are always welcome.

WNIHL Division 2 North – Final Table 2022/23

Team	GP	W	L	T	GF	GA	PTS
Solway Sharks	14	14	0	0	105	20	28
Widnes Wild	14	11	3	0	95	48	22
Telford Wrekin Raiders	14	9	4	1	101	34	19
Leeds Roses	14	7	5	2	83	47	16
Whitley Bay Beacons B	13	4	7	2	26	46	10
Sheffield Shadows B	14	4	8	2	32	67	10
Grimsby Wolves	14	1	12	1	28	123	3
Kingston Diamonds C	13	1	12	0	25	110	2

Top Points Scorers

Player	Team	GP	G	A	Pts	PIM
C.J. Harrison	Leeds Roses	13	25	13	38	4
Leen de Decker	Widnes Wild	14	27	9	36	0
Katie Fairclough	Widnes Wild	13	20	12	32	10
Taylor Simmonds	Leeds Roses	11	9	22	31	4
KathTrachtenberg	Solway Sharks	8	19	8	27	4
Natalia Tamas	Telford Wrekin	9	12	14	26	2
Maureen Muir	Solway Sharks	12	11	14	25	4
Preston Gennoe	Widnes Wild	12	13	10	23	4
Emma Allender	Leeds Roses	13	15	6	21	8
Michelle Madziak	Telford Wrekin	9	14	7	21	2
Lauren Clark	Solway Sharks	12	12	8	20	6
Rose Abbott	Leeds Roses	13	11	7	18	6
Sarah Rowlands	Leeds Roses	13	9	9	18	2
Rachael Pearce	Widnes Wild	14	8	9	17	6

Top Netminders (Min 5 games)

Netminder	Team	GPI	TOI	SVS	GA	GAA	SV%	SO
Elizabeth Meikle	SOL	11	660	204	12	1.09	94.40	4
Teagan Hyatt	TEL	10	600	261	21	2.1	92.6	3
Stephanie Drinkwater	WID	8	384	163	17	2.66	90.6	0
Ellie Green	WID	6	217	109	11	3.05	90.8	0
Megan Quigley	LEE	5	300	173	18	3.6	90.6	0
Jessica Kinghorn	WHI	7	420	363	31	4.42	92.1	0
Shannon Schneider	SHE	9	540	314	40	4.44	88.7	0
Ruth Palmer	GRI / LEE	9	540	408	72	8	85	0
Lucy Noble	KIN	9	511	350	79	9.29	81.6	0

Note: Placed in order of GAA. SV% gives a different result.

DMUK Widnes Wild Women Fixtures & Results – 2022/23

Date	Comp	Home			Away	WDL
01/10/2022	D2N	Solway Sharks	8	4	Widnes Wild	L
16/10/2022	D2N	Widnes Wild	9	0	Whitley Bay	W
30/10/2022	D2N	Widnes Wild	7	5	Sheffield Shadows	W
20/11/2022	D2N	Leeds Roses	1	9	Widnes Wild	W
27/11/2022	D2N	Whitley Bay	0	1	Widnes Wild	Wab*
08/01/2023	D2N	Widnes Wild	5	4	Telford Wrekin	W
21/01/2023	D2N	Telford Wrekin	11	1	Widnes Wild	L
29/01/2023	D2N	Sheffield Shadows	1	4	Widnes Wild	W
05/02/2023	D2N	Widnes Wild	15	2	Kingston Diamonds	W
18/02/2023	D2N	Grimsby Wolves	5	12	Widnes Wild	W
05/03/2022	D2N	Widnes Wild	7	2	Grimsby Wolves	W
26/03/2023	D2N	Widnes Wild	0	6	Solway Sharks	L
02/04/2023	D2N	Kingston Diamonds	1	12	Widnes Wild	W
23/04/2023	D2N	Widnes Wild	9	2	Leeds Roses	W
27/05/2023	POSF	Cardiff Comets	3	1	Widnes Wild	L

Note: The away game at Whitley was abandoned on 25 minutes after a player injury. The score was 0-1 to Widnes at the time and the result was allowed to stand.*

2022/23 Season Introduction

The Widnes Wild Ladies team are now in their 8th year – but only their 7th competitive season as the league was suspended for 2020/21 due to Covid restrictions.

In the wake of an eventful year in the Women's Premier League and a subsequent rebranding of the leagues during the summer, the Wild Women will be playing in the new WNIHL Division 2 North for the new 2022/23 season.

It is an 8-team league with each team playing all the others once home and once away and the new division will see the Ladies' team renew acquaintances with previous adversaries such as Solway, Whitley, Telford, Sheffield and Grimsby with new teams from Kingston (Hull) and Leeds.

The Wild Ladies team were league champions when they last played at this level in the 2019/20 season and there is much to look forward to this season as well.

101 And Counting!

The 2023 Play Off Semi Final was the team's 101st match since forming as the Wild Women for the start of the 2015/16 season.

In that time they have won 34 games, lost 56 and drawn 11 – scoring 389 goals and conceding 562.

The 101 figure purposely ignores the fact that the away game at Chelmsford in April 2019 was not actually played and awarded as a 5-0 win to the opposition after the time and venue were changed at the last minute, and that the away game at Nottingham in April 2020 was cancelled due to the Covid Pandemic and awarded as a 0-0 draw.

Both games were included as results in the final league tables, so make of it what you will...

DMUK Widnes Wild Women's Team - Season 2022/23 (Photo by Wil Evans)
Back Row: Adam Lappin (Head Coach), Sophia Green, Laura Marcroft, Suzie Miller, Catherine Fell, Rachael Pearce, Preston Gennoe, Natalie Buckles, Karyn Cooper, Charlotte Cramp, Katie Adshead, Jennifer Hickey, Victoria Connelly, Steve Furber (Coach).
Front Row: Lucy Kirkham, Lise Gillen, Danielle Skilander, Stephanie Drinkwater, Vanessa Crickmore-Clarke, Leen de Decker, Katie Fairclough, Ellie Green, Phoebe Patient, Ellen Tyrer, Pauline Hayward.

Widnes Wild Women Player Statistics – Season 2022/23
Regular Season Only

	GP	G	A	Pts	PIM
Leen de Decker	14	24	11	34	0
Katie Fairclough	13	20	12	32	10
Preston Gennoe	12	13	10	23	4
Rachael Pearce	14	8	9	17	6
Charlotte Cramp	14	2	9	11	0
Danielle Skilander	12	5	6	11	0
Lucy Kirkham	12	2	8	10	0
Laura Marcroft	13	4	3	7	0
Phoebe Patient	13	3	3	6	0
Catherine Fell	11	0	6	6	6
Lise Gillen	10	2	4	6	0
Sophia Green	7	1	5	6	12
Ellen Tyrer	12	2	3	5	0
Victoria Connelly	10	3	2	5	6
Jennifer Hickey	14	1	3	4	2
Katie Adshead	13	1	3	4	6
Sav Sumner	3	2	1	3	2
Karyn Cooper	13	0	2	2	2
Suzie Miller	10	0	2	2	0
Elizabeth Loss	9	0	2	2	0
Vanessa Crickmore-Clarke	8	1	0	1	6
Natalie Buckles	6	1	0	1	2
Pauline Hayward	2	0	1	1	0
Stephanie Drinkwater	10	0	0	0	0
Olivia Wilson	9	0	0	0	0
Ellie Green	8	0	0	0	0
Rebecca Donnelley	3	0	0	0	0
Sophie Hill	1	0	0	0	0

Widnes Wild Women Player Statistics – Season 2022/23

	League		POSF		All Games				
	GP	Pts	GP	Pts	GP	G	A	Pts	PIM
Leen de Decker	14	34	1	1	15	25	11	35	0
Katie Fairclough	13	32	1	0	14	20	12	32	10
Preston Gennoe	12	23	1	0	13	13	10	23	6
Rachael Pearce	14	17	1	1	15	8	10	18	6
Charlotte Cramp	14	11	1	1	15	2	10	12	0
Danielle Skilander	12	11	1	0	13	5	6	11	0
Lucy Kirkham	12	10	1	0	13	2	8	10	0
Laura Marcroft	13	7	1	0	14	4	3	7	0
Phoebe Patient	13	6	1	0	14	3	3	6	0
Catherine Fell	11	6	1	0	12	0	6	6	6
Lise Gillen	10	6	0	0	10	2	4	6	0
Sophia Green	7	6	1	0	8	1	5	6	12
Ellen Tyrer	12	5	1	0	13	2	3	5	0
Victoria Connelly	10	5	0	0	10	3	2	5	6
Jennifer Hickey	14	4	1	0	15	1	3	4	2
Katie Adsead	13	4	1	0	14	1	3	4	6
Sav Sumner	3	3	0	0	3	2	1	3	2
Karyn Cooper	13	2	1	0	14	0	2	2	2
Suzie Miller	10	2	1	0	11	0	2	2	0
Elizabeth Loss	9	2	1	0	10	0	2	2	0
Vanessa C/m-Clarke	8	1	1	0	9	1	0	1	6
Natalie Buckles	6	1	1	0	7	1	0	1	2
Pauline Hayward	2	1	0	0	2	0	1	1	0
Stephanie Drinkwater	10	0	1	0	11	0	0	0	0
Olivia Wilson	9	0	1	0	10	0	0	0	0
Ellie Green	8	0	1	0	9	0	0	0	0
Rebecca Donnelley	3	0	0	0	3	0	0	0	0
Sophie Hill	1	0	0	0	1	0	0	0	0

Netminder Statistics – All Games

Netminder	Comp	GPI	Mins	SA	GA	GAA	SA%	SO
Charlotte Cramp	D2N	1	60	32	8	8	75	0
Ellie Green	D2N	7	276.5	135	12	2.6	91.11	1
	POSF	1	27.25	32	0	0.00	100.00	1
	Total	8	303.75	167	12	2.37	92.81	1
Rebecca Donnelley	D2N	2	85	43	11	7.76	74.42	1
Steph Drinkwater	D2N	8	383.5	172	17	2.66	90.12	1
	POSF	1	32.75	35	3	5.50	91.43	0
	Total	9	416.25	207	20	2.88	90.34	1

Netminding Breakdown – Season 2022/23

Game	Netminder	GPI	Mins	SA	GA	GAA	Sv%
Away @ Solway	Cramp	1	60	32	8	8.00	75.00
Home v Whitley	Drinkwater	1	32	5	0	0.00	100.00
	Green	1	28	5	0	0.00	100.00
Home v Sheffield	Drinkwater	1	60	28	5	5.00	82.14
Away @ Leeds	Green	1	60	15	1	1.00	93.33
Away @ Whitley	Donnelly	1	25	12	0	0.00	100.00
Home v Telford	Drinkwater	1	30	20	0	0.00	100.00
	Green	1	30	20	4	8.00	80.00
Away @ Telford	Donnelly	1	60	31	11	11.00	64.52
Away @ Sheffield	Drinkwater	1	60	18	1	1.00	94.44
Home v Kingston	Drinkwater	1	31	15	2	3.87	86.67
	Green	1	29	9	0	0.00	100.00
Away @ Grimsby	Green	1	60	54	5	5.00	90.74
Home v Grimsby	Green	1	60	29	2	2.00	93.10
Home v Solway	Drinkwater	1	60	40	6	6.00	85.00
Away @ Kingston	Drinkwater	1	60	28	1	1.00	96.43
Home v Leeds	Drinkwater	1	50	18	2	2.40	88.89
	Green	1	10	3	0	0.00	100.00
POSF V Cardiff	Drinkwater	1	32	38	3	5.63	92.11
	Green	1	28	12	0	0.00	100.00

The Wild women in action away at Solway
(Photo by Mad Mac Photography)

Saturday 1st October 2022 – WNIHL Div 2 (N)
Solway Sharks Ladies 8 - Widnes Wild Ladies 4

The Widnes Wild Ladies team put in a battling performance away to Solway Sharks Ladies in Dumfries on Saturday in their first league game of the new season but ultimately lost out 8-4.

As is usual in ice hockey, there has been a lot of player movement during the summer months and this game saw Wild debuts for three new signings.

Canadian born Lise Gillen hails from Victoria, British Columbia, and recently played 3 seasons for Guildford Lightning in the English Women's Elite League.

Joining her on the Wild bench for the game were Victoria Connelly, who has also played Elite League hockey for

Guildford and Rachael Pearce who has previously played for Blackburn Thunder.

Sophia Green, who also plays for the Wild Academy Under 16 team, was given her first senior women's call up and the squad was further boosted by the return of former Wild women's players Lucy Kirkham - who has spent a few years away from league hockey - and Sav Sumner, who played last season with Whitley in the Elite League.

The game itself was much closer than the final scoreline suggests and Widnes were hampered by the fact that they didn't have a recognised netminder available to make the trip north of the border.

In the end, attacking player Charlotte Cramp bravely donned the pads – having only ever gone in goal once before in a training session – and went on to give a very good account of herself.

Solway took the lead after 3 minutes but Widnes equalised just 60 seconds later with a goal from last season's top scorer Preston Gennoe.

The Wild Ladies took the lead with a goal from Leen de Decker in the 6th minute but were eventually pegged back and the score stood at 2-2 at the first period break.

Widnes took the lead again on 25 minutes with a second goal from Gennoe but the hosts fought back and three unanswered goals within 4 minutes of each other saw them leading 5-3 at the end of the second period.

Solway extended the lead to 6-3 on 46 minutes but a hat-trick goal for Gennoe on 50 minutes gave the Wild Ladies hope of mounting a late fight back.

Unfortunately, while they were pressing forward in an attempt to salvage something from the game, Solway fired in two late goals – to give a final score of 8-4 to the Sharks.

After the game, stand-in netminder Charlotte Cramp was named MVP for the Wild after stopping 24 of the 32 shots that she faced.

Charlotte Cramp with the MVP award after playing in goal against Solway (Photo by Mad Mac Photography)

Wild Ladies team head coach Adam Lappin said afterwards:

"This was a very good first outing for this team and the new signings have brought a good depth to the squad."

"This would have been a different contest had we had our goalies available, but Charlotte Cramp has to be commended for stepping up and volunteering to play in goal; the score line did not reflect how well she played in her first game as a goalie!"

"We have a few points to work on from the game, but lots of positives for the Ladies to take away from today."

Lise Gillen receives the MVP award from match volunteer Rebecca Clayton (Photo by Paul Breeze)

Sunday 16th October 2022 - WNIHL Div 2N
Widnes Wild Ladies 9 – Whitley Bay Beacons 0

The Widnes Wild Ladies team put in superb performance in their first home game of the new WNIHL Division 2 North season beating last season's league champions Whitley Bay Beacons 9-0 at Planet Ice Widnes on Sunday.

Following a difficult year in the Women's Premier League last season - and with competitive ice hockey having been suspended before that due to the Covid pandemic - this was, in fact, their first women's league win since March 2020 and their first shut-out since a 0-2 win away in Nottingham back in December 2017, so there was a lot to be pleased about.

The game saw home debuts for summer signings Lise Gillen, Rachel Pearce and Victoria Connelly as well as the first senior appearance for 17 year old netminder Ellie Green, who played last season for the Wild Academy Under 18 team.

Widnes opened the scoring with just 79 seconds gone on the clock with a well taken goal from team captain and Belgian international Leen de Decker and the lead was doubled on 7 minutes with a strike from Katie Fairclough.

The Whitley team had travelled with a short bench while the Wild women had a full playing roster to ice so this game was pretty much one way traffic from the off. Widnes outshot the visitors by 34 to 2 in the first period and were it not for the efforts of Elite League netminder Jessica Kinghorn in the Beacons' net, the game would probably have been a complete rout.

As it was, de Decker made it 3-0 to Widnes with 3 minutes left in the first period and the score remained the same at the first break.

Three more goals followed in the opening stages of the second period – from de Decker, Preston Gennoe and Danielle Skilander – and Widnes looked comfortably in control. At the mid-point of the game, Ellie Green came on to take over in goal from Stephanie Drinkwater and, with the game already as good as won, the challenge was now to try and protect a much-coveted shut-out.

A goal for Ellen Tyrer with just 19 seconds to go in the period further extended the Widnes lead and the score stood at 7-0 at the second break.

The third period was pretty much all Widnes again as they outshot Whitley by 30 to 4. Two well taken goals by

Katie Fairclough gave her a hat-trick for the night and rounded off the scoring for the game.

The Kate Luard Memorial MVP awards – sponsored by Poet-in-Residence Lucy London – were presented by match timekeeper Rebecca Clayton and went to Rebecca Boardman for Whitley and Lise Gillen for Widnes.

Halton Huskies rec netminder Rebecca Donnelly played two games in goal for the Wild Women this season - the abandoned win away at Whitley and the defeat away at Telford (Photo by @haganovaphoto)

Ellen Tyrer, Ellie Green and Phoebe Patient showing off the new MVP awards for the season (Photo by Paul Breeze)

Lucy London Sponsors MVP Awards

The Widnes Wild Ladies team have some impressive new trophies for their Most Valuable Player (MVP) awards at their home games this season thanks to the continued sponsorship of the Wild club's Poet in Residence Lucy London.

This is the fourth year in a row that Lucy has sponsored the MVP awards for the Wild Women's ice hockey team's home matches and, in keeping with her other main activity – that of researching and raising awareness of the roles of women in the Great War - Lucy has decided to dedicate this year's awards to the memory of British nurse Kate Luard, RRC and Bar (1872 - 1962), who served for two years in South Africa during the Second Boer War (1899 - 1902) and then in France during the First World War.

Rachael Pearce in action against Sheffield (Photo by Wil Evans)

Sunday 30th October - WNIHL Div 2 N
Widnes Wild Ladies 7 – Sheffield Shadows 5

The Widnes Wild Ladies team gave their title challenge a boost with a highly entertaining 7-5 win over Sheffield Shadows at Planet Ice Widnes on Sunday.

The game saw a Wild league debut for Rebecca Donnelly and a first home appearance of the new campaign for Sav Sumner - who was the first ever Widnes born and trained player to play in a league ice hockey fixture in the town back in 2016 and is back with the Wild women after playing for Whitley Bay in the Women's Elite League last season.

This was a very topsy-turvy game with both teams playing with a lot of spirit and enthusiasm and fortunes quickly switching in the end to end encounter.

Sheffield actually took the lead on 6 minutes with a powerplay goal and then doubled the advantage just 90 seconds later to take a 0-2 lead into the first period break

Widnes flew out of the blocks for the second period and pulled a goal back after just 64 seconds with a strike from Sav Sumner - and then equalised 15 seconds later with a first Wild goal for summer signing Rachael Pearce.

A third goal followed just 90 seconds after that – a debut strike from Lise Gillen – and Widnes were suddenly in the lead.

After a fairly even first period in terms of shots on goal (17-10) and puck possession, Widnes had the upper hand for much of the second period. A Sheffield player picked up a 5 minute major penalty for boarding on 27 minutes and the Shadows had to play 4 on 5 for that entire time.

The Wild women piled the pressure on the Sheffield defence and looked as if they might score again at any moment. But the visitors held out and actually went on to score an equalising goal as soon as the 5 minute penalty had finished.

Despite Widnes having heavily outshot their opponents by 20 to 5 over the course of the second period, the score remained at a finely balanced 3-3 at the second break.

Widnes came out for the third period and edged back into the lead with a goal from Katie Fairclough on 42 minutes. A second goal for Fairclough followed 5 minutes later and then a strike from team captain Leen de Decker made the score 6-3 to Widnes with 12 minutes left to play.

Sheffield pulled back a short handed goal on the 50 minute mark but the Wild women re-established the 3-goal cushion with a second goal from de Decker just 49 seconds later. Another Shadows goal with just over 2 minutes left to play brought the score to 7-5 and meant that the closing stages were a little more nerve-wracking than they might otherwise have been but the Widnes Ladies held on to secure a well earned victory.

The Kate Luard Memorial MVP awards – sponsored by Poet-in-Residence Lucy London – were presented by match timekeeper Conner Dakin and went to Morgan Walker for Sheffield and Lucy Kirkham for Widnes.

MVPs Lucy Kirkham (left) and Morgan Walker

Preston Gennoe scored 2 goals away at Leeds
(Photo by Mad Mac Photography)

Sunday 20th November 2022 – WNIHL Div 2 N
Leeds Roses 1 - Widnes Wild Ladies 9

The Widnes Wild Ladies team moved clear into second place in the WNIHL North 2 league table after an emphatic 1-9 away win over Leeds Roses on Sunday.

The Roses are a new team in the league for this season and this was the Wild Ladies first ever visit to the new Leeds rink so this encounter was always going to be a bit of an unknown quantity.

Widnes took the lead with a goal from Charlotte Cramp after 80 seconds and made it 0-2 with a strike from captain Leen de Decker on 8 minutes.

Three more Widnes goals followed in the first period – from Preston Gennoe on 9 minutes, Laura Marcroft on 14 and Victoria Connelly just 44 seconds after that – before

Leeds finally found the back of the net themselves and the score stood at 1-5 at the first period break.

A powerplay goal from Sav Sumner on 25 minutes was the only goal in the second period and Widnes looked well in control heading into the third with a 1-6 lead.

Leen de Decker scored her second goal of the game 3 minutes into the third period and Lisa Gillen further extended the lead on 50 minutes. Preston Gennoe completed her brace in the 57th minute and that rounded off the scoring for the match, handing Widnes an impressive 1-9 victory in their first ever visit to Leeds.

The win sees the Wild women in second place in the league table with 6 points from their 4 league games to date. Early season leaders Solway Sharks Ladies are 2 points ahead with a 100% record of 4 wins from 4 starts.

Sunday 27th November 2022 – WNIHL Div 2 N
Whitley Bay Beacons 0 – Widnes Wild Ladies 1

The Widnes Wild Ladies team's game away at Whitley Bay on Sunday was abandoned 5 minutes into the second period after a player injury. The Wild women were leading 0-1 at the time.

Following various failed attempts to rearrange the game, the league management committee decided to award it as a 0-1 win to Widnes.

Leen de Decker scored the single goal and Rebecca Donnelly picked up a shut-out for her 25 minute stint in goal.

Wild Women's head coach Adam Lappin on the bench (Photo by Wil Evans)

WILD LADIES TEAM SET TO RENEW TITLE CHALLENGE

The Widnes Wild Ladies team return to match action this Sunday 8th January with a crunch home game against the Telford Wrekin Raiders at Planet Ice Widnes, 4.15pm face off.

Telford have historically been one of the top teams in this division and the last time that the Wild women played at this level, they were locked in a 3-way battle for the top places with the Raiders and Solway Ladies for most of the season.

It is still early days in the women's leagues and Widnes have only played 4 games out of their 16-match regular schedule so far. They currently occupy 3rd place in the

WNIHL North 2 table with 3 wins out of 4 and are 1 point behind Telford, who have played the same number of games, and 4 points behind early leaders Solway who have played 2 games more.

Telford finished off the calendar year with home and away wins over Grimsby while the Wild women haven't completed a competitive game since their win away to Leeds in mid-November.

Wild Ladies head coach Adam Lappin explained how the team have been preparing for this Sunday's game – and who he thinks are the teams to watch this season:

"We have been training regularly and continuing with our structured programme. We, as a coaching team, have looked at the lessons identified from previous games to tailor the training needs and requirements of the team."

"Things can move quite quickly in this league so any team can produce great results, but Solway are always strong contenders in this league, as are Whitley. Telford were tough opponents last time we played them, so we will see what they bring to the next home game."

As with every year in British ice hockey, the Ladies team saw a number of players join their ranks for this season and the team has an exciting blend of youth and experience. Talking about the strength of the Widnes roster this season, Lappin said:

"There have been a number of new players, but also a number of returning players from previous seasons. They have settled in well and have very quickly adjusted to the team ethos and work ethic. They have each brought something to the team, and this has contributed very much to the successes we have seen in the latter part of 2022."

"I am extremely happy with the ladies we have. Whether they are younger or more experienced players, they all contribute well to the squad as a whole. It has ensured a depth and resilience to the squad, which has in turn enabled us to take an almost full roster to every away game so far this season; a luxury I am sure most other teams do not have!"

As regards his own involvement with the Widnes Ladies team, Lappin said:

"Having been appointed as Head Coach at the start of the pre-season, on the back of a difficult stint in the Premier Division last season, it has been a real privilege to be part of our growth so far this season. From a good recruitment drive over the off season, to the four weeks of pre-season training, leading into a very positive start to this year's campaign, the players and coaching staff have worked together well to work on set lines and flowing team hockey.

"This team is coming together very well, not just as a group of players who train and compete together, but also as an extended family. This is a very good baseline for the rest of the season and the seasons to come. I can see us in the top third this season, with a very realistic chance of a playoff place. Looking into the next season and beyond, I can see this team staying strong. That is a combination of the players, coaching staff and management committee, which contributes to the successes of the wider team. We have a good dynamic, which is only getting stronger and increasingly more fun to be a part of."

The Wild Ladies team are at home this Sunday 8th January when they take on Telford, 4.15pm face off.

Wild woman Charlotte Cramp receives the MVP award from match volunteer Howard Smith (Photo by Paul Breeze)

Sunday 8th January – WNIHL Div 2 N
Widnes Wild Women 5 – Telford Wrekin Raiders 4

The Widnes Wild ladies team got the new year off to a flying start with a 5-4 victory over title rivals Telford Wrekin Raiders at Planet Ice Widnes on Sunday.

The last time that the Wild women played at this level, they spent the majority of the season locked in a three-way battle for the title with Solway Sharks and Telford, so positive results against those teams are vitally important if the Ladies are to mount a serious challenge again this season.

The opening phase was very close - with both teams testing each other out - and the first goal did not come until the 13th minute when Katy Fairclough finally broke the deadlock in Widnes' favour.

A second Fairclough goal followed with just 29 seconds left in the period and Widnes were able to take a 2 goal lead into the first break.

The Widnes attack looked formidable in these early stages and they went 3-0 up on 26 minutes with a goal from captain Leen de Decker. Telford had their own chances in front of goal and gained more puck possession as the game went on, but they were thwarted at every turn as Wild netminder Stephanie Drinkwater performed heroics to keep them out.

A 4th goal at the mid-way point in the game scored by Danielle Skilander looked to have put Widnes well in charge but things can change very quickly in ice hockey.

A routine netminder change saw 18 year old Ellie Green take over from Drinkwater in the Wild goal. Telford thought they had scored with their very next attack but Green managed to smother the puck and, after some discussion, the match officials decided that it hadn't crossed the line.

Just 2 minutes later, Widnes went 5 goals ahead with a second strike of the game from De Decker and looked to be cruising but Telford had other ideas.

After a roller-coaster second period during which they actually outshot the Wild team by 2 to 1, the Raiders eventually scored their first goal of the game in the 37th minute

Widnes still looked pretty secure with a 5-1 lead after two periods but Telford scored again just 2 minutes after the restart – and alarm bells began to ring.

Two more goals followed for Telford on 54 and 56 minutes with the clock ticking down much slower than anybody in the Widnes camp would have liked. The Wild bench called a timeout after the 4th Telford goal to discuss last gasp defensive tactics and the tension around the rink went up a couple of notches.

Telford put in a battling display in the last few minutes but the Widnes defence stood strong and held out to secure the win.

The Kate Luard Memorial MVP awards – sponsored by Poet-in-Residence Lucy London – were presented by match timekeeper Howard Smith and went to Tegan Hyatt for Telford and Charlotte Cramp for Widnes.

The result sees the Widnes Ladies leapfrog Telford into second place in the Division 2 North table with 4 wins from 5 games. Leeds Roses also move above Telford after their 7-0 win over Whitley at the weekend and join Widnes on 8 points. Solway Sharks Ladies currently lead the table with 10 points, having won all 5 of their league games to date.

The Wild women are next in action on Saturday 21st January when they play the return match away in Telford and they are then away to Sheffield on Sunday 29th January. They are next at home on Sunday 5th February when they take on Kingston Diamonds at Planet Ice Widnes, 4.15pm face off.

Saturday 21st January – WNIHL Div 2 N
Telford Wrekin Raiders 11 – DMUK Widnes Wild Women 1

The DMUK Widnes Wild women's team lost ground at the top of the league table after an 11-1 away defeat at the hands of fellow title chasers Telford Wrekin Raiders.

Despite the one-sided scoreline, the Wild ladies didn't, in fact, play badly and actually matched their hosts in terms of shots on goal during the game as a whole.

The difference was in the finishing in front of goal and Telford took the lead after just 32 seconds of the game. The score was 5-0 at the end of the first period and 7-0 at the end of the second.

The Raiders had racked up a 10-0 lead by the time that Widnes scored their consolation goal on 57 minutes and that came from the stick of Phoebe Patient – her first goal for the club. An extra strike for the home side with 70 seconds left to play rounded off the scoring for the game.

The result sees Telford replace Widnes in 3rd place in the league table with the Wild Ladies now 4 points behind unbeaten leaders Solway Sharks, having played the same number of games.

The chasing pack are still very closely matched with second placed team Leeds with 10 points from 8 games, Telford with 9 from 6 and Widnes with 8 from 6.

The Wild women are next in action on Sunday 29th January when they are away to Sheffield Shadows. They are next at home on Sunday 5th February when they take on Kingston Diamonds of Hull at Planet Ice Widnes, 4.15pm face off.

Katie Fairclough, Ellie Green and Ellen Tyrer show off the new DMUK sponsored playing shirts (Photo by Paul Breeze)

DMUK Sponsor the Wild Women

The Wild ladies' team have agreed a title sponsorship deal with Sale-based company Debt Movement UK to run for the rest of the season. The team will now be known as the "DMUK Widnes Wild Women" and they have smart new playing shirts bearing the company logo.

DMUK provide professional debt guidance and solutions that help people move out of debt. This empowers people to take control of their finances so they can live their best lives again.

The team wore the home shirts for the first time in their last home game against Telford and the new away shirt on Sunday but both will be formally launched at the women's next home game on 5th February when representatives of DMUK will be present as VIP guests.

Sunday 29th January - WNIHL North 2
Sheffield Shadows 1 – DMUK Widnes Wild Women 4

The DMUK Widnes Wild Women moved up to second place in the Division2 North league table after a 1-4 win away over Sheffield Scimitars on Sunday.

Widnes were comfortably on top for much of the game, outshooting their hosts by almost 3 to 1, and their first goal came from Rachael Pearce in the 8th minute. The score remained 0-1 at the first period break but the Wild women edged further ahead just 54 seconds from the restart with a goal from Katie Fairclough.

Six minutes later, it was 0-3 to Widnes with a goal from Preston Gennoe but Sheffield eventually found the back of the net themselves at the mid-way point of the game and the score stood at 1-3 at the end of the second period.

The only goal of the third period came on 55 minutes and was scored by Leen de Decker to hand the Wild women a useful 1-4 victory.

The win sees the Wild women move up into second place in the league table, overtaking both Telford and Leeds who didn't play at the weekend. The only other game in the division saw Solway Sharks Ladies win 2-4 away at Kingston, which means they lead the table with a 100% record of 7 wins from 7 starts. Widnes are 4 points behind them, having played the same number of games.

The DMUK Wild Women are next in action this Sunday 5th February when they take on the Kingston Diamonds at Planet Ice Widnes, 4.15pm face off. Representatives from the new team sponsors Debt Movement UK will be in attendance as VIP guests to formally launch the new DMUK branded home and away shirts.

Widnes netminder Stephanie Drinkwater makes a save against Kingston (Photo by Wil Evans)

Sunday 5th February 2023 – WNIHL Div 2 (N)
Widnes Wild Women 15 – Kingston Diamonds 2

The DMUK Widnes Wild women's team notched up a comprehensive 15-2 victory in a bad tempered encounter with the Hull–based Kingston Diamonds at Planet Ice Widnes on Sunday.

Widnes got off to a flying start and took the lead with a Preston Gennoe goal after just 53 seconds. Team captain Leen de Decker doubled the advantage on 6 minutes and Katie Fairclough made it 3-0 to the Wild women 6 minutes later. Hull pulled a goal back on 14 minutes to stay in contention and the score stood at 3-1 at the first period break

Widnes remained the dominant force in the second period, although the Hull team never gave up and did give a good account of themselves in patches. Katie

Adshead scored her first ever Widnes goal on 23 minutes and Victoria Connelly edged the Wild women further ahead with a goal just 27 seconds later. This was countered on 25 minutes by another Kingston strike to bring the score to 5-2 but then the floodgates opened and the Wild women fired in 5 unanswered goals in an incredible 5 minute spell.

A second strike for Connelly was followed up by a first senior goal for Sophia Green, then two more for Katie Fairclough and second of the game for de Decker racked the score up to 10-2 by the end of the second period.

The Widnes "goal rush" continued in the third period with a second strike from Gennoe just 79 seconds from the restart, a goal for Laura Marcroft 90 seconds later and a hat-trick goal for Gennoe 104 seconds after that.

Katie Fairclough scored her 4th goal of the game in the 50th minute and then things started to get a bit "tetchy". With the score standing at 14-2 with just 10 minutes left to play, the game was obviously out of the reach of the struggling Diamonds team and some of the niggles that had started earlier in the game began to surface.

At 50.50 on the clock a mass scuffle broke out in the corner by the Diamonds goal involving most of the players on the ice. This is quite unusual in the normally sedate "non-contact " sport of women's ice hockey and it took the match officials a little while to sort things out.

The Kingston instigator of the melée was given a 5 + game penalty for fighting while Sophia Green had to sit out a 10 minute misconduct for Widnes.

The scoring for the game was rounded off with a 5th goal for Fairclough with just 58 seconds left to play and the Wild women were able to celebrate their biggest margin of victory since they beat Nottingham Vipers 15-1 back in January 2020 in their Division 1 North title winning season.

The Kate Luard Memorial MVP awards – sponsored by Poet-in-Residence Lucy London – were presented by special guests Laura Prescott and her daughter Emily. Laura is the CEO of Debt Movement UK who are the Wild womens' team's title sponsors for the season. The awards went to Tiya Dhillon for Kingston and Karyn Cooper for Widnes.

The DMUK Widnes Wild Women are next in action on Saturday 18th February when travel to Lincolnshire to play the Grimsby Wolves. They are next at home on Sunday 5th March when they face the same opposition at Planet Ice Widnes, 4.15pm face off.

Karyn Cooper receives the Widnes MVP award from VIP guests Laura and Emily Prescott (Photo by Paul Breeze)

Laura Prescott from Debt Movement UK officially presents the sponsored shirts to Wild players Danielle Skilander and Karyn Cooper, helped by her daughter Emily (Photo by Paul Breeze)

Saturday 18th February – WNIHL Div 2 North
Grimsby Wolves 5 – DMUK Widnes Wild Women 12

The DMUK Widnes Wild women's team kept up the pressure at the top of the Division 2 North table with a 5-12 away win over Grimsby Wolves on Saturday.

The Lincolnshire side had only won one game all season and were bottom of the league table before this game, so a Widnes win always looked on the cards but the Grimsby ice surface is famously small and difficult to play on and the Wild women still had a job to do.

The Wild took the lead after just 93 seconds with a goal from Charlotte Cramp and then doubled the advantage with a Leen de Decker strike on 7 minutes.

Grimsby pulled a goal back just 43 seconds later and went on to equalise on 11 minutes but a goal from Phoebe Patient on 17 minutes saw the Wild women take a slender 2-3 lead into the first period break.

The Wolves equalised again just 2 minutes into the second period but Widnes edged back into the lead with a goal from Katie Fairclough 30 seconds later and further widened the gap with a second goal from de Decker on 30 minutes and strikes from Ellen Tyrer and Lucy Kirkham.

With the score standing at 3-7 to Widnes after 2 periods, the Wild women now had a bit of breathing space with 20 minutes left to play. Three unanswered goals followed for Widnes early in the third period with a strike from de Decker - for her hat-trick - Laura Marcroft and de Decker again.

Grimsby scored again to bring the score back to 4-10 but the game was well and truly over as a contest by that point. A second goal for Katie Fairclough and a fifth of the game for Leen de Decker raised the Wild tally to a dozen and a 5th goal for the hosts on 57 minutes rounded off the scoring for the game.

Sunday 5th March – WNIHL Division 2 North
DMUK Widnes Wild Women 7 – Grimsby Wolves 2

The DMUK Widnes Wild women made it 4 wins in a row with a 7-2 victory over the league's bottom team Grimsby Wolves at Planet Ice Widnes on Sunday.

Despite the comfortable final winning margin, the Grimsby team gave a good account of themselves and matched the Wild for lengthy spells before finally running out of steam later in the game. In fact, it was the visitors who were quickest out of the blocks and they scored with their very first attack after 44 seconds.

Widnes eventually equalised on 6 minutes with a goal from Preston Gennoe but the Wolves edged ahead again on 16 minutes and took a 1-2 lead into the first period break.

The Wild women began to stamp their authority on the game more in the second period and a goal from Laura Marcroft on 28 minutes tied the score at 2-2. Two further goals late in the period – a powerplay strike from Vanessa Crickmore-Clarke and a goal from team captain Leen de Decker – put some daylight between the two teams and the Wild women led 4-2 at the second break.

A goal on 42 minutes from Ellen Tyrer increased the Widnes lead still further and two more for Leen de Decker, giving her a hat-trick, rounded off the scoring for the match.

The Kate Luard Memorial MVP awards – sponsored by Poet-in-Residence Lucy London – were presented by match volunteer Howard Smith and went to Sophie Hill for Widnes and the netminder for Grimsby.

Laura Marcroft in action for Widnes against Grimsby (Photo by Annie Bennison)

Sophie Hill receives the Widnes MVP award from Howard Smith (Photo by Paul Breeze)

Stephanie Drinkwater receives the Wild MVP award against Solway from match volunteer Andy Patient (Photo by Paul Breeze)

Sunday 26th March 2023 – WNIHL Div2 N
Widnes Wild Women 0 – Solway Sharks Ladies 6

The DMUK Widnes Wild women's team put in a spirited performance in their top of the table clash with league leaders Solway Sharks Ladies but ultimately slumped to a disappointing 0-6 defeat at Planet Ice Widnes on Sunday.

The game actually started well for the Wild women and they gave as good as they got in the early stages. When Solway finally opened the scoring in the 12th minute, it felt as if it was against the run of play and, even when they doubled their advantage less than 60 seconds after that, it only seemed to be a blip in what still promised to be a closely contested game between the two title contenders.

Unfortunately, this "blip" continued into the second period and Solway edged further ahead with a third goal just 80 seconds from the restart. Widnes had their own chances but were unable to break down a very solid Solway defence and the score remained a frustrating 0-3 at the second period break.

The latter half of the game was littered with minor penalties for both sides as things began to get niggly but Solway coped the better with the disruption and scored three more unanswered goals in the third period.

The Kate Luard Memorial MVP awards – sponsored by Poet-in-Residence Lucy London – were presented by match volunteer Andy Patient and went to Rosaline Adey for Solway and netminder Stephanie Drinkwater for Widnes.

Sunday's result sees Solway extend their impressive 100% record for the season to 11 wins from 11 starts with a 4 point advantage at the top of the league table.

Widnes remain in second place but, with only two games left to play, are now unable to overtake the Sharks to win the league title.

There is still plenty to play for, however, as the top two finishing teams in the league will qualify for the end of season play offs with a chance to win promotion to Division 1 for next season.

As things stand, there is a 3-way battle for the two play off places between Widnes, Solway and Telford Wrekin Raiders. Telford are currently in 3rd place but have games in hand over the top two teams. They still have a slim mathematical chance of winning the league title and play Solway on 6th May in a game that will go a long way towards deciding the league's final top three.

Sunday 2nd April – WNIHL Div 2 N
Kingston Diamonds 1 – Widnes Wild Women 12

The DMUK Widnes Wild women's team bounced back from their disappointing home defeat against Solway Sharks last week to notch up a comprehensive 1-12 win away to Kingston Diamonds in Hull on Sunday.

The Wild women were on top from the start and outshot their hosts by 76 to 28 over the course of the 60 minutes. Preston Gennoe opened the scoring for Widnes with just 78 seconds on the clock and further goals from Katie Fairclough and Rachael Pearce saw them leading comfortably 0-3 at the first period break.

The - largely - one way traffic continued in the second period and a second Gennoe goal followed 70 seconds from the restart.

Two more goals from Pearce, one from Jennifer Hickey and from captain Leen de Decker just 9 seconds after that gave the Wild women an 8-goal lead before Kingston scored what was to be their only goal of the game on 38 minutes.

The third period saw two more goals each for Fairclough and de Decker, meaning that along with Rachael Pearce, three Wild players scored hat-tricks in the game.

The 1-12 win means that Widnes remain in second place in the league table, 2 points behind leaders Solway who have games in hand.

The Wild women play their last game of the regular season on Sunday 23rd April when they take on Leeds Roses at Planet Ice Widnes, 4.25pm face off, in a game that they need to win to have a chance of reaching the end of season play offs.

Natalie Buckles receives the Widnes MVP award from match volunteer Helen Patient (Photo by Paul Breeze)

Sunday 23rd April – WNIHL North 2
DMUK Widnes Wild Women 9 – Leeds Roses 2

The DMUK Widnes Wild women's team rounded off their regular season with a comprehensive 9-2 win over Leeds Roses at Planet Ice Widnes on Sunday.

Leeds are a new team in the league this season, so it was their first visit to Widnes and the outcome was especially important as the Wild women needed a win to improve their chances of reaching the end of season play offs.

Despite the somewhat one-sided final scoreline, this was a very entertaining game to watch, with plenty of flowing end to end hockey, and the fledgling Leeds team gave a very good account of themselves.

Widnes took the lead on 8 minutes with a goal from Rachael Pearce but the Roses struck back with an equaliser straight from the resulting face off.

It took another 10 minutes for the Wild women to break down the stubborn Leeds defence again and they edged back into the lead on 18 minutes with a strike from Lucy Kirkham.

Some late pressure on the Leeds net as the clock ticked down towards the end of the period paid off as Leen de Decker forced home another goal with just 6 seconds left to play and Widnes led 3-1 at the first break.

The second period was all Widnes and they scored 4 unanswered goals – from de Decker, Natalie Buckles (her first ever competitive goal for the Wild women), Katie Fairclough and Pearce – to lead comfortably 7-1 at second break.

Leeds scored their second, and final, goal of the game 44 seconds into the third period but the 6 goal cushion was restored just 49 seconds after that with a hat-trick goal from Rachael Pearce.

The tempo eased off somewhat after that as the result was, by then, fairly clear cut and Ellie Green came in goal for Widnes for the final 10 minutes, making some impressive saves to register a cameo "shut out".

A second goal of the game from Katie Fairclough with 72 seconds left on the clock rounded off the scoring for the match and the Wild women were able to celebrate a 9-2 victory.

The result means that Widnes remain in second place in the league table behind Solway Sharks who have already been confirmed champions.

The Wild women have a good chance of qualifying for the end of season play offs, which will be held in Sheffield at the end of May, but that is now out of their hands.

Telford Wrekin Raiders – who are currently in third place – have games yet to play and, if they win all of their remaining matches, they will overtake Widnes as runners up and secure the other play off spot.

The Kate Luard Memorial MVP awards for Sunday's game – sponsored by Poet-in-Residence Lucy London – were presented by match volunteer Helen Patient and went to Rosie Steedman for Leeds and Natalie Buckles for Widnes.

The Wild women's team after their last league game of the season at home to Leeds (Photo by Paul Breeze)

Wild Women Qualify For Play Offs

The DMUK Widnes Wild women's team have qualified for the end of season play offs - to be held in Sheffield at the end of the Month.

They achieved this without even having to step out onto the ice after their closest rivals Telford lost a crunch match against already confirmed champions Solway Sharks, meaning that they will no longer be able to overtake the Wild Women in the league table.

The Widnes ladies had already finished their regular season schedule with a 9-2 win over Leeds Roses at the end of April but the WNIHL season runs until the end of May and other teams in the division still have games to complete. The Telford match result means that the Wild women are confirmed in second place in the table with 11 wins from their 14 league games, and can look forward to the Play Off weekend at iceSheffield.

This will be the first time that Widnes have appeared in the end of season tournament since 2017 when they finished 4th in the Women's Premier League and lost to Streatham Storm in the semi final. In the normal run of events, they would also have played in the 2020 tournament after having won the Division 1 North title that season but all sports were suspended due to the Covid pandemic and the Play Offs never took place.

This year's event will see the top two teams from Division 2 North – Solway and Widnes – take on the top two finishing teams from Division 2 south – Cardiff and Peterborough – in semi finals and final to decide an overall winner. The team that wins the final will also be eligible for promotion to Women's Division 1 for next season.

The women's play off weekend takes place at iceSheffield over the Bank Holiday Weekend of 27th to 29th May and features teams from all 6 women's competitions - Elite League, Division 1, Division 2 North and South and Under 16 girls North and South - with 13 games over the 3 days.

The WNIHL Division 2 Semi Finals take place at 6pm and 8.15pm on the Saturday and the final will be played at 3pm on the Sunday.

Leen de Decker in action against Grimsby
(Photo by Annie Bennison)

De Decker Leading Points Scorer Ahead Of Play Offs.

DMUK Widnes Wild women captain Leen de Decker finished up as the team's top points scorer for the regular season with 24 goals and 11 assists. The Belgium national team record holder for international appearances, she was one of four ever present players to have played in all 14 league games, along with Rachael Pearce, Charlotte Cramp and Jennifer Hickey.

De Decker was pushed all the way in the scoring standings by former GB Under18 international Katie Fairclough, who finished just 3 points behind with 20 goals and 12 assists from 13 games – including 2 hat tricks and an impressive 5-goal haul in the home game against Kingston Diamonds.

Last season's top scorer Preston Gennoe weighed in with 13 goals and 10 assists while Pearce, Cramp, Danielle Skilander and Lucy Kirkham also made double figures.

De Decker is one of the longest serving players on the Wild women's team, having been part of the group that moved to Widnes from Altrincham in 2015 to set up the new club.

Stephanie Drinkwater, Lucy Kirkham, Vanessa Crickmore-Clarke, Elizabeth Loss and Catherine Fell are the other founder member of the Wild women still to be playing with the club and, with a combined total of over 450 appearances between them, the team will be relying heavily on their experience when it comes to the play offs over the Bank Holiday weekend.

Wild woman Rachael Pearce scored back-to-back hat tricks in April – in the away game at Kingston Diamonds and the home game against Leeds Roses.

The Wild women's team at the WNIHL Play Offs
(Photo by Mike Lennon)

Saturday 27th May 2023 – Play Off Semi Final:
Cardiff Comets 3 – DMUK Widnes Wild Women 1

The DMUK Widnes Wild women put in a spirited performance against Cardiff Comets in the Division 2 Play Off semi final before losing out 3-1 at iceSheffield on Saturday.

This was first time that the Wild women had ever played against Cardiff, so they were very much an unknown quantity, and taking on the South Division champions was always likely to be a bit of an uphill struggle.

Widnes had featured in two playoff semi finals before – in the Women's Premier League back in 2016 and 2017 - and, on both occasions were beaten by Streatham but any hopes that this might have been a case of "third time lucky" were soon dashed as the Wild women got off to a nightmare start and conceded the first goal just 30 seconds into the game.

Two more Cardiff goals followed and Widnes were left trailing 3-0 at the end of the first period. They steadied the ship somewhat in the second - which played out goal-less - but this still left them with a metaphorical mountain to climb in the third period if they were to have any chance of progressing to the final.

Widnes had more of the play in the 3rd period and they were finally rewarded with a goal with 6 minutes left in the game when Leen de Decker beat the Cardiff netminder with a long range shot from out by the blue line.

The Wild women put the Cardiff net under increasing pressure in the latter stages, forcing several defensive penalties, but were unable to make the most of the resulting powerplay and the score remained 3-1 at the end of the game.

The other semi final saw D2 North champions Solway Sharks beat South runners up Peterborough 5-1 to reach the final, where they overcame Cardiff to take the overall Division 2 National title.

In the Division 1 play off final, Whitley Bay Beacons beat Swindon Topcats 5-1 while Solihull Vixens were beaten 1-3 by the Queen Bees in the Elite League final.

Laura Marcroft receives her Unsung Hero award from Thomas Horner (coach), Leen de Decker (captain) and Steve Furber (coach)

10th June: Wild Women's Awards Night

The DMUK Widnes Wild women's team recently held their end of season awards evening at the Village Hotel in Warrington, where the following accolades were presented for the 2022/23 season:

Coaches' Award - Charlotte Cramp
Best Defence - Lucy Kirkham
Best Forward - Phoebe Patient
Most Points - Leen De Decker
Players' Player - Charlotte Cramp
Unsung Hero - Laura Marcroft
Most Improved - Sophie Hill

Popular cult figure Pauline Hayward was also presented with a light hearted award for being the "Toughest Player" after continuing to play through the home game against Grimsby with a fractured patella!

The Wild Women's team at the 25th BWIHF Tournament in Bristol

24th & 25th June: Wild Women At Bristol Tournament

The DMUK Widnes Wild women's team enjoyed a roller coaster weekend down in the South west, as they took part in the annual BWIHF Tournament in Bristol for the first time since 2018.

The "Bristol Women's International Friendship Tournament" – to give its full title – is now in its 25th year and was played for a number of years at Swindon after the previous Bristol rink closed down and a replacement facility was being built.

It is a fairly unique competition as it involves teams from the different EIHA divisions – Elite League, Division 1 and Divisions 2 North & South - all playing against each other in one big qualifying group and there have been teams from abroad taking part in previous years as well.

This was the first time that the Wild women have taken part in the BWIF tournament since 2018 and they did fairly well on their previous visits, finishing second in the tournament in 2017 - where they lost out to the host Swindon Elite League team 3-0 in the final – and coming mid-table in 2018 but winning the Fair Play award.

The tournament is a veritable masterpiece of planning and logistics and this year's schedule features 10 teams playing a total of 48 games. The group games are just 15 minutes each in duration, with running clock, and the next game follows immediately afterwards with a brief pause for ice cutting at certain points during the day.

Over the course of the Saturday - and the early part of Sunday - all the teams play each other and the top four in the final group standings go on to play in semi-finals and then a final – played with a slightly longer match time - on the Sunday evening.

Widnes actually led the table after the first round of games after a 6-0 slaughtering of the Cardiff team who had beaten them in the Play Off semi final 4 weeks earlier.

An eye watering 20 shots peppered the Cardiff net over the 15 minute game and the goals came from Katie Fairclough (2), Lise Gillen (2), Catherine Fell & Rachael Pearce. Widnes netminder Stephanie Drinkwater ended up with the bizarre combination of a shut out and a 0% Save Percentage, as the overwhelmed Cardiff team didn't manage a single shot on goal.

The Wild women went on to draw 0-0 with Caledonia Steel Queens, lose 3-1 to Nottingham – with the Widnes goal coming from Ellen Tyrer - beat Streatham 1-0 (goal from Lise Gillen) and then lose 4-0 to hosts Bristol to end the day in 6th place in the table with 5 points from 5 games.

Sunday's group games saw a 3-0 win over Oxford – with goals from Katie Fairclough, Victoria Connelly and Leen de Decker - a 1-1 draw with the Firebees (goal from Rachael Pearce) and a 3-0 win over Coventry (Fairclough, Connelly & Laura Marcroft).

This led to an exciting finale in the group stage where Widnes played their last game knowing that they needed to beat Milton Keynes to climb into 4th place in the table and qualify for the semi final. Unfortunately, MK won that game 1-0 leaving the Wild women in 6th place overall out of 10 teams with a record of 4 wins, 3 losses and 2 draws.

The semi finals saw Bristol beat Caledonia 1-0 and Nottingham beat Milton Keynes 3-2. In a bit of a shock result, Nottingham then beat Bristol 3-2 in the final - the only game that the host team had lost all weekend.

Katie Fairclough was the Wild women's top points scorer for the weekend with 4 goals and 2 assists in the 9 group games. Leen de Decker was second with 1+3, Lise Gillen weighed in with 3+0 while Rachael Pearce and Victoria Connelly both contributed 2+1.

Bristol Women's Ice Hockey Friendship Tournament 2023
Played at Planet Ice Bristol 24th & 25th June

Group Table	GP	W	L	T	GF	GA	PTS
Bristol	9	8	0	1	21	1	17
Milton Keynes	9	7	2	0	14	2	14
Nottingham	9	6	2	1	21	9	13
Caledonia	9	6	2	1	14	4	13
Fire Bees	9	4	2	3	17	4	11
Widnes	9	4	3	2	15	9	10
Coventry	9	2	6	1	4	12	5
Streatham	9	2	6	1	5	14	5
Oxford	9	1	8	0	5	21	2
Cardiff	9	0	9	0	0	40	0

Player Statistics	GP	G	A	PTS	PIM
Fairclough, Katherine #11	9	4	2	6	2
De Decker, Leen #5	9	1	3	4	0
Pearce, Rachael #13	9	2	1	3	0
Connelly, Victoria #88	9	2	1	3	0
Gillen, Lise #10	7	3	0	3	0
Gennoe, Preston #53	9	0	2	2	0
Marcroft, Laura #93	9	1	0	1	0
Fell, Catherine #73	9	1	0	1	1
Tyrer, Ellen #23	9	1	0	1	0
Wilson, Olivia #51	9	0	0	0	0
Cooper, Karyn #65	9	0	0	0	0
Hickey, Jennifer #22	9	0	0	0	0
Hill, Sophie #74	9	0	0	0	0
Adshead, Katie #12	9	0	0	0	0
Patient, Phoebe #44	9	0	0	0	0
Drinkwater, Stephanie #1	9	0	0	0	0

Netminder Stats	GPI	Mins	SA	GA	SV	GAA	SV%	SO
Drinkwater, S #1	9	135	72	9	63	1.07	87.50	5

Coach Lappin On Wild Women's Season

Following the end of the 2022/23 season WNIHL season, DMUK Widnes Wild women's team head coach Adam Lappin has commented on the team's achievements:

"The season went very well with some great development and growth from everyone. We were aiming for a top 3 finish and we hit form at the right time to achieve this."

"The playoffs were a good experience for all, as there were not many in the team who had been exposed to that environment. We had a good plan, but we wanted all players to play their game and use it as a stepping stone for the new season, and to use the playoff weekend as a learning experience. Overall, I cannot fault the ladies for their team spirit and overall team ethos."

Talking about the Bristol Friendship Tournament, Lappin said: "It was a good end to the season with no pressure. The ladies were able to go and enjoy a good weekend of hockey in prep for a nice summer off. Bring on pre-season!"

*****

The 2023 Play Off Semi Final was the team's 101st match since forming as the Wild Women for the start of the 2015/16 season. In that time they have won 34 games, lost 56 and drawn 11 – scoring 389 goals and conceding 562.

The Wild Women won the Division 1 North league title in the 2019/20 season and were runners up in the Women's Premier League in 2015/16 and Division 2 North this - 2022/23 – season.

DMUK Widnes Wild Women - Season 2023/24 (Photo by Paul Breeze)

Back Row: Adam Lappin, Suzie Miller, Charlotte McAdam, Jemma Brown, Rachael Pearce, Katya Oliver, Preston Gennoe, Laura Moran, Karyn Cooper, Katie Adshead, Jennifer Hickey, Eleanor Aldred, Leen de Decker, Thomas Horner. Front Row: Eleanor Johnson, Ellen Tyrer, Vanessa Crickmore-Clarke, Stephanie Drinkwater, Charlotte Cramp, Laura Marcroft, Elizabeth Loss, Phoebe Patient.
Missing from photo: Katie Fairclough, Sophie Hill, Lise Gillen, Catherine Fell, Victoria Connelly, Ellie Green, Natalie Buckles, Lucy Kirkham.

WNIHL Division 2 (North) – Season 2023/24

Final League Table	GP	W	D	L	GF	GA	Pts
Caledonia Steel Queens	14	14	0	0	115	23	28
Telford Wrekin Raiders	14	11	0	3	89	26	22
Sheffield Shadows	14	9	1	4	64	33	19
Leeds Roses	14	8	1	5	72	55	17
Widnes Wild	14	5	2	7	55	50	12
Whitley Bay Beacons	14	4	1	9	44	93	9
Kingston Diamonds	14	2	1	11	29	101	5
Grimsby Wolves	14	0	0	14	20	107	0

Top Points Scorers

Player	Team	GP	G	A	Pts	PIM
C.J. Harrison	Leeds Roses	14	20	20	40	8
Michelle Whitehouse	Telford Raiders	12	23	6	29	2
Kate Gillies	Caledonia S Queens	12	14	13	27	0
Laetitia Liu	Telford Raiders	13	12	11	23	2
Preston Gennoe	Widnes Wild	11	16	5	21	14
Heather Metcalf	Telford Raiders	13	9	12	21	4
Jessica Bridger	Caledonia SQueens	10	12	8	20	0
Morgan-Leigh Walker	Leeds Roses	11	12	8	20	6
Michelle Davidson	Caledonia SQueens	10	7	10	17	2
Rebecca Craig	Telford Raiders	12	6	11	17	0

Top Netminders

Netminder	Team	GPI	Mins	SA	GA	GAA	SV%	SO
Kirsty Robson	SHE	10	418	202	13	1.87	0.936	3
Alice Somerford	TEL	13	780	385	27	2.08	0.93	0
Steph Drinkwater	WID	10	471	347	29	3.7	0.916	2
Shan Schneider	SHE	10	423	223	20	2.84	0.91	4
Megan Quigley	LEE	10	468	344	36	4.62	0.895	1
Lucy Noble	KIN	11	435	440	57	7.86	0.87	0
Sienna Bugg	GRI	10	284	242	41	8.69	0.831	0

DMUK Widnes Wild Women Fixtures & Results
Season 2023/24

Date	Home			Away	Res
01/10/2023	Widnes Wild	5	0	Grimsby Wolves	W
14/10/2023	Caledonia S/Qs	10	1	Widnes Wild	L
04/11/2023	Leeds Roses	8	2	Widnes Wild	L
12/11/2023	Sheffield Shadows	5	4	Widnes Wild	L
25/11/2023	Telford W Raiders	8	1	Widnes Wild	L
10/12/2023	Widnes Wild	10	2	Kingston Diamonds	W
07/01/2024	Widnes Wild	5	0	Whitley Bay	W
27/01/2024	Kingston Diamonds			Widnes Wild	Da[1]
04/02/2024	Widnes Wild	2	4	Caledonia S/Qs	L
24/02/2024	Grimsby Wolves	0	5	Widnes Wild	Wa[2]
09/03/2024	Whitley Bay	3	15	Widnes Wild	W
24/03/2024	Widnes Wild	1	5	Telford W Raiders	L
28/04/2024	Widnes Wild	2	2	Sheffield Shadows	D
12/05/2024	Widnes Wild	2	3	Leeds Roses	L

Notes:

1) *The away game at Kingston on 27th January had to be cancelled as the Hull Jets NIHL team needed the ice slot for a Moralee Cup semi final match. It was not possible to re-arrange the game so it was awarded as a 0-0 draw with 1 point for each team.*

2) *The away game at Grimsby on 24th February was abandoned at 16.47 minutes due to a serious injury to a Grimsby player. The score was 4-1 to Grimsby at the time with the Wild goal coming from Charlotte Cramp (assist Rachael Pearce). The game was not rescheduled and was later awarded as a 0-5 win to Widnes.*

DMUK Widnes Wild Women Player Statistics Season 2023/24

Player	GP	G	A	Pts	PIM
Preston Gennoe	11	16	5	21	14
Katie Fairclough	10	10	5	15	12
Katya Oliver	9	3	5	8	2
Ellen Tyrer	10	5	2	7	0
Rachael Pearce	12	2	2	4	4
Jennifer Hickey	12	2	2	4	2
Charlotte Cramp	11	1	3	4	0
Jemma Brown	10	2	2	4	0
Sophie Hill	5	2	2	4	0
Lise Gillen	4	2	2	4	0
Laura Marcroft	11	2	1	3	2
Katie Adshead	10	1	2	3	2
Victoria Connelly	4	3	0	3	6
Phoebe Patient	10	2	0	2	4
Suzie Miller	11	0	1	1	0
Laura Moran	10	0	1	1	2
Karyn Cooper	10	0	1	1	4
Catherine Fell	8	0	1	1	0
Elizabeth Loss	9	0	0	0	0
Vanessa Crickmore-Clarke	8	0	0	0	4
Abigail Aldred	7	0	0	0	4
Natalie Buckles	7	0	0	0	2
Eleanor Johnson	6	0	0	0	0
Charlotte McAdam	4	0	0	0	0
Lucy Kirkham	3	0	0	0	0
Stephanie Drinkwater	10	0	0	0	0
Ellie Green	8	0	0	0	0

Netminder Statistics – Season 2023/24

	GPI	Mins	SA	GA	GAA	Sv%	SO
Drinkwater	10	473m50s	347	32	4.68	90.78	2
Green	8	245m50s	170	18	4.33	89.41	2
Empty	1	00m20s	0	0	0.00	100	
Totals	**12**	**720m00s**	**517**	**50**	**4.17**	**90.33**	**2**

Breakdown of Netminder Statistics – Season 2023/24

Match	Netminder	GPI	Mins	SA	GA	GAA	Sv%	SO
H v GRI	Drinkwater	1	30.30	9	0	0.00	100.00	1
	Green	1	29.30	14	0	0.00	100.00	1
A @ CAL	Drinkwater	1	60	78	10	10.00	87.18	0
A @ LEE	Drinkwater	1	32	18	7	13.13	61.11	0
	Green	1	28	16	1	2.14	93.75	0
A @ SHE	Drinkwater	1	59.40	49	5	5.05	89.80	0
	Empty	1	00.20	0	0	0.00	100	0
A @ TEL	Green	1	60	47	8	8.00	82.98	0
H v KIN	Drinkwater	1	30	10	1	2.00	90.00	0
	Green	1	30	14	1	2.00	92.86	0
H v WHI	Drinkwater	1	52.40	28	0	0.00	100.00	1
	Green	1	7.20	3	0	0.00	100.00	1
A @ KIN			*Match Not Played*					
H v CAL	Green	1	60	53	4	4.00	92.45	0
A @ GRI	*Kirkham**		*16.47*	*19*	*4*	*13.33*	*78.95*	*0*
A @ WHI	Drinkwater	1	60	47	3	3.00	93.62	0
H v TEL	Drinkwater	1	40	36	2	3.00	94.44	0
	Green	1	20	15	3	9.00	80.00	0
H v SHE	Drinkwater	1	45	32	1	1.33	96.88	0
	Green	1	15	8	1	4.00	87.50	0
H v LEE	Drinkwater	1	60	40	3	3.00	92.50	0
Totals		**12**	**720**	**517**	**50**	**4.55**	**90.33**	**2**

Note: The game away at Grimsby was abandoned after 16.47 minutes and was later awarded as a 0-5 win to Widnes. As a result of this decision, the netminder statistics are not officially recorded for this game -although they do appear on Elite Prospects...

Stephanie Drinkwater (Photo by Flyfifer Photography)

Katie Fairclough (Photo by David Law)

Vanessa Crickmore-Clarke (Photo by Stephen Fairclough)

Summer Signing Announcements

The DMUK Widnes Wild women's team are back in training after a short summer break and preparations are well under way for the new 2023/24 WNIHL season, which starts in October.

Last season's coaching team of Adam Lappin, Steve Furber and Thomas Horner are back for another season and are building a competitive team roster in the hope of improving on last season's runners up spot in Division 2 North.

Two early signings to the team are returnees Stephanie Drinkwater and Vanessa Crickmore-Clarke, who have both been with the Wild team since it relocated to Widnes from Altrincham back in 2015.

Netminder Drinkwater has played over 100 competitive games in total – some 75 for Widnes – and was a member of the Wild women's team that won the Division 1 North league title in the 2019/20 season to add the title she won at Altrincham in 2014/15.

She played in 9 games last season and ended up with a very impressive Save Percentage of 90.34%, a Goals Against Average of 2.88 and 1 shut out.

Crickmore-Clarke is a highly experienced attacker turned defender who won 5 league titles with the Sunderland Scorpions in her native north east and then spent 9 seasons playing at Deeside and Altrincham before the move to Widnes.

Like Drinkwater, she also won the Division 1 North title with Altrincham in 2014 and Widnes in 2020 and, in an impressive career to date, has played over 250 competitive games in total. She also played in 9 games last season, scoring 1 goal from her defensive position.

Talking about her return to the team, Vanessa said: "I am really pleased to be re-signing with the Wild again and can't wait to get back on the ice with the team. We had a successful 22/23 season for our league team, as well as the successful growth and progression of our development players and hopefully we'll be in for a chance of reaching out for the silverware again."

Preston Gennoe (Photo by Brian Noble)

Laura Marcroft (Photo by David Law)

The DMUK Widnes Wild women's team have added some firepower to their roster for the new 2023/24 WNIHL season with the return of 3 more players from last season's team.

Between them, Katie Fairclough, Preston Gennoe and Laura Marcroft notched up 37 goals and 25 assists in the Wild Women's Division 2 North campaign, which saw them finish runners up in the final league table.

Katie Fairclough first joined the Wild in 2017 and will be back for her sixth season in Widnes colours.

She originally started off playing Roller Hockey and was a GB International in that sport before switching to playing on ice. Since taking up ice hockey, Katie has gained international honours at GB Women's Under 18 level and was a league title winner with the Wild women in 2020.

Last season, Fairclough was the Wild women's second highest scorer with 20 goals and 12 assists in 13 games and, overall, she has played 62 games for Widnes, scoring 29+20 with 71 penalty minutes.

She also played 17 games for the Manchester University teams last season, scoring 11 goals and 2 assists.

Looking ahead to the new season, Fairclough said:

"After the amazing season we just had, I'm looking forward to what should be another great season this year. While we narrowly missed out on promotion, I think we're in with a good shot this year. It's been great to see so many new players on the team, but at the same time we have a very strong base of well established players who can bring in the results at the same time as developing the newer members of the squad. I can't wait to get back on the ice for the first game!"

Preston Gennoe joined the Wild women for the 2021/22 season and is returning for her third campaign. She was the team's top scorer in the Women's Premier League that year and, in 26 games overall, has contributed 21 goals and 14 assists, with 32 penalty minutes.

Talking about her re-signing, Gennoe said: ""I'm feeling excited about the new season. It's my 3rd season with the Wild and I couldn't ask for a better group of girls to play and progress with."

Laura Marcroft has played for the Wild women for 4 seasons overall and was another member of the team that won the Division 1 North title in 2020.

Overall she has scored 5 goals and 9 assists in 53 games, picking up just 4 penalty minutes in that time and last season was her most productive to date in terms of points, as she scored 4+2 and was also awarded the Hardest Worker award by the coaches.

Marcroft said of her return for the new season: "I'm looking forward to the season ahead, to see how we can build on the last season as a team. Taking part in the playoffs was a huge boost for the team and for me as a player. I hope as a player I can continue to improve and contribute to some more goals this year. All in all, I am looking forward to the year ahead and what it will bring."

Ellie Green, Phoebe Patient and Ellen Tyrer (Photo by Paul Breeze)

Ellie Green, Phoebe Patient and Ellen Tyrer have all previously played junior hockey for the Wild Academy and are a shining example of how developing local talent is reaping positive benefits for the Widnes senior teams.

Ellie Green began her career at Blackburn but played for the Wild Academy Under 18 team for the 2021/22 season and made her senior debut last season for the Wild women, when the team finished as runners up in the league.

She played in 9 league and play off games, facing a total of 167 shots and conceding just 12 goals, for a hugely impressive Save % of 92.81 and a Goals Against Average of 2.37.

Phoebe Patient played for the Wild Academy Under 15 and Under 18 teams and made her Wild women's senior debut in the Women's Premier League in the 2021/22 season.

In 29 league, play off and challenge games over her two seasons with the Wild women so far, she has scored 3 goals and 4 assists and was named Best Forward at End of Season Award for last season.

Talking about her resigning, Patient said: "I'm excited about the season ahead and seeing how the team develops even more with new and established players. I have high hopes after last season's brilliant performance as a team"

Ellen Tyrer also played for the Wild Academy Under 15 and Under 18 teams and made her Wild women's senior debut in the Women's Premier League in the 2021/22 season.

In 28 league, play off and challenge games over her two seasons with the Wild women so far, she has also scored 3 goals and 4 assists and, like Patient and Green, was a member of the Wild women's team who finished second in the WNIHL Division 2 North last season.

With regard to her return to the Wild women for another season, Ellen said:

"I'm really looking forward to the upcoming season after the year we just had and watching the team grow closer and improve throughout."

"I'm incredibly excited to have some new players joining us and becoming part of this brilliant team. I'm sure it will be an awesome season with lots of fun and memorable moments."

Charlotte Cramp (photo by Anne Bennison)

More Signings For Wild Women

The DMUK Widnes Wild women's team continue to prepare for their 2023/24 WNIHL Division 2 North league title challenge with the return of 4 more players from last season's squad.

Forward **Charlotte Cramp** returns to the Wild women for her third season, having joined the team in 2021 from a background of university hockey with Manchester Metros.

In her two seasons with the Wild to date, she has played 31 games and scored 5 goals and 11 assists.

Cramp is very versatile and even played in goal for the first game of last season, picking up the MVP award away at Solway. She is also a qualified Level 3 match official and regularly referees junior matches and can cover senior men's games at NIHL 2 level if required.

Charlotte also has an IIHF licence, which allows her to officiate at international women's tournaments.

She will be the captain of the Wild women's team for the new season.

Karyn Cooper has re-signed for her 5th season with the Wild women, having joined the team from the 2018/19 season. She also played University hockey for the Manchester Metros team, clocking up 43 games in 4 years.

In her 4 seasons to date at Widnes, Karyn has played in 52 league, playoff and challenge matches, contributing 6 assists.

She is also the Wild women's team manager and puts in a huge amount of work behind the scenes.

Karyn Cooper (photo by Wil Evans)

Rachael Pearce only joined the Wild women last season, but she has a fascinating background in ice hockey and brings a wealth of experience to the team.

Rachael originally played with the Blackpool women's team in the late 1980s and then joined the Blackburn Falcons rec team at the then newly opened East Lancs rink. She then had a 20 year break from ice hockey, playing football up to county level, before playing for the Wyre Seagulls at the SubZero rink in Cleveleys in 2011/12 and then joining the Blackburn Thunder women's team the following year.

She played 6 seasons for the Thunder from 2012 to 2018, finishing as a runner-up in the Division 1 North table before the team sadly folded at the end of that season.

4 years later, Pearce joined the Wild women's team where she was an ever-present for the 2022/23 season,

having her best campaign in terms of points with 8 goals and 10 assists in 15 league and play off games.

Talking about re-joining the Wild women for the new season, Rachael said:

“Joining Widnes last season I couldn't have wished for a better bunch of team-mates to play with as I have learnt so much more in this last season and it has, once again, renewed my passion to keep playing this amazing sport as long as I can!”

“This year, I hope to keep assisting and scoring goals - and hopefully get to the playoffs once again at the end of the season, with teamwork and a great bunch of people!”

Jemma Brown (Photo by Geoff White)

Laura Moran – playing for Oxford against Widnes at the Bristol Tournament (Photo by Flyfifer Photography)

More Signings For Wild Women

The DMUK Widnes Wild women's team have a new player to boost their squad for the forthcoming 2023/24 WNIHL North season, as well as the return of a familiar face.

Laura Moran has played for the Oxford Midnight Stars in Division 2 South for the past 8 years and has over 70 WNIHL matches under her belt. In that time she contributed 4 goals and 11 assists from her defensive role and notched up 42 penalty minutes.

Moran also played University hockey for 4 seasons with the UEA (University Of East Anglia) Avalanche, scoring 1+2 in 18 games.

Talking about her move to the Wild women, Laura said: “I can’t wait to get this season started with Widnes! I was sad to be leaving Oxford at the end of last season after 8 years but Widnes have been so welcoming. I’m looking forward to getting to know all the girls more and seeing how much we can achieve on the ice this year!”

Returnee Jemma Brown needs no introduction to Widnes fans as she played three seasons for the Wild women from 2018 to 2022 before taking a break from competitive hockey last year.

In that time she played 38 league and challenge matches scoring 6 goals and 8 assists and was a member of the Wild women’s team that won the Division 1 North title in 2019/20.

Before joining Widnes, Jemma had played for the Kingston Diamonds in the Women’s Premier League as well as junior hockey for Blackburn and Trafford and has over 90 competitive games to her record.

She said of her return to the Wild women’s team: “I am incredibly excited to be returning back to playing for the women after having a season off. After seeing how well the team performed last season, I am excited to see how well the team performs this season.”

“I’m sure it will be an amazing season with new team members and some very experienced players with lots of fun and exciting memories for us all to remember as a team.”

Three more players from last season’s squad have also returned to the Wild women for the new campaign.

Ontario-born Lise Gillen brings a wealth of experience having played 3 seasons for the Guildford Lightning in the Womens' Elite League, as well as playing in her native Canada. She played 10 games for Widnes last season, scoring 2 goals and 4 assists

Victoria Connelly also played 10 games for Widnes last season, scoring 3 goals and 2 assists she is also a former Guildford Lightning Elite player, previously playing for the Bracknell Fire Bees and, in total, has made over 50 WNIHL appearances.

Jennifer Hickey joined the Wild women for the 2021/22 season and has played in all 30 games that the team have played since then. She has contributed 3 goals and 4 assists and picked up just 4 penalty minutes.

Hickey also plays University hockey for the Manchester Metros, scoring 6+9 in 28 games over two seasons.

The DMUK Widnes Wild women play their first game of the new season on Sunday 1st October when they take on the Grimsby Wolves at Planet Ice Widnes, 4.25pm face off.

Top: Lise Gillen (Photo by Wil Evans)

Above left: Victoria Connelly with Rambo in Edinburgh

Above right: Jennifer Hickey

Wild Women's Roster Complete

The DMUK Widnes Wild women's team have completed their roster for the forthcoming 2023/24 WNIHL season with the return of 6 more players from last year's team and the arrival of a new player.

Experienced centre Elizabeth Loss was one of the original Manchester Phoenix team that moved to Widnes in 2015 and, in her 6 seasons with the Wild women, has played 45 games, scoring 4 goals and 16 assists - and never picking up a single penalty minute.

Liz was a key member of the Widnes team that won the 2019/20 Division 1 North league title and finished as runners up last season.

Commenting on her return for the new season, Loss said: "I'm feeling very positive about this season. We had a really good season last year and we know what we need to work on to get to the play offs again and win this year."

Suzie Miller is back for her 4th season in Widnes colours, having originally joined the Wild women for the 2019/20 title winning season. In that time she has played 31 games, contributing 3 assists from her defensive role. Behind the scenes, Suzie is also a qualified coach and manager.

Miller said on her re-signing: "I am excited to go into the new season with an existing team who have come together well, with some new faces ready for the upcoming challenges".

Katie Adshead returns for 5th season with the team, having originally joined as part of the big experiment 2018/19 season. She has notched up 53 matches in that time, scoring 2 goals and 6 assists with 22 penalty minutes and was another key member of the 2019/20 title winning season.

Natalie Buckles joined the Wild women for the post-Covid 2021/22 WPL season and is now back for her third campaign. She has played 18 games for Widnes, scoring 1 goal and 1 assist. Buckles is also a qualified coach, has occasionally helped on the bench at Wild NIHL men's games and also works with the juniors. She also plays recreational hockey with the Widnes-based Earle Road Elks and Cheshire Pistons teams.

Olivia Wilson returns to the Wild women for her third season in Widnes colours, having originally joined in 2021. She previously played WNIHL league hockey for the Whitley Bay Squaws but also has an impressive background in University Hockey where she has notched up almost 100 games playing for Newcastle, London and Scottish teams.

Wilson has played 22 games for Widnes to date, contributing 1 assist.

Sophie Hill was a new player to the Wild women's team last season. She has made just 1 appearance so far – against Grimsby in March - but scored an assist and was named Most Valuable Player for the game.

The new arrival on the Wild women's team is Katya Oliver who previously played for the Chelmsford Cobras in the Women's Premier League and U16 girls' hockey for Bracknell. She has most recently played two seasons of university hockey with Manchester Metros, making 30 appearances and scoring 3+5.

Elizabeth Loss (by Wil Evans) & Katie Adshead (by David Law)

Natalie Buckles & Suzie Miller (by John Lewis)

The DMUK Widnes Wild women's team have put together a strong roster mixing youth and experience for the forthcoming 2023/24 WNIHL season where they will, once again, be competing in Division 2 North.

They will be hoping to go one better after finishing as runners up to champions Solway Sharks Ladies last season and regain the title that they won themselves back in the 2019/20 season.

WNIHL North 2 comprises 8 teams again this year with promoted Solway being replaced by another Scottish team – the Caledonia Steel Queens from Edinburgh - and all teams play each other once home and once away for a 14-game regular season.

The Wild women's league fixtures for the 2023/24 WNIHL season are:

1st Oct: Home v Grimsby Wolves, 4.25pm face off
14th Oct: Away @ Caledonia Steel Queens, 10.15pm
4th Nov: Away @ Leeds Roses, 7.30pm
12th Nov: Away @ Sheffield Shadows, 5pm
25th Nov: Away @ Telford Wrekin Raiders, 4.15pm
10th Dec: Home v Kingston Diamonds, 4.25pm
7th Jan: Home v Whitley Bay Beacons, 4.25pm
27th Jan: Away @ Kingston Diamonds, 6.30pm
4th Feb: Home v Caledonia Steel Queens, 4.25pm
24th Feb: Away @ Grimsby Wolves, 1.10pm
9th Mar: Away @ Whitley Bay Beacons, 12.00 noon
24th Mar: Home v Telford Wrekin Raiders, 4.25pm
28th April: Home v Sheffield Shadows, 4.25pm
12th May: Home v Leeds Roses, 4.25pm

Duo debut for Wild in pre-season challenge

Women get off to five-star start to season

League leaders prove too powerful for Wild

Match Reports & News Items Season 2023/24

Wild duo break new ground in GB match

Five-star start to the year for Wild Women

Diamond display has Women back on track

Title shot for Edwardson

Plucky comeback in vain as Wild miss out

Understrength Wild Women fall to Queens

SPORT

Leeds loss brings down Wild curtain

Laura Moran was the Widnes MVP against Grimsby (Photo by Paul Breeze)

Sunday 1st October 2023 – WNIHL Division 2 North DMUK Widnes Wild Women 5 - Grimsby Wolves 0

The DMUK Widnes Wild women got their 2023/24 Division 2 North campaign off to the best possible start with a 5-0 win over Grimsby Wolves at Planet Ice Widnes on Sunday.

The game saw debuts for new signings Laura Moran, Katya Oliver and Eleanor Johnson and a return to the team after a year away for Jemma Brown.

The Wild women opened the scoring after just 48 seconds with a goal from Preston Gennoe and then two goals within a minute of each other around the 10 minute mark – from Katya Oliver and Katie Fairclough – handed them a commanding lead.

A superb piece of individual play saw Fairclough score her second goal of the game in the 17th minute and Widnes were able to take a 4-goal lead into the first period break.

The Wild women outshot Grimsby by over 2 to 1 over the course of the game and it was no great surprise when Fairclough scored her straight hat trick goal just 4 ½ minutes into the second after sustained pressure around the Wolves net.

With the score standing at 5-0 – and with 35 minutes still to play - Widnes took their foot off the gas a bit and took the opportunity to give the whole of the bench plenty of ice time.

There was no more scoring after that and Ellie Green came on to replace Stephanie Drinkwater in the Wild goal for the final 30 minutes to take a share in the resulting shutout.

The Wild Women's Most Valuable Player awards for this season have been sponsored by Lucy London - Poet In Residence for the 5th year in a row and consist of goodie bags containing a limited edition MVP teddy bear and a selection of Body Shop products provided by Running Mum Beauty.

The awards were presented by Wild Women matchday volunteer co-ordinator Clair Johnson and went to Erin Dommett for Grimsby and Laura Moran for Widnes.

The Caledonia and Widnes teams after the first ever women's league match in Edinburgh (Photo by Steel Queens IHC)

Saturday 14th October - WNIHL Div2 North Caledonia Steel Queens 10 – DMUK Widnes Wild Women 1

The DMUK Widnes Wild women's team underwent a baptism of fire on their first ever visit to Edinburgh as they suffered a 10-1 defeat at the hands of the Caledonia Steel Queens on Saturday.

The Steel Queens are a new team in the division for this season, having originally started out as a University team and Saturday saw their first ever league game. That match faced off at the somewhat unsociable hour of 10.15pm, although that was actually an improvement - as far as the Wild women were concerned - on the original start time of 7.30pm on the Sunday, which would have meant getting home on the Monday morning milk train.

The game saw the Wild women on the back foot for much of the time but overall gave a good account of themselves. They were heavily outshot over the course of the 60 minutes playing time but, despite this, they actually took the lead on 17 minutes with a goal from Victoria Connelly and the score remained 0-1 to Widnes at the first period break.

The Steel Queens scored their first ever league goal on 23 minutes then edged into the lead with a further strike on 36 minutes. With the score standing at 2-1 at the end of the second period, there was still hope of a Wild fightback but that was all scuppered with two quick Caledonia goals within 10 seconds of each other right at the start of the third period.

More goals followed in quick succession and, by the end of a disastrous final 20 minutes, the Wild women found themselves 10-1 down.

Over the course of the game, the Steel Queens outshot Widnes by 78 to 21 but overworked netminder Stephanie Drinkwater put in an heroic performance in the Wild goal and stopped an incredible 68 of them to end up with an 87.18 Save Percentage.

The Wild women are next in action on Saturday 4th November when they travel across the Pennines to face the Leeds Roses.

After that, they have games away to Sheffield Shadows (12th November) and Telford Wrekin Raiders (25th November) before their next home game on Sunday 10th December when they entertain Kingston Diamonds at Planet Ice Widnes.

Saturday 4th November – WHIHL Div 2 North
Leeds Roses 8 – DMUK Widnes Wild Women 2

The DMUK Widnes Wild women's team slumped to their second away defeat in a row with an 8-2 loss away to Leeds Roses on Saturday.

After a fairly close start, Leeds took the lead on 8 minutes and, 3 minutes later, the score was 2-0 to the hosts. Two more goals followed late in the period to give the home side a 4-0 lead at the first period break.

The second period played out goal-less, giving the Wild women some hope of bouncing back in the third, but it was not to be. The Roses further extended their lead just 51 seconds in and then two more goals within 20 seconds of each other on 42 minutes effectively killed off the game at 7-0.

Widnes finally found the back of the net for themselves with a well taken breakaway goal from Katya Oliver, making the most of a powerplay to pick up on a superb pass from Preston Gennoe, but there was never much chance of the Wild women making up the deficit by that stage.

Leeds scored their 8th goal of the game on 54 minutes and Widnes rounded off the goals for the night with a powerplay strike from Rachael Pearce with 2 minutes left on the clock.

The Wild women have two more away games - at Sheffield Shadows (12th November) and Telford Wrekin Raiders (25th November) - before their next home game on Sunday 10th December when they entertain Kingston Diamonds at Planet Ice Widnes.

Sunday 12th November – WNIHL Div 2 North
Sheffield Shadows 5 – DMUK Widnes Wild Women 4

The DMUK Widnes Wild women put in a battling performance away to Sheffield Shadows on Sunday but narrowly lost out 5-4 in an entertaining game at iceSheffield.

Widnes took the lead in the 8th minute with a goal from Lise Gillen but Sheffield equalised late in the period and the score stood at 1-1 at the first break.

The second period went badly for the Wild women and they conceded three unanswered goals to trail 4-1 after 40 minutes playing time. Sheffield scored a fifth goal just 2 minutes into the third period but this seemed to spur the Wild team into mounting a late rally.

A shorthanded goal from Gillen narrowed the score on 50 minutes and then a brace from Preston Gennoe just 45 seconds apart on 55 minutes brought the deficit down to just a single goal.

Widnes piled pressure on the Shadows net and withdrew goaltender Stephanie Drinkwater for the last minute in favour of an extra attacker in an attempt to force a late breakthrough. Unfortunately, it was to no avail, and Sheffield held on to record a 5-4 victory.

The Wild women have one more away game - at Telford Wrekin Raiders on 25th November - before their next home game on Sunday 10th December when they entertain Kingston Diamonds at Planet Ice Widnes.

Saturday 25th October – WNHIL Div2 North Telford Wrekin Raiders 8 – DMUK Widnes Wild Women 1

The DMUK Widnes Wild women's team slumped to their 4th defeat in a row with an 8-1 loss away to Telford Wrekin Raiders on Saturday.

The game was the last of a difficult run of 4 back-to-back road trips that has taken them to Edinburgh, Leeds, Sheffield and now Shropshire and has seen them concede 31 goals, while scoring just 8.

The game started badly for the Wild women as they went behind after just 25 seconds. Telford scored a second goal on 8 minutes to double the lead and then an amazing two goals within 3 seconds of each other on 12 minutes effectively ended the match as a contest.

A fifth goal on 17 minutes saw the home side edge even further ahead, leaving the Wild women the proverbial mountain to climb.

Widnes tightened up their game in the second period and matched their opponents for shots on goal, but were unable to make any sort of breakthrough and two more goals for Telford brought the score to 7-0. Telford had scored their 8th and final goal of the game by the time that the Wild women finally broke their duck – with a consolation strike from Katie Fairclough on 50 minutes.

The DMUK Widnes Wild women will be looking to get back to winning ways with their first home game for over 2 months when they take on the Kingston Diamonds at Planet Ice Widnes on Sunday 10th December, 4.25pm face off.

Laura Moran was the Widnes MVP against Kingston (Photo by Paul Breeze)

Sunday 10th December – WNIHL Div2N
Widnes Wild Women 10 – Kingston Diamonds 2

The DMUK Widnes Wild women's team got back to winning ways with a comprehensive 10-2 demolition of the Kingston Diamonds from Hull at Planet Ice Widnes on Sunday.

It was the Wild women's first home game in over two months and came off the back of 4 consecutive away defeats that had left the team in an uncomfortable position in the lower half of the Division 2 North league table.

As it turned out, Widnes were on top throughout and outshot their plucky opponents by 60 to 24 over the course of the game, with Stephanie Drinkwater and Ellie Green sharing the Wild netminding duties 50/50.

The first goal came from Preston Gennoe on 3 minutes and this was quickly followed by strikes from Katie Fairclough and Jennifer Hickey to give the Wild Women a 3-0 lead at the first break.

Kingston pulled a goal back on 25 minutes but Widnes restored the 3-goal advantage just 16 seconds later with a second goal of the game from Katie Fairclough. The lead was then extended to 5-1 with a goal from Phoebe Patient with 90 seconds left to go in the second period.

The third period went the same way as the previous two with Widnes comfortably in charge. A second goal of the night from Gennoe on 47 minutes edged the home side further ahead and then two goals within 20 seconds of each other – a powerplay goal from Laura Marcroft and a hat trick strike from Gennoe – handed the Wild Women an 8-1 lead.

Two more quick-fire goals came within 27 seconds of each other on 53 minutes – a fourth from Gennoe and one for Rachael Pearce – to put the Wild into double figures and Kingston fired in a late strike to round off the scoring for the game.

The Wild Women's Most Valuable Player awards for this season have been sponsored by Lucy London - Poet In Residence for the 5th year in a row and consist of goodie bags containing a limited edition MVP teddy bear and a selection of Body Shop products provided by Running Mum Beauty. The awards were presented by match volunteer Colin Ellis and went to Neveah Allsopp for Kingston and Laura Moran for Widnes.

The DMUK Widnes Wild Women are next in action on Sunday 7th January when they take on Whitley Bay at Planet Ice Widnes, 4.25pm face off.

DMUK Widnes Wild Women End Of Year Report

Like the Wild NIHL team, The DMUK Widnes Wild women's team also find themselves in the bottom half of the league table at the end of the calendar year with two wins from their 6 league games this season so far.

They have won both of their home games by a comfortable margin – beating Grimsby Wolves 5-0 and Kingston Diamonds 10-2 - but an unfortunate run of 4 defeats in 4 consecutive away games has left them with a lot of catching up to do in the second half of the season.

Katie Fairclough is the leading points scorer thus far for the Wild Women with 6 goals and 5 assists in 6 games while Preston Gennoe is just behind with 8+2. Katya Oliver – a new player on the team this season – weighs in with 1+5 in third.

The team to beat so far this season is Caledonia Steel Queens, who are a new team to the league, based in Edinburgh. The Wild Women lost 10-1 in the first ever WNIHL league match to be played in the Scottish capital and the Steel Queens have a 100% record of 4 wins from their 4 games played. Leeds Roses are in second place with 3 wins from 3 games

The Wild Women's first game of the new year is on Sunday 7th January, when they take on the Whitley Bay Beacons at Planet Ice Widnes, 4.25pm face off. The Beacons are currently third in the league table with 3 wins and 1 defeat from their 4 games to date and this is a game that Widnes will be keen to win in order to keep their season's hopes alive.

Phoebe Patient was the Widnes MVP against Whitley (Photo by Paul Breeze)

Sunday 7th January – WNIHL Div 2N
Widnes Wild Women 5 – Whitley Bay Beacons 0

The DMUK Widnes Wild Women got 2024 off to the best possible start with a 5-0 win over the Whitley Bay Beacons at Planet Ice Widnes on Sunday.

It took until the 16th minute for the first goal and this fell to the Wild's Jemma Brown. This was quickly followed by strikes from Victoria Connelly, Preston Gennoe and Ellen Tyrer and Widnes were able to take a 4-0 lead into the first break.

The goal rush did not extend into the second period and this was much closer in terms of puck possession and shots on goal.

Here again, it took over 15 minutes for the next breakthrough and the chance, when it came, fell to Laura Marcroft to fire away the puck.

Widnes led 5-0 at the second break and, with the third period playing out goal-less, that turned out to be the final score.

Wild netminder Stephanie Drinkwater put in a superb performance, turning away all 28 shots that she faced. Ellie Green replaced her for the final 7½ minutes to complete the shut out.

The Wild Women's Most Valuable Player awards for this season have been sponsored by Lucy London - Poet In Residence for the 5th year in a row and consist of goodie bags containing a limited edition MVP teddy bear and a selection of Body Shop products provided by Running Mum Beauty.

The awards were presented by match volunteer Lynda Bird and went to Claire Wilson for Whitley and Phoebe Patient for Widnes.

The Wild women are next in action away to Kingston Diamonds in Hull on Saturday 27th January and are next at home on Sunday 4th February when they take on the Caledonia Steel Queens from Edinburgh at Planet Ice Widnes, 4.25pm face off.

Wild Women Hull Trip Off

The DMUK Widnes Wild women's team's away game with the Kingston Diamonds that was scheduled for this Saturday 27th January has been postponed due to an ice availability issue at Hull Arena.

The Hull Jets NIHL team have qualified for the semi-finals of the Moralee Cup and need to stage their home leg on that date, so the women's game will have to be rescheduled.

This means that the Wild women's next game will be at home the following Sunday 4th February when they take on league leaders Caledonia Steel Queens at Planet Ice Widnes, 4.25pm face off.

The Edinburgh based Steel Queens, who are in their first season of league competition, currently lead the WNIHL Div2 North league table with a 100% record of 5 wins from their 5 games to date – the most recent being a highly impressive 2-4 win away to regular title challengers Telford.

The Wild women lost 10-1 to the Steel Queens in the first meeting between the two teams – the first WNIHL match ever to be played at the Murrayfield Ice Rink - back in October at the, admittedly, rather unsociable face off time of 10.15pm on a Saturday night.

However, they are unbeaten in all 3 of their home games so far this season – with a mean defensive record of having conceded just 2 goals in a total 180 minutes playing time – and it is hoped that Sunday will provide a close–fought and entertaining game.

Charlotte Cramp was the Widnes MVP against Caledonia (Photo by Paul Breeze)

Sunday 4th February 2024 – WNIHL Div 2 North Widnes Wild Women 2 – Caledonia Steel Queens 4

The DMUK Widnes Wild women put in a battling performance against league leaders Caledonia Steel Queens before ultimately losing out 2-4 in a highly entertaining game at Planet Ice Widnes on Sunday.

The showing was all the more impressive as the Wild women were missing several regular players due to illness.

For a "non-checking" women's game, this was quite a physical encounter but - to their credit – the match officials let the game flow and didn't keep blowing the whistle for niggly penalties. In fact, Caledonia managed to stay clear of the sin bin all match and Widnes only picked up 6 minutes in total.

After a high octane opening phase, with lots of breathless end to end hockey, the visitors took the lead on 10 minutes but Widnes drew level 5 minutes later with a goal from Victoria Connelly. Caledonia edged into the lead once again with 2 minutes left in the period and took a less than convincing 1-2 lead into the break.

The visitors scored again just two minutes into the second period to put daylight between the teams but Widnes hit back just 45 seconds later with a superb individual breakaway goal from Preston Gennoe to keep themselves in contention.

The clock ticked down, the hockey continued to flow and, just as it looked as if the second period might finish up 1-1, Widnes picked up one of those rare penalties and Caledonia scored on the resulting powerplay with just 50 seconds left to play.

That late blow left a 2-goal deficit to overcome in the third period but the Wild women took to their task with gritty determination. Contrary to all Widnes hopes, the last 20 minutes played out goal-less but stand out performances in every position on the ice still gave the home crowd plenty to cheer about.

Despite being heavily out-shot over the course of the game – by 53 to 16 – Widnes never really looked out of it and a superb performance by Ellie Green in the Wild net meant that she ended up with a better Save % overall than the Caledonia keeper by 92.45% to 87.50%.

The Wild Women's Most Valuable Player awards for this season have been sponsored by Lucy London - Poet In Residence for the 5th year in a row and consist of goodie bags containing a limited edition MVP teddy bear and a selection of Body Shop products provided by Running Mum Beauty.

The awards were presented by match volunteer Callum Rose and went to Caitlyn Monk for Caledonia and Charlotte Cramp for Widnes.

Lucy Kirkham played in goal away at Grimsby
(Photo by Anne Bennison)

Saturday 24th February 2024 – WNIHL Div 2 N
Grimsby Wolves – DMUK Widnes Wild Women

The DMUK Widnes Wild women's team's game away at Grimsby was abandoned in the first period after a Wolves player suffered a broken ankle on the ice.

The home side were leading 4-1 at the time of the stoppage, although the Wild Women had travelled without a regular netminder and senior player Lucy Kirkham bravely took up the pads and played in goal. The sole Wild goal was scored by team captain Charlotte Cramp.

There are hopes that the game will be rescheduled for a later date if a suitable ice time slot can be arranged at the Lincolnshire rink.

Ellen Tyrer scored a hat-trick away at Whitley (Photo by Wil Evans)

Saturday 9th March 2024 – WNIHL Div2 N
Whitley Bay Beacons 3 – DMUK Widnes Wild Women 15

The DMUK Widnes Wild women finally broke their road trip hoodoo with an emphatic 3-15 win away to Whitley Bay Beacons on Saturday.

The Wild women had lost their first 4 away games of the season and then seen two more postponed or abandoned for various reasons, but everything fell into place for this potentially tricky visit to the North East.

Widnes took the lead with a goal from Katie Adshead on 3 minutes and then doubled the advantage with a Preston Gennoe strike just 40 seconds later.

Whitley hit back with two goals of their own to tie the score but further goals from Ellen Tyrer and Jennifer Hickey saw the Wild women leading 2-4 at the first period break.

Katie Fairclough edged the Wild further into the lead with a goal just 2 minutes into the second period and then the floodgates opened with 5 more unanswered goals – from Gennoe (2), Tyrer, Phoebe Patient and Tyrer again – to put the game well out of reach of the home side at 2-10 after 40 minutes of play.

The third period saw Widnes keep the pressure up and 5 more goals followed – from Fairclough (2) Sophie Hill (2, her first for the club) and Preston Gennoe for her fourth of the game.

The resulting 3-15 victory is the Wild women's biggest win of the season so far and their highest score since their 15-2 home win over Kingston in March 2023.

They are next in action Sunday 24th March when they take on Telford Wrekiin Raiders at Planet Ice Widnes, 4.25pm face off

Karyn Cooper was the Wild women's MVP against Telford
(Photo by Paul Breeze)

24th March 2024 – WNIHL Div2 N
DMUK Widnes Wild Women 1 – Telford Wrekin Raiders 5

The DMUK Widnes Wild women's team suffered a 1-5 defeat at the hands of play off contenders Telford Wrekin Raiders at Planet Ice Widnes on Sunday.

Following on from their comprehensive 3-15 away victory over Whitley Bay in their previous game, there were hopes that the Wild women might be able to launch a late charge to qualify for the play offs themselves but Telford proved to be a much tougher challenge altogether.

The game saw home debuts for Charlotte McAdam and Eleanor Johnson but Widnes were missing a couple of regular players and had to juggle their usual lines, meaning that it took them a while to get going.

Telford scored the first goal mid-way through the first period and then added a second on 17 minutes, taking full advantage of a powerplay for a Wild penalty.

The score remained 0-2 to the Raiders at the first period break but, with them having outshot Widnes by 6 to 18, it could have been worse had Stephanie Drinkwater not been on form in the Wild goal.

The second period saw a tighter Widnes defensive performance and, while they were still heavily outshot, the resulting 0-0 period score gave rise to hopes that there might be a late rally in the final 20 minutes of play.

These hopes were dashed by a third Telford goal just 55 seconds into the period – before incoming netminder Ellie Green had time to settle – and further goals on 42 and 44 minutes put the game well beyond Widnes' reach.

The Wild breakthrough finally came with 45.33 on the clock when Widnes captain Charlotte Cramp slotted the puck past the Telford netminder, rounding off the scoring for the game.

The Wild Women's Most Valuable Player awards for this season have been sponsored by Lucy London - Poet In Residence for the 5th year in a row and consist of goodie bags containing a limited edition MVP teddy bear and a selection of Body Shop products provided by Running Mum Beauty.

The awards were presented by match volunteer Fiona Tyrer and went to Rebecca Craig for Telford and Karyn Cooper for Widnes.

The 1-5 result means that Telford remain in a good position to challenge for a top two spot and a place in the end of season play offs while Widnes look resigned to battling for the mid-table places.

The Wild women have two more home games left to play and await a league management decision regarding two outstanding away games for which no suitable replay date has been found.

The Wild Women are next in action on Sunday 28th April when they take on Sheffield Shadows at Planet Ice Widnes, 4.25pm face off.

Wild Women v Sheffield Preview

The DMUK Widnes Wild women's team play their first game in over a month when they take on Sheffield Shadows this Sunday 28th April at Planet Ice Widnes, 4.25pm face off.

The Wild women have had a bit of an "up and down" season and have narrowly lost their last two home games – to league champions Caledonia Steel Queens and play off contenders Telford – and will be keen to bounce back from those defeats.

Sunday's opponents Sheffield are above Widnes in the league table with 6 wins from their 10 games to date, as opposed to the Wild's 4 wins from the same number of games. The away game in Sheffield back in November was very close and saw the Wild women fight back from being 5-1 down early in the third period to almost snatching a point in a 5-4 defeat, so there are hopes that the game on Sunday will be just as keenly contested and entertaining.

Sheffield are in 4th place in the Division 2 North table at present and are still harbouring hopes of qualifying for the end of season Play Offs.

The Caledonia Steel Queens have already secured the first spot in the play offs, having won the Division 2 North league title with games still to play but qualification for the second spot is still wide open with a chasing pack of 5 teams still in the running.

As the league table stands at present, the Wild Women could – mathematically, at least – still snatch second spot in the table and take the other play off berth if a rather unlikely series of events were to take place.

Firstly they would have to win both of their remaining league games – which is certainly possible - then hope that everybody else takes points off each other – which is less likely – and, finally, hope that they get a favourable decision from the League Management Committee on the allocation of points from two unplayed games that can't be rescheduled.

With that over-complicated scenario seeming rather improbable, it looks as if the Wild Women might miss out on the Play Offs this season, which may be a blessing in disguise as there is a bit of a storm brewing in that direction.

The EIH(A) have announced that the Play Offs will take place at iceSheffield over three days on the weekend of 31st May to 2nd June. Last year they were played over the Bank Holiday weekend from Saturday to Monday - which was fine for most people - but this year, as the venue was, apparently, not available for that particular weekend, the event is being run from Friday to Sunday – with the first day being a normal working day for many players, officials and, of course, supporters.

Six semi final matches are scheduled to be played on the Friday, starting at 9am in the morning and running through until 10pm or later in the evening, and as the women's leagues don't officially finish until the end of May, some teams may not even know who has qualified for them until a few days beforehand.

This could cause a logistical nightmare in terms of getting time off work, booking hotels and travelling to Sheffield on a busy weekday and the scheduling for this year's event has provoked a lot of criticism from around the country.

Wild Women MVP v Sheffield Natalie Buckles (Photo by Paul Breeze)

Sunday 28th April – WNIHL Div 2N
DMUK Widnes Wild Women 2 – Sheffield Shadows 2

The DMUK Widnes Wild women had to make do with one point instead of two after the Sheffield Shadows snatched a 2-2 draw in a dramatic finish at Planet Ice Widnes on Sunday.

With the Shadows having won the corresponding away game back in November by a single goal, this game was also going to be a close one and it turned out to be one of the tensest encounters seen at the Widnes rink this season.

The Wild women took the lead with a goal from Jemma Brown in the 6th minute and despite numerous chances for both sides, the score remained 1-0 at the first period break.

Sheffield moved up a gear in the second period – outshooting the Wild by more than 2 to 1 - and this pressure was rewarded with an equalised goal in the 24th minute. However, Widnes bounced back and Phoebe Patient edged the Wild Women back in front with just 28 seconds to go in the second period, handing the home side a rather precarious 2-1 lead.

The third period was fascinating to watch with plenty of end to end hockey as the Wild women looked to extend their lead and Sheffield sought to draw level again. The atmosphere around the rink was electrifying and the pressure built up as the clock ticked slowly down.

With two minutes left to play, the period remained goal-less it looked as if the Wild Women might be able to hang on to their slender lead and record their first home win since January.

But then it all went wrong. A slashing penalty given at 58.26 meant that, at best, Widnes would have to play out the rest of the game a player short. Sheffield called a timeout at this point and replaced their netminder with an extra attacker meaning that Widnes had to defend the ensuing face off in their defensive zone with 4 players against 6.

Although this meant that the Shadows goal was undefended – and a well placed place shot out of defence might have settled the game with an empty net goal - the Wild Women found themselves under so much pressure at their own end that that opportunity never arose.

Sheffield surrounded the Widnes goal, determined to make the most of their two player advantage and the tactic paid off when netminder Ellie Green - clearly unsighted due to the sea of grappling bodies directly in front of her – was beaten by a close range shot with just 27 seconds left to play.

Widnes – now back to full strength after the goal wiped out the penalty – pushed forward to try and snatch a late winner but the clock ran down and the game finished as a 2-2 draw.

The Wild Women's Most Valuable Player awards for this season have been sponsored by Lucy London - Poet In Residence for the 5th year in a row and consist of goodie bags containing a limited edition MVP teddy bear and a selection of Body Shop products provided by Running Mum Beauty.

The awards were presented by match volunteer Anthony Stock and went to Hayley Reynolds for Sheffield and Natalie Buckles for Widnes.

The Wild Women are next in action on Sunday 12th May for their last match of the season when they take on Leeds Roses at Planet Ice Widnes, 4.25pm face off.

Team Captain for the day Laura Marcroft was the Wild Women's MVP in the match against Leeds (Photo by Paul Breeze)

Sunday 12th May – WNIHL Div2 N
DMUK Widnes Wild Women 2 – Leeds Roses 3

The DMUK Widnes Wild women's team put in a battling performance but ended up on the wrong end of a 2-3 scoreline against Leeds Roses in their last game of the season at Planet Ice Widnes on Sunday.

The Wild Women had lost 8-2 in the away fixture against Leeds earlier in the season and then suffered a huge disappointment in their last home game against Sheffield when an equalising goal with just 27 seconds left to play robbed them of a win, so there was a lot of cross-Pennine pride at stake in this final league game.

The match started well for Widnes and they opened the scoring in the 7th minute with a well-taken goal from Preston Gennoe. There were numerous chances for both teams and the visitors had a slight edge in terms of shots on goal, but Stephanie Drinkwater water looked very composed in the Wild net and the score remained 1-0 at the first period break.

The second period was as closely contested as the first – with lots of end to end action - and Leeds eventually equalised with a goal on 25 minutes. Widnes hit straight back, however, and a second goal from Gennoe on 29 minutes edged the home side back in front.

The score stood at a tantalisingly close 2-1 to Widnes at the second interval and the Wild Women just needed to carry on as they were and hang on for another 20 minutes to bring their season to a winning conclusion.

Having managed to keep penalty free during the first two periods, it all began to go wrong in the third as the clock ticked down and the game began to get niggly. Leeds pushed forward in an attempt to force an equaliser and Widnes were forced into conceding penalties to keep them at bay.

The game changing moment came when the Wild women were 35 seconds into a slashing call and Leeds were able to make the most of their player advantage to level the score with 12 minutes still to play. This gave the Roses a huge boost and they went on to take the lead 3 minutes later.

The Wild women pushed hard to try and find a way back into the game but they were unable to make any headway against the stubborn Leeds defence in the last

10 minutes and the game ended in a narrow 2-3 victory for the visitors.

The Wild Women's Most Valuable Player awards for this season have been sponsored by Lucy London - Poet In Residence for the 5th year in a row and consist of goodie bags containing a limited edition MVP teddy bear and a selection of Body Shop products provided by Running Mum Beauty. The awards were presented by match volunteer Colin Ellis and went to Emma Allender for Leeds and Laura Marcroft for Widnes.

Wild Women Awarded Points In League Decision

The DMUK Widnes Wild women's team have finished the WNIHL Division 2 North season with three extra league points following a decision by the League Management Committee regarding two unresolved games.

The first game was the away fixture at Kingston Diamonds that was due to be played on 27th January but had to be postponed as the Hull Jets NIHL (men's) team needed the ice slot for a Moralee Cup semi final match, which had to be played that weekend.

It was not subsequently possible to re-arrange the women's game for a mutually convenient date and time so the result was eventually awarded as a 0-0 draw with 1 point for each team.

With Widnes having already beaten Kingston 10-2 at home in their first encounter of the season back in December - and considering the fact that the Diamonds' only wins all season came at the expense of bottom team Grimsby - having this game awarded as draw comes across as a bit of a gift as the Wild women would, probably have won the re-arranged game had it been played.

The other decision was a bit more complicated as the away game at Grimsby on 24th February had to be abandoned at 16.47 minutes due to a serious injury to a Grimsby player.

It was nobody's fault and there was no foul play involved - the player concerned just fell badly and needed to be taken to hospital with a broken leg.

Widnes had travelled to the game without a recognised netminder so senior player Lucy Kirkham bravely stepped in to play in goal. At the time of the abandonment, the score was 4-1 to Grimsby, with the sole Widnes goal coming from team captain Charlotte Cramp.

When a similar thing happened in a Wild women's game the previous season - and a Widnes player was injured in a game away at Whitley - the score had been 0-1 to the Wild at the time of the incident and the result had been allowed to stand.

This time, however, the LMC decided to award the abandoned game as a 0-5 forfeit win to Widnes, suggesting that there must have been other aspects that needed to be considered.

The Grimsby team may well feel aggrieved that they missed out on their only chance of a win for the season when the game was called off but – here again - a full strength Widnes team would almost certainly have won the re-arranged game, had it been played.

With the result being awarded as a 0-5 forfeit, it means that the goals and assists scored by both sides do not get counted in the official records and, sadly, nor does Lucy

Kirkham's heroic 16 minute stint in goal during which she saved 15 of the 19 shots she faced.

The league decision means that the Wild women now finish the season with five wins, two draws and seven defeats from their 14 league matches.

They end up in 5th place in the 8-team table with12 points - 5 behind Leeds Roses who finish 4th and 3 ahead of Whitley Bay Beacons who finish 6th.

The Wild women's top points scorer for the season was Preston Gennoe with 16 goals and 5 assists from 11 games

Katie Fairclough was second with 10+5 from 10 games and Katya Oliver third with 3+5 from 9 games.

Wild Women's most improved player Jennifer Hickey with coach Steve Furber (Photo by Vanessa Crickmore–Clarke)

Widnes Wild Women's Awards Night

The DMUK Widnes Wild women's team held their end of season Presentation Evening at the Mercure Hotel, Haydock, at the weekend and the following awards were presented:

Top Points For Season - Preston Gennoe

Best Forward - Ellen Tyrer

Best Defence - Katie Adshead

Most Improved Player - Jennifer Hickey

Coaches Player Of The Season - Katya Oliver

Unsung Hero - Karyn Cooper

Players' Player of the Season – Rachael Pearce

WNIHL Division 2 North – Season 2024/25

Final Table	GP	W	D	L	GF	GA	GD	Pts
Widnes Wild Women	12	7	4	1	56	36	20	18
Telford Wrekin Raiders	12	7	2	3	72	31	41	16
Sheffield Shadows	12	8	0	4	55	29	26	16
Leeds Roses	12	6	3	3	75	32	43	15
Whitley Bay Beacons	12	5	1	6	50	50	0	11
Kingston Diamonds	12	3	2	7	33	74	-41	8
Caledonia Bees	12	0	0	12	28	117	-89	0

Top Points Scorers

Player	Team	GP	G	A	Pts	PIM
C.J. Harrison	Leeds Roses	11	19	9	28	2
Jasmin Daniel	Leeds Roses	10	16	9	25	0
Tiffany-Jayne Miller	Telford Raiders	11	11	14	25	6
Leen de Decker	Widnes Wild	10	15	6	21	0
Heather Metcalf	Telford Raiders	12	8	13	21	8
Maggie Whitmore	Telford Raiders	11	14	6	20	8
Isabella Oswin	Kingston D'monds	9	12	6	18	4
Chloe Carter	Sheffield Shadows	10	12	4	16	12
Athene Idiabor-Moses	Sheffield Shadows	11	5	10	15	4
Charlotte Cramp	Widnes Wild	10	8	6	14	0

Top Netminders

Netminder	Team	GPI	Mins	SA	GA	GAA	SV%	SO
Kirsty Robson	SHE	11	409	200	15	2.2	92.50%	2
Teagan Hyatt	TEL	7	420	241	16	2.29	93.40%	1
Emily Johnson	KIN	8	403	292	21	3.13	92.80%	0
Barthe McCormick	LEE	4	227	151	11	2.92	92.70%	0
Shannon Schneider	SHE	2	40	13	1	1.5	92.30%	1
Dawn Dickinson	KIN	1	49	35	3	3.74	91.40%	0
Alice Somerford	TEL/LEE	5	300	158	14	2.8	91.10%	1
Keira Daniel	LEE	2	120	77	7	3.5	90.90%	0
Steph Drinkwater	WID	11	647	418	39	3.62	90.70%	1
Ruth Palmer	WHI	12	720	345	50	4.17	85.50%	0

Widnes Wild Women Player Statistics – 2024/25
WNIHL Division 2 North

Player	GP	G	A	Pts	PIM
Leen de Decker	10	15	6	21	0
Charlotte Cramp	10	9	6	15	0
Lise Gillen	8	8	4	12	4
Amanda Armstrong	7	5	5	10	0
Jennifer Hickey	11	2	6	8	2
Phoebe Patient	7	4	2	6	2
Ellen Tyrer	7	2	4	6	2
Karyn Cooper	11	0	6	6	2
Ruth Leopold	12	4	1	5	2
Jemma Brown	11	4	1	5	4
Victoria Connelly	7	1	4	5	0
Rachael Pearce	12	0	5	5	8
Abigail Aldred	7	2	2	4	0
Charlotte McAdam	8	1	2	3	0
Catherine Fell	8	0	3	3	8
Katie Fairclough	8	1	1	2	31
Eleanor Johnson	10	0	2	2	2
Jennifer Greenwood	8	0	1	1	2
Lucy Kirkham	6	0	1	1	2
Savannah Sumner	3	0	1	1	2
Suzie Miller	10	0	0	0	2
Katie Adshead	10	0	0	0	4
Elizabeth Loss	9	0	0	0	2
Vanessa Crickmore-Clarke	8	0	0	0	2
Laura Moran	8	0	0	0	6
Sophie Hill	6	0	0	0	0
Niamh Horsfield	2	0	0	0	0
Nicole Rainey	1	0	0	0	0
Stephanie Drinkwater	11	0	0	0	0
Charlotte Jackson	1	0	0	0	0

Netminder	GPI	Min	SA	GA	GAA	Save %	SO
Stephanie Drinkwater	11	646	421	32	2.97	92.40	1
Charlotte Jackson	1	60	38	4	4.00	89.47	0
Totals	12	706	459	36	3.06	92.16	1

Please note that the goals and assists for the away game at Caledonia were taken from Wild Women's team coach Paddy Horner's notes and NOT from the official gamesheet, so our player stats for the season may not tally with other official figures.

Widnes Wild Women Player Statistics – 2024/25
WNIHL Division 2 North Cup

Player	GP	G	A	Pts	PIM
Katie Fairclough	3	4	1	5	0
Leen de Decker	4	1	4	5	2
Rachael Pearce	4	2	2	4	4
Catherine Fell	4	1	2	3	2
Karyn Cooper	4	2	0	2	0
Amanda Armstrong	2	1	1	2	0
Jemma Brown	2	1	1	2	0
Cath Thornton	3	1	0	1	0
Suzie Miller	4	0	0	0	0
Jennifer Hickey	4	0	0	0	0
Jennifer Greenwood	4	0	0	0	0
Eleanor Johnson	4	0	0	0	0
Katie Adshead	3	0	0	0	0
Charlotte McAdam	3	0	0	0	0
Elizabeth Loss	2	0	0	0	0
Ruth Leopold	2	0	0	0	0
Niamh Horsfield	2	0	0	0	0
Sophie Hill	2	0	0	0	0
Ellen Tyrer	1	0	0	0	0
Lucy Kirkham	1	0	0	0	0
Charlotte Cramp	1	0	0	0	0
Vanessa Crickmore-Clarke	1	0	0	0	0
Stephanie Drinkwater	3	0	0	0	0
Charlotte Jackson	1	0	0	0	0

Netminder	GPI	Min	SA	GA	GAA	Save %	SO
Stephanie Drinkwater	3	161.3	157	22	8.18	85.99	0
Charlotte Jackson	1	60	59	13	13.00	77.97	0
Totals	4	221.3	216	35	9.49	83.80	0

Widnes Wild Women Player Statistics – 2024/25
WNIHL D2N Play Offs

Player	GP	G	A	Pts	PIM
Leen de Decker	1	1	0	1	0
Lise Gillen	1	0	1	1	0
Eleanor Johnson	1	0	1	1	0
Charlotte Cramp	1	0	0	0	0
Jennifer Hickey	1	0	0	0	0
Phoebe Patient	1	0	0	0	0
Karyn Cooper	1	0	0	0	0
Ruth Leopold	1	0	0	0	2
Jemma Brown	1	0	0	0	0
Victoria Connelly	1	0	0	0	0
Rachael Pearce	1	0	0	0	0
Abigail Aldred	1	0	0	0	2
Charlotte McAdam	1	0	0	0	0
Catherine Fell	1	0	0	0	0
Suzie Miller	1	0	0	0	0
Katie Adshead	1	0	0	0	0
Elizabeth Loss	1	0	0	0	0
Vanessa Crickmore-Clarke	1	0	0	0	0
Laura Moran	1	0	0	0	2
Stephanie Drinkwater	1	0	0	0	0

Netminder	GPI	Min	SA	GA	GAA	Save %	SO
Stephanie Drinkwater	1	60	50	8	8.00	84.00	0

Widnes Wild Women Player Statistics – 2024/25

All Matches (includes League, Cup & Play Offs

Player	GP	G	A	Pts	PIM
Leen de Decker	15	17	10	27	2
Charlotte Cramp	12	9	6	15	0
Lise Gillen	9	8	5	13	4
Amanda Armstrong	9	6	6	12	0
Rachael Pearce	17	2	7	9	12
Jennifer Hickey	16	2	6	8	2
Karyn Cooper	16	2	6	8	2
Jemma Brown	14	5	2	7	4
Katherine Fairclough	11	5	2	7	31
Catherine Fell	13	1	5	6	10
Phoebe Patient	8	4	2	6	2
Ellen Tyrer	8	2	4	6	2
Ruth Leopold	15	4	1	5	4
Victoria Connelly	8	1	4	5	0
Abigail Aldred	8	2	2	4	2
Eleanor Johnson	15	0	3	3	2
Charlotte McAdam	12	1	2	3	0
Jennifer Greenwood	12	0	1	1	2
Lucy Kirkham	7	0	1	1	2
Savannah Sumner	3	0	1	1	2
Cath Thornton	3	1	0	1	0
Suzanne Miller	15	0	0	0	2
Stephanie Drinkwater	15	0	0	0	0
Katie Adshead	14	0	0	0	4
Elizabeth Loss	12	0	0	0	2
Vanessa Crickmore-Clarke	10	0	0	0	2
Laura Moran	9	0	0	0	8
Sophie Hill	8	0	0	0	0
Niamh Horsfield	4	0	0	0	0
Charlotte Jackson	2	0	0	0	0
Nicole Rainey	1	0	0	0	0

Netminder	Comp	GPI	Mins	SA	GA	GAA	Save %	SO
Stephanie Drinkwater	League	11	646.05	421	32	2.97	92.40	1
	Cup	3	161.19	157	22	8.18	85.99	0
	Play Offs	1	60.00	50	8	8.00	84.00	0
	Totals	15	867.24	628	62	4.29	90.13	1
Charlotte Jackson	Cup	1	60.00	59	13	13.00	77.97	0
	League	1	60.00	38	4	4.00	89.47	0
	Totals	2	120.00	97	17	8.50	82.47	0

Netminding Break-Down – Season 2024/25

League	Netminder	GPI	Min	SA	GA	GAA	Save %	SO
@ KIN	Drinkwater	1	60	39	4	4.00	89.74	0
@ SHE	Drinkwater	1	60	33	1	1.00	96.97	0
@ WHI	Drinkwater	1	60	55	6	6.00	89.09	0
v WHI	Drinkwater	1	60	43	5	5.00	88.37	0
@ CAL	Jackson	1	60	38	4	4.00	89.47	0
@ TEL	Drinkwater	1	60	37	2	2.00	94.59	0
V TEL	Drinkwater	1	60	39	4	4.00	89.74	0
V SHE	Drinkwater	1	60	49	2	2.00	95.92	0
v KIN	Drinkwater	1	60	32	4	4.00	87.50	0
v LEE	Drinkwater	1	60	49	1	1.00	97.96	0
V CAL	Drinkwater	1	60	16	0	0.00	100.00	1
@ LEE	Drinkwater*	1	46[2]	29	3	3.91	89.66	0
	Totals	**12**	**706**	**459**	**36**	**3.06**	**92.16**	**1**

Cup	Netminder	GPI	Min	SA	GA	GAA	Save %	SO
v SHE	Drinkwater	1	60	59	10	10.00	83.05	0
@ SHE	Drinkwater	1	60	50	7	7.00	86.00	0
v TEL	Drinkwater	1	41.3[1]	48	5	7.26	89.58	0
@ TEL	Jackson	1	60	59	13	13.00	77.97	0
	Totals	**4**	**221.3**	**216**	**35**	**9.49**	**83.80**	**0**

Play Offs	Netminder	GPI	Min	SA	GA	GAA	Save %	SO
v STR	Drinkwater	1	60	50	8	8.00	84.00	0

1: Game abandoned at 41.10 due to a player injury. Result recorded as a 5-5 draw – the score at the time of the stoppage.

2: Game abandoned at 46.05 due to a player injury. Result recorded as a 3-3 draw – the score at the time of the stoppage.

Widnes Wild Women - Season 2024/25 (Photo by Wil Evans)

Back Row: Steve Furber, Katie Adshead, Grace Teinert, Jennifer Greenwood, Jennifer Hickey, Sophie Hill, Laura Moran, Karyn Cooper, Leen de Decker, Eleanor Johnson, Amanda Armstrong, Niamh Horsfield, Ruth Leopold, Natalie Buckles, Thomas Horner. Front Row: Suzie Miller, Charlotte McAdam, Elizabeth Loss, Charlotte Cramp, Stephanie Drinkwater, Rachael Pearce, Ellen Tyrer, Phoebe Patient, Lise Gillen, Victoria Connelly

Widnes Wild Women Results - Season 2024/25

Date		Home			Away	
29/9/24	D2N	Kingston Diamonds	4	4	Widnes Wild	D
12/10/24	D2N	Sheffield Shadows	1	2	Widnes Wild	W
27/10/24	D2N	Whitley Bay Beacons	6	4	Widnes Wild	L
24/11/24	D2N	Widnes Wild	6	5	Whitley Bay Beacons	W
7/12/24	D2N	Caledonia Queen Bees	4	12	Widnes Wild	W
15/12/24	Cup	Widnes Wild	2	10	Sheffield Shadows	L
12/1/25	D2N	Telford Wrekin Raiders	2	2	Widnes Wild	D
26/1/25	D2N	Widnes Wild	5	4	Telford Wrekin Raiders	W
2/2/25	Cup	Sheffield Shadows	7	3	Widnes Wild	L
16/2/25	Cup	Widnes Wild	5	5	Telford Wrekin Raiders	Da[1]
9/3/25	D2N	Widnes Wild	4	2	Sheffield Shadows	W
16/3/25	D2N	Widnes Wild	4	4	Kingston Diamonds	D
13/4/25	D2N	Widnes Wild	2	1	Leeds Roses	W
27/4/25	D2N	Widnes Wild	8	0	Caledonia Queen Bees	W
3/5/25	Cup	Telford Wrekin Raiders	13	3	Widnes Wild	L
10/5/25	D2N	Leeds Roses	3	3	Widnes Wild	Da[2]
24/05/25	POS	Widnes Wild	1	8	Streatham Storm	L

1: Game abandoned at 41.19 due to a player injury. Result recorded as a 5-5 draw – the score at the time of the stoppage.

2: Game abandoned at 46.05 due to a player injury. Result recorded as a 3-3 draw – the score at the time of the stoppage.

Wild Women Season Preview

The Widnes Wild women's team have announced their leadership teams in preparation for the new 2024/25 WNIHL season, which starts this weekend.

The Head Coach for the new season is Steve Furber, with Thomas (Paddy) Horner as Assistant Coach. Leen De Decker, Katie Fairclough and Suzie Miller will all be Player / Coaches.

Charlotte Cramp returns as team captain in the role that she filled so admirably last season and Rachael Pearce and Elizabeth Loss are Alternate Captains.

The Wild Women will, once again, be playing in WNIHL Division 2 North where they will take on opposition from: Hull, Sheffield, Whitley Bay, Edinburgh, Telford and Leeds.

Last year's strugglers Grimsby withdrew from the league during the summer and a new 3-team Northern Cup competition has been introduced between Widnes, Telford and Sheffield to provide extra matches to make up the shortfall.

The Wild Women start their season with a trip to Hull and back this Sunday 29th September when they take on the Kingston Diamonds. They then have two more away fixtures before their first home game against Whitley Bay Beacons on Sunday 24th November at Planet Ice Widnes, 4.25pm face off.

The full fixture list for the 2024/25 season is:

29th Sept: away @ Kingston
12th Oct: away @ Sheffield
27th Oct: away @ Whitley
24th Nov: home v Whitley
7th Dec: away @ Caledonia
15th Dec: home v Sheffield (Cup)
12th Jan: away @ Telford
26th Jan: home v Telford
2nd Feb: away @ Sheffield (Cup)
16th Feb: home v Telford (Cup)
9th Mar: home v Sheffield
16th Mar: home v Kingston
22nd Mar: away @ Leeds
13th April: home v Leeds
27th April: home v Caledonia
3rd May: away @ Telford (Cup)

Meet The Wild Women – 2024/25

#1 Stephanie Drinkwater: Netminder Stephanie is one of the original Wild Women players who moved to Widnes when the club was relocated from Altrincham in the wake of the Manchester Phoenix fiasco back in 2015.

She has played over 100 competitive league games in total – some 85 for Widnes – and was a member of the Wild women's team that won the Division 1 North league title in the 2019/20 season to add the title she won at Altrincham in 2014/15.

She played in 10 games last season and ended up with a very impressive Save Percentage of 90.78% and 2 shut outs. She returns for her 9th season in Widnes colours this season.

#5 Leen De Decker. Leen is another original Wild Woman and had previously played 8 seasons for Kingston Diamonds before arriving at Widnes via Altrincham. She was, until recently, the most capped player for her native Belgium with 52 World Championship games under her belt, along with 3 WC bronze medals and 1 silver medal.

Leen has played in 7 of the Wild Women's 8 seasons – having been behind the scenes in a coaching capacity last season – and has scored 86 goals and 34 assists in 72 competitive matches. She was an important member of the Wild women's team that won the Division 1 North league title in the 2019/20 season and was team captain for the 2022/23 season when they were league runners up.

#6 Vanessa Crickmore-Clarke. Vanessa is a highly experienced attacker turned defender who won 5 league titles with the Sunderland Scorpions in her native north east and then spent 9 seasons playing at Deeside and Altrincham before the move to Widnes. Like Drinkwater and de Decker, she also won the Division 1 North title with Altrincham in 2015 and Widnes in 2020 and, in an impressive career to date, has played over 250 competitive games in total. She played in 8 games for Widnes last season.

#7: Ruth Leopold. Ruth is new face in a Widnes shirt this season but has been very well-known around the women's game for many years. She started playing for the Blackpool Blades women' team in 1987/88 and then moved to the Blackburn Falcons. She joined the newly formed Sheffield Shadows for the 1993/94 season – scoring the club s' first ever goal – then moved down to Bristol for work and joined the Swindon Top Cats in 1995. Ruth won a number of Division One titles with Swindon and also had a WPL title-winning year with Slough in 1998/99 before returning to the Top Cats and later Bristol Huskies.

Talking about joining Widnes for the coming season, Leopold said; "I moved back up to Lytham last year and thought I had retired, but was inspired by Rachael (Pearce) to come back and started training with Blackburn women. I enjoyed that so wanted to play league hockey again, and I decided to come along to Widnes. I am really looking forward to the season, where I hope my experience can be an asset to help the team. I am very grateful to the Wild for giving me a chance to continue playing the sport I have loved for 37 years!"

#8 Suzie Miller: Suzie is back for her 5th season in Widnes colours, having originally joined the Wild women for the 2019/20 title winning season. In that time she has played 42 games, contributing 4 assists from her defensive role. Behind the scenes, Suzie is also a qualified coach and manager.

#9 Natalie Buckles: Non playing coach this season.

#10 Lise Gillen: Ontario-born Lise Gillen brings a wealth of experience having played 3 seasons for the Guildford Lightning in the Womens' Elite League, as well as playing in her native Canada. She has played 14 games for Widnes over the past 2 seasons, scoring 4 goals and 6 assists

#11: Katie Fairclough. Katie first joined the Wild in 2017 and will be back for her seventh season in Widnes colours. She has gained international honours at GB Women's Under 18 level and was a league title winner with the Wild women in 2020. Last season, Fairclough was the Wild women's second highest scorer with 10 goals and 5 assists in 10 games and, overall, she has played 72 games for Widnes, scoring 39+25 with 83 penalty minutes. Katie is also a qualified coach and match official.

#12 Katie Adshead: Katie returns for her 6th season with the Wild team, having originally joined for the 2018/19 season. She has notched up 63 matches in that time, scoring 3 goals and 8 assists with 24 penalty minutes and was another key member of the 2019/20 title winning season.

#13 Rachael Pearce: Rachael is back for her 3rd season with the Wild women's team and brings a huge amount of experience, stretching back to the Blackpool women's team in the late 1980s, the Blackburn Falcons team in the early 1990s and then more recently with the Wyre Seagulls and the Blackburn Thunder women's team. She has been an "ever present" since joining the Wild Women and has scored 10 goals and 12 assists in 27 league and play off games.

#15 Laura Moran. Laura returns for her second season in Wild colours with over 80 WNIHL matches under her belt, having previously played for 8 years for the Oxford Midnight Stars in Division 2 South. She has 4 career goals and 12 assists from her defensive role and has notched up 44 penalty minutes. Moran also played University hockey for 4 seasons with the UAE (University Of East Anglia) Avalanche, scoring 1+2 in 18 games.

#18: Grace Teinert. Grace is a new player to the team, having come up through the highly respected Hockey Basics and Hockey Excellence programmes at the Widnes rink. She is a development player and this will be her first season of competitive ice hockey. Her brother Daniel is a Wild Academy junior player and her father Mike is a two time Summer Cup winner with the Riverside Raiders recreational team.

#19: Cath Thornton. Cath is a new face to Widnes fans but she played league ice hockey for the Deeside-based Flintshire Furies – alongside fellow Wild women Catherine Fell and Vanessa Crickmore-Clarke - for four seasons, scoring 7 goals and 4 assists in 48 competitive matches. She has most recently been playing for the Connah's Quay Cobras recreational team at Deeside.

#22: Jennifer Hickey. Jennifer joined the Wild women for the 2021/22 season and has played in all 42 games that the team have played since then. She has contributed 5 goals and 6 assists and picked up just 6 penalty minutes. Hickey also plays University hockey for the Manchester Metros, scoring 7+12 in 52 games over three seasons.

#23: Ellen Tyrer. Ellen also made her Wild women's senior debut in the Women's Premier League in the 2021/22 season, having previously played for the Wild Academy Under 15 and Under 18 teams. In 38 league, play off and challenge games over her three seasons with the Wild women so far, she has also scored 8 goals and 6 assists.

#26: Niamh Horsfield. A new player to the WNIHL for this season, Niamh has a background in university hockey, having played for the Whitley Bay based North East Angels - who are a team compromised of women's players from the various universities in the North East of England such as Newcastle, Northumbria and Durham - and also with Manchester Metros.

#27: Lucy Kirkham. Lucy will be back for her 6th season as a Wild player, having originally moved with the Phoenix contingent from Altrincham in 2015 but spending the period 2018 to 2022 away from the game. She has played 51 competitive matches for the Wild Women, scoring 11 goals and 20 assists. She played in 3 games last season - and even went in goal for 20 minutes for the abandoned match away at Grimsby.

#29: Charlotte Cramp. Charlotte returns to the Wild women for her fourth season, having joined the team in 2021 from a background of university hockey with Manchester Metros. In her three seasons with the Wild to date, she has played 42 games and scored 6 goals and 14 assists. She will again be the captain of the Wild women's team for the new season, having admirably fulfilled the role last term. She is also a qualified match official.

#34: Elizabeth Loss. Experienced centre Elizabeth was one of the original Manchester Phoenix team that moved to Widnes in 2015 and, in her 7 seasons with the Wild women, has played 54 games, scoring 4 goals and 16 assists - and never picking up a single penalty minute. Liz was a key member of the Widnes team that won the 2019/20 Division 1 North league title.

#44: Phoebe Patient. Phoebe also played for the Wild Academy Under 15 and Under 18 teams and made her Wild women's senior debut in the Women's Premier League in the 2021/22 season. In 39 league, play off and challenge games over her three seasons with the Wild women so far, she has scored 5 goals and 4 assists.

#54: Charlotte Jackson. Netminder Charlotte was another member of the Wild women's team that won the North 1 league title in the 2019/20 season and also played in the 2012/22 post-Covid Premier League campaign. Since then, she has been away at Nottingham University studying for a Criminology degree and playing for the Mavericks University side. She also plays roller hockey, has represented GB in the past and won a number of tournaments with the Sirens team. Charlotte's brother, Tom Jackson, is the player coach of the Widnes Wild Moralee Division men's team.

#65: Karyn Cooper. Karyn returns for her 5th season with the Wild women, having originally joined the team for the 2018/19 season. She also played University hockey for the Manchester Metros team, clocking up 43 games in 4 years. In her 5 seasons to date at Widnes, Karyn has played in 62 league, playoff and challenge matches, contributing 7 assists. She is also the Wild women's Team Manager and puts in a huge amount of work behind the scenes.

#66: Jemma Brown. Jemma also returns for her 5th season at Widnes, having previously played for the Kingston Diamonds in the Women's Premier League as well as junior hockey for Blackburn and Trafford. She was a member of the Wild women's team that won the Division 1 North title in 2019/20 and has played 48 league and challenge matches for Widnes scoring 8 goals and 10 assists.

#68: Abigail Aldred. Abigail returns for her second season with Widnes, having played 7 games last season. In a busy year all round, she also played with the Nottingham Vipers womens team in WNIHL Division 1 and the Manchester Storm mixed Under 18 team last season. She has previously played with the Manchester Under 16 girls' team and is an assistant coach with them for this season.

#71: Amanda Armstrong. Amanda was another of the original Wild Women who moved from Altrincham in 2015 and went on to play for Widnes for 4 seasons until 2019.

In an impressive career spanning over 20 years, she has played some 250 competitive games and has been Head Coach of the Manchester Storm Under 16 girls' team for the past 2 seasons. During her previous stint with Widnes, she scored 15 goals and 13 assists in 39 games.

#72: Savannah Sumner. Sav was the first Widnes-born and trained player ever to play a competitive match for a Wild team when she and fellow local girl Sal Roberts took to the ice against Milton Keynes Falcons in the first game of the 2016/2017 season.

She played for the Wild Women for 4 seasons and was part of the team that won the 2019/20 Division 1 North title before moving to play for Whitley Bay in the Women's Elite League. She played 3 more games for Widnes in the 2022/23 season bringing her total in Wild colours to 48 games, scoring 18 goals and 12 assists.

#73: Catherine Fell. Catherine returns for her 8th season with the Wild Women, having been another of the "originals" who moved from Altrincham 2015.

Fell began playing hockey with the Blackburn Thunder team in 1999 season and played 8 seasons with them and 6 seasons with the Deeside-based Flintshire Furies, before joining the Manchester Phoenix Women's Team for their 2014/2015 Division 1 North winning season.

She has played 60 competitive matches for the Wild Women, scoring 20 goals and 16 assists and was a member of the team that won the league title in 2019/20.

#74: Sophie Hill. Sophie returns for her third season with Widnes. She has played 6 games in the past two seasons, scoring 2 goals and 3 assists.

#77 Jennifer Greenwood. Previously played 3 seasons with Blackburn Thunder in Division 1 North, 2004-07.

#79: Nicole Rainey. A Manchester Storm junior player who played 9 games with their U16 girls' team last season.

#88: Victoria Connelly. Victoria is back for her third season as a Widnes player. She is a former Guildford Lightning Elite player, previously playing for the Bracknell Fire Bees and has made 14 appearances for the Wild Women over the past 2 seasons, scoring 6 goals and 2 assists.

#95: Eleanor Johnson. Eleanor made her senior debut with the Wild Women last season, icing in 6 WNIHL matches. She also played for the Manchester Storm Under 16 girls' team and will be splitting her time this season between Widnes and the new Under 16s girls' team at Deeside.

#97: Charlotte McAdam. Charlotte returns for her second season in Widnes colours. Last season was her first in competitive hockey and she played in 4 games for the Wild Women.

New Wild Women signing Ruth Leopold
(Photo by Natalie Buckles)

Sunday 29th September 2024 – WNIHL Div 2 (N)
Kingston Diamonds 4 – Widnes Wild Women 4

The Widnes Wild women's team started their 2024/25 Division 2 North season with a 4-4 draw away to the Kingston Diamonds in Hull on Sunday.

The game saw Wild debuts for new signings Jennifer Greenwood, Ruth Leopold, Nicole Rainey and Niamh Horsfield – and returns to the team for Sav Sumner and Charlotte Jackson after spending some time away with other clubs.

The two teams were very closely matched throughout this game and the first period remained goal-less until the very last minute when Jennifer Hickey opened the scoring for the Wild with just 35 seconds left on the clock.

Two goals early in the second period put the Diamonds in the lead and they edged further ahead with a goal on 30 minutes to lead 3-1 at the second interval.

The Wild Women visibly upped their game in the third period and two goals in two minutes – from Katie Fairclough and Leen de Decker – put them on level terms with 13 minutes left to play.

Kingston got their noses back in front with a 4th goal on 50 minutes but de Decker equalised again with 4 minutes left on the clock to secure the point for Widnes.

The Wild Women have two more away fixtures - at Sheffield on 12th October and Whitley Bay on 27th October - before their first home game against Whitley Bay Beacons on Sunday 24th November at Planet Ice Widnes, 4.25pm face off.

*****

Ruth Leopold is a new face in a Widnes shirt this season but has been very well-known around the women's game for many years. She started playing for the Blackpool Blades women's team in 1987/88 and then moved to the Blackburn Falcons in 1991.

She joined the newly formed Sheffield Shadows for the 1993/94 season – scoring the club's first ever goal – then moved down to Bristol for work and joined the Swindon Top Cats in 1995.

Ruth won a number of Division One titles with Swindon and also had a WPL title-winning year with Slough in 1998/99 before returning to the Top Cats and later playing for the Bristol Huskies.

Talking about joining Widnes for the new season, Leopold said;

“I moved back up to Lytham last year and thought I had retired, but was inspired by Rachael (Pearce) to come back and started training with Blackburn women. I enjoyed that so wanted to play league hockey again, and I decided to come along to Widnes.”

“I am really looking forward to the season, where I hope my experience can be an asset to help the team. I am very grateful to the Wild for giving me a chance to continue playing the sport I have loved for 37 years!”

Netminder Stephanie Drinkwater was the Wild Women's MVP away at Sheffield

Saturday 12th October 2024 – WNIHL Div 2N
Sheffield Shadows 1 – Widnes Wild Women 2

The Widnes Wild women's team continued their unbeaten start to the new season with a 1-2 win away to Sheffield Shadows on Saturday.

As the score suggests, this was a very close game and the result could have gone either way until the very last seconds.

Sheffield took the lead in the 5th minute but Widnes drew level on 10 minutes with a goal from former Belgium international player Leen de Decker. The Wild Women went ahead on 15 minutes with another de Decker strike, this time a powerplay goal punishing a Sheffield stick-holding penalty.

The score remained 1-2 at the first period break and, despite numerous chances for both sides, it also ended up as the final score.

Sheffield upped the pressure as the game progressed, looking for an equaliser forcing Widnes into taking a few defensive penalties as they battled to keep them at bay. Wild netminder Stephanie Drinkwater put in a superb performance in front of goal keeping out 32 of the 33 shots that she faced - and was named MVP for the Wild women.

The Wild Women have another away fixture - at Whitley Bay on 27th October - before their first home game of the season against Whitley Bay Beacons on Sunday 24th November at Planet Ice Widnes, 4.25pm face off.

Leen de Decker (Photo by Wil Evans)

Leen De Decker is one of the original Wild Women players who moved to Widnes when the club was relocated from Altrincham in the wake of the Manchester Phoenix fiasco back in 2015, and had previously played 8 seasons for Kingston Diamonds before arriving at Widnes via Altrincham.

She was, until recently, the most capped player for her native Belgium with 52 World Championship games under her belt, along with 3 WC bronze medals and 1 silver medal.

Leen has played in 7 of the Wild Women's 8 seasons – having been behind the scenes in a coaching capacity last season – and in that time, scored 86 goals and 34 assists in 72 competitive matches. She was an important member of the Wild women's team that won the Division 1 North league title in the 2019/20 season and was team captain for the 2022/23 season when they were league runners up.

Previous Wild Women's team sponsor Laura Prescott from Debt Movement UK (Photo by Paul Breeze)

Widnes Wild Women Seeking Sponsors

The WIdnes Wild women's team are looking for sponsors to support them during the 2024/25 Womens National Ice Hockey League season.

The Wild Women are a not-for-profit women's ice hockey team with players ranging across from 14 years to 50+ years old, playing out of the Planet Ice rink in Widnes. They are playing this season in the women's Division 2 North and are hoping to make it to play offs in May for promotion to the national Division 1 for next year.

The 2024/25 season runs until the end of May and sees the Wild women travelling far and wide across the country, facing opposition from Hull, Sheffield, Leeds, Telford, Whitley Bay and Edinburgh.

There are a number of sponsorship package options, which include company promotion such as:

- Company logo on playing jerseys
- Ceremonial puck drops & MVP presentations
- Regular social media coverage
- Company announcements on match days

Another sponsorship option, which has been popular in previous years is an individual, player sponsorship. The benefits of Individual Player Sponsorship include:

- Company logo on the player's home and away jerseys
- Company name announcements at every home game, and when your player scores or is awarded MVP
- Tagged in social media posts about the player

Interested parties are requested to contact the Wild Women's team in the first instance via their Facebook page.

The Wild Women are away to Whitley Bay Beacons this Sunday 27th October, 5pm face off, and play their first home game of the season against the same opposition on Sunday 24th November at Planet Ice Widnes, 4.25pm face off.

Stephanie Drinkwater and Jennifer Greenwood defend the Wild goal away at Whitley (Photo by Mark Bird Sports Photography)

Sunday 27th October 2024 – WNIHL Div 2 N
Whitley Bay Beacons 6 - Widnes Wild Women 4

The Widnes Wild Women's team suffered their first defeat of the season with a 6-4 loss away to Whitley Bay Beacons on Sunday.

The Wild Women made the long trip to the North East with a strong squad and were boosted by the return of former player coach Amanda Armstrong, who has rejoined the club after 5 seasons away from playing.

Whitley opened the scoring on 2 minutes and were 2-0 up 5 minutes later. Widnes pulled a goal back with a strike from Phoebe Patient on 15 minutes but Whitley restored the two-goal cushion heading into the last minute of the period.

A goal from Jemma Brown with just 6 seconds left on the clock narrowed the deficit again and the score stood at 3-2 at the first interval.

The Beacons made the score 4-2 with a goal 2 minutes into the second period but Widnes fought back and goals from returnee Amanda Armstrong and team captain Charlotte Cramp – on 25 and 28 minutes respectively - saw them level at the second period break.

Unfortunately, Widnes were unable to carry this momentum into the third period and two unanswered goals late in the game handed Whitley the 6-4 win.

The Wild Women are next in action on Sunday 24th November when they play their first home game of the season – again against Whitley Bay Beacons – at Planet Ice Widnes, 4.25pm face off.

Amanda Armstrong (Photo by Flyfifer Photography)

Amanda Armstrong (formerly Williams) is one of the original Wild Women players who moved to Widnes when the club was relocated from Altrincham back in 2015, and went on to play for Widnes for 4 seasons until 2019.

In an impressive career spanning over 20 years - including 13 seasons at Blackburn Thunder – she has played some 250 competitive games and has been Head Coach of the Manchester Storm Under16 girls' team for the past 2 seasons. During her previous stint with Widnes, Amanda scored 15 goals and 13 assists in 39 games

Charlotte Cramp (Photo by Mark Bird Sports Photography)

Charlotte Cramp Selected For GB Students Team

Widnes Wild women's team captain Charlotte Cramp has been selected to play for the Great Britain students' team at the World Students Games in Italy in January.

The 2025 FISA World University Games will take place in the Piedmonte region around Turin from 13th to 23rd January and will feature a variety of outdoor and indoor winter sports.

Alpine skiing, snowboarding, and freestyle will be staged in Bardonecchia, cross-country skiing, biathlon, and ski orienteering in Pragelato, and ski mountaineering in Sestriere.

The indoor sports of figure skating, short track speed skating and curling will be held in Turin and ice hockey matches will be divided around three venues - in Pinerolo, Torre Pellice and Turin.

The GB Students team will come up against opposition from Canada, Chinese Taipei, Czech Republic, Japan, Kazakhstan, Slovakia, and the USA.

Talking about her GB selection, Charlotte said:

“I'm so excited to have been selected to compete in the FISU World University Games with the GB Students Ice Hockey Team. Being selected for any form of team or competition is amazing, however this opportunity is an absolute dream come true.”

“I am extremely grateful and excited for the opportunity to represent GB Students in Torino, Italy in January 2025.Over the next few months I will be putting in a lot of hard work both on and off the ice to ensure I am ready for the challenges at the World University Games. Bring on Italy!”

Charlotte Cramp is now playing in her fourth season with the Wild women, having joined the team in 2021 from a background of university hockey with Manchester Metros.

In her previous three seasons with the Wild, she played 42 games and scored 6 goals and 14 assists.

She is captain of the Wild women’s team for the second season in a row, having admirably fulfilled the role last term.

Charlotte is also a qualified match official and regularly officiates at Moralee and Laidler Division matches in the NIHL.

Jemma Brown was the Wild Women's MVP against Whitley (Photo by Mark Bird Sports Photography)

Sunday 24th November 2024 – WNIHL Division 2 North
Widnes Wild Women 6 – Whitley Bay Beacons 5

The Widnes Wild Women's team won their first home game of the season by the narrowest of margins with a 6-5 victory over Whitley Bay Beacons at Planet Ice Widnes on Sunday.

This was a highly entertaining match to watch with plenty of end to end action throughout and numerous chances for both sides.

Whitley had the better of the first period, outshooting the Wild women by some 2 to 1. They took the lead in the 10th minute and were 0-2 up by the first period break.

Widnes visibly upped their game in the second period and pulled a goal back through Jemma Brown on 27 minutes, however, that was the only goal action of the second period and the score stood 1-2 to the Beacons with 20 minutes left to play.

The third period saw a veritable scoring-fest, with 8 goals being fired in, and the result remaining open to question until the very last seconds.

Whitley scored again just 34 seconds in to lead 1-3 but 2 goals within a minute of each other - from team captain Charlotte Cramp and Phoebe Patient – saw the Wild Women draw level.

Just when it looked as if Widnes would go on to take control of the match, Katie Fairclough picked up a game misconduct penalty for slashing and the Wild women had to play 5 minutes shorthanded. Despite coming under intense pressure, they managed to weather this storm with staunch team defending and netminder Stephanie Drinkwater performing heroics in the Widnes goal.

A strike from Leen de Decker on 52 minutes put Widnes ahead for the first time in the game and a second goal from Cramp just 27 seconds after that extended the home advantage. Two goals from Whitley levelled the score again but Leen de Decker fired home the winning goal with just over 2 minutes left on the clock.

The Wild Women are next in action on Saturday 7th December when they make the long journey north of the border to play the Caledonia Bees in Edinburgh, 4pm face off, and are next at home on Sunday 15th December when they take on Sheffield Shadows at Planet Ice Widnes, 4.25pm start.

Charlotte Cramp at the Women's World Championship in 2024

International Calls Up For Match Officials

Three match officials with Widnes connections have been selected by the International Ice Hockey Federation (IIHF) to officiate across the world at international tournaments during the current 2024/25 season.

Charlotte Cramp is the current Widnes Wild women's team captain and she also officiates at men's NIHL Moralee and Laidler Division matches.

She has officiated at the women's playoffs weekend for the last 3 seasons, and the most recent season did the men's Laidler Division play offs and was on the crew for the women's Elite final

This is her second year officiating at international level as she was a linesman at the Women's Under 18 World Championships Division II Group B in Sofia, Bulgaria, last year. In March, Charlotte will be officiating at the senior Women's World Championships Division IIIA in Belgrade, Serbia.

Philippa MacKinnon (previously Wheeler) played for the Widnes women's team in the 2018/19 Women's Premier League season and also played league hockey for Peterborough and Nottingham. She officiates at NIHL Moralee Division level and has only recently returned to the ice after having a baby 4 months ago.

She was a linesman at the Youth Olympics in Switzerland in 2020, the Women's U18 World Championships in Istanbul Turkey in 2022 and again in Dumfries in 2023. In January she will be officiating at the Women's Under 18 World Championship Division III in Zagreb, Croatia.

David Good is an experienced Elite League referee who previously played as netminder for his hometown Hull Jets in the NIHL.

He was drafted in by the Wild as an emergency loan player for two games at the 2016 Laidler Division Play Off weekend after regular Widnes netminder Greg Ruxton suffered an injury late in the season.

Widnes beat Nottingham Lions 2-1 in the semi-final and lost out to league champions Deeside Dragons 5-2 in the final. As a result of this, Good has an impressive all time Widnes netminding record of 90.40 Save Percentage from his two games.

He was a referee at the World Youth Olympics in Lausanne in 2020 and the Under 20 World Championships in Iceland in 2023.

Charlotte McAdam scored her first Wild Women's goal away at Caledonia (Photo by Mark Bird Sports Photography)

Saturday 7th December – WNIHL Div 2N
Caledonia Queen Bees 4 - Widnes Wild Women 12

The Widnes Wild women's team battled through hurricane conditions to head north to Scotland but it was all worthwhile as they came home with a 4-12 victory over the Caledonia Queen Bees on Saturday.

The Queen Bees are a new team in the league this season and are a second team to the Caledonia Steel Queens, who won the league title last season and are now playing in the higher WNIHL Division 1.

The match was played at the Border Ice Rink in Kelso which the Caledonia club use quite often and, as it is a good 50 miles further south than their regular home rink of Murrayfield in Edinburgh, is a bit easier to get to.

This was the Wild women's first visit to that compact and bijou venue and it took them a while to get used to the unusual surroundings.

It was quite a close game in its early stages and the Queen Bees took the lead after just 2 minutes of play. Jemma Brown equalised for the Wild skating the whole length of the ice to do so - on 12 minutes and then Lise Gillen fired Widnes in front three minutes later.

Caledonia equalised with 2 minutes left on the clock and the score stood at 2-2 at the first period break.

Two quick goals within 45 seconds of each other at the start of the second period - from Gillen and Amanda Armstrong – put Widnes back in front and they never really looked back from there.

The Wild Women fired in two more goals – from Abigail Aldred (her first ever competitive goal), and team captain Charlotte Cramp – before Caledonia eventually pulled a goal back on 38 minutes.

Charlotte McAdam had left the game early in the first period after a hefty collision with the boards but bravely returned to the ice and was rewarded with her first Wild women's goal with 54 seconds left in the second. The score stood at 3-7 at the second interval and the Wild Women looked well in control.

Caledonia scored their 4th goal 50 seconds into the third period but any hopes of their mounting a late comeback were well and truly scotched with 5 unanswered goals - from Victoria Connelly, Gillen again for a hat-trick and three more from Cramp – handing the Wild Women an emphatic 4-12 victory.

The Wild Women are next in action this Sunday 15th December when they take on Sheffield Shadows at Planet Ice Widnes, 4.25pm face off.

In a break from the league programme, this match is part of new cup competition that was introduced for this season to make up the number of games after the Grimsby team withdrew from competing.

Alongside their league meetings, Widnes will play Sheffield and Telford once home and once away in a three team “round robin” cup group that will decide an overall winner.

*****

The Wild Women had THREE players called Charlotte in their team on Saturday – Charlotte Cramp, Charlotte McAdam and netminder Charlotte Jackson.

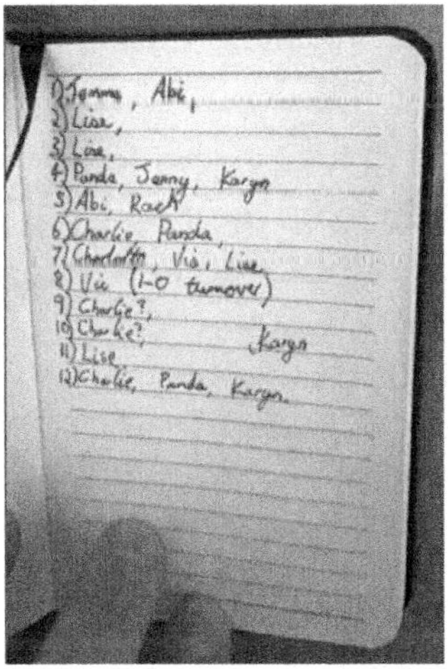

Please note that the goalscorer details for this report have been taken from Wild Women’s team coach Paddy Horner’s notes and NOT from the official gamesheet - so there may be some discrepancies with “official” figures

Sunday 15th December 2024 – WNIHL North Cup: Widnes Wild Women 2 – Sheffield Shadows 10

The Widnes Wild women's team had a difficult start to their WNIHL North Cup campaign with a surprise 2-10 defeat at home to Sheffield Shadows at Planet Ice Widnes on Sunday.

When the two teams met in the league earlier in the season away at iceSheffield, the game had finished in a very close 1-2 win for the Wild, so this result was rather unexpected.

This is the first year that the WNIHL has run a separate cup alongside the league competition and it has been introduced for this season to make up the number of games after the Grimsby team withdrew from this season's WNIHL Division 2 North. Alongside their league meetings, Widnes are playing Sheffield and Telford once home and once away in a three team "round robin" cup group that will decide an overall winner. A separate cup competition also sees Leeds, Kingston and Caledonia meeting in a similar format.

Sheffield came out of the blocks the quickest and took the lead after just 3 minutes. They doubled their advantage three minutes later and Widnes had to wait until the 14th minute to open their own account with a goal from Katie Fairclough. The score stood at a fairly manageable 1-2 to Sheffield at the first period break with both sides very much in contention.

Two more goals early in the second period saw the Shadows edge further ahead but Fairclough found the back of the net once again to bring the score to 2-4 at the second interval.

Widnes still looked in with a shout at this point but the floodgates opened up in the third period as Sheffield outshot the Wild Women by a massive 24 to 5 and their efforts were duly rewarded. 6 unanswered goals swept past overworked netminder Stephanie Drinkwater in the final 20 minutes of play, helping Sheffield to a higher margin of victory than the Wild performance possibly deserved.

The Wild Women have a few weeks' break now to lick their wounds and regroup before the season restarts in January. They travel to Telford to face the Wrekin Raiders in the league on Sunday12th January and are next at home on Sunday 26th January when they take on the same opposition at Planet Ice Widnes, 4.25pm face off.

Sunday's game saw a Widnes debut for recent signing Cath Thornton. Cath may be a new face to Widnes fans but she played league ice hockey for the Deeside-based Flintshire Furies – alongside fellow Wild women Catherine Fell and Vanessa Crickmore-Clarke - for four seasons from 2005 to 2010, scoring 7 goals and 4 assists in 48 competitive matches.

She has most recently been playing for the Connah's Quay Cobras recreational team at Deeside.

Thornton was named MVP for the Wild Women in her first game at Widnes.

The Wild Women's team enjoy their annual fancy dress Christmas scrimmage (Photo by Rachael Pearce)

Widnes Wild Women Top Of The League For New Year

The Widnes Wild women's team finish the year proudly occupying top spot in the Division 2 North league table, with 3 wins, 1 draw and 1 defeat from their 5 league games to date.

They are being stalked, however, by Leeds Roses and Telford Wrekin Raiders who are just 1 point behind and each with a game in hand, but there is still a long way to go in this year's league title chase.

It is a fascinating competition this season with no one team dominating and everybody looking capable of beating everybody else.

The only exception to this might be the Edinburgh based Caledonia Queen Bees who are a new team for this season and are a development team for the Steel Queens team who won the league last season and were promoted to Division 1. They have lost all 5 of their league games so far this season, conceding 67 goals, of which 12 came in the Wild Women's visit north of the border in early December.

Team captain Charlotte Cramp is the Wild Women's leading scorer at this early stage of the season with 7 goals and 5 assists from 5 games. Former Belgium international player Leen de Decker is second with 6+3 and recently returned Amanda Armstrong is just behind them with 3+4.

The goals and assists have been widely spread around the squad this season with Lise Gillen, Jemma Brown, Phoebe Patient, Jennifer Hickey, Victoria Connelly, Abigail Aldred, Katie Fairclough and Charlotte McAdam all having found the net and 6 other players all contributing assists.

Katie Fairclough is the current leader by some distance in the Division 2 North "Bad Girl" stakes with 31 penalty minutes, due mainly to her 5+game for slashing in the home game against Whitley.

Katie is beaten, however, in the overall Division 2 penalty standings by three players from South 2 who all have 45 PIMs despite each having played fewer games than her.

The Wild Women are also taking part in a cup competition for the first time this season – playing Sheffield and Telford home and away in a 3-team round robin.

They lost their opening game 2-10 at home to Sheffield just before Christmas so have a bit of ground to make up if they are going to have any chance in that competition.

The Wild Women are back in action on Sunday 12th January when they travel to Telford to face the Wrekin Raiders for a league game.

Wild Women In Top Of The Table Clash

The Widnes Wild women's team will be hoping that the weather has improved enough for them to be able to travel to Telford on Sunday 12th January for a top of the table clash against the Wrekin Raiders in their first match of the new year.

The Wild women topped the Division 2 North table over the festive period but a narrow 2-1 win for Telford over Whitley Bay Beacons on Saturday saw them leapfrog them into top spot and they now head the table by 1 point, having played the same number of games.

The Wild women are then at home to Telford on Sunday 26th January at Planet Ice Widnes, 4.25pm face off.

Sunday 12th January 2025 – WNIHL Division 2 North
Telford Wrekin Raiders 2 – Widnes Wild Women 2

The Widnes Wild women's team put in a superb performance in their top of the table clash away to Telford Wrekin Raiders to come home from Shropshire with a creditable 2-2 on Sunday.

It is the first time in 4 attempts that the Wild women have ever picked up a point away to the perennial title contenders and it will stand them in good stead should the teams finish locked on points at the end of the season, when league positions are decided by results between the two teams.

Telford opened the scoring with just 18 seconds on the clock but Widnes equalised 51 seconds later with a goal from Leen de Decker and the score remained 1-1 at the first period break.

The Wild Women took the lead 47 seconds into the second period with a Lise Gillen strike and it took Telford until the 35th minute to manage a reply. There was absolutely nothing to choose between the two teams as they went into the third period at a finely balanced 2-2.

Despite numerous chances at both ends, neither side was able to break the deadlock and the game finished as a draw.

The situation at the top of the Women's Division 2 North is extremely close after the weekend's games. Telford remain top with 9 points from 6 games and Widnes are second with 8 points from 6.

Kingston Diamonds are just one point behind them and Leeds and Sheffield both follow on 6 points each.

The fascinating title battle will continue when the Wild women play host to Telford at home on Sunday 26th January at Planet Ice Widnes, 4.25pm face off.

Wild Women Aim To Top Table in Crunch Encounter

The Widnes Wild women's team have the chance to go back to the top of the WNIHL Division 2 North table this weekend as they take on current league leaders Telford Wrekin Raiders this Sunday 26th January at Planet Ice Widnes, 4.25pm face off.

The two teams drew 2-2 in a very close and nail biting encounter in Shropshire two weeks ago – the first time that the Wild women have ever taken a point away to Telford – and they will be keen to go one better on Sunday.

A win for the Wild women would see them leapfrog the Raiders and take a narrow 1 point lead at the top. With just 2 points being awarded for a win in the women's leagues – as opposed to three for a regulation time victory in the men's NIHL – the league positions are very close with just three points separating the top 5 teams.

Telford currently lead the table with 9 points from their 6 games to date while Widnes are second with 8 points from 6 games. Kingston Diamonds have also played 6 games and are in third place with 7 points, while Leeds and Sheffield are close behind with 6 points each from 5 games played.

The Wild women previously won the league title at this level back in the 2019/20 season, when it was known as Division 1 North.

Katie Fairclough was the Wild Women's MVP in the win over Telford (Photo by Paul Breeze)

Sunday 26th January 2025 – WNIHL Div 2 N
Widnes Wild Women 5 – Telford Wrekin Raiders 4

The Widnes Wild women's team moved back to the top of the Division 2 North table after a close-fought and highly entertaining 5-4 victory over erstwhile league leaders Telford Wrekin Raiders at Planet Ice Widnes on Sunday.

The division's top two teams had played out a fascinating chess-match like 2-2 draw down in Shropshire two weeks earlier and this game was just as nerve-wracking and finely poised - and the result could easily have gone either way right until the final seconds.

Telford took the lead in the 7th minute and, despite Widnes out-shooting the visitors by more than 2 to 1, the score remained 0-1 at the first period break.

The continued Wild pressure was eventually rewarded in the 24th minute when Leen de Decker fired in a delayed penalty goal punishing a Telford holding call.

Telford edged ahead again just 90 seconds later but the Wild Women levelled once more three minutes after that with a goal from Lise Gillen. A further Raiders goal on 35 minutes put Telford noses back in front and the score stood at 2-3 at the second interval.

The third period saw Telford on top in terms of shots on goal and they scored a fourth goal 4 minutes in to open up a two-goal lead.

Ellen Tyrer pulled a goal back for Widnes two minutes later and this sparked a late fight back by the home side. De Decker fired home on a powerplay on 52 minutes to level the score once again and the Wild took the lead for the first time in the game with Gillen's second goal of the night on 56 minutes.

The Wild women held on in the last few minutes to secure a 5-4 victory - which could be highly significant for the league title race. Having drawn the away game with Telford 2-2, this win means that, should the two teams finish level on points in the league table at the end of the season, Widnes would take the higher position based on results between the two teams.

Sunday 2nd February 2025 – WNIHL D2N Cup: Sheffield Shadows 7 - Widnes Wild Women 3

It looks as if the Widnes Wild women's team will be able to "concentrate on the league" after a frustrating 7-3 cup defeat away to Sheffield Shadows on Sunday.

This is the first time that the women's league have organised a separate cup competition and the three-way tournament between Widnes, Sheffield and Telford offers additional games to pad out the regular league schedule.

However, despite doing well in the league and currently topping the Division 2 North table, Widnes have struggled in the cup and lost their opening match 2-10 at home to Sheffield back in December.

The away game on Sunday was a much better performance and was closely fought for much of its duration. Widnes actually scored first, with Rachael Pearce firing home in the 3rd minute and it took Sheffield right up until the 19th minute to equalise, leaving the score at a finely-balanced 1-1 at the first period break.

The only goal of the second period saw Sheffield take the lead on 23 minutes and, despite numerous chances at both ends, they remained 2-1 ahead at the second interval.

Widnes equalised 9 minutes into the third period – some 25 minutes after the previous goal – with a strike from Leen de Decker but they were unable to push on from this breakthrough and take control of the game. Sheffield edged back in front on 50 minutes and two more goals within 77 seconds saw them open up a 5-2 lead.

Jemma Brown pulled a goal back for the Wild Women on 53 minutes but the damage had already been done and two late strikes for the Shadows gave the final score a more lop-sided look than the Widnes performance possibly deserved.

The Wild Women still have two more cup games to play – at home to Telford on Sunday 16th February and away in Shropshire on 3rd May – but even if they win both of those, the results in the games between Sheffield and Telford will probably determine the winners of this inaugural cup competition.

Sunday 16th February 2025 – WNIHL North Cup

Widnes Wild Women 5
Telford Wrekin Raiders 5

(Match abandoned at 41.19)

Cath Thornton scored her first goal for the Wild Women (Photo by Paul Breeze)

The Widnes Wild women's team saw their cup game against Telford Wrekin Raiders abandoned early in the 3rd period - with the score standing at 5-5 - after an injury to a Telford player at Planet Ice Widnes on Sunday.

The game had started well for Widnes as Katie Fairclough fired them into the lead after just 2 minutes. Telford hit back with two quick goals but a second from Fairclough on 10 minutes levelled the score again.

The Raiders edged back into the lead just two minutes later and then 2 quick fire goals within 8 seconds of each other in the last minute of the period put them 2-5 ahead.

Widnes pulled a goal back on 24 minutes with a strike from Amanda Armstrong and then a goal from Cath Thornton – her first in Widnes colours – on 29 minutes – narrowed the deficit to just one.

There followed a tense spell of end- to-end hockey with chances at both ends but it took until the last minute of the period for the next goal – which fell to the Wild's

Rachael Pearce to level the score at a finely balanced 5-5.

A barnstorming third period looked to be on the cards but, sadly, it was not to be as with only 1.19 played, a Telford player suffered a heavy collision against the boards and collapsed onto the ice.

There was a significant delay while she received medical attention in–situ and, by the time that she could be safely moved from the ice, there wasn't enough ice time left to play out the remainder of the game.

The two team coaches and the match officials decided to call off the game at that point and it was officially abandoned.

According to the official England Ice Hockey regulations, in the case of a match being abandoned due a medical emergency with neither team being at fault:

"Where less than 2 periods of the match have been played, a 0-0 draw will be declared with each team being awarded one point. Where more than 2 periods of the match have been played, the result at the point of abandonment will stand."

This would suggest that the match will be recorded as a 5-5 draw, but that will still have to be decided by the League Management Committee after considering reports from the various officials involved.

The Wild Women are next in action on Sunday 9th March when they take on Sheffield Shadows in a league game at Planet Ice Widnes, 4.25pm face off.

Ellen Tyrer was the Wild Women's MVP against Sheffield (Photo by Suzie Miller)

Sunday 9th March 2025 – WNIHL Division 2 North Widnes Wild Women 4 – Sheffield Shadows 2

The Widnes Wild women's team maintained their Division 2 North league title challenge with a hard fought 4-2 win over Sheffield Shadows at Planet Ice Widnes on Sunday.

Sheffield opened the scoring after just two minutes and it took until later into the period for Widnes to open their own account. Two quick fire goals from Leen de Decker just 38 seconds apart on 17 minutes drew the Wild Women level and then gave them a slender lead going into the first break.

Another Widnes goal – from Amanda Armstrong on 22 minutes – edged the Wild Women further ahead but Sheffield pulled a goal back at the midway point of the game and the score stood at a tantalisingly close 3-2 at the second interval.

Sheffield actually out-shot Widnes by some margin, with the overall tally for the game amounting to 18 to 49 and it took an inspirational performance from Stephanie Drinkwater in the Wild goal to keep the Shadows attack at bay.

Widnes nerves were eased by de Decker's hat–trick on 50 minutes and with no more scoring after that, the Wild were able to celebrate a 4-2 victory.

The Widnes Wild Women are at home again this Sunday 16th March when they take on Kingston Diamonds at Planet Ice Widnes, 4.25pm face off.

Ruth Leopold was the Wild Women's MVP against Kingston (Photo by Paul Breeze)

Sunday 16th March 2025 – WNIHL Division 2 North Widnes Wild Women 4 – Kingston Diamonds 4

The Widnes Wild women's team battled hard to salvage a well deserved point in their 4-4 draw against Kingston Diamonds at Planet Ice Widnes on Sunday.

After a very nervy and close opening phase, Kingston eventually opened the scoring in the 15th minute. They scored again 60 seconds later and took a 0-2 lead into the first period break.

A powerplay strike from Lucy Kirkham 2 minutes into the second period, punishing a Kingston boarding call, pulled a goal back for Widnes but a powerplay goal for the

Diamonds just 3 minutes later restored their 2-goal advantage.

Ruth Leopold pulled another goal back for Widnes two minutes after that and then a Phoebe Patient strike on 38 minutes put the Wild Women on level terms at 3-3 heading into the third period.

Kingston edged back in front again with a goal on 48 minutes but a well-taken short handed goal from Leen de Decker tied the score for Widnes once again with 5 minutes left to play.

Unfortunately, they were unable to build on this and the game finished in a 4-4 draw – the same score as in the away game between the two teams earlier in the season.

The Widnes Wild women's team's game that was scheduled to be played away against Leeds Roses on Saturday was postponed and will now take place on 10th May. The game will be played at Bradford due to a lack of available ice time at the Leeds rink and it will be the first time that the Wild Women have ever played at that venue.

The Wild Women's next game is at home to Leeds on Sunday 13th April at Planet Ice Widnes, 4.25pm face off.

Stephanie Drinkwater was the Wild Women's MVP against Leeds (Photo by Paul Breeze)

Sunday 13th April 2025 – WNIHL Division 2 North
Widnes Wild Women 2 – Leeds Roses 1

The Widnes Wild Women maintained their Division 2 North title challenge with a hard fought 2-1 win over Leeds Roses at Planet Ice Widnes on Sunday.

This was a very entertaining game to watch – with the result remaining in doubt until the very last seconds - and many observers agreed that it was quite possibly one of the best women's matches ever seen at the Widnes rink.

Leeds opened the scoring with a goal on 9 minutes and the score remained 0-1 at the first period break. Widnes equalised on 24 minutes with a strike from Ruth Leopold and, despite chances for both teams, the score stood at 1-1 at the second interval.

This game was end to end action throughout, although the Roses had the edge in terms of shots on goal – out-shooting the Wild Women by 49 to 36 over the whole 60 minutes. However, they came up against Stephanie Drinkwater who was in fine form in the Widnes goal and made a succession of stunning saves, keeping out an impressive 48 of the 49 shots that she faced, for a 97.96 save percentage.

Widnes eventually took the lead on 47 minutes with a first Wild goal for Jennifer Greenwood, setting up a nail-biting finale.

Despite the closeness of this game and its significance for the league standings, it was played in good spirit throughout, with very few penalties being awarded.

Just 4 minutes of penalties were handed out to each side over the course of the game and two each of these came in the third period when Widnes were defending their slender lead.

The Wild Women managed to fend off the Leeds assault when they were a player down and were unable to take advantage when the tables were turned with 6 minutes left to play.

The clock slowly ticked down and, despite a late flurry of pressure from Leeds, Widnes were able to hold on and record an important victory.

The MVP awards - sponsored this season by niche publishers Ice Hockey Review – were presented by match volunteer Lynda Bird and went to Kirsty Hodgins for Leeds and Stephanie Drinkwater for Widnes.

The Wild women now have 6 wins, three draws and one defeat from their 10 league games to date. The other teams in the mix for the league title have games to catch up on so the table standings for Division 2 are far from clear at present.

Widnes play their last home game of the season on Sunday 27th April when they take on Caledonia Bees at Planet Ice Widnes. The game has a later than usual face off time of 5.45pm.

They then finish off their regular league schedule with an away game to Leeds Roses on 10th May – which will be played at Bradford Ice Rink due to a lack of available ice time at Leeds.

The Wild Women celebrate their 2020 title win
(Photo by Mo Muir)

Wild Women's Title Push – 21st April 2025

The Widnes Wild Women play their last home game of the season this Sunday 27th April when they take on Caledonia Bees at Planet Ice Widnes and their mission is clear. If they can win this game and then win their final league game away at Leeds Roses on 10th May, they will secure the Division 2 North league title.

The Wild Women currently top the Division 2 North league table with 15 points - a playing record of six wins, three draws and one defeat from their 10 games to date. There is a chasing pack of three more teams who are also still in with a chance of the title – perennial challengers Telford Wrekin Raiders, Sheffield Shadows and Leeds Roses. Sheffield and Telford are currently vying for second place and have 14 and 13 points respectively from 10 games.

Leeds are playing catch up in the fixture list and have 2 games in hand. The good news for the Wild Women is that the Roses have games against both Telford and Sheffield over the weekend of 3rd and 4th May so it is likely that, depending on those results, one or more of those teams will be played out of the title race by the time Widnes play Leeds the weekend after.

With there only being 12 matches in the league schedule this season, the table is very tight and the title may well be decided by a single point margin or less. This works in Widnes' favour at present as teams that finish on the same number of points are separated by results in matches played between them.

With the Wild Women having beaten Sheffield both home and away and also having beaten Telford narrowly at home after a draw away in Shropshire, they would take the top spot if they were to finish on the same number of points as either of those two teams.

On paper, the home game against Caledonia should be the easier of the two games in the Wild Women's title run-in. The Edinburgh-based Bees are a new team in the division for this season and are a development team for the Caledonia Steel Queens who play in Division 1.

They are bottom of the league table, having lost all 11 of their games to date, with a goal difference of minus 81. The Wild Women beat them 4-12 when they ventured north of the border back in December.

But there is no such thing as a certainty in ice hockey and games still need to be won - so the Wild women will need to be at their very best on Sunday.

The away game at Leeds is likely to be a very different kettle of fish entirely and the Wild Women only very narrowly beat them 2-1 in the recent encounter in Widnes. Depending on the other results in the intervening period, the game on 10th May could well be a deciding “winner takes all” clash for the league title.

The Wild Women previously won the league title in the 2019/20 season. They finished second in the league in 2022/23.

Wild Women MVP Jennifer Hickey (Photo by Paul Breeze)

27th April 2025 – WNIHL Div2 North
Widnes Wild Women 8 – Caledonia Bees 0

The Widnes Wild women's team took a step closer to winning the league title with an 8-0 win over Caledonia Bees at Planet Ice Widnes on Sunday.

The Edinburgh-based Bees are a new team in the division for this season and are a development team for the Caledonia Steel Queens who play in Division 1. They arrived bottom of the league table, having lost all 11 of their previous games and the Wild Women beat them 4-12 when they ventured north of the border back in December, so this game always seemed likely to be a bit of a home banker.

The match was actually very close in its early stages and a single goal – scored by Leen de Decker on 6 minutes - saw the Wild Women take a very slender 1-0 lead into the first period break.

A second goal for the Wild – from Ellen Tyrer - just 90 seconds into the second period settled any nerves that might have been lingering and then a goal from Jennifer Hickey just 60 seconds after that put the Wild Women well and truly in the driving seat.

The score remained 3-0 at the second interval but the flood gates opened in the third period and 5 unanswered goals – from Charlotte Cramp, de Decker again, Phoebe Patient and a brace for Ruth Leopold - saw Widnes sweep to the win.

While the end result was quite conclusive, this was far from a one-sided game and the Bees put in a very good showing. They looked dangerous going forward and Stephanie Drinkwater was called upon to make a number of spectacular saves to secure a first shut out of the season.

The win means that Widnes remain top of the Division 2 North table with 17 points from 11 games. With title rivals Leeds Roses beating Kingston Diamonds 3-0 at the weekend, the run-in for the league championship remains very tight. Leeds have games in hand to play and need to win them all if they are to have any chance of overtaking Widnes.

The two teams meet in their last game of the league season - in what may well be a title decider - in Bradford on 10th May.

Wild Women in celebratory mood (Photo by Wil Evans)

Wild Women Are Champions!

The Widnes Wild Women's team secured the Division 2 North league title after a fascinating weekend of ice hockey saw their rivals for the crown knock each other out of contention.

Widnes actually lost their own game 13-3 away to Telford on Saturday - but that was a cup game and had no bearing on the outcome of the league, which as it turned out, was decided by results elsewhere.

The Wild Women went into the weekend leading the D2N table with 17 points from their 11 league games – and one match still to play, away to Leeds Roses on 10th May.

Sheffield Shadows were in second with 14 points from 10 games and could still snatch the title if they won their remaining games and Widnes lost away at Leeds. Leeds themselves were also still in the running with 11 points from 9 games, knowing that 3 wins in their last 3 games could possibly see them overtake Widnes on the last day of the season

Somewhat fortuitously for the Wild Women, the fixture list pitched Leeds and Sheffield up against each other in Leeds on Saturday night, with the Roses winning 5-2. That result meant that Sheffield could no longer overtake the Wild Women at the top of the league table, even if they won their last remaining game.

Leeds, however, could still snatch the title if they won their two remaining matches and could beat Widnes in the last game of the season on 10th May.

Telford – who are perennial title challengers themselves but have dropped off the pace a little this year - did the Wild Women a huge favour by holding the Roses to a 2-2 draw in Shropshire on Sunday night meaning that Leeds are now also unable to deny Widnes top spot.

The weekend results mean that the Wild Women take the league title irrespective of what happens in the remaining games of the regular season.

They have also qualified for the end of season play offs, which take place over the Bank Holiday weekend of 24th to 26th May in Sheffield, where the top 2 teams in Division 2 North will compete with the top teams from Division 2 South for promotion to Division 1 for next season.

Saturday 3rd May 2025 – WNIHL North Cup
Telford Wrekin Raiders 13 – Widnes Wild Women 3

The Widnes Wild Women lost their final game in the WNIHL North Cup 13-3 away to Telford Wrekin Raiders on Saturday.

In competitive terms, this game was a bit of a dead rubber as neither team could win the cup, having both already lost twice to Sheffield Shadows, who are the other team in this three-way tournament, but pride was still very much on the line.

The earlier cup game between these two teams had ended in a 5-5 draw in Widnes after being abandoned early in the third period due to a player injury and with the two league meetings both going the way of Widnes - with a narrow 5-4 win at home and a 2-2 draw away in Shropshire - Telford probably felt they had a point to prove.

Telford took the lead in the 7th minute but Widnes equalised just 60 seconds later with a goal from Catherine Fell.

Telford edged back in front on 13 minutes but a strike from Karyn Cooper – her first ever goal for the Wild women on 16 minutes levelled the scores once again. However, the Wild Women were unable to build on this and two more goals late in the period gave Telford a 4-2 lead at the first break.

The damage was all done in the second period when Telford fired in 7 goals before Widnes were able to summon up a reply. A second goal of the game from Cooper with just 3 seconds left in the period gave the travelling contingent something to cheer about but, with the score standing at 11-3 at the second interval, the game was already well and truly over as a contest.

Telford eased their foot off the gas in the third period - quite possibly saving some energy for their league encounter with title challengers Leeds Roses the following night - and the game finished as a 13-3 win for the Raiders.

Despite the one-sided scoreline, Charlotte Jackson put in a good performance in the Widnes goal, turning away an impressive 46 of the 59 shots that she faced over the 60 minutes.

Karyn Cooper was named MVP for the Wild Women after her two goal haul, having played up front instead of in her usual defensive role in a make-shift playing line-up.

The Wild Women play their last league game of the season away to Leeds Roses this Saturday 10th May, face off 4pm. The game is being played at Bradford Ice Rink due to a lack of available ice time at Leeds.

Jemma Brown scored the first Widnes goal at Leeds and was named MVP for the Wild Women (Photo by Paul Breeze)

Saturday 10th May 2025 – WNIHL Div2N
Leeds Roses 3 – Widnes Wild Women 3
(Match Abandoned 46m)

The Widnes Wild women's team saw their league title winning season come to a rather subdued end after their final game away to Leeds was abandoned midway through the third period due to a player injury.

The score stood at 3-3 at the time and, subject to official confirmation, that is likely to be recorded as the final result.

While it is always nice to win, the result of this game didn't really matter too much to the Wild Women as they had already accrued enough points to secure the league championship.

Leeds, however, really needed to win to have a chance of finishing in second position in the league and clinching the remaining play off place.

Player injuries and match abandonments aside, it was a fascinating end to the season as three teams went into the final weekend level on 14 points – Leeds, Telford and Sheffield - any of whom could have finished in the runners up spot.

The game at Leeds – as the result suggests - was very close. It took until the 15th minute for the deadlock to be broken and a Jemma Brown goal fired the Wild Women into the lead.

40 seconds later it was 0-2 to Widnes after a strike from Lise Gillen and the score remained 0-2 at the first break.

Gillen found the back of the net again 4 minutes into the second period to put Widnes 0-3 up but then Leeds began to fight back.

They pulled a goal back just 70 seconds later and then further narrowed the deficit at the midway point of the game. The score stood at a tantalisingly close 2-3 at the second interval and Leeds went on to draw level on 44 minutes.

Unfortunately, we will never know what might have happened next as the game was called to a halt shortly after that.

Draws are fairly rare in ice hockey – especially in recent seasons since many leagues have adopted overtime and penalties shots to decide tied matches.

However, assuming that Saturday's game remains a draw, it will mean that the Wild Women have had an incredible FIVE draws from their 16 games this season.

They drew 2-2 away at Telford in the league, drew 4-4 both home and away against Kingston Diamonds and then saw their home cup game against Telford also end in a 5-5 draw, another game that was stopped early due to a player injury.

The draw away at Leeds means that Widnes finish top of the Division 2 North table with 18 points from their 12 league games.

With Leeds only drawing on Saturday, this meant they finished the league campaign on 15 points. Sheffield beat Whitley Bay Beacons 7-2, also on Saturday, and thus finished their season on 16 points putting them above Leeds and in the driving seat for the runners up spot – at least overnight.

The matter was eventually settled on Sunday when Telford Wrekin Raiders hammered Kingston Diamonds 17-0 to match the Shadows on points but secure second place with a superior goal difference of +41 to +26.

As things turned out, the point that Leeds dropped in the abandoned drawn game wouldn't have been enough to send them to the playoffs anyway as Telford would still have come out on top of the chasing pack due to the way that the league separate teams that have finished level in the table.

Wild Women at the Play Offs in 2017 (left to right): Sav Sumner, Sophie Sinclair Reeks, Tegan Lavery, Abigail Hayes, Beckie Elliott, Leen de Decker, Lucy Kirkham, Katie Hills, Sarah Roberts & Emma Pearson. (Photo by MyTeamPhoto.com)

Wild Women Off To Play Offs

The Widnes Wild women's team head to Sheffield at the weekend to take part in the Women's National Ice Hockey League (WNIHL) Play Offs, which will run over 3 days and feature 13 games in total.

As champions of Division 2 North, the Wild Women will take on Streatham Storm (2nd team), who finished second in Division 2 South, in their semi final - giving them a, possibly, slightly easier match than if they had finished second themselves and then had to face D2S champions Cambridge.

They will play in the second semi final, which faces off at 8.15pm on Saturday evening. The other semi final sees Telford take on Cambridge with a 6pm start time. The Division 2 final is at 2.45pm on the Sunday and the winner will secure the Play Off title as well as promotion to Division 1 for next season.

The other games over the weekend see the semi finals and final for the Division 1, the Women's Elite League and the Girls' Under 16 championship, as well as the promotion / relegation match between the winners of the D1 final and the bottom team in the Elite League.

This is the Wild Women's 4th trip to the play offs. On each previous occasion, they have bowed out at the semi final stage and have never yet got through to the final.

They reached the Play Offs two seasons running in their early years when they were in the Women's Premier League (now called WNIHL Division 1). They were runners up in the league in 2015/16 and narrowly lost 2-1 to Streatham Storm (1st team) in the play off semi final and finished 4th in 2016/17, losing to the same opposition again 6-1.

The Wild Women won the Division 1 North league title (which is now the equivalent of Division 2 North) in the 2019/20 season and qualified for the play offs once again, but they never took place because of the Coronavirus pandemic.

They came second in the third tier in the 2022/23 season and lost 3-1 in the play-off semi final to D2S champions Cardiff, so will be hoping to go one better this time around.

Wild Women Division 2 North champions (Photo by Stewart Cutting)

Saturday 24th May 2025 – WNIHL Play Off Semi Final Widnes Wild Women 1 – Streatham Storm 8

The Widnes Wild women's team put in a battling performance in their Play Off semi final at iceSheffield on Saturday, ultimately losing out 1-8 to Streatham Storm – but they, at least, had something to celebrate as they were presented with the trophy and medals for winning the Division 2 North League championship.

The Wild Women arrived at the Play Offs missing a few regular players and also had to contend with being the last game of the day, which didn't face off until 8.15pm. Streatham were a bit of an unknown quantity as WNIHL North and South teams don't usually play each other, although Widnes had played the Storm's first team a few times back in their Women's Premier League days.

As it turned out, the game was fairly even in its early stages with the two sides cautiously testing each other out. Just as it looked as if the first period would play out goal-less, Streatham fired in a goal to take the lead just 41 seconds from the buzzer. 73 seconds into the second period, the score was 0-2 to the southerners and on 25 minutes they went 0-3 ahead.

Widnes eventually found the back of the net themselves on 29 minutes with a goal from Leen de Decker, who picked up the puck behind the Storm goal and guided it around inside the right hand post – but that was about as good as things got for the Wild Women. Although they pushed forward, trying to build on this, Streatham scored again 4 minutes after that and the score remained 1-4 at the second period break.

The Widnes net bulged once again 34 seconds into the third period and, with Streatham leading 1-5 by then, the game was pretty much over as a contest. The Wild Women had their chances but were kept out by a stubborn Storm defence. This led to their own goal being put under intense pressure and only a string of impressive saves from Wild netminder Stephanie Drinkwater kept the score from being higher than it was.

The pressure continued, however, and three goals in the latter stages of the game handed Streatham a convincing 1-8 victory.

With Telford Wrekin Raiders also losing 8-1 in their semi final to Division 2 South champions Cambridge Kodiaks, this set up an all-south final on Sunday, which Cambridge went on to win 4-1.

After Saturday's semi-final, the Wild Women were presented with the league championship trophy for their

Division 2 North title win and the players were all given commemorative medals. This was an extra special moment for the Widnes team as the last time they won the league title - back in 2020 - the playoffs were cancelled due to the coronavirus pandemic, and the presentations were never made.

The Wild Women have their end of season presentation evening this weekend and can then enjoy a few weeks' break before preparations begin for the new 2025/26 WNIHL season.

The Wild Women's team celebrate the Division 2 North championship outside iceSheffield (Photo by Stewart Cutting)

Ruth Leopold, Rachael Pearce & Vanessa Crickmore Clarke with medals (Photo by Stewart Cutting)

For the sake of completeness, the full list of the WNIHL Play Off weekend results were as follows:

Saturday 24th May
Division 1 Semi Final 1: Bristol Huskies 2 – Caledonia Steel Queens 1
Division 1 Semi Final 2: Kingston Diamonds 1 – Swindon Topcats 4
Elite Semi Final 1: Solihull Vixens – Guildford Lightning 1
Elite Semi Final 2: Queen Bees 7 – Whitley Bay 2
Division 2 Semi Final 1: Cambridge Kodiaks 8 – Telford Wrekin Raiders 1
Division 2 Semi Final 2: Widnes Wild Women 1- Streatham Storm 8

Sunday 25th May
Under 16 Semi Final 1: Chelmsford Rattlesnakes 10 – Manchester Storm 1
Under 16 Semi Final 2: Whitley 5 – Bristol 1
Division 1 Final: Bristol Huskies 3 – Swindon Topcats 2
Division 2 Final: Cambridge Kodiaks 4 – Streatham Storm 1
Elite Final: Solihull Vixens 0 - Queen Bees 2

Monday 26th May
Under 16 Final: Chelmsford 4 - Whitley 3
Elite v Div 1 Relegation Match: Kingston Diamonds v Bristol Huskies

Stephanie Drinkwater with head coach Steve Furber
(Photo by Ellen Tyrer)

Wild Women's Presentation Evening

The Widnes Wild Women's team rounded off their successful Division 2 North title winning season with their annual awards evening at the weekend.

The player awards for the 2024/25 season were:

Best Defence: Jennifer Greenwood
Best Forward: Ruth Leopold
Most Improved Player: Eleanor Johnson
Coaches' Player Of The Season: Stephanie Drinkwater
Players' Player Of The Season: Stephanie Drinkwater
Unsung Hero: Rachael Pearce

Ruth Leopold had actually retired from playing after an impressive 37 year career with Blackpool, Sheffield, Swindon and Bristol but was tempted back onto the ice after a year away to play for the Wild Women this season.

She summed up her feelings thus: "Thank you so, so much to all at Widnes Wild Women's ice hockey team for such an enjoyable season. To get a league winners medal (and hat!) - and to top it off with an unexpected Best Forward award - and some very kind words from the coaches at the end of season do tonight, was amazing and emotional for me! I appreciate it so much."

As well as being named Coaches' Player and Players' Player of the season, inspirational netminder Stephanie Drinkwater was the first inductee to the Wild Womens' 100 Club, which has been newly set up to celebrate various playing milestones.

Drinkwater passed 100 appearances for the Wild Women this season – the first player on the team to do so.

She has been with the Wild Women since the team first started 10 years ago following its relocation from Altrincham. This season is actually her third title win overall as she also won the Division 1 North title (as it was then called) with Widnes in 2020, and with the previous Manchester Phoenix team in 2015.

In that time, Drinkwater has notched up 104 appearances for the Wild Women, and it would probably have been more had the league not been suspended for the 2020/21 season due to the Coronavirus pandemic.

Hot on her heels in the "Appearances Stakes" are two more original Wild Women and triple title winners, Catherine Fell with 92 games and Leen De Decker with

91. De Decker was also inducted into the 100 Club for having passed 100 goals for the team. She has 104 goals from her 91 games, and her tally of 46 assists and 150 points overall are also the all time highs for the Wild Women.

Talking about her hat-trick of accolades, Stephanie Drinkwater said:

"What an end to this year's season. I am lost for words after receiving Coaches' Player and Players' Player awards last night! Also being inducted into the 100 Club with officially playing 100 games for the Wild Women. It has been an amazing year and I have so much love for this team - forever my girls!"

The Wild Women now have a few weeks' well-earned rest before they return to the ice to prepare for the 2025/26 WNIHL season.

They are always keen to attract new players – especially anybody with league or international experience - and anybody interested is asked to contact the team via their Facebook page in the first instance.

Eleanor Johnson with Assistant coach Paddy Horner (Photo by Ellen Tyrer)

Widnes Wild Women
10 Year Statistics, 2015-2025

Widnes Wild Women Results 2015-2025
(see also "season by season" sections)

#	Date	Comp	Home			Away	WDL
1	12.9.15	WPL	Slough Phantoms	3	4	Widnes Wild	W
2	11.10.15	WPL	Streatham Storm	1	3	Widnes Wild	W
3	8.11.15	WPL	Swindon Topcats	1	0	Widnes Wild	L
4	21.2.16	WPL	Widnes Wild	1	2	MK Falcons	L
5	28.2.16	WPL	Widnes Wild	7	2	Slough Phantoms	W
6	5.3.16	WPL	Widnes Wild	3	3	Streatham Storm	D
7	26.3.16	WPL	Widnes Wild	3	3	Swindon TopCats	D
8	3.4.16	WPL	Chelmsford Cobras	2	10	Widnes Wild	W
9	10.4.16	WPL	Widnes Wild	5	4	Chelmsford Cobras	W
10	17.4.16	WPL	Nottingham Vipers	6	8	Widnes Wild	W
11	24.4.16	WPL	Whitley Squaws	2	10	Widnes Wild	W
12	1.5.16	WPL	MK Falcons	1	1	Widnes Wild	D
13	8..5.16	WPL	Widnes Wild	2	3	Whitley Squaws	L
14	15.5.16	WPL	Widnes Wild	5	3	Nottingham Vipers	W
15	28.05.16	POS	Streatham Storm	2	1	Widnes Wild	L
16	11.09.16	WPL	Widnes Wild	1	5	MK Falcons	L
17	25.09.16	WPL	Chelmsford Cobras	7	6	Widnes Wild	L
18	23.10.16	WPL	Widnes Wild	3	3	Slough Phantoms	D
19	30.10.16	WPL	Widnes Wild	3	2	Nottingham Vipers	W
20	27.11.16	WPL	Widnes Wild	6	4	Kingston Diamonds	W
21	11.12.16	WPL	Nottingham Vipers	4	2	Widnes Wild	L
22	08.01.17	WPL	Streatham Storm	5	1	Widnes Wild	L
23	15.01.17	WPL	Widnes Wild	2	3	Streatham Storm	L
24	12.02.17	WPL	Widnes Wild	4	4	Chelmsford Cobras	D
25	30.04.17	WPL	Slough Phantoms	2	9	Widnes Wild	W
26	07.05.17	WPL	MK Falcons	4	5	Widnes Wild	W
27	27.05.17	WPL	Kingston Diamonds	2	3	Widnes Wild	W
28	03.06.17	POS	Streatham Storm	6	1	Widnes Wild	L
29	15.10.17	WPL	Widnes Wild	3	5	Nottingham Vipers	L
30	5.11.17	WPL	Widnes Wild	0	3	Swindon Top Cats	L
31	3.12.17	WPL	Widnes Wild	4	6	MK Falcons	L
32	17.12.17	WPL	Nottingham Vipers	0	2	Widnes Wild	W
33	14.01.18	WPL	Widnes Wild	5	6	Chelmsford Cobras	L
34	10.02.18	WPL	Bracknell Firebees	6	1	Widnes Wild	L
35	11.02.18	WPL	Swindon Top Cats	5	1	Widnes Wild	L
36	18.02.18	WPL	Kingston Diamonds	3	1	Widnes Wild	L

37	25.02.18	WPL	Widnes Wild	1	5	Kingston Diamonds	L
38	18.03.18	WPL	Widnes Wild	4	4	Bracknell Firebees	D
39	15.04.18	WPL	MKeynes Falcons	8	0	Widnes Wild	L
40	06.05.18	WPL	Chelmsford Cobras	6	6	Widnes Wild	D
41	16.9.18	WPL	MK Falcons	10	3	Widnes Wild	L
42	13.10.18	WPL	Sheffield Shadows	3	1	Widnes Wild	L
43	28.10.18	WPL	Nottingham Vipers	11	2	Widnes Wild	L
44	11.11.18	WPL	Kingston Diamonds	6	0	Widnes Wild	L
45	9.12.18	WPL	Widnes Wild	1	9	Whitley Squaws	L
46	6.1.19	WPL	Bracknell Firebees	7	0	Widnes Wild	L
47	20.1.19	WPL	Widnes Wild	3	9	Nottingham Vipers	L
48	10.2.19	WPL	Widnes Wild	2	9	Chelmsford Cobras	L
49	3.3.19	CH	Solway Sharks	7	7	Widnes Wild	D
50	10.,3.19	WPL	Widnes Wild	1	4	MK Falcons	L
51	7.4.19	WPL	Widnes Wild	2	14	Bracknell Firebees	L
52	21.4.19	WPL	Chelmsford Cobras	5	0	Widnes Wild	LA
53	28.4.19	WPL	Widnes Wild	1	13	Kingston Diamonds	L
54	19.05.19	WPL	Widnes Wild	0	8	Sheffield Shadows	L
55	26.05.19	WPL	Whitley Squaws	7	0	Widnes Wild	L
56	11.08.19	Chall	Solway Sharks	6	10	Widnes Wild	W
57	22.09.19	Chall	Widnes Wild	8	8	Solway Sharks	D
58	06.10.19	D1N	Widnes Wild	7	2	Sheffield Shadows	W
59	16.11.19	D1N	Telford W Raiders	7	2	Widnes Wild	L
60	15.12.19	D1N	Widnes Wild	9	5	Solway Sharks	W
61	21.12.19	D1N	Sheffield Shadows	5	9	Widnes Wild	W
62	05.01.20	D1N	Widnes Wild	15	1	Nottingham Vipers	W
63	11.01.20	D1N	Grimsby Wolves	3	8	Widnes Wild	W
64	16.2.20	D1N	Widnes Wild	12	2	Grimsby Wolves	W
65	01.03.20	D1N	Widnes Wild	8	1	Telford W Raiders	W
66	14.03.20	D1N	Solway Sharks	2	4	Widnes Wild	W
67	18.04.20	D1N	Nottingham Vipers	0	0	Widnes Wild	Da
68	11/07/2021	Chall	Sheffield Shadows	10	2	Widnes Wild	L
69	24/07/2021	Chall	Widnes Wild	7	9	Cal Steel Queens	L
70	28/08/2021	Chall	Widnes Wild	1	11	Bracknell Firebees	L
71	10/10/2021	WPL	Chelmsford Cobras	7	2	Widnes Wild	L
72	30/10/2021	WPL	Slough Sirens	10	4	Widnes Wild	L
73	06/11/2021	WPL	Sheffield Shadows	14	0	Widnes Wild	L
74	14/11/2021	WPL	Nottingham Vipers	5	5	Widnes Wild	D
75	21/11/2021	WPL	Widnes Wild	2	3	Nottingham Vipers	L

76	02/01/2022	WPL	Widnes Wild	0	9	Kingston Diamonds	L
77	09/01/2022	WPL	Widnes Wild	0	9	Sheffield Shadows	L
78	23/01/2022	WPL	Bristol Huskies	21	0	Widnes Wild	L
79	06/02/2022	WPL	Widnes Wild	4	13	Chelmsford Cobras	L
80	13/03/2022	WPL	Kingston Diamonds	15	0	Widnes Wild	L
81	20/03/2022	WPL	Widnes Wild	3	7	Firebees	L
82	03/04/2022	WPL	Widnes Wild	4	7	Slough Sirens	L
83	01/05/2022	WPL	Widnes Wild	0	20	Bristol Huskies	L
84	08/05/2022	WPL	Widnes Wild	2	14	MK Falcons	L
85	15/05/2022	WPL	MK Falcons	9	3	Widnes Wild	L
86	22/05/2022	WPL	Firebees	8	2	Widnes Wild	L
87	01/10/2022	D2N	Solway Sharks	8	4	Widnes Wild	L
88	16/10/2022	D2N	Widnes Wild	9	0	Whitley Bay	W
89	30/10/2022	D2N	Widnes Wild	7	5	Sheffield Shadows	W
90	20/11/2022	D2N	Leeds Roses	1	9	Widnes Wild	W
91	27/11/2022	D2N	Whitley Bay	0	1	Widnes Wild	W ab*
92	08/01/2023	D2N	Widnes Wild	5	4	Telford W Raiders	W
93	21/01/2023	D2N	Telford Raiders	11	1	Widnes Wild	L
94	29/01/2023	D2N	Sheffield Shadows	1	4	Widnes Wild	W
95	05/02/2023	D2N	Widnes Wild	15	2	Kingston Diamonds	W
96	18/02/2023	D2N	Grimsby Wolves	5	12	Widnes Wild	W
97	05/03/2022	D2N	Widnes Wild	7	2	Grimsby Wolves	W
98	26/03/2023	D2N	Widnes Wild	0	6	Solway Sharks	L
99	02/04/2023	D2N	Kingston Diamonds	1	12	Widnes Wild	W
100	23/04/2023	D2N	Widnes Wild	9	2	Leeds Roses	W
101	27/05/2023	POSF	Cardiff Comets	3	1	Widnes Wild	L
102	01/10/2023	D2N	Widnes Wild	5	0	Grimsby Wolves	W
103	14/10/2023	D2N	Cal Steel Queens	10	1	Widnes Wild	L
104	04/11/2023	D2N	Leeds Roses	8	2	Widnes Wild	L
105	12/11/2023	D2N	Sheffield Shadows	5	4	Widnes Wild	L
106	25/11/2023	D2N	Telford W Raiders	8	1	Widnes Wild	L
107	10/12/2023	D2N	Widnes Wild	10	2	Kingston Diamonds	W
108	07/01/2024	D2N	Widnes Wild	5	0	Whitley Bay	W
109	27/01/2024	D2N	Kingston Diamonds	0	0	Widnes Wild	Da
110	04/02/2024	D2N	Widnes Wild	2	4	Cal Steel Queens	L
111	24/02/2024	D2N	Grimsby Wolves	0	5	Widnes Wild	Wa
112	09/03/2024	D2N	Whitley Bay	3	15	Widnes Wild	W
113	24/03/2024	D2N	Widnes Wild	1	5	Telford W Raiders	L
114	28/04/2024	D2N	Widnes Wild	2	2	Sheffield Shadows	D
115	12/05/2024	D2N	Widnes Wild	2	3	Leeds Roses	L

116	29/09/2024	D2N	Kingston Diamonds	4	4	Widnes Wild	D
117	12/10/2024	D2N	Sheffield Shadows	1	2	Widnes Wild	W
118	27/10/2024	D2N	Whitley Beacons	6	4	Widnes Wild	L
119	24/11/2024	D2N	Widnes Wild	6	5	Whitley Bay	W
120	07/12/2024	D2N	Caledonia Bees	4	12	Widnes Wild	W
121	15/12/2024	Cup	Widnes Wild	2	10	Sheffield Shadows	L
122	12/01/2025	D2N	Telford W Raiders	2	2	Widnes Wild	D
123	26/01/2025	D2N	Widnes Wild	5	4	Telford Raiders	W
124	02/02/2025	Cup	Sheffield Shadows	7	3	Widnes Wild	L
125	16/02/2025	Cup	Widnes Wild	5	5	Telford W Raiders	Dab1
126	09/03/2025	D2N	Widnes Wild	4	2	Sheffield Shadows	W
127	16/03/2025	D2N	Widnes Wild	4	4	Kingston Diamonds	D
128	13/04/2025	D2N	Widnes Wild	2	1	Leeds Roses	W
129	27/04/2025	D2N	Widnes Wild	8	0	Caledonia Bees	W
130	03/05/2025	Cup	Telford W Raiders	13	3	Widnes Wild	L
131	10/05/2025	D2N	Leeds Roses	3	3	Widnes Wild	Dab2
132	24/05/2025	POS	Widnes Wild	1	8	Streatham Storm	L

Wild Women Results Summary – 2015-2025

	GP	W	D	L	GF	GA	Pts
WPL	68	14	8	46	182	424	36
D1N	10	8	1	1	72	28	17
D2N	40	23	6	11	216	134	52
Chall	6	1	2	3	35	51	4
Cup	4	0	1	3	13	35	1
POSF	4	0	0	4	4	19	0
Totals	**132**	**46**	**18**	**68**	**522**	**691**	**110**

Widnes Wild Women - Highs & Lows (2015-2025)

Biggest Win - Home

+/-	Date	Comp	Home			Away
14	05/01/2020	WD1N	Widnes Wild	15	1	Nottingham Vipers
13	05/02/2023	D2N	Widnes Wild	15	2	Kingston Diamonds
10	16/02/2020	WD1N	Widnes Wild	12	2	Grimsby Wolves

Biggest Win - Away

12	09/03/2024	D2N	Whitley Bay	3	15	Widnes Wild
11	02/04/2023	D2N	Kingston Diamonds	1	12	Widnes Wild
8	03/04/2016	WPL	Chelmsford Cobras	2	10	Widnes Wild
8	20/11/2022	D2N	Leeds Roses	1	9	Widnes Wild
8	24/04/2016	WPL	Whitley Squaws	2	10	Widnes Wild

Heaviest Defeat - Away

-21	23/01/2022	WPL	Bristol Huskies	21	0	Widnes Wild
-15	13/03/2022	WPL	Kingston Diamonds	15	0	Widnes Wild
-14	06/11/2021	WPL	Sheffield Shadows	14	0	Widnes Wild

Heaviest Defeat - Home

-20	01/05/2022	WPL	Widnes Wild	0	20	Bristol Huskies
-12	08/05/2022	WPL	Widnes Wild	2	14	MK Falcons
-12	07/04/2019	WPL	Widnes Wild	2	14	Bracknell Firebees
-12	28/04.2019	WPL	Widnes Wild	1	13	Kingston Diamonds

Highest Scoring Game - Home

20	01/05/2022	WPL	Widnes Wild	0	20	Bristol Huskies
17	06/02/2022	WPL	Widnes Wild	4	13	Chelmsford Cobras
17	05/02/2023	D2N	Widnes Wild	15	2	Kingston Diamonds

Highest Scoring Game - Away

17	18/02/2023	D2N	Grimsby Wolves	5	12	Widnes Wild
18	09/03/2024	D2N	Whitley Bay	3	15	Widnes Wild
21	23/01/2022	WPL	Bristol Huskies	21	0	Widnes Wild

Lowest Scoring Game - Home

3	13/04/2025	D2N	Widnes Wild	2	1	Leeds Roses
3	05/11/2017	WPL	Widnes Wild	0	3	Swindon Topcats
3	21/02/2016	WPL	Widnes Wild	1	2	MK Falcons

Lowest Scoring Game - Away

1	08/11/2015	WPL	Swindon Topcats	1	0	Widnes Wild
1	27/11/2022	D2N	Whitley Bay	0	1	Widnes Wild
2	17/12/2017	WPL	Nottingham Vipers	0	2	Widnes Wild

Winning & Losing Runs – 2015 to 2025

Longest Winning Streak

7 Games: 15/12/19 to 14/03/20 (D1N)
5 Games: 16/10/22 to 08/01/23 (D2N)
4 Games: 29/01/23 to 05/03/23 (D2N)
4 Games: 03/04/16 to 24/04/16 (WPL)

Longest Unbeaten Streak

8 Games: 15/12/19 to 18/4/20 - 7W 1D (D1N)
8 Games: 28/2/16 to 01/05/16 – 5W 3D (WPL)
5 Games: 16/02/25 to 27/04/25 – 3W 2D (D2N & Cup)

Longest Losing Streak

13 Games: 21/11/21 to 1/10/22 (WPL & D2N)
8 Games: 16/09/18 to 10/02/19 (WPL)

Longest Winless Streak

23 Games: 14/01/18 to 26/05/19 - 20L 3D (WPL)
21 Games: 18/04/20 to 01/10/22 – 19L 2D (D1N, Chall WPL, D2N)

Longest Goal-less Streak

3 Games: 02/01/22 to 23/01/22 (WPL)
206 minutes and 48 seconds without scoring a goal in a spell that saw 3 consecutive shut-outs

Widnes Wild Women Playing Record 2015-2025

Season	Comp	GP	W	D	L	GF	GA	+/-	Pts	Pos
2015/16	WPL	14	8	3	3	62	36	26	19	2 of 8
2016/17	WPL	12	5	2	5	45	45	0	12	4 of 7
2017/18	WPL	12	1	2	9	28	57	-29	4	6 of 7
2018/19	WPL	14	0	0	14	16	114	-98	-2	8 of 8
2019/20	D1N	10	8	1	1	74	28	46	16	1 of 7
2021/22	WPL	16	0	1	15	31	171	-140	1	9 of 9
2022/23	D2N	14	11	0	3	95	48	47	22	2 of 8
2023/24	D2N	14	5	2	7	55	50	5	12	5 of 8
2024/25	D2N	12	7	4	1	56	36	20	18	1 of 7
Totals		118	45	15	58	462	585	-123	102	
2015/16	POSF	1	0	0	1	1	2	-1	0	SF
2016/17	POSF	1	0	0	1	1	6	-5	0	SF
2022/23	POSF	1	0	0	1	1	3	-2	0	SF
2024/25	POSF	1	0	0	1	1	8	-7	0	SF
Totals		4	0	0	4	4	19	-15	0	
2024/25	Cup	4	0	1	3	13	35	-22	1	4 of 4
2018/19	Chall	1	0	1	0	7	7	0	1	
2019/20	Chall	2	1	1	0	18	14	4	4	
2021/22	Chall	3	0	0	3	10	30	-20	0	
Totals		6	1	2	3	35	51	-16	5	
Overall Total		**132**	**46**	**18**	**68**	**514**	**690**	**-176**	**108**	

10 Yr Summary	GP	W	D	L	GF	GA	+/-	Pts
League	118	45	15	58	462	585	-123	102
Play Offs	4	0	0	4	4	19	-15	0
Cup	4	0	1	3	13	35	-22	1
Challenge	6	1	2	3	35	51	-16	5
Overall	**132**	**46**	**18**	**68**	**514**	**690**	**-176**	**108**

Widnes Wild Women Versus....

Here is the Wild Women's playing record against each of their opponents from 2015 to 2025.

We appreciate that "points" aren't actually awarded for Play Off matches and Challenge games but have applied two points for a win and one point for a draw so as to allow for a proper comparison.

There is also an argument that we should separate out the results again 1st teams and 2nd second team - but that would just make it more complicated – and you can find that detail on subsequent pages should you wish to.

Opponents Sorted Alphabetically

Opponents	GP	W	D	L	GF	GA	Pts
Bracknell Firebees	7	0	1	6	13	57	1
Bristol Huskies	2	0	0	1	0	41	0
Caledonia Steel Queens	5	2	0	3	30	27	4
Cardiff Comets	1	0	0	1	1	3	0
Chelmsford Cobras	10	2	2	6	44	63	6
Grimsby Wolves	6	6	0	0	49	12	12
Kingston Diamonds	14	5	3	6	57	70	13
Leeds Roses	6	3	1	2	27	18	8
Milton Keynes Falcons	10	1	1	8	21	63	3
Nottingham Vipers	12	5	2	5	40	49	12
Sheffield Shadows	15	6	1	8	47	84	13
Slough Phantoms	6	3	1	2	31	27	7
Solway Sharks	7	3	2	2	42	42	8
Streatham Storm	7	1	1	5	12	28	3
Swindon TopCats	4	0	1	3	4	12	1
Telford Wrekin Raiders	10	3	2	5	33	50	8
Whitley Bay	10	6	0	4	53	35	12

Opponents Sorted by Widnes Points Gained

Opponents	GP	W	D	L	GF	GA	Pts
Kingston Diamonds	14	5	3	6	57	70	**13**
Sheffield Shadows	15	6	1	8	47	84	**13**
Grimsby Wolves	6	6	0	0	49	12	**12**
Nottingham Vipers	12	5	2	5	40	49	**12**
Whitley Bay	10	6	0	4	53	35	**12**
Leeds Roses	6	3	1	2	27	18	**8**
Solway Sharks	7	3	2	2	42	42	**8**
Telford Wrekin Raiders	10	3	2	5	33	50	**8**
Slough Phantoms	6	3	1	2	31	27	**7**
Chelmsford Cobras	10	2	2	6	44	63	**6**
Caledonia Steel Queens	5	2	0	3	30	27	**4**
Milton Keynes Falcons	10	1	1	8	21	63	**3**
Streatham Storm	7	1	1	5	12	28	**3**
Bracknell Firebees	7	0	1	6	13	57	**1**
Swindon TopCats	4	0	1	3	4	12	**1**
Bristol Huskies	2	0	0	1	0	41	**0**
Cardiff Comets	1	0	0	1	1	3	**0**

Opponents Sorted by Widnes Win%

Opponents	GP	W	D	L	GF	GA	Pts	Win%
Grimsby Wolves	6	6	0	0	49	12	12	**100.00%**
Whitley Bay	10	6	0	4	53	35	12	**60.00%**
Leeds Roses	6	3	1	2	27	18	8	**50.00%**
Slough Phantoms	6	3	1	2	31	27	7	**50.00%**
Solway Sharks	7	3	2	2	42	42	8	**42.86%**
Nottingham Vipers	12	5	2	5	40	49	12	**41.67%**
Sheffield Shadows	15	6	1	8	47	84	13	**40.00%**
Caledonia SQs	5	2	0	3	30	27	4	**40.00%**
Kingston Diamonds	14	5	3	6	57	70	13	**35.71%**
Telford Wr Raiders	10	3	2	5	33	50	8	**30.00%**
Chelmsford Cobras	10	2	2	6	44	63	6	**20.00%**
Streatham Storm	7	1	1	5	12	28	3	**14.29%**
Milton K Falcons	10	1	1	8	21	63	3	**10.00%**
Bracknell Firebees	7	0	1	6	13	57	1	**0.00%**
Swindon TopCats	4	0	1	3	4	12	1	**0.00%**
Bristol Huskies	2	0	0	1	0	41	0	**0.00%**
Cardiff Comets	1	0	0	1	1	3	0	**0.00%**

Widnes Wild Women Versus....

Bracknell Firebees

Home

18/03/2018	WPL	Widnes Wild	4	4	Bracknell Firebees	D
07/04/2019	WPL	Widnes Wild	2	14	Bracknell Firebees	L
28/08/2021	Chall	Widnes Wild	1	11	Bracknell Firebees	L
20/03/2022	WPL	Widnes Wild	3	7	Firebees	L

Away

10/02/2018	WPL	Bracknell Firebees	6	1	Widnes Wild	L
06/01/2019	WPL	Bracknell Firebees	7	0	Widnes Wild	L
22/05/2022	WPL	Firebees	8	2	Widnes Wild	L

	GP	W	D	L	GF	GA	Pts
Home	4	0	1	3	10	36	1
Away	3	0	0	3	3	21	0
Total	7	0	1	6	13	57	1

Note: after their home rink closed in Bracknell as a result of the Coronavirus pandemic, the team dropped the name Bracknell and have just played on as the Firebees at Slough instead.

Bristol Huskies

Home

01/05/2022	WPL	Widnes Wild	0	20	Bristol Huskies	L

Away

23/01/2022	WPL	Bristol Huskies	21	0	Widnes Wild	L

	GP	W	D	L	GF	GA	Pts
Home	1	0	0	1	0	20	0
Away	1	0	0	1	0	21	0
Total	2	0	0	1	0	41	0

Caledonia Steel Queens

Home

24/07/2021	Chall	Widnes Wild	7	9	Caledonia Steel Queens	L
04/02/2024	D2N	Widnes Wild	2	4	Caledonia Steel Queens	L
27/04/2025	D2N	Widnes Wild	8	0	Caledonia Queen Bees	W

Away

14/10/2023	D2N	Caledonia Steel Queens	10	1	Widnes Wild	L
07/12/2024	D2N	Caledonia Queen Bees	4	12	Widnes Wild	W

	GP	W	D	L	GF	GA	Pts
Home	3	1	0	2	17	13	2
Away	2	1	0	1	13	14	2
Total	5	2	0	3	30	27	4

Note: the Bees are the Caledonia Steel Queens' second team. They are referred to elsewhere as the Caledonia Bees.

Cardiff Comets

Neutral

27/05/2023	POSF	Cardiff Comets	3	1	Widnes Wild	L

	GP	W	D	L	GF	GA	Pts
Neutral	1	0	0	1	1	3	0

Chelmsford Cobras

Home

10/04/2016	WPL	Widnes Wild	5	4	Chelmsford Cobras	W
12/02/2017	WPL	Widnes Wild	4	4	Chelmsford Cobras	D
14/01/2018	WPL	Widnes Wild	5	6	Chelmsford Cobras	L
10/02/2019	WPL	Widnes Wild	2	9	Chelmsford Cobras	L
06/02/2022	WPL	Widnes Wild	4	13	Chelmsford Cobras	L

Away

3.4.16	WPL	Chelmsford Cobras	2	10	Widnes Wild	W
25.09.16	WPL	Chelmsford Cobras	7	6	Widnes Wild	L
06.05.18	WPL	Chelmsford Cobras	6	6	Widnes Wild	D
21.4.19	WPL	Chelmsford Cobras	5	0	Widnes Wild	LA*
10/10/2021	WPL	Chelmsford Cobras	7	2	Widnes Wild	L

	GP	W	D	L	GF	GA	Pts
Home	5	1	1	3	20	36	3
Away	5	1	1	3	24	27	3
Total	10	2	2	6	44	63	6

Note: away game on 21st April 2019 was rescheduled at short notice to an inconvenient time and venue and Widnes declined to participate. Game was awarded as a 5-0 forfeit to Chelmsford.

Grimsby Wolves

Home

16/02/2020	D1N	Widnes Wild	12	2	Grimsby Wolves	W
05/03/2022	D2N	Widnes Wild	7	2	Grimsby Wolves	W
01/10/2023	D2N	Widnes Wild	5	0	Grimsby Wolves	W

Away

11.01.20	D1N	Grimsby Wolves	3	8	Widnes Wild	W
18/02/2023	D2N	Grimsby Wolves	5	12	Widnes Wild	W
24/02/2024	D2N	Grimsby Wolves	0	5	Widnes Wild	Wa*

	GP	W	D	L	GF	GA	Pts
Home	3	3	0	0	24	4	6
Away	3	3	0	0	25	8	6
Total	6	6	0	0	49	12	12

Kingston Diamonds

Home

27/11/2016	WPL	Widnes Wild	6	4	Kingston Diamonds	W
25/02/2018	WPL	Widnes Wild	1	5	Kingston Diamonds	L
28/04/2019	WPL	Widnes Wild	1	13	Kingston Diamonds	L
02/01/2022	WPL	Widnes Wild	0	9	Kingston Diamonds	L
05/02/2023	D2N	Widnes Wild	15	2	Kingston Diamonds	W
10/12/2023	D2N	Widnes Wild	10	2	Kingston Diamonds	W
16/03/2025	D2N	Widnes Wild	4	4	Kingston Diamonds	D

Away

27/05/2017	WPL	Kingston Diamonds	2	3	Widnes Wild	W
18/02/2018	WPL	Kingston Diamonds	3	1	Widnes Wild	L
11/11/2018	WPL	Kingston Diamonds	6	0	Widnes Wild	L
13/03/2022	WPL	Kingston Diamonds	15	0	Widnes Wild	L
02/04/2023	D2N	Kingston Diamonds	1	12	Widnes Wild	W
27/01/2024	D2N	Kingston Diamonds	0	0	Widnes Wild	Da
29/09/2024	D2N	Kingston Diamonds	4	4	Widnes Wild	D

	GP	W	D	L	GF	GA	Pts
Home	7	3	1	3	37	39	7
Away	7	2	2	3	20	31	6
Total	14	5	3	6	57	70	13

Note: Kingston Diamonds WPL and Kingston Diamonds D2N are separate teams

Leeds Roses

Home

23/04/2023	D2N	Widnes Wild	9	2	Leeds Roses	W
12/05/2024	D2N	Widnes Wild	2	3	Leeds Roses	L
13/04/2025	D2N	Widnes Wild	2	1	Leeds Roses	W

Away

20/11/2022	D2N	Leeds Roses	1	9	Widnes Wild	W
04/11/2023	D2N	Leeds Roses	8	2	Widnes Wild	L
10/05/2025	D2N	Leeds Roses	3	3	Widnes Wild	Dab2

	GP	W	D	L	GF	GA	Pts
Home	3	2	0	1	13	6	5
Away	3	1	1	1	14	12	3
Total	6	3	1	2	27	18	8

Milton Keynes Falcons

Home

21/02/2016	WPL	Widnes Wild	1	2	MK Falcons	L
11/09/2016	WPL	Widnes Wild	1	5	MK Falcons	L
03/12/2017	WPL	Widnes Wild	4	6	MK Falcons	L
10/03/2019	WPL	Widnes Wild	1	4	MK Falcons	L
08/05/2022	WPL	Widnes Wild	2	14	MK Falcons	L

Away

01/05/2016	WPL	MK Falcons	1	1	Widnes Wild	D
07/05/2017	WPL	MK Falcons	4	5	Widnes Wild	W
15/04/2018	WPL	MK Falcons	8	0	Widnes Wild	L
16/09/2018	WPL	MK Falcons	10	3	Widnes Wild	L
15/05/2022	WPL	MK Falcons	9	3	Widnes Wild	L

	GP	W	D	L	GF	GA	Pts
Home	5	0	0	5	9	31	0
Away	5	1	1	3	12	32	3
Total	10	1	1	8	21	63	3

Nottingham Vipers

Home

15/05/2016	WPL	Widnes Wild	5	3	Nottingham Vipers	W
30/10/2016	WPL	Widnes Wild	3	2	Nottingham Vipers	W
15/10/2017	WPL	Widnes Wild	3	5	Nottingham Vipers	L
20/01/2019	WPL	Widnes Wild	3	9	Nottingham Vipers	L
05/01/2020	D1N	Widnes Wild	15	1	Nottingham Vipers	W
21/11/2021	WPL	Widnes Wild	2	3	Nottingham Vipers	L

Away

17/04/2016	WPL	Nottingham Vipers	6	8	Widnes Wild	W
11/12/2016	WPL	Nottingham Vipers	4	2	Widnes Wild	L
17/12/2017	WPL	Nottingham Vipers	0	2	Widnes Wild	W
28/10/2018	WPL	Nottingham Vipers	11	2	Widnes Wild	L
18/04/2020	D1N	Nottingham Vipers	0	0	Widnes Wild	Da
14/11/2021	WPL	Nottingham Vipers	5	5	Widnes Wild	D

	GP	W	D	L	GF	GA	Pts
Home	6	3	0	3	31	23	6
Away	6	2	2	2	19	26	6
Total	12	5	2	5	40	49	12

Sheffield Shadows

Home

19/05/2019	WPL	Widnes Wild	0	8	Sheffield Shadows	L
06/10/2019	D1N	Widnes Wild	7	2	Sheffield Shadows	W
09/01/2022	WPL	Widnes Wild	0	9	Sheffield Shadows	L
30/10/2022	D2N	Widnes Wild	7	5	Sheffield Shadows	W
28/04/2024	D2N	Widnes Wild	2	2	Sheffield Shadows	D
15/12/2024	Cup	Widnes Wild	2	10	Sheffield Shadows	L
09/03/2025	D2N	Widnes Wild	4	2	Sheffield Shadows	W

Away

13/10/2018	WPL	Sheffield Shadows	3	1	Widnes Wild	L
21/12/2019	D1N	Sheffield Shadows	5	9	Widnes Wild	W
11/07/2021	Chall	Sheffield Shadows	10	2	Widnes Wild	L
06/11/2021	WPL	Sheffield Shadows	14	0	Widnes Wild	L
29/01/2023	D2N	Sheffield Shadows	1	4	Widnes Wild	W
12/11/2023	D2N	Sheffield Shadows	5	4	Widnes Wild	L
12/10/2024	D2N	Sheffield Shadows	1	2	Widnes Wild	W
02/02/2025	Cup	Sheffield Shadows	7	3	Widnes Wild	L

	GP	W	D	L	GF	GA	Pts
Home	7	3	1	3	22	38	7
Away	8	3	0	5	25	46	6
Total	15	6	1	8	47	84	13

Slough Phantoms

Home

28/02/2016	WPL	Widnes Wild	7	2	Slough Phantoms	W
23/10/2016	WPL	Widnes Wild	3	3	Slough Phantoms	D
03/01/2022	WPL	Widnes Wild	4	7	Slough Sirens	L

Away

12/09/2015	WPL	Slough Phantoms	3	4	Widnes Wild	W
30/04/2017	WPL	Slough Phantoms	2	9	Widnes Wild	W
30/10/2021	WPL	Slough Sirens	10	4	Widnes Wild	L

	GP	W	D	L	GF	GA	Pts
Home	3	1	1	1	14	12	3
Away	3	2	0	1	17	15	4
Total	6	3	1	2	31	27	7

Solway Sharks

Home

22/09/2019	Chall	Widnes Wild	8	8	Solway Sharks	D
15/12/2019	D1N	Widnes Wild	9	5	Solway Sharks	W
26/03/2023	D2N	Widnes Wild	0	6	Solway Sharks	L

Away

03/03/2019	Chall	Solway Sharks	7	7	Widnes Wild	D
11/08/2019	Chall	Solway Sharks	6	10	Widnes Wild	W
14/03/2020	D1N	Solway Sharks	2	4	Widnes Wild	W
01/10/2022	D2N	Solway Sharks	8	4	Widnes Wild	L

	GP	W	D	L	GF	GA	Pts
Home	3	1	1	1	17	19	3
Away	4	2	1	1	25	23	5
Total	7	3	2	2	42	42	8

Streatham Storm

Home

05/03/2016	WPL	Widnes Wild	3	3	Streatham Storm	D
15/01/2017	WPL	Widnes Wild	2	3	Streatham Storm	L

Away

11/10/2015	WPL	Streatham Storm	1	3	Widnes Wild	W
08/01/2017	WPL	Streatham Storm	5	1	Widnes Wild	L

Neutral

28/05/2016	POS	Streatham Storm	2	1	Widnes Wild	L
03/06/2017	POS	Streatham Storm	6	1	Widnes Wild	L
24/05/2025	POS	Widnes Wild	1	8	Streatham Storm	L

	GP	W	D	L	GF	GA	Pts
Home	2	0	1	1	5	6	1
Away	2	1	0	1	4	6	2
Neutral	3	0	0	3	3	16	0
Total	7	1	1	5	12	28	3

2016 and 2017 POS were against Streatham 1st team. 2025 POS was against Streatham 2nd team

Swindon TopCats

Home

26/03/2016	WPL	Widnes Wild	3	3	Swindon TopCats	D
05/11/2017	WPL	Widnes Wild	0	3	Swindon Top Cats	L

Away

08/11/2015	WPL	Swindon TopCats	1	0	Widnes Wild	L
11/02/2018	WPL	Swindon TopCats	5	1	Widnes Wild	L

	GP	W	D	L	GF	GA	Pts
Home	2	0	1	1	3	6	1
Away	2	0	0	2	1	6	0
Total	4	0	1	3	4	12	1

Telford Wrekin Raiders

Home

01/03/2020	D1N	Widnes Wild	8	1	Telford Raiders	W
08/01/2023	D2N	Widnes Wild	5	4	Telford Raiders	W
24/03/2024	D2N	Widnes Wild	1	5	Telford Raiders	L
26/01/2025	D2N	Widnes Wild	5	4	Telford Raiders	W
16/02/2025	Cup	Widnes Wild	5	5	Telford Raiders	Dab1

Away

16/11/2019	D1N	Telford Raiders	7	2	Widnes Wild	L
21/01/2023	D2N	Telford Raiders	11	1	Widnes Wild	L
25/11/2023	D2N	Telford Raiders	8	1	Widnes Wild	L
12/01/2025	D2N	Telford Raiders	2	2	Widnes Wild	D
03/05/2025	Cup	Telford Raiders	13	3	Widnes Wild	L

	GP	W	D	L	GF	GA	Pts
Home	5	3	1	1	24	19	7
Away	5	0	1	4	9	41	1
Total	10	3	2	5	33	50	8

Whitley Bay Squaws / Beacons

Home

08/05/2016	WPL	Widnes Wild	2	3	Whitley Squaws	L
09/12/2018	WPL	Widnes Wild	1	9	Whitley Squaws	L
16/10/2022	D2N	Widnes Wild	9	0	Whitley Bay	W
07/01/2024	D2N	Widnes Wild	5	0	Whitley Bay	W
24/11/2024	D2N	Widnes Wild	6	5	Whitley Bay	W

Away

24/04/2016	WPL	Whitley Squaws	2	10	Widnes Wild	W
26/05/2019	WPL	Whitley Squaws	7	0	Widnes Wild	L
27/11/2022	D2N	Whitley Bay	0	1	Widnes Wild	Wa
09/03/2024	D2N	Whitley Bay	3	15	Widnes Wild	W
27/10/2024	D2N	Whitley Bay	6	4	Widnes Wild	L

	GP	W	D	L	GF	GA	Pts
Home	5	3	0	2	23	17	6
Away	5	3	0	2	30	18	6
Total	10	6	0	4	53	35	12

Whitley Squaws were the WPL team and Whitley Bay Beacons are a more recent and separate - D2N team. All Whitley women's teams are now branded as Whitley Bay Beacons.

Wild Women Player Appearances 2015-2025

	Player	GP	G	A	Pts	PIM
1	Drinkwater, Stephanie	104	0	0	0	6
2	Fell, Catherine	92	22	33	55	60
3	De Decker, Leen	91	104	46	150	10
4	Fairclough, Katie	83	44	27	71	114
5	Cooper, Karyn	78	2	13	15	12
6	Adshead, Katie	77	3	8	11	28
7	Crickmore-Clarke, Vanessa	72	3	1	4	26
8	Loss, Elizabeth	66	4	5	9	2
9	Marcroft, Laura	64	7	10	17	6
10	Brown, Jemma	62	13	12	25	20
11	Kirkham, Lucy	61	11	20	31	4
12	Hickey, Jennifer	58	6	12	18	8
13	Miller, Suzie	57	0	4	4	2
14	Sumner, Savannah	56	25	17	42	36
15	Pearson, Emma	55	30	33	63	79
16	Cramp, Charlotte	54	15	20	35	0
17	Williams, Amanda (also Armstrong)	50	22	20	42	6
18	Patient, Phoebe	47	9	6	15	8
19	Tyrer, Ellen	46	10	10	20	4
20	Pearce, Rachael	44	12	19	31	22
21	Skilander, Danielle	43	9	10	19	2
22	Gennoe, Preston	37	37	19	56	46
23	Chapman, Charlene	37	14	11	25	10
24	Hayward, Pauline	36	0	2	2	4
25	Sinclair-Reeks, Sophie	35	3	5	8	12
26	Elliott, Beckie	34	2	3	5	2
27	Hills, Katie	31	31	19	50	54
28	McPhee, Charlotte	30	2	0	2	0
29	Hayes, Abigail	29	3	3	6	20
30	Bowen-Fell, Megan	26	1	2	3	96
31	Garner, Kathryn	25	4	6	10	8
32	Buckles, Natalie	25	1	1	2	8
33	Gillen, Lise	23	12	8	20	4
34	Connelly, Victoria	22	7	6	13	12
35	Aldred, Abigail	22	2	2	4	10
36	Boyle, Samantha Joann	22	0	1	1	8
37	Wilson, Olivia	22	0	1	1	0
38	Jackson, Charlotte	22	0	0	0	0

39	Johnson, Eleanor	21	0	3	3	2
40	Martin, Emma (also Downe)	19	2	3	5	0
41	Moran, Laura	19	0	1	1	10
42	Lloyd-Hazlegreaves, Daisy	18	1	2	3	4
43	Roberts, Sarah	18	0	1	1	8
44	Holt, Shannon	17	1	2	3	2
45	Green, Ellie	17	0	0	0	0
46	Venables, Victoria	16	1	5	6	16
47	McAdam, Charlotte	16	1	2	3	0
48	Leopold, Ruth	15	4	1	5	4
49	Hill, Sophie	14	2	2	4	0
50	Wright, Elizabeth Amy	14	0	3	3	14
51	Walsh-O'Neill, Ellie	14	2	0	2	2
52	Aspinall, Sarah-Louise	13	6	5	11	2
53	Wheeler, Philippa	13	2	3	5	4
54	Greenwood, Jennifer	12	0	1	1	2
55	Moran, Josie	12	0	0	0	0
56	Culshaw, Abigail	11	10	6	16	6
57	England, Pamela	11	0	0	0	0
58	Gustavsson, Madeleine	10	1	3	4	0
59	Oliver, Katya	9	3	5	8	2
60	Green, Sophia	8	1	5	6	12
61	Middleton, Emma	8	0	2	2	0
62	Boyle, Jodie Alexandra	8	0	0	0	0
63	Winstanley, Daisy	7	0	1	1	0
64	Fairbairn, Rachel	7	0	0	0	0
65	Horsfield, Alice	7	0	0	0	0
66	Duncan Jakki	6	0	2	2	2
67	Holliday, Katherine	4	0	0	0	0
68	Horsfield, Niamh	4	0	0	0	0
69	Cartwright, Rachel	3	2	1	3	0
70	Hutchinson, Sarah	3	0	2	2	4
71	Thornton, Cath	3	1	0	1	0
72	Bevan, Emma	3	0	0	0	0
73	Donnelley, Rebecca	3	0	0	0	0
74	Kerr,Kaitlin	2	2	2	4	2
75	Lavery, Tegan	2	0	0	0	0
76	Scott, Rebekah	2	0	0	0	0
77	Wilde, Rebecca Jade	2	0	0	0	0
78	Fletcher, Penelope	1	0	0	0	0
79	Rainey, Nicole	1	0	0	0	0

Widnes Wild Women Points Scorers 2015-2025

Player	GP	G	A	Pts	PIM
De Decker, Leen	91	104	46	**150**	10
Fairclough, Katie	83	44	27	**71**	114
Pearson, Emma	55	30	33	**63**	79
Gennoe, Preston	37	37	19	**56**	46
Fell, Catherine	92	22	33	**55**	60
Hills, Katie	31	31	19	**50**	54
Sumner, Savannah	56	25	17	**42**	36
Williams, Amanda	50	22	20	**42**	6
Cramp, Charlotte	54	15	20	**35**	0
Kirkham, Lucy	61	11	20	**31**	4
Pearce, Rachael	44	12	19	**31**	22
Brown, Jemma	62	13	12	**25**	20
Chapman, Charlene	37	14	11	**25**	10
Tyrer, Ellen	46	10	10	**20**	4
Gillen, Lise	23	12	8	**20**	4
Skilander, Danielle	43	9	10	**19**	2
Hickey, Jennifer	58	6	12	**18**	8
Marcroft, Laura	64	7	10	**17**	6
Culshaw, Abigail	11	10	6	**16**	6
Cooper, Karyn	78	2	13	**15**	12
Patient, Phoebe	47	9	6	**15**	8
Connelly, Victoria	22	7	6	**13**	12
Adshead, Katie	77	3	8	**11**	28
Aspinall, Sarah-Louise	13	6	5	**11**	2
Garner, Kathryn	25	4	6	**10**	8
Loss, Elizabeth	66	4	5	**9**	2
Sinclair-Reeks, Sophie	35	3	5	**8**	12
Oliver, Katya	9	3	5	**8**	2
Hayes, Abigail	29	3	3	**6**	20
Venables, Victoria	16	1	5	**6**	16
Green, Sophia	8	1	5	**6**	12
Elliott, Beckie	34	2	3	**5**	2
Martin, Emma (also Downe)	19	2	3	**5**	0
Leopold, Ruth	15	4	1	**5**	4
Wheeler, Philippa	13	2	3	**5**	4
Crickmore-Clarke, Vanessa	72	3	1	**4**	26
Miller, Suzie	57	0	4	**4**	2
Aldred, Abigail	22	2	2	**4**	10
Hill, Sophie	14	2	2	**4**	0

Gustavsson, Madeleine	10	1	3	**4**	0
Kerr, Kaitlin	2	2	2	**4**	2
Bowen-Fell, Megan	26	1	2	**3**	96
Johnson, Eleanor	21	0	3	**3**	2
Lloyd-Hazlegreaves, Daisy	18	1	2	**3**	4
Holt, Shannon	17	1	2	**3**	2
McAdam, Charlotte	16	1	2	**3**	0
Wright, Elizabeth Amy	14	0	3	**3**	14
Cartwright, Rachel	3	2	1	**3**	0
Hayward, Pauline	36	0	2	**2**	4
McPhee, Charlotte	30	2	0	**2**	0
Buckles, Natalie	25	1	1	**2**	8
Walsh-O'Neill, Ellie	14	2	0	**2**	2
Middleton, Emma	8	0	2	**2**	0
Duncan Jakki	6	0	2	**2**	2
Hutchinson, Sarah	3	0	2	**2**	4
Boyle, Samantha Joann	22	0	1	**1**	8
Wilson, Olivia	22	0	1	**1**	0
Moran, Laura	19	0	1	**1**	10
Roberts, Sarah	18	0	1	**1**	8
Greenwood, Jennifer	12	0	1	**1**	2
Winstanley, Daisy	7	0	1	**1**	0
Thornton, Cath	3	1	0	**1**	0

Leaders by "Points Per Game Average" (PPGAv)

Player	**GP**	**G**	**A**	**Pts**	**PIM**	**PPGAv**
Kerr, Kaitlin	2	2	2	**4**	2	**2.0000**
De Decker, Leen	91	104	46	**150**	10	**1.6484**
Hills, Katie	31	31	19	**50**	54	**1.6129**
Gennoe, Preston	37	37	19	**56**	46	**1.5135**
Culshaw, Abigail	11	10	6	**16**	6	**1.4545**
Pearson, Emma	55	30	33	**63**	79	**1.1455**
Cartwright, Rachel	3	2	1	**3**	0	**1.0000**
Oliver, Katya	9	3	5	**8**	2	**0.8889**
Gillen, Lise	23	12	8	**20**	4	**0.8696**
Fairclough, Katie	83	44	27	**71**	114	**0.8554**
Aspinall, Sarah-Louise	13	6	5	**11**	2	**0.8462**
Williams, Amanda	50	22	20	**42**	6	**0.8400**
Sumner, Savannah	56	25	17	**42**	36	**0.7500**
Green, Sophia	8	1	5	**6**	12	**0.7500**
Pearce, Rachael	44	12	19	**31**	22	**0.7045**

Widnes Wild Women Goal Scorers 2015-2025

Player	GP	G	A	Pts	PIM
De Decker, Leen	91	**104**	46	150	10
Fairclough, Katie	83	**44**	27	71	114
Gennoe, Preston	37	**37**	19	56	46
Hills, Katie	31	**31**	19	50	54
Pearson, Emma	55	**30**	33	63	79
Sumner, Savannah	56	**25**	17	42	36
Fell, Catherine	92	**22**	33	55	60
Williams, Amanda	50	**22**	20	42	6
Cramp, Charlotte	54	**15**	20	35	0
Chapman, Charlene	37	**14**	11	25	10
Brown, Jemma	62	**13**	12	25	20
Pearce, Rachael	44	**12**	19	31	22
Gillen, Lise	23	**12**	8	20	4
Kirkham, Lucy	61	**11**	20	31	4
Tyrer, Ellen	46	**10**	10	20	4
Culshaw, Abigail	11	**10**	6	16	6
Patient, Phoebe	47	**9**	6	15	8
Skilander, Danielle	43	**9**	10	19	2
Marcroft, Laura	64	**7**	10	17	6
Connelly, Victoria	22	**7**	6	13	12
Hickey, Jennifer	58	**6**	12	18	8
Aspinall, Sarah-Louise	13	**6**	5	11	2
Loss, Elizabeth	66	**4**	5	9	2
Garner, Kathryn	25	**4**	6	10	8
Leopold, Ruth	15	**4**	1	5	4
Adshead, Katie	77	**3**	8	11	28
Crickmore-Clarke, Vanessa	72	**3**	1	4	26
Sinclair-Reeks, Sophie	35	**3**	5	8	12
Hayes, Abigail	29	**3**	3	6	20
Oliver, Katya	9	**3**	5	8	2
Cooper, Karyn	78	**2**	13	15	12
Elliott, Beckie	34	**2**	3	5	2
McPhee, Charlotte	30	**2**	0	2	0
Aldred, Abigail	22	**2**	2	4	10
Martin, Emma (also Downe)	19	**2**	3	5	0
Hill, Sophie	14	**2**	2	4	0
Walsh-O'Neill, Ellie	14	**2**	0	2	2
Wheeler, Philippa	13	**2**	3	5	4
Cartwright, Rachel	3	**2**	1	3	0

Kerr, Kaitlin	2	**2**	2	4	2
Bowen-Fell, Megan	26	**1**	2	3	96
Buckles, Natalie	25	**1**	1	2	8
Lloyd-Hazlegreaves, Daisy	18	**1**	2	3	4
Holt, Shannon	17	**1**	2	3	2
Venables, Victoria	16	**1**	5	6	16
McAdam, Charlotte	16	**1**	2	3	0
Gustavsson, Madeleine	10	**1**	3	4	0
Green, Sophia	8	**1**	5	6	12
Thornton, Cath	3	**1**	0	1	0

Leaders by "Goals Per Game Average" (GPGAv)

Player	GP	G	A	Pts	PIM	GPGAv
De Decker, Leen	91	**104**	46	150	10	**1.1429**
Gennoe, Preston	37	**37**	19	56	46	**1.0000**
Hills, Katie	31	**31**	19	50	54	**1.0000**
Kerr, Kaitlin	2	**2**	2	4	2	**1.0000**
Culshaw, Abigail	11	**10**	6	16	6	**0.9091**
Cartwright, Rachel	3	**2**	1	3	0	**0.6667**
Pearson, Emma	55	**30**	33	63	79	**0.5455**
Fairclough, Katie	83	**44**	27	71	114	**0.5301**
Gillen, Lise	23	**12**	8	20	4	**0.5217**
Aspinall, Sarah-Louise	13	**6**	5	11	2	**0.4615**

Widnes Wild Women Assists 2015-2025

Player	GP	G	A	Pts	PIM
De Decker, Leen	91	104	**46**	150	10
Fell, Catherine	92	22	**33**	55	60
Pearson, Emma	55	30	**33**	63	79
Fairclough, Katie	83	44	**27**	71	114
Kirkham, Lucy	61	11	**20**	31	4
Cramp, Charlotte	54	15	**20**	35	0
Williams, Amanda	50	22	**20**	42	6
Pearce, Rachael	44	12	**19**	31	22
Gennoe, Preston	37	37	**19**	56	46
Hills, Katie	31	31	**19**	50	54
Sumner, Savannah	56	25	**17**	42	36
Cooper, Karyn	78	2	**13**	15	12
Brown, Jemma	62	13	**12**	25	20
Hickey, Jennifer	58	6	**12**	18	8
Chapman, Charlene	37	14	**11**	25	10
Marcroft, Laura	64	7	**10**	17	6
Tyrer, Ellen	46	10	**10**	20	4
Skilander, Danielle	43	9	**10**	19	2
Adshead, Katie	77	3	**8**	11	28
Gillen, Lise	23	12	**8**	20	4
Patient, Phoebe	47	9	**6**	15	8
Garner, Kathryn	25	4	**6**	10	8
Connelly, Victoria	22	7	**6**	13	12
Culshaw, Abigail	11	10	**6**	16	6
Loss, Elizabeth	66	4	**5**	9	2
Sinclair-Reeks, Sophie	35	3	**5**	8	12
Venables, Victoria	16	1	**5**	6	16
Aspinall, Sarah-Louise	13	6	**5**	11	2
Oliver, Katya	9	3	**5**	8	2
Green, Sophia	8	1	**5**	6	12
Miller, Suzie	57	0	**4**	4	2
Elliott, Beckie	34	2	**3**	5	2
Hayes, Abigail	29	3	**3**	6	20
Johnson, Eleanor	21	0	**3**	3	2
Martin, Emma (also Downe)	19	2	**3**	5	0
Wright, Elizabeth Amy	14	0	**3**	3	14
Wheeler, Philippa	13	2	**3**	5	4
Gustavsson, Madeleine	10	1	**3**	4	0
Hayward, Pauline	36	0	**2**	2	4

Bowen-Fell, Megan	26	1	**2**	3	96
Aldred, Abigail	22	2	**2**	4	10
Lloyd-Hazlegreaves, Daisy	18	1	**2**	3	4
Holt, Shannon	17	1	**2**	3	2
McAdam, Charlotte	16	1	**2**	3	0
Hill, Sophie	14	2	**2**	4	0
Middleton, Emma	8	0	**2**	2	0
Duncan Jakki	6	0	**2**	2	2
Hutchinson, Sarah	3	0	**2**	2	4
Kerr,Kaitlin	2	2	**2**	4	2
Crickmore-Clarke, Vanessa	72	3	**1**	4	26
Buckles, Natalie	25	1	**1**	2	8
Boyle, Samantha Joann	22	0	**1**	1	8
Wilson, Olivia	22	0	**1**	1	0
Moran, Laura	19	0	**1**	1	10
Roberts, Sarah	18	0	**1**	1	8
Leopold, Ruth	15	4	**1**	5	4
Greenwood, Jennifer	12	0	**1**	1	2
Winstanley, Daisy	7	0	**1**	1	0
Cartwright, Rachel	3	2	**1**	3	0

Leaders by "Assists Per Game Average" (APGAv)

Player	GP	G	A	Pts	PIM	APGAv
Kerr, Kaitlin	2	2	**2**	4	2	**1.0000**
Hutchinson, Sarah	3	0	**2**	2	4	**0.6667**
Green, Sophia	8	1	**5**	6	12	**0.6250**
Hills, Katie	31	31	**19**	50	54	**0.6129**
Pearson, Emma	55	30	**33**	63	79	**0.6000**
Oliver, Katya	9	3	**5**	8	2	**0.5556**
Culshaw, Abigail	11	10	**6**	16	6	**0.5455**
Gennoe, Preston	37	37	**19**	56	46	**0.5135**
De Decker, Leen	91	104	**46**	150	10	**0.5055**
Pearce, Rachael	44	12	**19**	31	22	**0.4318**
Williams, Amanda	50	22	**20**	42	6	**0.4000**

Widnes Wild Women Penalties 2015-2025

Player	GP	G	A	Pts	PIM
Fairclough, Katie	83	44	27	71	**114**
Bowen-Fell, Megan	26	1	2	3	**96**
Pearson, Emma	55	30	33	63	**79**
Fell, Catherine	92	22	33	55	**60**
Hills, Katie	31	31	19	50	**54**
Gennoe, Preston	37	37	19	56	**46**
Sumner, Savannah	56	25	17	42	**36**
Adshead, Katie	77	3	8	11	**28**
Crickmore-Clarke, Vanessa	72	3	1	4	**26**
Pearce, Rachael	44	12	19	31	**22**
Brown, Jemma	62	13	12	25	**20**
Hayes, Abigail	29	3	3	6	**20**
Venables, Victoria	16	1	5	6	**16**
Wright, Elizabeth Amy	14	0	3	3	**14**
Cooper, Karyn	78	2	13	15	**12**
Sinclair-Reeks, Sophie	35	3	5	8	**12**
Connelly, Victoria	22	7	6	13	**12**
Green, Sophia	8	1	5	6	**12**
De Decker, Leen	91	104	46	150	**10**
Chapman, Charlene	37	14	11	25	**10**
Aldred, Abigail	22	2	2	4	**10**
Moran, Laura	19	0	1	1	**10**
Hickey, Jennifer	58	6	12	18	**8**
Patient, Phoebe	47	9	6	15	**8**
Garner, Kathryn	25	4	6	10	**8**
Buckles, Natalie	25	1	1	2	**8**
Boyle, Samantha Joann	22	0	1	1	**8**
Roberts, Sarah	18	0	1	1	**8**
Drinkwater, Stephanie	104	0	0	0	**6**
Marcroft, Laura	64	7	10	17	**6**
Williams, Amanda	50	22	20	42	**6**
Culshaw, Abigail	11	10	6	16	**6**
Kirkham, Lucy	61	11	20	31	**4**
Tyrer, Ellen	46	10	10	20	**4**
Hayward, Pauline	36	0	2	2	**4**
Gillen, Lise	23	12	8	20	**4**

Lloyd-Hazlegreaves, Daisy	18	1	2	3	**4**
Leopold, Ruth	15	4	1	5	**4**
Wheeler, Philippa	13	2	3	5	**4**
Hutchinson, Sarah	3	0	2	2	**4**
Loss, Elizabeth	66	4	5	9	**2**
Miller, Suzie	57	0	4	4	**2**
Skilander, Danielle	43	9	10	19	**2**
Elliott, Beckie	34	2	3	5	**2**
Johnson, Eleanor	21	0	3	3	**2**
Holt, Shannon	17	1	2	3	**2**
Walsh-O'Neill, Ellie	14	2	0	2	**2**
Aspinall, Sarah-Louise	13	6	5	11	**2**
Greenwood, Jennifer	12	0	1	1	**2**
Oliver, Katya	9	3	5	8	**2**
Duncan Jakki	6	0	2	2	**2**
Kerr, Kaitlin	2	2	2	4	**2**

Leaders by "Penalties Per Game Average" (PIMPGAv)

Player	**GP**	**G**	**A**	**Pts**	**PIM**	**PIMPGAv**
Bowen-Fell, Megan	26	1	2	3	**96**	**3.69**
Hills, Katie	31	31	19	50	**54**	**1.74**
Green, Sophia	8	1	5	6	**12**	**1.50**
Pearson, Emma	55	30	33	63	**79**	**1.44**
Fairclough, Katie	83	44	27	71	**114**	**1.37**
Hutchinson, Sarah	3	0	2	2	**4**	**1.33**
Gennoe, Preston	37	37	19	56	**46**	**1.24**
Venables, Victoria	16	1	5	6	**16**	**1.00**
Wright, Elizabeth Amy	14	0	3	3	**14**	**1.00**
Kerr,Kaitlin	2	2	2	4	**2**	**1.00**

Widnes Wild Women - Player A To Z

Player	Season	Comp	GP	G	A	Pts	PIM
Adshead, Katie	2018/19	WPL	13	0	0	0	2
Adshead, Katie	2018/19	Chall	1	1	0	1	0
Adshead, Katie	2018/19	Total	14	1	0	1	2
Adshead, Katie	2019/20	D1N	8	0	2	2	12
Adshead, Katie	2019/20	Chall	2	0	0	0	0
Adshead, Katie	2019/20	Total	10	0	2	2	12
Adshead, Katie	2021/22	WPL	13	0	1	1	2
Adshead, Katie	2021/22	Chall	2	0	0	0	0
Adshead, Katie	2021/22	Total	15	0	1	1	2
Adshead, Katie	2022/23	D1N	13	1	3	4	6
Adshead, Katie	2022/23	POSF	1	0	0	0	0
Adshead, Katie	2022/23	Total	14	1	3	4	6
Adshead, Katie	2023/24	D2N	10	1	2	3	2
Adshead, Katie	2024/25	D2N	10	0	0	0	4
Adshead, Katie	2024/25	POSF	1	0	0	0	0
Adshead, Katie	2024/25	Cup	3	0	0	0	0
Adshead, Katie	2024/25	Total	14	0	0	0	4
Adshead, Katie	Totals		77	3	8	11	28
Aldred, Abigail	2023/24	D2N	7	0	0	0	4
Aldred, Abigail	2023/24	D2N	7	0	0	0	4
Aldred, Abigail	2024/25	D2N	7	2	2	4	0
Aldred, Abigail	2024/25	POSF	1	0	0	0	2
Aldred, Abigail	2024/25	Total	8	2	2	4	2
Aldred, Abigail	Totals		22	2	2	4	10
Armstrong, Amanda (see Williams)							
Aspinall, Sarah	2019/20	D1N	9	5	4	9	0
Aspinall, Sarah	2019/20	Chall	2	1	1	2	2
Aspinall, Sarah	2019/20	Total	11	6	5	11	2
Aspinall, Sarah	2021/22	WPL	1	0	0	0	0
Aspinall, Sarah	2021/22	Chall	1	0	0	0	0
Aspinall, Sarah	2021/22	Total	2	0	0	0	0
Aspinall, Sarah	Totals		13	6	5	11	2

Player	Season	Comp	GP	G	A	Pts	PIM
Bevan, Emma	2015/16	WPL	1	0	0	0	0
Bevan, Emma	2016/17	WPL	2	0	0	0	0
Bevan, Emma	Totals		3	0	0	0	0
Bowen Fell, Catherine (see Fell)							
Bowen-Fell, Megan	2015/16	WPL	12	1	2	3	26
Bowen-Fell, Megan	2015/16	POSF	1	0	0	0	0
Bowen-Fell, Megan	2015/16	Total	13	1	2	3	26
Bowen-Fell, Megan	2016/17	WPL	7	0	0	0	64
Bowen-Fell, Megan	2017/18	WPL	6	0	0	0	6
Bowen-Fell, Megan	Totals		26	1	2	3	96
Boyle, Jodie	2015/16	WPL	7	0	0	0	0
Boyle, Jodie	2015/16	POSF	1	0	0	0	0
Boyle, Jodie	2015/16	Total	8	0	0	0	0
Boyle, Jodie	Totals		8	0	0	0	0
Boyle, Samantha	2015/16	WPL	12	0	0	0	6
Boyle, Samantha	2015/16	POSF	1	0	0	0	0
Boyle, Samantha	2015/16	Total	13	0	0	0	6
Boyle, Samantha	2017/18	WPL	9	0	1	1	2
Boyle, Samantha	Totals		22	0	1	1	8
Brown, Jemma	2018/19	WPL	12	0	2	2	2
Brown, Jemma	2018/19	Chall	1	0	0	0	0
Brown, Jemma	2018/19	Total	13	0	2	2	2
Brown, Jemma	2019/20	D1N	8	1	1	2	10
Brown, Jemma	2019/20	Chall	2	3	2	5	0
Brown, Jemma	2019/20	Total	10	4	3	7	10
Brown, Jemma	2021/22	WPL	13	2	2	4	4
Brown, Jemma	2021/22	Chall	2	0	1	1	0
Brown, Jemma	2021/22	Total	15	2	3	5	4
Brown, Jemma	2023/24	D2N	10	2	2	4	0
Brown, Jemma	2024/25	D2N	11	4	1	5	4
Brown, Jemma	2024/25	POSF	1	0	0	0	0
Brown, Jemma	2024/25	Cup	2	1	1	2	0
Brown, Jemma	2024/25	Total	14	5	2	7	4
Brown, Jemma	Totals		62	13	12	25	20

Player	Season	Comp	GP	G	A	Pts	PIM
Buckles, Natalie	2021/22	WPL	9	0	1	1	4
Buckles, Natalie	2021/22	Chall	2	0	0	0	0
Buckles, Natalie	2021/22	Total	11	0	1	1	4
Buckles, Natalie	2022/23	D1N	6	1	0	1	2
Buckles, Natalie	2022/23	POSF	1	0	0	0	0
Buckles, Natalie	2022/23	Total	7	1	0	1	2
Buckles, Natalie	2023/24	D2N	7	0	0	0	2
Buckles, Natalie	Totals		25	1	1	2	8
Cartwright, Rachel	2015/16	WPL	3	2	1	3	0
Cartwright, Rachel	Totals		3	2	1	3	0
Chapman, Charlene	2015/16	WPL	14	5	3	8	6
Chapman, Charlene	2015/16	POSF	1	0	0	0	0
Chapman, Charlene	2015/16	Total	15	5	3	8	6
Chapman, Charlene	2016/17	WPL	10	6	6	12	0
Chapman, Charlene	2017/18	WPL	12	3	2	5	4
Chapman, Charlene	Totals		37	14	11	25	10
Connelly, Victoria	2022/23	D1N	10	3	2	5	6
Connelly, Victoria	2023/24	D2N	4	3	0	3	6
Connelly, Victoria	2024/25	D2N	7	1	4	5	0
Connelly, Victoria	2024/25	POSF	1	0	0	0	0
Connelly, Victoria	2024/25	Total	8	1	4	5	0
Connelly, Victoria	Totals		22	7	6	13	12
Cooper, Karyn	2018/19	WPL	11	0	0	0	2
Cooper, Karyn	2018/19	Chall	1	0	0	0	0
Cooper, Karyn	2018/19	Total	12	0	0	0	2
Cooper, Karyn	2019/20	D1N	9	0	2	2	0
Cooper, Karyn	2019/20	Chall	2	0	0	0	0
Cooper, Karyn	2019/20	Total	11	0	2	2	0
Cooper, Karyn	2021/22	WPL	14	0	2	2	0
Cooper, Karyn	2021/22	Chall	1	0	0	0	0
Cooper, Karyn	2021/22	Total	15	0	2	2	2
Cooper, Karyn	2022/23	D1N	13	0	2	2	2
Cooper, Karyn	2022/23	POSF	1	0	0	0	0
Cooper, Karyn	2022/23	Total	14	0	2	2	2

Player	Season	Comp	GP	G	A	Pts	PIM
Cooper, Karyn	2023/24	D2N	10	0	1	1	4
Cooper, Karyn	2024/25	D2N	11	0	6	6	2
Cooper, Karyn	2024/25	POSF	1	0	0	0	0
Cooper, Karyn	2024/25	Cup	4	2	0	2	0
Cooper, Karyn	2024/25	Total	16	2	6	8	2
Cooper, Karyn	Totals		78	2	13	15	12
Cramp, Charlotte	2021/22	WPL	15	2	1	3	0
Cramp, Charlotte	2021/22	Chall	1	1	1	2	0
Cramp, Charlotte	2021/22	Total	16	3	1	5	0
Cramp, Charlotte	2022/23	D1N	14	2	9	11	0
Cramp, Charlotte	2022/23	POSF	1	0	1	1	0
Cramp, Charlotte	2022/23	Total	15	2	10	12	0
Cramp, Charlotte	2023/24	D2N	11	1	3	4	0
Cramp, Charlotte	2024/25	Cup	1	0	0	0	0
Cramp, Charlotte	2024/25	D2N	10	9	6	15	0
Cramp, Charlotte	2024/25	POSF	1	0	0	0	0
Cramp, Charlotte	2024/25	Total	12	9	6	15	0
Cramp, Charlotte	Totals		54	15	20	36	0
Crickmore-Clarke, Vanessa	2015/16	WPL	8	0	1	1	6
Crickmore-Clarke,V	2015/16	POSF	1	0	0	0	0
Crickmore-Clarke,V	2015/16	Total	9	0	1	1	6
Crickmore-Clarke,V	2016/17	WPL	6	2	0	2	0
Crickmore-Clarke,V	2017/18	WPL	9	0	0	0	2
Crickmore-Clarke,V	2018/19	WPL	8	0	0	0	2
Crickmore-Clarke,V	2019/20	D1N	4	0	0	0	4
Crickmore-Clarke,V	2021/22	WPL	9	0	0	0	0
Crickmore-Clarke,V	2022/23	D1N	8	1	0	1	6
Crickmore-Clarke,V	2022/23	POSF	1	0	0	0	0
Crickmore-Clarke,V	2022/23	Total	9	1	0	1	6
Crickmore-Clarke,V	2023/24	D2N	8	0	0	0	4
Crickmore-Clarke,V	2024/25	D2N	8	0	0	0	2
Crickmore-Clarke,V	2024/25	POSF	1	0	0	0	0
Crickmore-Clarke,V	2024/25	Cup	1	0	0	0	0
Crickmore-Clarke,V	2024/25	Total	10	0	0	0	2
Crickmore-Clarke,V	Totals		72	3	1	4	26

Player	Season	Comp	GP	G	A	Pts	PIM
Culshaw, Abigail	2015/16	WPL	8	7	4	11	6
Culshaw, Abigail	2015/16	POSF	1	0	0	0	0
Culshaw, Abigail	2015/16	Total	9	7	4	11	6
Culshaw, Abigail	2016/17	WPL	2	3	2	5	0
Culshaw, Abigail	Totals		11	10	6	16	6
De Decker, Leen	2015/16	WPL	14	15	4	19	2
De Decker, Leen	2015/16	POSF	1	1	0	1	0
De Decker, Leen	2015/16	Total	15	16	4	20	2
De Decker, Leen	2016/17	WPL	11	12	5	17	2
De Decker, Leen	2016/17	POSF	1	1	0	1	0
De Decker, Leen	2016/17	Total	12	13	5	18	2
De Decker, Leen	2017/18	WPL	9	4	5	9	0
De Decker, Leen	2018/19	WPL	3	3	0	3	0
De Decker, Leen	2018/19	Total	3	3	0	3	0
De Decker, Leen	2019/20	D1N	7	20	8	28	0
De Decker, Leen	2021/22	WPL	14	6	3	9	4
De Decker, Leen	2021/22	Chall	1	0	0	0	0
De Decker, Leen	2021/22	Total	15	6	3	9	4
De Decker, Leen	2022/23	D1N	14	24	11	34	0
De Decker, Leen	2022/23	POSF	1	1	0	1	0
De Decker, Leen	2022/23	Total	15	25	11	35	0
De Decker, Leen	2024/25	D2N	10	15	6	21	0
De Decker, Leen	2024/25	Cup	4	1	4	5	2
De Decker, Leen	2024/25	POSF	1	1	0	1	0
De Decker, Leen	2024/25	Total	15	17	10	27	2
De Decker, Leen	Totals		91	104	46	150	10
Donnelley, Rebecca	2022/23	D1N	3	0	0	0	0
Donnelley, Rebecca	Totals		3	0	0	0	0

Downe, Emma (see Martin)

Player	Season	Comp	GP	G	A	Pts	PIM
Drinkwater, Stephanie	2015/16	WPL	13	0	0	0	0
Drinkwater, Stephanie	2015/16	POSF	1	0	0	0	0
Drinkwater, Stephanie	2015/16	Total	14	0	0	0	0
Drinkwater, Stephanie	2016/17	WPL	7	0	0	0	0
Drinkwater, Stephanie	2016/17	POSF	1	0	0	0	0
Drinkwater, Stephanie	2016/17	Total	8	0	0	0	0
Drinkwater, Stephanie	2017/18	WPL	10	0	0	0	2
Drinkwater, Stephanie	2018/19	WPL	13	0	0	0	4
Drinkwater, Stephanie	2018/19	Chall	1	0	0	0	0
Drinkwater, Stephanie	2018/19	Total	14	0	0	0	4
Drinkwater, Stephanie	2019/20	D1N	7	0	0	0	0
Drinkwater, Stephanie	2019/20	Chall	1	0	0	0	0
Drinkwater, Stephanie	2019/20	Total	8	0	0	0	0
Drinkwater, Stephanie	2021/22	WPL	14	0	0	0	0
Drinkwater, Stephanie	2021/22	Total	14	0	0	0	0
Drinkwater, Stephanie	2022/23	D1N	10	0	0	0	0
Drinkwater, Stephanie	2022/23	POSF	1	0	0	0	0
Drinkwater, Stephanie	2022/23	Total	11	0	0	0	0
Drinkwater, Stephanie	2023/24	D2N	10	0	0	0	0
Drinkwater, Stephanie	2024/25	D2N	11	0	0	0	0
Drinkwater, Stephanie	2024/25	Cup	3	0	0	0	0
Drinkwater, Stephanie	2024/25	POSF	1	0	0	0	0
Drinkwater, Stephanie	2024/25	Total	15	0	0	0	0
Drinkwater, Stephanie	Totals		104	0	0	0	6
Duncan Jakki	2015/16	WPL	6	0	2	2	2
Duncan Jakki	Totals		6	0	2	2	2
Elliott, Beckie	2015/16	WPL	12	1	1	2	2
Elliott, Beckie	2015/16	Total	12	1	1	2	2
Elliott, Beckie	2016/17	WPL	12	0	2	2	0
Elliott, Beckie	2016/17	POSF	1	0	0	0	0
Elliott, Beckie	2016/17	Total	13	0	2	2	0
Elliott, Beckie	2017/18	WPL	2	0	0	0	0
Elliott, Beckie	2021/22	WPL	7	1	0	1	0
Elliott, Beckie	2021/22	Total	7	1	0	1	0
Elliott, Beckie	Totals		34	2	3	5	2

Player	Season	Comp	GP	G	A	Pts	PIM
England, Pamela	2018/19	WPL	9	0	0	0	0
England, Pamela	2021/22	WPL	1	0	0	0	0
England, Pamela	2021/22	Chall	1	0	0	0	0
England, Pamela	2021/22	Total	2	0	0	0	0
England, Pamela	Totals		11	0	0	0	0
Fairbairn, Rachel	2016/17	WPL	7	0	0	0	0
Fairbairn, Rachel	Totals		7	0	0	0	0
Fairclough, Katie	2017/18	WPL	11	0	1	1	29
Fairclough, Katie	2018/19	WPL	12	0	1	1	4
Fairclough, Katie	2018/19	Chall	1	0	0	0	0
Fairclough, Katie	2018/19	Total	13	0	1	1	4
Fairclough, Katie	2019/20	D1N	9	2	3	5	20
Fairclough, Katie	2019/20	Chall	2	2	1	3	4
Fairclough, Katie	2019/20	Total	11	4	4	8	24
Fairclough, Katie	2021/22	WPL	13	5	2	7	4
Fairclough, Katie	2021/22	Chall	0	0	0	0	0
Fairclough, Katie	2021/22	Total	13	5	2	7	4
Fairclough, Katie	2022/23	D1N	13	20	12	32	10
Fairclough, Katie	2022/23	POSF	1	0	0	0	0
Fairclough, Katie	2022/23	Total	14	20	12	32	10
Fairclough, Katie	2023/24	D2N	10	10	5	15	12
Fairclough, Katie	2024/25	Cup	3	4	1	5	0
Fairclough, Katie	2024/25	D2N	8	1	1	2	31
Fairclough, Katie	2024/25	Total	11	5	2	7	31
Fairclough, Katie	Totals		83	44	27	71	114
Fell, Catherine	2015/16	WPL	13	10	4	14	4
Fell, Catherine	2015/16	POSF	1	0	0	0	0
Fell, Catherine	2015/16	Total	14	10	4	14	4
Fell, Catherine	2016/17	WPL	1	0	0	0	0
Fell, Catherine	2016/17	POSF	0	0	0	0	
Fell, Catherine	2016/17	Total	1	0	0	0	0
Fell, Catherine	2017/18	WPL	7	0	1	1	4
Fell, Catherine	2019/20	D1N	7	6	3	9	4
Fell, Catherine	2019/20	Chall	1	1	1	2	0
Fell, Catherine	2019/20	Total	8	7	4	11	4
Fell, Catherine	2021/22	WPL	12	4	1	5	20

Player	Season	Comp	GP	G	A	Pts	PIM
Fell, Catherine	2021/22	Chall	1	0	0	0	0
Fell, Catherine	2021/22	Total	13	4	1	5	20
Fell, Catherine	2022/23	D1N	11	0	6	6	6
Fell, Catherine	2022/23	Total	12	0	6	6	6
Fell, Catherine	2022/23	POSF	1	0	0	0	0
Fell, Catherine	2023/24	D2N	8	0	1	1	0
Fell, Catherine	2024/25	D2N	8	0	3	3	8
Fell, Catherine	2024/25	POSF	1	0	0	0	0
Fell, Catherine	2024/25	Cup	4	1	2	3	2
Fell, Catherine	2024/25	Total	13	1	5	6	10
Fell, Catherine	Totals		92	22	33	55	60

Note: played as Catherine Bowen Fell 2013 to 2020

Player	Season	Comp	GP	G	A	Pts	PIM
Fletcher, Penelope	2015/16	WPL	1	0	0	0	0
Fletcher, Penelope	Totals		1	0	0	0	0
Garner, Kathryn	2018/19	WPL	12	0	0	0	2
Garner, Kathryn	2018/19	Chall	1	0	1	1	2
Garner, Kathryn	2018/19	Total	13	0	1	1	4
Garner, Kathryn	2019/20	D1N	9	1	5	6	2
Garner, Kathryn	2019/20	Chall	2	1	0	1	2
Garner, Kathryn	2019/20	Total	11	2	5	7	4
Garner, Kathryn	2021/22	Chall	1	2	0	2	0
Garner, Kathryn	Totals		25	4	6	10	8
Gennoe, Preston	2021/22	WPL	12	7	4	11	26
Gennoe, Preston	2021/22	Chall	1	0	0	1	0
Gennoe, Preston	2021/22	Total	13	8	4	12	26
Gennoe, Preston	2022/23	D1N	12	13	10	23	4
Gennoe, Preston	2022/23	POSF	1	0	0	0	2
Gennoe, Preston	2022/23	Total	13	13	10	23	6
Gennoe, Preston	2023/24	D2N	11	16	5	21	14
Gennoe, Preston	Totals		37	37	19	56	46

Player	Season	Comp	GP	G	A	Pts	PIM
Gillen, Lise	2022/23	D1N	10	2	4	6	0
Gillen, Lise	2022/23	POSF	0	0	0	0	0
Gillen, Lise	2022/23	Total	10	2	4	6	0
Gillen, Lise	2023/24	D2N	4	2	2	4	0
Gillen, Lise	2024/25	D2N	8	8	1	12	4
Gillen, Lise	2024/25	POSF	1	0	1	1	0
Gillen, Lise	2024/25	Total	9	8	2	13	4
Gillen, Lise	Totals		23	12	8	23	4
Green, Ellie	2022/23	D1N	8	0	0	0	0
Green, Ellie	2022/23	POSF	1	0	0	0	0
Green, Ellie	2022/23	Total	9	0	0	0	0
Green, Ellie	2023/24	D2N	8	0	0	0	0
Green, Ellie	Totals		17	0	0	0	0
Green, Sophia	2022/23	D1N	7	1	5	6	12
Green, Sophia	2022/23	POSF	1	0	0	0	0
Green, Sophia	2022/23	Total	8	1	5	6	12
Green, Sophia	Totals		8	1	5	6	12
Greenwood, Jennifer	2024/25	D2N	8	0	1	1	2
Greenwood, Jennifer	2024/25	Cup	4	0	0	0	0
Greenwood, Jennifer	2024/25	Total	12	0	1	1	2
Greenwood, Jennifer	Totals		12	0	1	1	2
Gustavsson, Madeleine	2015/16	WPL	10	1	3	4	0
Gustavsson, Madeleine	Totals		10	1	3	4	0
Hayes, Abigail	2015/16	WPL	10	0	0	0	12
Hayes, Abigail	2015/16	POSF	1	0	0	0	0
Hayes, Abigail	2015/16	Total	11	0	0	0	12
Hayes, Abigail	2016/17	WPL	9	1	2	3	2
Hayes, Abigail	2016/17	POSF	1	0	0	0	
Hayes, Abigail	2016/17	Total	10	1	2	3	2
Hayes, Abigail	2017/18	WPL	8	2	1	3	6
Hayes, Abigail	Totals		29	3	3	6	20

Player	Season	Comp	GP	G	A	Pts	PIM
Hayward, Pauline	2017/18	WPL	10	0	1	1	0
Hayward, Pauline	2018/19	WPL	12	0	0	0	4
Hayward, Pauline	2018/19	Chall	1	0	0	0	0
Hayward, Pauline	2018/19	Total	13	0	0	0	4
Hayward, Pauline	2019/20	D1N	7	0	0	0	0
Hayward, Pauline	2019/20	Chall	2	0	0	0	0
Hayward, Pauline	2019/20	Total	9	0	0	0	0
Hayward, Pauline	2021/22	WPL	2	0	0	0	0
Hayward, Pauline	2022/23	D1N	2	0	1	1	0
Hayward, Pauline	Totals		36	0	2	2	4
Hickey, Jennifer	2021/22	WPL	14	1	0	1	2
Hickey, Jennifer	2021/22	Chall	1	0	1	1	0
Hickey, Jennifer	2021/22	Total	15	1	1	2	2
Hickey, Jennifer	2022/23	D1N	14	1	3	4	2
Hickey, Jennifer	2022/23	POSF	1	0	0	0	0
Hickey, Jennifer	2022/23	Total	15	1	3	4	2
Hickey, Jennifer	2023/24	D2N	12	2	2	4	2
Hickey, Jennifer	2024/25	D2N	11	2	6	8	2
Hickey, Jennifer	2024/25	POSF	1	0	0	0	0
Hickey, Jennifer	2024/25	Cup	4	0	0	0	0
Hickey, Jennifer	2024/25	Total	16	2	6	8	2
Hickey, Jennifer	Totals		58	6	12	18	8
Hill, Sophie	2022/23	D1N	1	0	0	0	0
Hill, Sophie	2023/24	D2N	5	2	2	4	0
Hill, Sophie	2024/25	D2N	6	0	0	0	0
Hill, Sophie	2024/25	Cup	2	0	0	0	0
Hill, Sophie	2024/25	Total	8	0	0	0	0
Hill, Sophie	Totals		14	2	2	4	0
Hills, Katie	2015/16	WPL	14	15	8	23	10
Hills, Katie	2015/16	POSF	1	0	1	1	0
Hills, Katie	2015/16	Total	15	15	9	24	10
Hills, Katie	2016/17	WPL	10	10	6	16	42
Hills, Katie	2016/17	POSF	1	0	1	1	
Hills, Katie	2016/17	Total	11	10	7	17	42
Hills, Katie	2017/18	WPL	5	6	3	9	2
Hills, Katie	Totals		31	31	19	50	54

Player	Season	Comp	GP	G	A	Pts	PIM
Holliday, Katherine	2015/16	WPL	4	0	0	0	0
Holliday, Katherine	Totals		4	0	0	0	0
Holt, Shannon	2019/20	D1N	4	1	2	3	2
Holt, Shannon	2021/22	WPL	12	0	0	0	0
Holt, Shannon	2021/22	Chall	1	0	0	0	0
Holt, Shannon	2021/22	Total	13	0	0	0	0
Holt, Shannon	Totals		17	1	2	3	2
Horsfield, Alice	2017/18	WPL	7	0	0	0	0
Horsfield, Alice	Totals		7	0	0	0	0
Horsfield, Niamh	2024/25	D2N	2	0	0	0	0
Horsfield, Niamh	2024/25	Cup	2	0	0	0	0
Horsfield, Niamh	2024/25	Total	4	0	0	0	0
Horsfield, Niamh	Totals		4	0	0	0	0
Hutchinson, Sarah	2015/16	WPL	3	0	2	2	4
Hutchinson, Sarah	Totals		3	0	2	2	4
Jackson, Charlotte	2019/20	D1N	8	0	0	0	0
Jackson, Charlotte	2019/20	Chall	2	0	0	0	0
Jackson, Charlotte	2019/20	Total	10	0	0	0	0
Jackson, Charlotte	2021/22	WPL	8	0	0	0	0
Jackson, Charlotte	2021/22	Chall	2	0	0	0	0
Jackson, Charlotte	2021/22	Total	10	0	0	0	0
Jackson, Charlotte	2024/25	D2N	1	0	0	0	0
Jackson, Charlotte	2024/25	Cup	1	0	0	0	0
Jackson, Charlotte	2024/25	Total	2	0	0	0	0
Jackson, Charlotte	Totals		22	0	0	0	0
Johnson, Eleanor	2023/24	D2N	6	0	0	0	0
Johnson, Eleanor	2024/25	D2N	10	0	2	2	2
Johnson, Eleanor	2024/25	POSF	1	0	1	1	0
Johnson, Eleanor	2024/25	Cup	4	0	0	0	0
Johnson, Eleanor	2024/25	Total	15	0	3	3	2
Johnson, Eleanor	Totals		21	0	3	3	2
Kerr, Kaitlyn	2021/22	Chall	2	2	2	4	2
Kerr, Kaitlyn	Totals		2	2	2	4	2

Player	Season	Comp	GP	G	A	Pts	PIM
Kirkham, Lucy	2015/16	WPL	13	2	3	5	2
Kirkham, Lucy	2015/16	POSF	1	0	0	0	0
Kirkham, Lucy	2015/16	Total	14	2	3	5	2
Kirkham, Lucy	2016/17	WPL	11	4	4	8	0
Kirkham, Lucy	2016/17	POSF	1	0	0	0	
Kirkham, Lucy	2016/17	Total	12	4	4	8	0
Kirkham, Lucy	2017/18	WPL	12	3	4	7	0
Kirkham, Lucy	2022/23	D1N	12	2	8	10	0
Kirkham, Lucy	2022/23	POSF	1	0	0	0	0
Kirkham, Lucy	2022/23	Total	13	2	8	10	0
Kirkham, Lucy	2023/24	D2N	3	0	0	0	0
Kirkham, Lucy	2024/25	D2N	6	0	1	1	2
Kirkham, Lucy	2024/25	Cup	1	0	0	0	0
Kirkham, Lucy	2024/25	Total	7	0	1	1	2
Kirkham, Lucy	Totals		61	11	20	31	4
Lavery, Tegan	2016/17	WPL	1	0	0	0	0
Lavery, Tegan	2016/17	POSF	1	0	0	0	0
Lavery, Tegan	2016/17	Total	2	0	0	0	0
Lavery, Tegan	Totals		2	0	0	0	0
Leopold, Ruth	2024/25	D2N	12	4	1	5	2
Leopold, Ruth	2024/25	Cup	2	0	0	0	0
Leopold, Ruth	2024/25	POSF	1	0	0	0	2
Leopold, Ruth	2024/25	Total	15	4	1	5	4
Leopold, Ruth	Totals		15	4	1	5	4
Lloyd-Hazlegreaves, Daisy	2018/19	WPL	12	0	0	0	2
Lloyd-Hazlegreaves, Daisy	2019/20	D1N	6	1	2	3	2
Lloyd-Hazlegreaves, Daisy	Totals		18	1	2	3	4

Player	Season	Comp	GP	G	A	Pts	PIM
Loss, Elizabeth	2015/16	WPL	1	0	0	0	0
Loss, Elizabeth	2016/17	WPL	1	0	0	0	0
Loss, Elizabeth	2018/19	WPL	11	1	1	2	0
Loss, Elizabeth	2019/20	D1N	9	2	1	3	0
Loss, Elizabeth	2019/20	Chall	2	1	1	2	0
Loss, Elizabeth	2019/20	Total	11	3	2	5	0
Loss, Elizabeth	2021/22	WPL	10	0	0	0	0
Loss, Elizabeth	2021/22	Chall	1	0	0	0	0
Loss, Elizabeth	2021/22	Total	11	0	0	0	0
Loss, Elizabeth	2022/23	D1N	9	0	2	2	0
Loss, Elizabeth	2022/23	POSF	1	0	0	0	0
Loss, Elizabeth	2022/23	Total	10	0	2	2	0
Loss, Elizabeth	2023/24	D2N	9	0	0	0	0
Loss, Elizabeth	2024/25	D2N	9	0	0	0	2
Loss, Elizabeth	2024/25	POSF	1	0	0	0	0
Loss, Elizabeth	2024/25	Cup	2	0	0	0	0
Loss, Elizabeth	2024/25	Total	12	0	0	0	2
Loss, Elizabeth	Totals		66	4	5	9	2
Marcroft, Laura	2018/19	WPL	12	0	1	1	0
Marcroft, Laura	2018/19	Chall	1	0	2	2	0
Marcroft, Laura	2018/19	Total	13	0	3	3	0
Marcroft, Laura	2019/20	D1N	8	1	2	3	4
Marcroft, Laura	2019/20	Chall	2	0	0	0	0
Marcroft, Laura	2019/20	Total	10	1	2	3	4
Marcroft, Laura	2021/22	WPL	14	0	0	0	0
Marcroft, Laura	2021/22	Chall	2	0	0	1	0
Marcroft, Laura	2021/22	Total	16	0	1	1	0
Marcroft, Laura	2022/23	D1N	13	4	3	7	0
Marcroft, Laura	2022/23	POSF	1	0	0	0	0
Marcroft, Laura	2022/23	Total	14	4	3	7	0
Marcroft, Laura	2023/24	D2N	11	2	1	3	2
Marcroft, Laura	Totals		64	7	10	17	6

Player	Season	Comp	GP	G	A	Pts	PIM
Martin, Emma	2019/20	D1N	9	2	2	4	0
Martin, Emma	2019/20	Chall	1	0	1	1	0
Martin, Emma	2019/20	Total	10	2	3	5	0
Martin, Emma	2021/22	WPL	7	0	0	0	0
Martin, Emma	2021/22	Chall	2	0	0	0	0
Martin, Emma	2021/22	Total	9	0	0	0	0
Martin, Emma	Totals		19	2	3	5	0
Martin, Emma							
McAdam, Charlotte	2023/24	D2N	4	0	0	0	0
McAdam, Charlotte	2024/25	Cup	3	0	0	0	0
McAdam, Charlotte	2024/25	D2N	8	1	2	3	0
McAdam, Charlotte	2024/25	POSF	1	0	0	0	0
McAdam, Charlotte	2024/25	Total	12	1	2	3	0
McAdam, Charlotte	Totals		16	1	2	3	0
McPhee, Charlotte	2017/18	WPL	5	0	0	0	0
McPhee, Charlotte	2018/19	WPL	13	0	0	0	0
McPhee, Charlotte	2018/19	Chall	1	2	0	2	0
McPhee, Charlotte	2018/19	Total	14	2	0	2	0
McPhee, Charlotte	2019/20	D1N	8	0	0	0	0
McPhee, Charlotte	2019/20	Chall	2	0	0	0	0
McPhee, Charlotte	2019/20	Total	10	0	0	0	0
McPhee, Charlotte	2021/22	WPL	0	0	0	0	0
McPhee, Charlotte	2021/22	Chall	1	0	0	0	0
McPhee, Charlotte	2021/22	Total	1	0	0	0	0
McPhee, Charlotte	Totals		30	2	0	2	0
Middleton, Emma	2015/16	WPL	4	0	2	2	0
Middleton, Emma	2016/17	WPL	4	0	0	0	0
Middleton, Emma	Totals		8	0	2	2	0

Player	Season	Comp	GP	G	A	Pts	PIM
Miller, Suzie	2019/20	D1N	4	0	0	0	0
Miller, Suzie	2021/22	WPL	14	0	1	1	0
Miller, Suzie	2021/22	Chall	2	0	0	0	0
Miller, Suzie	2021/22	Total	16	0	1	1	0
Miller, Suzie	2022/23	D1N	10	0	2	2	0
Miller, Suzie	2022/23	POSF	1	0	0	0	0
Miller, Suzie	2022/23	Total	11	0	2	2	0
Miller, Suzie	2023/24	D2N	11	0	1	1	0
Miller, Suzie	2024/25	D2N	10	0	0	0	2
Miller, Suzie	2024/25	POSF	1	0	0	0	0
Miller, Suzie	2024/25	Cup	4	0	0	0	0
Miller, Suzie	2024/25	Total	15	0	0	0	2
Miller, Suzie	Totals		57	0	4	4	2
Moran, Josie	2018/19	WPL	10	0	0	0	0
Moran, Josie	2018/19	Chall	1	0	0	0	0
Moran, Josie	2018/19	Total	11	0	0	0	0
Moran, Josie	2019/20	Chall	1	0	0	0	0
Moran, Josie	Totals		12	0	0	0	0
Moran, Laura	2023/24	D2N	10	0	1	1	2
Moran, Laura	2024/25	D2N	8	0	0	0	6
Moran, Laura	2024/25	POSF	1	0	0	0	2
Moran, Laura	2024/25	Total	9	0	0	0	8
Moran, Laura	Totals		19	0	1	1	10
Oliver, Katya	2023/24	D2N	9	3	5	8	2
Oliver, Katya	Totals		9	3	5	8	2
Patient, Phoebe	2021/22	WPL	14	0	1	1	2
Patient, Phoebe	2021/22	Chall	1	0	0	0	0
Patient, Phoebe	2021/22	Total	15	0	1	1	2
Patient, Phoebe	2022/23	D1N	13	3	3	6	0
Patient, Phoebe	2022/23	POSF	1	0	0	0	0
Patient, Phoebe	2022/23	Total	14	3	3	6	0
Patient, Phoebe	2023/24	D2N	10	2	0	2	4
Patient, Phoebe	2024/25	D2N	7	4	2	6	2
Patient, Phoebe	2024/25	POSF	1	0	0	0	0
Patient, Phoebe	2024/25	Total	8	4	2	6	2
Patient, Phoebe	Totals		47	9	6	15	8

Player	Season	Comp	GP	G	A	Pts	PIM
Pearce, Rachael	2022/23	D1N	14	8	9	17	6
Pearce, Rachael	2022/23	POSF	1	0	1	1	0
Pearce, Rachael	2022/23	Total	15	8	10	18	6
Pearce, Rachael	2023/24	D2N	12	2	2	4	4
Pearce, Rachael	2024/25	D2N	12	0	5	5	8
Pearce, Rachael	2024/25	Cup	4	2	2	4	4
Pearce, Rachael	2024/25	POSF	1	0	0	0	0
Pearce, Rachael	2024/25	Total	17	2	7	9	12
Pearce, Rachael	Totals		44	12	19	31	22
Pearson, Emma	2015/16	WPL	6	1	4	5	2
Pearson, Emma	2015/16	POSF	1	0	0	0	2
Pearson, Emma	2015/16	Total	7	1	4	5	4
Pearson, Emma	2016/17	WPL	12	2	5	7	4
Pearson, Emma	2016/17	POSF	1	0	0	0	
Pearson, Emma	2016/17	Total	13	2	5	7	4
Pearson, Emma	2017/18	WPL	10	1	2	3	33
Pearson, Emma	2018/19	WPL	13	2	6	8	16
Pearson, Emma	2018/19	Chall	1	0	0	0	0
Pearson, Emma	2018/19	Total	14	2	6	8	16
Pearson, Emma	2019/20	D1N	9	21	15	36	22
Pearson, Emma	2019/20	Chall	2	3	1	4	0
Pearson, Emma	2019/20	Total	11	24	16	40	22
Pearson, Emma	Totals		55	30	33	63	79
Rainey, Nicole	2024/25	D2N	1	0	0	0	0
Rainey, Nicole	Totals		1	0	0	0	0
Roberts, Sarah	2016/17	WPL	10	0	0	0	2
Roberts, Sarah	2016/17	POSF	1	0	0	0	0
Roberts, Sarah	2016/17	Total	11	0	0	0	2
Roberts, Sarah	2017/18	WPL	7	0	1	1	6
Roberts, Sarah	Totals		18	0	1	1	8
Scott, Rebekah	2017/18	WPL	2	0	0	0	0
Scott, Rebekah	Totals		2	0	0	0	0

Player	Season	Comp	GP	G	A	Pts	PIM
Sinclair-Reeks, Sophie	2015/16	WPL	3	0	0	0	0
Sinclair-Reeks, Sophie	2015/16	POSF	1	0	0	0	0
Sinclair-Reeks, Sophie	2015/16	Total	4	0	0	0	0
Sinclair-Reeks, Sophie	2016/17	WPL	10	3	2	5	6
Sinclair-Reeks, Sophie	2016/17	POSF	1	0	0	0	0
Sinclair-Reeks, Sophie	2016/17	Total	11	3	2	5	6
Sinclair-Reeks, Sophie	2017/18	WPL	11	0	1	1	2
Sinclair-Reeks, Sophie	2018/19	WPL	8	0	1	1	4
Sinclair-Reeks, Sophie	2018/19	Chall	1	0	1	1	0
Sinclair-Reeks, Sophie	2018/19	Total	9	0	2	2	4
Sinclair-Reeks, Sophie	Totals		35	3	5	8	12
Skilander, Danielle	2018/19	WPL	10	1	1	2	0
Skilander, Danielle	2018/19	Chall	0	0	0	0	0
Skilander, Danielle	2018/19	Total	10	1	1	2	0
Skilander, Danielle	2019/20	D1N	9	1	2	3	0
Skilander, Danielle	2019/20	Chall	2	1	0	0	0
Skilander, Danielle	2019/20	Total	11	2	2	3	0
Skilander, Danielle	2021/22	WPL	8	0	1	1	2
Skilander, Danielle	2021/22	Chall	1	1	0	1	0
Skilander, Danielle	2021/22	Total	9	1	1	2	2
Skilander, Danielle	2022/23	D1N	12	5	6	11	0
Skilander, Danielle	2022/23	POSF	1	0	0	0	0
Skilander, Danielle	2022/23	Total	13	5	6	11	0
Skilander, Danielle	Totals		43	9	10	18	2
Sumner, Savannah	2016/17	WPL	12	1	2	3	10
Sumner, Savannah	2016/17	POSF	1	0	1	1	
Sumner, Savannah	2016/17	Total	13	1	3	4	10
Sumner, Savannah	2017/18	WPL	12	2	0	2	6
Sumner, Savannah	2018/19	WPL	12	6	2	8	8
Sumner, Savannah	2018/19	Chall	1	2	0	2	0
Sumner, Savannah	2018/19	Total	13	8	2	10	8
Sumner, Savannah	2019/20	D1N	9	7	7	14	6
Sumner, Savannah	2019/20	Chall	2	4	3	7	2
Sumner, Savannah	2019/20	Total	11	11	10	21	8
Sumner, Savannah	2021/22	Chall	1	1	0	1	0
Sumner, Savannah	2022/23	D1N	3	2	1	3	2
Sumner, Savannah	2024/25	D2N	3	0	1	1	2
Sumner, Savannah	Totals		56	25	17	42	36

Player	Season	Comp	GP	G	A	Pts	PIM
Thornton, Cath	2024/25	Cup	3	1	0	1	0
Thornton, Cath	Totals		3	1	0	1	0
Tyrer, Ellen	2021/22	WPL	14	1	1	2	2
Tyrer, Ellen	2021/22	Chall	1	0	0	0	0
Tyrer, Ellen	2021/22	Total	15	1	1	2	2
Tyrer, Ellen	2022/23	D1N	12	2	3	5	0
Tyrer, Ellen	2022/23	POSF	1	0	0	0	0
Tyrer, Ellen	2022/23	Total	13	2	3	5	0
Tyrer, Ellen	2023/24	D2N	10	5	2	7	0
Tyrer, Ellen	2024/25	D2N	7	2	4	6	2
Tyrer, Ellen	2024/25	Cup	1	0	0	0	0
Tyrer, Ellen	2024/25	Total	8	2	4	6	2
Tyrer, Ellen	Totals		46	10	10	20	4
Venables, Victoria	2018/19	WPL	7	0	1	1	8
Venables, Victoria	2019/20	D1N	8	1	3	4	8
Venables, Victoria	2019/20	Chall	1	0	1	1	0
Venables, Victoria	2019/20	Total	9	1	4	5	8
Venables, Victoria	Totals		16	1	5	6	16
Walsh-O'Neill, Ellie	2021/22	WPL	14	2	0	2	2
Walsh-O'Neill, Ellie	Totals		14	2	0	2	2
Wheeler, Philippa	2018/19	WPL	11	0	0	0	4
Wheeler, Philippa	2018/19	Chall	1	1	0	1	0
Wheeler, Philippa	2018/19	Total	12	1	0	1	4
Wheeler, Philippa	2019/20	Chall	1	1	3	4	0
Wheeler, Philippa	Totals		13	2	3	5	4
Wilde, Rebecca	2015/16	WPL	2	0	0	0	0
Wilde, Rebecca	Totals		2	0	0	0	0

Player	Season	Comp	GP	G	A	Pts	PIM
Williams, Amanda	2015/16	WPL	10	2	4	6	0
Williams, Amanda	2015/16	POSF	1	0	1	1	2
Williams, Amanda	2015/16	Total	11	2	5	7	2
Williams, Amanda	2016/17	WPL	9	4	4	8	0
Williams, Amanda	2016/17	Total	9	4	4	8	0
Williams, Amanda	2017/18	WPL	9	7	3	10	0
Williams, Amanda	2018/19	WPL	11	3	2	5	4
Williams, Amanda	2018/19	Chall	1	0	0	0	0
Williams, Amanda	2018/19	Total	12	3	2	5	4
Williams, Amanda*	2024/25	Cup	2	1	1	2	0
Williams, Amanda*	2024/25	D2N	7	5	5	10	0
Williams, Amanda*	2024/25	Total	9	6	6	12	0
Williams, Amanda	Totals		50	22	20	42	6
Wilson, Olivia	2021/22	WPL	11	0	1	1	0
Wilson, Olivia	2021/22	Chall	1	0	0	0	0
Wilson, Olivia	2021/22	Total	12	0	1	1	0
Wilson, Olivia	2022/23	D1N	9	0	0	0	0
Wilson, Olivia	2022/23	POSF	1	0	0	0	0
Wilson, Olivia	2022/23	Total	10	0	0	0	0
Wilson, Olivia	Totals		22	0	1	1	0
Winstanley, Daisy	2021/22	WPL	7	0	1	1	0
Winstanley, Daisy	Totals		7	0	1	1	0
Wright, Elizabeth	2015/16	WPL	13	0	3	3	14
Wright, Elizabeth	2015/16	POSF	1	0	0	0	0
Wright, Elizabeth	2015/16	Total	14	0	3	3	14
Wright, Elizabeth	Totals		14	0	3	3	14

Amanda Williams played as Amanda Armstrong for the 2024/25 season

Netminders – Season By Season

2015/16	**Comp**	**GPI**	**Mins**	**SA**	**GA**	**GAA**	**Save %**	**SO**
Stephanie Drinkwater	WPL	13	774	365	33	2.56	90.96	0
Stephanie Drinkwater	POS	1	45	18	2	2.67	88.89	0
Stephanie Drinkwater	Totals	14	819	383	35	2.56	90.86	0
Emma Bevan	WPL	1	60	25	3	3.00	88.00	0
2016/17	**Comp**	**GPI**	**Mins**	**SA**	**GA**	**GAA**	**Save %**	**SO**
Drinkwater	WPL	7	400	254	26	3.90	89.76	0
Emma Bevan	WPL	2	120	71	5	2.50	92.96	0
Rachel Fairbairn	WPL	3	140	90	12	5.14	86.67	0
Tegan Lavery	WPL	1	60	39	2	2.00	94.87	0
Tegan Lavery	POS	1	60	40	6	6.00	85.00	0
Tegan Lavery	Totals	2	120	79	8	4.00	89.87	0
2017/18	**Comp**	**GPI**	**Mins**	**SA**	**GA**	**GAA**	**Save %**	**SO**
Stephanie Drinkwater	WPL*	10	600	459	48	4.80	89.54	1
Rebekah Scott	WPL*	2	120	84	9	4.50	89.29	0
2018/19								
Stephanie Drinkwater	WPL	13	780	965	109	8.38	88.70	0
Stephanie Drinkwater	Chal	1	60	44	7	7.00	84.09	0
Stephanie Drinkwater	Totals	14	840	1009	116	8.29	88.50	0
2019/20	**Comp**	**GPI**	**Mins**	**SA**	**GA**	**GAA**	**Save %**	**SO**
Stephanie Drinkwater	D1N*	7	360	215	14	2.33	93.49	0
Stephanie Drinkwater	Chall	1	90	17	2	1.33	88.24	0
Stephanie Drinkwater	Totals	8	420	232	16	2.29	93.10	0
Charlotte Jackson	D1N*	8	240	104	14	3.50	86.54	0
Charlotte Jackson	Chall	2	90	50	12	8.00	76.00	0
Charlotte Jackson	Totals	10	360	154	26	4.33	83.12	0
2021/22	**Comp**	**GPI**	**Mins**	**SA**	**GA**	**GAA**	**Save %**	**SO**
Stephanie Drinkwater	WPL*	14	780	903	124	9.54	86.27	0
Charlotte Jackson	WPL*	8	180	220	47	15.67	78.64	0
Charlotte Jackson	Chall	2	120	98	20	10.00	79.59	0
Charlotte Jackson	Totals	10	300	318	67	13.40	78.93	0
2022/23	**Comp**	**GPI**	**Mins**	**SA**	**GA**	**GAA**	**Save %**	**SO**
Charlotte Cramp	D2N	1	60	32	8	8.00	75.00	0
Ellie Green	D2N	7	276.5	135	12	2.60	91.11	1
Ellie Green	POSF	1	27.25	32	0	0.00	100.00	1
Ellie Green	Totals	8	303.75	167	12	2.37	92.81	1
Rebecca Donnelley	D2N	2	85	43	11	7.76	74.42	1
Stephanie Drinkwater	D2N	8	383.5	172	17	2.66	90.12	1
Stephanie Drinkwater	POSF	1	32.75	35	3	5.50	91.43	0
Stephanie Drinkwater	Totals	9	416.25	207	20	2.88	90.34	1
2023/24	**Comp**	**GPI**	**Mins**	**SA**	**GA**	**GAA**	**Save %**	**SO**
Stephanie Drinkwater	D2N	10	474	347	32	4.68	90.78	2
Ellie Green	D2N	8	245	170	18	4.33	89.41	2
Lucy Kirkham^	D2N	1	16	19	4	13.33	78.95	0

2024/25	Comp	GPI	Mins	SA	GA	GAA	Save %	SO
Stephanie Drinkwater	D2N	11	646	421	32	2.97	92.40	1
Stephanie Drinkwater	Cup	3	161.3	157	22	8.18	85.99	0
Stephanie Drinkwater	POSF	1	60	50	8	8.00	84.00	0
Stephanie Drinkwater	Totals	15	867.3	628	62	4.29	90.13	1
Charlotte Jackson	Cup	1	60	59	13	13.00	77.97	0
Charlotte Jackson	D2N	1	60	38	4	4.00	89.47	0
Charlotte Jackson	Totals	2	120	97	17	8.50	82.47	0

Notes:

* *Estimated figures as the Fixtures Live system didn't keep a proper record of "Mins" played (Time On Ice), thus making Goals Against Average (GAA) difficult to calculate and making comparisons between seasons otherwise impossible.*

^ *Lucy Kirkham – somewhat bravely - played in goal for the away game at Grimsby. The match was abandoned after 16 minutes due to a player injury, with the score standing at 4-1 to Grimsby. It was later awarded as a 5-0 forfeit win to Widnes so Lucy's netminding figures are "unofficial".*

Widnes Wild Women Netminders- 2015-2025

Emma Bevan

Season	Comp	GPI	Mins	SA	GA	GAA	Sv %	SO
2015/16	WPL	1	60	25	3	3.00	88.00	0
2016/17	WPL	2	120	71	5	2.50	92.96	0
Totals		3	180	96	8	2.67	91.67	0

Charlotte Cramp

Season	Comp	GPI	Mins	SA	GA	GAA	Sv %	SO
2022/23	D2N	1	60	32	8	8.00	75.00	0
Totals		1	60	32	8	8.00	75.00	0

Rebecca Donnelley

Season	Comp	GPI	Mins	SA	GA	GAA	Sv %	SO
2022/23	D2N	2	85	43	11	7.76	74.42	0
Totals	D2N	2	85	43	11	7.76	74.42	0

Rachel Fairbairn

Season	Comp	GPI	Mins	SA	GA	GAA	Sv %	SO
2016/17	WPL	3	140	90	12	5.14	86.67	0
Totals		3	140	90	12	5.14	86.67	0

Tegan Lavery

Season	Comp	GPI	Mins	SA	GA	GAA	Sv %	SO
2016/17	WPL	1	60	39	2	2.00	94.87	0
2016/17	POS	1	60	40	6	6.00	85.00	0
Totals		2	120	79	8	4.00	89.87	0

Rebekah Scott

Season	Comp	GPI	Mins	SA	GA	GAA	Sv %	SO
2017/18	WPL*	2	120	84	9	4.50	89.29	0
Totals		2	120	84	9	4.50	89.29	0

Charlotte Jackson

Season	Comp	GPI	Mins	SA	GA	GAA	Sv %	SO
2019/20	D1N	8	240	104	14	3.50	86.54	0
2019/20	Chall	2	90	50	12	8.00	76.00	0
2019/20	Total	10	360	154	26	4.33	83.12	0
2021/22	WPL	8	180	220	47	15.67	78.64	0
2021/22	Chall	2	120	98	20	10.00	79.59	0
2021/22	Total	10	300	318	67	13.40	78.93	0
2024/25	Cup	1	60	59	13	13.00	77.97	0
2024/25	D2N	1	60	38	4	4.00	89.47	0
2024/25	Total	2	120	97	17	8.50	82.47	0
Totals		22	780	569	110	8.46	80.67	0

Ellie Green

Season	Comp	GPI	Mins	SA	GA	GAA	Sv %	SO
2022/23	D2N	7	276.5	135	12	2.60	91.11	1
2022/23	POSF	1	27.25	32	0	0.00	100.00	0
2022/23	Total	8	303.75	167	12	2.37	92.81	1
2023/24	D2N	8	245	170	18	4.33	89.41	2
Total		16	548.75	337	30	3.28	91.10	3.00

Lucy Kirkham*

Season	Comp	GPI	Mins	SA	GA	GAA	Sv %	SO
2023/24	D2N	1	16	19	4	13.33	78.95	0
Totals		1	16	19	4	13.33	78.95	0

**Unofficial figures – see note in previous section*

Stephanie Drinkwater

Season	Comp	GPI	Mins	SA	GA	GAA	Sv %	SO
2015/16	WPL	13	774	365	33	2.56	90.96	0
2015/16	POSF	1	45	18	2	2.67	88.89	0
2015/16	Total	14	819	383	35	2.56	90.86	0
2016/17	WPL	7	400	254	26	3.90	89.76	0
2017/18	WPL	10	600	459	48	4.80	89.54	1
2018/19	WPL	13	780	965	109	8.38	0.89	0
2018/19	Chall	1	60	44	7	7.00	84.10	0
2018/19	Total	14	840	1009	116	8.29	0.89	0
2019/20	D1N	7	360	215	14	2.33	0.93	0
2019/20	Chall	1	90	17	2	1.33	0.88	0
2019/20	Total	8	420	232	16	2.29	0.93	0
2021/22	WPL	14	780	903	124	9.54	86.27	0
2022/23	D2N	8	383.5	172	17	2.66	90.12	1
2022/23	POSF	1	32.75	35	3	5.50	91.43	0
2022/23	Total	9	416.25	207	20	2.88	90.34	1
2023/24	D2N	10	474	347	32	4.68	90.78	2
2024/25	D2N	11	646	421	32	2.97	92.40	1
2024/25	Cup	3	161.3	157	22	8.18	85.99	0
2024/25	POSF	1	60	50	8	8.00	84.00	0
2024/25	Total	15	867.3	628	62	4.29	90.13	1
Totals		**101**	**5616.55**	**4422**	**479**	**5.12**	**89.17**	**5**

Lucy with referees Stephen French and Ray Ormes at a Wild women's match at Widnes in December 2018

(Photo by Paul Breeze)

Lucy London – Poet In Residence

Lucy London was appointed honorary "Poet In Residence" for the Widnes Wild club in September 2017 and has since made it her mission to immortalise their exploits in verse.

She had previously watched ice hockey for a number of years at Peterborough, Altrincham, Blackburn and Blackpool / Cleveleys and has followed the Wild since moving closer to the area in 2015.

Lucy was an EIHA off-ice game official at Widnes for several seasons from 2017 to 2020, the match scorer for Riverside Raiders home games and has been the sponsor of the MVP awards for the Wild women's team for the past four seasons. Unfortunately, she has been laid low by poor health recently and is currently supporting from a distance.

Lucy is an experienced writer and broadcaster and has had two volumes of her own poems published as well as a song book, numerous short stories and various feature articles.

She has also become a bit of an authority on lesser known poetry of the First World War since being asked to put together an exhibition of women poets for the Wilfred Owen Story museum in Birkenhead back in 2012.

She has since edited and published numerous books on the subject of women poets, inspirational women and forgotten male poets of World War One and has staged exhibitions across the UK and in Ireland, France and the USA.

Back in September 2017, it was thought to be the first time that an ice rink had appointed a Poet In Residence and it is just another example that helps reinforce Widnes Wild's commitment to building strong links across the wider community.

Lucy London has a dedicated Facebook page for her poetry residency at Planet Ice Widnes and is keen to encourage other people to explore and develop their own artistic and literary talents.

You can follow her poetic musings on the goings on at Widnes at www.facebook.com/Lucy-Poet-In-Residence

And find information about Lucy's other First World War projects and other publications here: http://femalewarpoets.blogspot.co.uk/

Lucy says:

I love watching the Wild women's team play and am always surprised at how they manage to look so graceful with all that kit on!

My sister was a professional ballet dancer and that is another discipline where a lot of hard work and training behind the scenes goes on to make the final product look smooth and almost effortless…

Here's a poem that I wrote at one of the first Wild women's games that I saw:

Ballet Shoes and Skating Boots

(Started at the Ice Hockey Match Widnes Wild women v. Slough Phantoms, 28th February 2016, Silver Blades Ice Rink, Widnes).

Like ballet shoes, the skaters' boots are laced and worn with care
And for every discipline, they need a different pair
For speed or hockey, dance on ice or even figure skating
The blade and boot are different, as is of course the lacing.

With ballet there are character boots, shoes with blocks and more
Almost as hard as ice are the wood blocks on the floor
Pirouettes or passing pucks both keep you on your toes
Your equipment is expensive – that's where the money goes!

Whether it's the ice pad or "treading the boards"
The referee's shrill whistle or Tchaikowsky's rousing chords,
Dedication, commitment, practice and passion
Are all important for the stars but so is following fashion.

Lucy London, 8th September 2016.

We wish you well Widnes Wild Women as you ice against Solway
In your first home match this season - we know you played them away.
Widnes Wild Women – it will be interesting to see
How the Team gel together and who wins the MVP.

Lucy London, 21st September 2019

No ice hockey on Sunday? Don't sit at home and moan
For Widnes Wild Women's Team are at home
No need to miss out on the action or simply hang around
Face Off is at 5.30 and admission is just a pound.

Widnes Wild Women v. Sheffield Shadows in their first Women's Division One North League Game of the Season - Planet Ice Widnes. Face Off 5.30 p.m.

Lucy London, 3rd October 2019

Widnes Wild women players Catherine Fell, Sav Sumner, Emma Pearson & Kat Garner (Photo by Paul Breeze)

The Wild women's team after their 7-2 win over Sheffield Shadows (Photo by Paul Breeze)

7 - 2

Our thanks to all the sponsors and to all those who came
To watch the Widnes Wild Women's ice hockey game
At Planet Ice last Sunday versus Sheffield Shadows
The Wild Women deserved a win – goodness only knows.

Our thanks to the mascot and to the referees –
For that match Ethan Arnold and Josh Humphreys -
Thanks to the bench coaches and the volunteers unseen
And to the Widnes Wild Women's Ice Hockey Team!
And though it is a busy time, we hope you'll all remember
The Wild Women're at home again on the 15th of December.

Lucy Poet in Residence

While YKK Widnes Wild ice at Deeside away,
Widnes Wild Women's team at home will play.
So lots of ice hockey treats in store
This weekend – to find out more
Check out these websites:
www.widneswild.co.uk / www.icehockeyreview.co.uk

Lucy Poet in Residence

Shannon Holt – Wild women's MVP away at Grimsby
(Photo by David Law Photography)

Widnes Wild Women went to Grimsby
Where they won eight to three
And Shannon Holt was M V P.

LL, 12th January 2020

Lines for the Wild Weekend 4th and 5th January 2020

Congratulations Widnes Wild Ice HockeyTeams
Widnes Wild Men, Wild Women and Under Fifteens
You did us proud this past weekend –
Here's hoping that this starts a trend.

Lucy Poet in Residence 7th January 2020

Lines for Widnes Wild Women's match v. Telford Wrekin Raiders 1st March 2020, Planet Ice, Widnes

Yesterday's Wild Women's match was AMAZING – thanks to everyone who came
And to all of those who contributed to the success of the game
The players in teams Widnes Wild Women and Telford Raiders from Wrekin
Coaches Howard Hughes, Gareth Davies, Charles Humphreys and Michael Parkin
To Ryan Morris, Nicky Jackson and Shannon Holt for their wonderful 50/50 collection
And to everyone else involved – these names are just a selection:
Widnes teams have an amazing fan base – they are all really super.
Thanks to the mascots and to the goal judges Howard Smith and Conor Cooper
Thanks to Julia Shutt and Gary Eddleston for penalty box help and to Andrew Shutt for doing the clock
And to Paul Breeze for announcements and music to make us rock
To Colin Ellis for all his help and for his fantastic game videos
(And of course for Time to go Wild, Colin's amazing radio shows)
To all the staff at Planet Ice in Widnes behind the scenes
And Oh Dear Me, I almost forgot – thanks to the referees.
With sincere apologies to anyone I have left out.

Lucy Poet in Residence, 2nd March 2020

Match action shot from the Wild women's important win over Grimsby (Photo by John Lewis)

Widnes Wild Women v. Grimsby Wolves, Sunday, 16th February 2020

Well done Widnes Wild Women for winning 12 – 2
Oh! How I wish I could have been there watching you
But thanks to Bex Clayton - who does the Wild Men's team Tweets
On Match Days – I was able to keep up with your feats.

Lucy Poet in Residence, 18th February 2020

Widnes Wild women's players Katie Fairclough, Ellie Green and Ellen Tyrer model the new DMUK sponsored home shirts (Photo by Paul Breeze)

Thank you to the company DMUK
Who are sponsoring Wild Women's shirts home and away
They are launching the shirts during the match today.

Lucy Poet in Residence, 5 February 2023

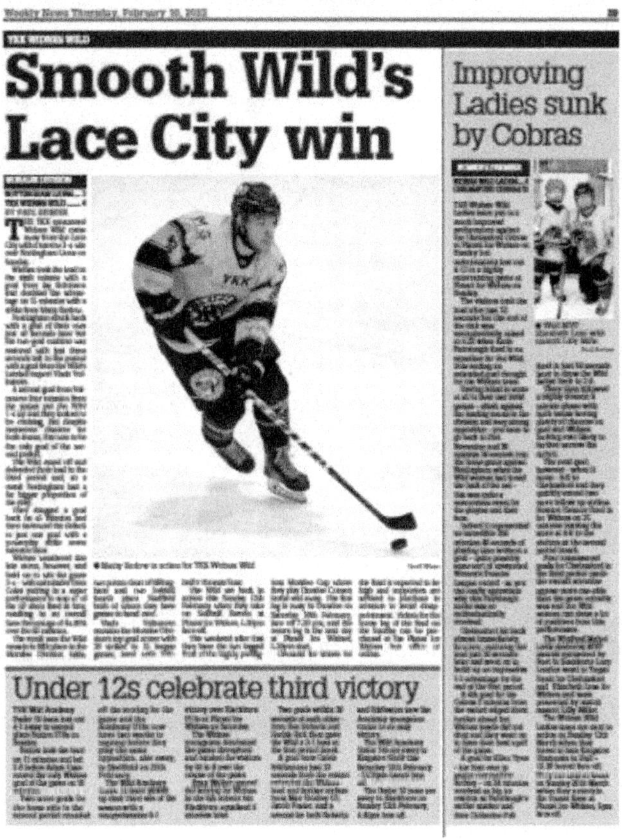

Smooth Wild's Lace City win

Improving Ladies sunk by Cobras

Under 12s celebrate third victory

Widnes Weekly News 10th February 2022, Page 29

Girls and boys come out to play
Ice hockey – hip hooray!
The Wild Men won away
The Women lost but have upped their game
Win or lose, Wild, we love you just the same.

Lucy Poet in Residence, 9th February 2022

Too many Wild men on the ice, alas, alack
But three Wild women scored hatricks
I'm sure the Wild Men, like the phoenix from the flame,
Will arise and find their winning streak again.

LL, 3.4.2023

Pauline Hayward helping to launch the 2019/20 Wild women's MVP awards (Photo by Paul Breeze)

Pauline Hayward

Sometime ago I posted this little poem on my Facebook page:

"Over the River"

Across the River Mersey my thoughts often float
Drifting and dreaming with the River's flow
Light and happy in an imaginary boat.
Won't you tell me, please where your thoughts go?

LL 18th March 2020

(Inspired by the 1958 DDR song "Uber die Elbe", lyrics by Heribert Klein)

My friend Pauline Hayward, who I met because she played for the Widnes Wild Women's Ice Hockey Team, replied with this delightful verse, so I asked her if we could include it:

Oooh when my mind drifts, it's on ice that I glide,
Frictionless; thrilling, I never collide;
Match day excitement, the ping of a puck; mad ref decisions and slices of luck.
*But the wildest of dreams; due to greatest fatigue - nothing compares quite, to winning the league**

Pauline agreed and sent me a bit about herself and some photos for us to use.

"I'd describe myself as "late to the party. Prompted by Sport England's "This Girl Can" programme which sponsored ten weeks of free coaching at Widnes, I learned to skate and began to play ice hockey as a total beginner in my sixties."

"Before I knew it, I was playing with the Widnes Wild ladies, with the best team-mates anyone could ever wish for I've been playing and partying ever since."

"I knew I had gone completely "Wild" when I agreed to join some of the others in Tough Mudder. If there's anything that you have always wanted to do, my advice is "go for it". You'll surprise yourself!"

(*To the best of our knowledge, Pauline is the oldest ever player to have won a competitive league title when she was a member of the Widnes Wild women's team that won the WNIHL Division 1 North title during the 2019/20 season.)

Pauline's Bitch

There's a player comically known as "Pauline's Bitch"
Out of politeness to him, I won't say which.
But she knocked him flat, across the ice
I bet he won't let THAT happen twice!

PB 22nd July 2023
(Inspired while washing up)

///LUCY

POET IN RESIDENCE

lucy-poet-in-residence
facebook

"Lucy Match Scorer" caricature by Manga Mark

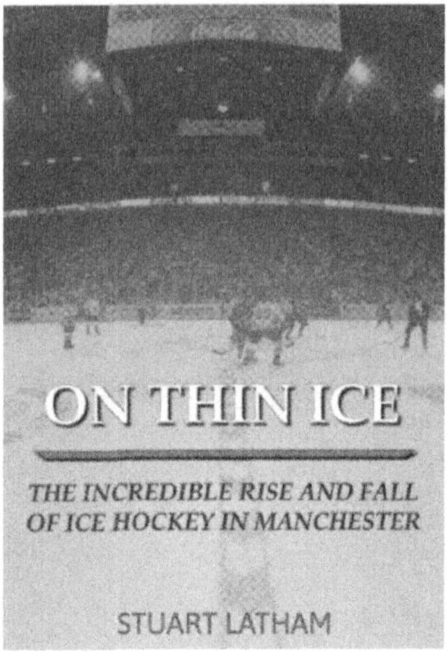

BOOK REVIEW

"On Thin Ice"
By Stuart Latham

(Originally published on icehockeyreview.co.uk on 25th June 2024)

When I was a young lad growing up in Stanground - which, if you don't happen to know it, is a pleasant leafy suburb of the historic cathedral city of Peterborough – I once saw a very odd sight which has stayed in the back of my mind all these years.

I was walking to the sweet shop when I saw a chap – maybe late teens / early 20s (when you are 9 or 10, everybody else just looks "old" to you...) – ride by on a bike. BUT he was riding no-handed and reading a book at the same time.

Now, this was back in the mid 1970s in the days when the liberal consensus and permissive society and everything else were all in full swing and nobody had ever heard of "Health & Safety" but even then, I figured this might have been a bit of a dangerous thing to do.

As far as I can remember, he had a small paperback book balanced against the handlebars held loosely in position by his thumbs, so may well have had a modicum of control over his machine, but he certainly wasn't looking where he was going.

I don't know who he was, where he was going or what happened later – he could have come to a sticky end a bit further up the road for all I knew – but the vision of this bloke on this bike with this book has always stuck with me.

So – why am I telling you this? Well, not that I would EVER encourage or condone anybody attempting to doing anything quite so dangerous and illegal on a public road, putting themselves and others in harm's way, and however clever this particular bloke was with reading books on bicycles, I bet that he would NOT have been able to do it with Stuart Latham's new publication "On Thin Ice" – which is a fascinating comprehensive account of ice hockey in Manchester from 1961 onwards.

I have commented before on the "huge-ness" of some of Stuart's other books – the Alloa Athletic one still lays stubbornly where I first put it down because it is too heavy for me to pick up and put away anywhere - and this is another very impressive example of literary huge-ity. It is certainly too big to prop up against the handlebars and read while you arc pedalling along.

If you want facts and figures to back up this assertion – or "stats", as we like to call them in the ice hockey world – I will givc you some.

"On Thin Ice" has a whopping 734 pages and weighs 1.3kg! It is a hardback, which gives it that nice classic quality feel and, as the spine is 4.5cm wide, it will stand nicely on your bookshelf without falling over or flopping. It is 26.5cm tall – which is actually 1cm taller than most of Stuart's other B5 format ice hockey books – but that just means that it is easier to find on the shelf in the dark.

Now, if you are a keen collector of ice hockey books in general - and Stuart Latham's books in particular - you will probably have come across a lot of this material before as he has previously produced separate volumes about the Altrincham Aces, Manchester Phoenix and Manchester Storm teams but, even so – it's nice to have all this stuff together in one tidy edition.

This book goes right back to the early days when the original Devonshire Road rink in Altrincham first opened and boasts such well known names of the day as Chick Zamick and Art Hodgins on the Aces bench.

We then navigate through the Trafford Metros era of the late 1980s and early 90s, the first Manchester Storm team in the Superleague, the Manchester Phoenix period from 2002 to 2017 and finish up with the modern Storm and Aces teams.

As you'd expect from a Stuart Latham publication, it is packed with league tables, stats and photos. There are loads of player profiles and some great memories from people who were involved, such as

Daryl Lipsey, Hilton Ruggles and John Lawless (Storm)

Neil Morris, Tony Hand and Peter Hagan (Phoenix)

Tom Revesz, James Ashton and Sarah Hutchinson (Aces)

and there's even a bit from me in there as well…

So, there we have it: "On Thin Ice – The Incredible Rise And Fall Of Ice Hockey In Manchester".

BOOK REVIEW

Gone But Not Forgotten

(Originally published on icehockeyreview.co.uk on 20th December 2024)

I have said, in the past, that you can "never have too many ice hockey books". And, while I WOULD say that because I do, occasionally, sell the odd one or two to help fund my Twiglet habit, this book is not one of mine.

Yep, just when I was wondering how I was going to cope over the festive period without any NIHL hockey to watch or report on (we in the lower reaches don't have Boxing Day games etc like the "Elite" boys and National Division do...) this latest offering from the fine stable of Stuart Latham ice hockey club histories has landed on the doormat.

"Gone But Not Forgotten" is an interesting book as it covers a number of different teams from different eras.

Depending on how old you are and how much you might have read about past glories in British ice hockey, you may have heard of a lot of these teams already, but it is nice to see so much information all gathered up in one place.

And what we have here covers:

Kensington Corinthians (1930s)

Richmond Hawks (1930s)

Earls Court Royals (1930s)

Grosvenor House Canadians (1930s)

Wembley Canadians (1930s)

Wembley Monarchs (1930s & 40s)

Wembley Vets (1970s)

London Phoenix Flyers (Richmond – 1970s)

Richmond Flyers (1980s)

Earls Court Rangers (1930s & 40s)

London Lions (1920s & 30s)

London Lions (1970s - exhibition team)

Wembley Lions (1930s, 40s & 50s)

Milton Keynes Kings (1990s & 00s)

Ashfield Islanders (1980s & 90s)

Bournemouth Stags (1980s & 90s)

As you'd expect with a Stuart Latham compilation, the book is packed with league tables, player statistics and fascinating photos and is bound to be of interest to ice hockey fans of all the various eras.

Now if I were being picky here, (picky – moi? shurely not...) - but if I WAS being picky, I would have expected the 1980s London All Stars team (Dave Richards, Bob Mitura et al) to be worthy of a page or two in this as well. Ice hockey fans of a particular vintage may well recall that they won the 1984/85 British League Division 2 South title.

That was quite an achievement for them because – like Ashfield Islanders - they had to play all of their games away for double points, as their home ice at the Sobell Centre in Islington wasn't suitable for playing league matches.

There was, actually, quite a lot of that went on during those halcyon Heineken-fuelled "expansion" days of the mid 80s – check out Brighton and Hastings as well (oops! - he hasn't included them, either...)

But I am not being picky today. The last train to Picky-Ville has departed "ohne mich" - so I won't mention any of them...

Anyway, despite that, this book is all very interesting and represents a very good record of a lot of teams that have fallen by the wayside over the years.

So, there we have it: "Gone But Not Forgotten.

To order your copy, drop Stuart a line via Facebook or send him an email to stuartlatham65@sky.com - and get him to tell you about his other ice hockey books as well.

MORE ICE HOCKEY BOOKS BY STUART LATHAM

ISBN	Title	RRP £
9781838116507	60 Years Of The Altrincham Aces	£15.99
9781838116521	Ice Hockey in Bristol	£15.99
9781838116538	The Deeside Dragons	£15.99
9781838116545	The Manchester Storm	£15.99
9781838116569	The Rise and Fall of the Manchester Phoenix	£15.99
9781838116590	The Cardiff Devils	£16.99
9781838332808	Ice Hockey Memories	£18.99
9781838332822	The History of the Slough Jets	£17.99
9781838332846	More Ice Hockey Memories	£17.99
9780953060863	Blood Sweat and Tears Ice Hockey in Peterborough	£24.99
9780953060870	Swindon Wildcats 1986-2016	£22.99
9780953060887	The History of the Bracknell Bees	£24.99
9781838332853	Ice Hockey in Edinburgh	£18.99
9781838332891	Stars Wars - The Oxford City Stars	£16.99
9781838460907	Swindon Ice Hockey Statistically Speaking 1986-2021	£17.99
9781838460914	In Their Own Words - Swindon Ice Hockey Memories	£16.99
9781838460938	Hockey in Haringey	£17.99
9781838460952	Ice Hockey In Solihull	£18.99
9781838460983	The NHL IN The UK	£19.99
9781915697042	Ice Hockey In Guildford	£21.99

Available by mail order from Waterstones.com, brownbfs.co.uk, foyles.co.uk and other major outlets.

For more details, contact stuartlatham65@sky.com or tel: +44 7702035951

ICE HOCKEY BOOKS
by Michael A Chambers

THE COMPLETE WORKS: Compendium of the Nottingham Panthers Ice Hockey Team

This is the third book on the Nottingham Panthers and is an extension to the two previous about the club with additional statistics and facts. It is an update of the recent seasons 2007-08 to 2022-23 and is filled with lots of player pictures or events not published before. Also a complete list and register of every player to have put on the Panthers jersey from 1946 – this has never been documented until now.
It's a complete history of all of the competitions in all the seasons. Cartoons, drawings and more.

300 Pages A4 Paperback - ISBN: 979-8365711198

UK ICE HOCKEY - *Featuring:*

History of English & Scottish Leagues, Season By Season League Tables, Cup And Play Off Competitions,

Full Lists of Title & Trophy Winners, UK clubs in European Competitions, Great Britain National Team, All Star Teams

226 pages A4 paperback - ISBN: 978-0-9539398-4-8

ICE COLD MURDER –

an ice hockey murder mystery

ISBN: 978-0953939831

When a body is found within hockey owner Mark Atkin's establishment, Inspector Dilley has to unravel this terrible scene in order to find out what happened. Amongst a complexity of doors, keys and camera pictures which have much to do with it all.

Many people have much to do with the events that occur this day which puts them 'in the frame' within this much troubled club. Who did it?

Copies available from the author. Contact Michael via e-mail at: spikc2004@yahoo.co.uk

PB TRANSLATING

Over 30 years' experience of translation & interpreting in industry & commerce - specialising in English / French /German.

Also involvement with Italian, Spanish, Dutch, Russian, Czech & Polish.

For enquiries, please e-mail to pbtranslating@gmail.com

ICE HOCKEY REVIEW

www.icehockeyreview.co.uk

NIHL Yearbook Back Issues Available

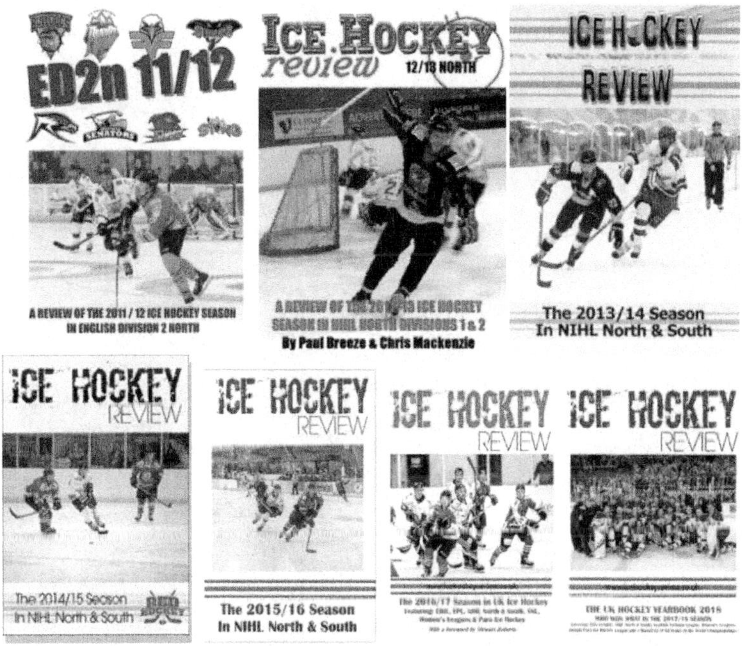

Available by mail order from www.poshupnorth.com, Amazon, icehockeyreview.co.uk and other quality outlets

www.icehockeyreview.co.uk

Celebrating 10 years 2014 –2024 and 1.000.000+ hits!

British grass-roots hockey news & reviews website

ICE HOCKEY REVIEW

www.icehockeyreview.co.uk

Available by mail order from** www.poshupnorth.com, **Amazon, icehockeyreview.co.uk and other quality outlets

FYLDE FLYERS
A Complete Record

The Fylde Flyers ice hockey team only existed for two seasons but they reignited interest in a sport that has a proud history in Blackpool dating back to the 1930s.

Their legacy goes on even though the team does not.

Here is the fascinating story of the Fylde Flyers.

Full Contents List:

Acknowledgements
About The Author
Historical Timeline
The SubZero Story
The "Small Ice Rink" Dilemma

2011/12 Season Summary
News Stories, Match Reports & Gamesheets
End Of Season Awards

2012/13 Season Summary
News Stories, Match Reports & Gamesheets
End Of The Line For Flyers

Fylde Flyers Fact File
Summary Of Player Statistics
Most Points
Most Goals
Most Assists
Most Appearances
Most Penalties
Netminder Statistics
Summary Of All Time League Results

Player Directory A - Z

ISBN: 9781909643130

Available by mail order from www.poshupnorth.com, Amazon, icehockeyreview.co.uk and other quality outlets

10 YEARS IN THE WILD

2013 to 2023

To celebrate the 10th anniversary of the founding of the Widnes Wild ice hockey team, we thought we'd gather up all the material that we have collected over the years and put it together in one single volume.

ISBN: 978-1-909643-54-3

Full Contents List:

Introduction
New Ice Rink Opens In Widnes
Widnes Wild Team Launch
How It All Began!
Widnes Wild's First Ever Game
Richard Charles Looks Back At The First Widnes Game
Craig Williams And The First Ever Widnes Wild Goal
Season by Season: 2013/14, 2014/15, 2015/16, 2016/17, 2017/18, 2018/19, 2019/20, 2020/21, 2021/22, 2022/23
10 Year Records
Roll Of Honour
Playing Record
Wild Player Top 10s
Head to Head Playing Records
Wild Player A To Z
Pukka Penguin
Team Staff, Off Ice Officials & Match Volunteers
Long Service Awards
Wild Shirt Retirements
NIHL Player Award Winners
Lucy London – Poet In Residence
Bookshelf

Various mail order options available
Visit www.icehockeyreview.co.uk for more details

RAPTORS, EAGLES & HAWKS 2 TOO...

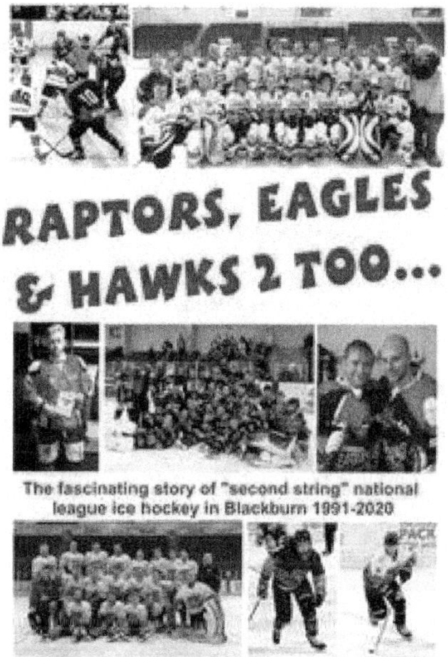

The fascinating story of "second string" national league ice hockey in Blackburn 1991-2020

ISBN: 978-1-909643-63-5

Full Contents List:

Introduction

Ice Hockey Arrives In Blackburn

1991-93: Blackburn Falcons

1993-97: Blackburn Seagulls

1997-98: Blackburn Phoenix

2007-12: Lancashire Raptors
Introduction
Season By Season
All Time Player Records

2012-17: Blackburn Eagles
Season By Season
All Time Player Records

2017-20: Blackburn Hawks 2
Season By Season
All Time Player Records

Overall Playing Record
– All Teams

A to Z Players Records
– All Teams

Bookshelf

Please note: the full colour version is available direct from the publisher via eBay. A budget black and white version is available via Amazon. Apart from colour photos, the actual content is the same in both versions.

Mail order links can be found on www.icehockeyreview.co.uk

DEESIDE DUCKS SEASON 2024/25

Contents:

Season 2024/25

ISBN: 978-1-909643-68-0

The fascinating story of the Deeside Ducks' first - and, indeed, only - season in the NIHL Laidler Division, as told in the Flintshire & Wrexham Leader newspaper and on the Ice Hockey Review website.

Includes: match reports, player stats, A to Z gallery, a few poems by Lucy and photos throughout.

Available by mail order from www.poshupnorth.com, Amazon, icehockeyreview.co.uk and other quality outlets

Paul & Lucy's
Best Kept Secrets
https://paulandlucysbestkeptsecrets.blogspot.com

Interesting Books...
...Fascinating Subjects!

POSH UP NORTH
Publishing
www.poshupnorth.com

Check out our audio and video archive in our dedicated "Paul & Lucy's Best Kept Secrets" YouTube channel at www.youtube.com.

Printed in Dunstable, United Kingdom

71827225R00352